VALUE AND CAPITAL

VALUE

AND

CAPITAL

AN INQUIRY INTO
SOME FUNDAMENTAL PRINCIPLES
OF ECONOMIC THEORY

BY

J. R. HICKS

FELLOW OF NUFFIELD COLLEGE, OXFORD

SECOND EDITION

OXFORD
AT THE CLARENDON PRESS

Oxford University Press, Walton Street, Oxford OX2 6DP

OXFORD LONDON GLASGOW
NEW YORK TORONTO MELBOURNE WELLINGTON
KUALA LUMPUR SINGAPORE HONG KONG TOKYO
DELHI BOMBAY CALCUTTA MADRAS KARACHI
NAIROBI DAR ES SALAAM CAPE TOWN

ISBN 0 19 828269 9

First published 1939
Reprinted 1939, 1941
Second Edition 1946
Reprinted 1948, 1950, 1953, 1957, 1961
1962, 1965, 1968, 1974, 1978, 1979

Printed in Great Britain
at the University Press, Oxford
by Eric Buckley
Printer to the University

PREFACE TO SECOND EDITION

THE majority of the alterations which I have made in this new edition are concerned with the correction of a technical slip in the argument as originally published. I had worked out the general conditions of stability in consumer's choice (as I still think) quite correctly; but I did not use all the conditions which were mathematically available, since there were some of them to which I could not give, at that time, any economic sense. In this I was wrong; as a result of more recent work (my own and others'), it now appears that the neglected conditions have a very important economic sense, and that later stages of my argument suffered by my failure to use them. Since the result was to make these later stages more complicated than they need have been, it has been very desirable to simplify by making the necessary corrections.

The general proposition, which I overlooked, is now set out in words on pp. 51–2. Consequential adjustments have been made on pp. 71, 72, 77, 102–4, 222, and in the corresponding places in the mathematical appendix. Further consequences of the new proposition are discussed in Additional Note A.

Another place where the original argument seems to have been defective did not lend itself to the same sort of correction. The text has therefore been left unchanged, and the matter is discussed in Additional Note B.

Technical amendments of this sort I have felt myself bound to make; but I have not felt the same compulsion to deal with those criticisms, however well founded, which have been concerned with more fundamental matters. When writing the Introduction to this book, I took care to emphasize that I made no pretensions to be putting forward a complete system of economic theory; I was simply following out a particular approach wherever it led me. *Value and Capital* is better left as a statement of things which can be reached by that route; its relations with other (and perhaps superior) routes can be better discussed elsewhere.

There is, however, one school of critics whose work has already resulted in a new construction—in a theory which differs from mine, though it is closely related to mine. A new edition of this book would look incomplete if it contained no reference to the work of Professor Samuelson and his collaborators; I have therefore commented upon it—though very briefly and inadequately—in the last of my Additional Notes.

OXFORD   J. R. H.

July 1946

PREFACE TO FIRST EDITION

THE ideas on which this book is based were conceived at the London School of Economics during the years 1930–5. They were not by any means entirely my own ideas; they came into being by a sort of social process which went on among the people who were working there, at that time, under the leadership of Professor Robbins. Those whom I remember particularly as having contributed were Mr. R. G. D. Allen, Mr. Kaldor, Mr. Lerner, Professor Hayek, Dr. Rosenstein-Rodan, and Dr. Edelberg. Each of these will probably be able to recognize something of his own in these pages. But imputation would be too difficult for me to attempt to make specific acknowledgements.

If the first stage in the development of this book was unusually social, later stages have been every bit as definitely individual. I have taken the ideas which sprouted at London, and given them a long development in directions for which I take sole responsibility. I have had some very useful criticism from Mr. Sraffa, and from one or two of those mentioned above. But physical separation has made it impossible to re-create the constant collaboration of the first years; I therefore put in the present work as my own personal report on the significance and the implications of the things we discovered.

The one debt I have to acknowledge, which runs all through, is that to my wife. She was a member of the group from which these ideas came; she watched over their later extensions; while the fact that this book was written alongside her *Finance of British Government* was, in several ways, a singular advantage to me. I think it is those parts of my book which deal with the Capital market which profited most; but there is no part which has not profited from the constant reminder which I have had from her work, that the place of economic theory is to be the servant of applied economics.

J. R. H.

MANCHESTER

October 1938

CONTENTS

Part I

THE THEORY OF SUBJECTIVE VALUE

Part II

GENERAL EQUILIBRIUM

PART III

THE FOUNDATIONS OF DYNAMIC ECONOMICS

PART IV

THE WORKING OF THE DYNAMIC SYSTEM

MATHEMATICAL APPENDIX

ADDITIONAL NOTES

INTRODUCTION

ALTHOUGH this book deals with a considerable proportion of those topics generally treated in works on economic theory, it has no claim to be a 'Principles of Economics'. Its aim is very different. The ideal which any writer of *Principles* ought to set before himself is that of the classical poet: 'What oft was thought but ne'er so well expressed'; I am almost entirely concerned with novelties. I shall confine myself to those aspects of each subject I treat on which I have something new to say; or at least I shall deal with familiar aspects quite cursorily.

This being so, it might be thought that the following pages, which seek to say something new on many branches of a well-developed science like economics, could only contain a series of essays, not a unified book. Yet I believe I have written a book. The basis for this claim lies not in unity of subject but in unity of method. I believe I have had the fortune to come upon a method of analysis which is applicable to a wide variety of economic problems. The method arises out of some of the simplest, most fundamental problems—so they have their place here; it is, perhaps, most illuminating when it is applied to the most complex problems (such as those of trade fluctuations)—so that they have their place here too.

One often hears, particularly from those who are engaged in the study of these most intricate questions, a wish for some method of dealing, at once, with more than two or three variables. Simple problems of two or three variables can be dealt with, quite efficiently, by geometrical diagrams; but when the problem becomes more complex, the familiar geometrical method fails. What is to be done? The obvious answer is, Have recourse to algebra. But, quite apart from the fact that many economists are not very good at algebra, the sort of algebraic methods commonly employed, while they are of some use in setting out problems, are much less efficient as a means of argument than diagrams appear to be, when diagrams can be used. It is to cope with this situation that I put forward my new method. The construction of this method, of course, involved mathematics, but fortunately it can be explained and used without anything more than a systematic use of diagrams;

I shall thus be able to dispense with mathematics almost entirely in the text of the book, though (for those who like such things) the relevant mathematics will be summarized at the end in an Appendix.[1]

It turns out, on investigation, that most of the problems of several variables, with which economic theory has to concern itself, are problems of the interrelation of markets. Thus, the more complex problems of wage-theory involve the interrelations of the market for labour, the market for consumption goods, and (perhaps) the capital market. The more complex problems of international trade involve the interrelations of the markets for imports and exports with the capital market. And so on. What we mainly need is a technique for studying the interrelations of markets.

When looking for such a technique we are naturally impelled to turn to the works of those writers who have specially studied such interrelations—that is to say, the economists of the Lausanne school, Walras and Pareto, to whom, I think, Wicksell should be added. The method of General Equilibrium, which these writers elaborated, was specially designed to exhibit the economic system as a whole, in the form of a complex pattern of interrelations of markets. Our own work is bound to be in their tradition, and to be a continuation of theirs.

Nevertheless, it is not possible to find in their work all of what we seek. Walras (*Éléments d'économie politique pure*, 1874) confined himself, in the main, to setting out the problem. His work is fairly adequately described by the dictum of Marshall (who clearly had Walras in mind when he wrote): 'The chief use of pure mathematics in economic questions seems to be in helping a person to write down quickly, shortly, and exactly, some of his thoughts for his own use; and to make sure that he has enough, and only enough, premisses for his conclusions (i.e. that his equations are neither more nor less in number than his unknowns).'[2] General Equilibrium had not accomplished much more than this in 1890;[3] nevertheless, it is a pity that the authority of Marshall

[1] A purely mathematical statement of my method (at least in so far as it applies to value theory) has already appeared in French—*Théorie mathématique de la Valeur* (Paris, Hermann).

[2] Marshall, *Principles*, Preface to First Edition.

[3] Even in the mere counting of equations and unknowns, when performed systematically, there is implied a great deal. See Chapter IV below, and my article, 'Léon Walras' (*Econometrica*, 1934).

has confirmed so many people in the belief that it *can* do no more than the counting of equations.

It was Pareto (*Manuel d'économie politique*, 1909) who began to take things farther. Yet Pareto's work, important as it is, and influential as it has been, is only a beginning; it is limited by a lack of attention to problems of capital and interest; and even on value theory, where it is strongest, it is vitiated by a lack of clearness on some vital points, to which we shall have to draw attention.

Wicksell cannot be blamed for a neglect of capital and interest, which problems were indeed his main preoccupation. But, writing before Pareto, he had not the advantage of being able to use Pareto's improvements in value theory; and (largely in consequence, I believe) his capital theory is limited to considering the artificial abstraction of a stationary state. Subject to this limitation, he did wonders; his theory of money and interest, in particular (*Geldzins und Güterpreise*, 1898), has been the foundation of modern monetary theory.

Our present task may therefore be expressed in historical terms as follows. We have to reconsider the value theory of Pareto, and then to apply this improved value theory to those dynamic problems of capital which Wicksell could not reach with the tools at his command.

Remembering that the works of Walras and Pareto are not available in English and are not, on the whole, very familiar to English readers, I shall summarize such parts of their work as I need in the course of my own argument. I shall take for granted not Pareto's value theory but the more familiar value theory of Marshall; and this will have some advantages, since I do not regard Pareto's theory as being superior to Marshall's in all respects. One of the things we have to do is to fill out Pareto's theory in those respects where it is defective compared with Marshall's.

Similarly, when we come to dynamic problems, I shall not neglect to pay attention to the important work which has been done in that field by Marshallian methods—I allude in particular to the work of Mr. Keynes. Mr. Keynes's *General Theory of Employment, Interest, and Money* (1936) appeared at a time when my own work was well under way, but was still incomplete in several respects. Since we were concerned with such similar fields, it was inevitable that I should be influenced by Mr. Keynes's work to a very great extent. The latter half of this book would have been very different if I had not had the *General Theory* at my disposal when writing. The final chapters of Part IV, in particular, are very Keynesian.

When I began to work on Capital, I had the hope that I should produce an entirely new Dynamic Theory—the theory which many writers had demanded, but which none, at that time, had produced. These hopes have been dashed, for Mr. Keynes has got in first.[1] Yet I still think it worth while to produce my own analysis, even if it looks pedestrian beside his. A more pedestrian approach has the advantage of being more systematic; further, I think I have cleared up several important things he left not very clear.[2]

I must confess that, as I have worked with Mr. Keynes's book, I have been amazed at the way he manages, without the use of any special apparatus, to cut through the tangle of difficulties that beset him, and to go straight for the really important things. He succeeds in doing so just because he makes free use of his superb intuition and acute observation of the real world, in order to be able to discard the inessentials and go straight for the essential. Yet this same power has its drawbacks, and sets obstacles in the way of many readers. 'Supposing,' they cannot help saying, 'supposing he is wrong; supposing the one set of influences is more important than he thinks, and the other less important; would it not make a great deal of difference?' This kind of question deserves to be answered. It is, indeed, particularly desirable for the reader to be able to separate out those things which are the fruit of pure logic, which he can thus be compelled to believe, from those things which are the fruit of Mr. Keynes's own point of view on social questions, where he may prefer to differ. Now we shall find ourselves, *vis-à-vis* Mr. Keynes, as *vis-à-vis* Wicksell, very free to dispense with special assumptions; we shall thus be able to see just why it is that Mr. Keynes reaches different results from earlier economists on crucial matters of social policy; and we shall be able

---

[1] The earlier stages of my own work are on record, for what they are worth, in three articles, written before I saw the *General Theory*: 'Gleichgewicht und Konjunktur' (*Zeitschrift für Nationalökonomie*, 1933); 'A Suggestion for Simplifying the Theory of Money' (*Economica*, 1935); 'Wages and Interest—the Dynamic Problem' (*Economic Journal*, 1935).

[2] See, in particular, my discussions of the relation between saving and investment (Ch. XIV, note), of the period of production (Ch. XVII), of short and long lending (Ch. XI), of why rigid wages are so important (Ch. XXI), of the process of capital accumulation (Ch. XXIII).

to walk round these disturbing considerations, surveying them from several points of view, and making up our own minds about them.

I expect that these parts of our investigations (contained in Parts III and IV) will seem to most readers the most interesting, as they are certainly the most important. I must apologize to the reader for putting them at the end of the book, where they are protected by the wire-entanglement of Part II, rather than at the beginning, where he might like to have them. This could not be helped; since it is the peculiar characteristic of our theory of capital that it depends upon our improved theory of value. The problems of capital and interest present, in fact, two sorts of complications: one is the complication proper to dynamic problems as such, but the other is simply the complication of inter-related markets, which can be dealt with separately. We shall find it an immense convenience, when we come to deal with dynamic problems, that we have already mastered this essentially irrelevant complication in Part II. We can then separate out the special dynamic difficulties—those involved in conceiving the process of price-formation, instead of the 'static' system of prices; these are dealt with in Part III, which is thus not specially dependent on our value theory. And the general problems—the most important problems—where we have to face both the dynamic complications and the complications of interrelated markets, will finally be dealt with in Part IV.

This is why I have to ask the reader to control his impatience to be reading about Saving and Investment, Interest and Prices, Booms and Slumps; and to be content to go back to school with Marginal Utility. Roundabout methods, it has been said, are sometimes more productive than direct methods; it is perhaps fitting that we should discuss the theory of capital in a setting which illustrates that famous principle.

The plan before us is thus as follows:

Part I deals with the theory of Subjective Value—'Wants and their Satisfaction'—the same subject as Book III of Marshall's *Principles*. What I have to say on this matter is needed for what comes later, but it also has a special interest of its own. My work on this subject began with the endeavour to supply a needed theoretical foundation for statistical demand studies; so that there is a definite relevance to that field. Other matters of fundamental methodological importance are thrown up as well.

Part II uses the results of our revised theory of Subjective Value to rework the General Equilibrium analysis of Walras and Pareto. Most important here is the opportunity thrown open to us to transcend the mere counting of equations and unknowns, and to lay down general laws for the working of a price-system with many markets. This is the main thing which needed to be done in order to free the Lausanne theory from the reproach of sterility brought against it by Marshallians. I believe I have done it. Nevertheless, Part II is a relatively arid tract. It is completely 'static'; although some notable economists have been content to mould most of their thought in such a frame as this, it leaves out far too much of the real problem to be a secure resting-place. Nevertheless, if it is regarded as no more than a formal theory of the interrelation of markets, it has its uses. That is how I wish it to be regarded here.

Part III deals with the Foundations of Dynamic Economics. It is concerned particularly with that setting-out of problems which, as we saw, was the main concern of General Equilibrium analysis in its Walrasian stage. I shall go into the matter in much greater detail than Walras did in his sketch of a theory of capital. Thus Part III will contain, for example, what I have to say on controverted questions like the Determination of the Rate of Interest. It will also contain a discussion of the meaning of some vital concepts, like Income and Saving.

Part IV deals with the Working of a Dynamic System. Here the results of Parts II and III are brought together to form a theory of the Economic Process in time. Part II will have given us the laws of the working of a system of interrelated markets in general; Part III will have acquainted us with the characteristics of some special sorts of markets of great importance, such as the capital market. The strands must cross before the working of the capital market can be fully understood.

The programme before us is thus rather extensive, and we have, I think, a right to limit it in some directions. One limitation to our analysis will soon become very obvious, and I had better own up to it at once. We shall proceed throughout under the assumption of perfect competition; that is to say, we shall almost always neglect the influence on supply which may arise from calculations made by sellers about the influence on prices of the sales they make themselves. (Similarly for demand.) In fact, many supplies and demands are probably influenced to some extent by such calculations; it may be that they are influenced to a very important extent. However, it is very difficult to make much allowance for this influence in any other than the simplest problems; so that, although the analysis of this book would certainly be improved if more attention were paid to imperfect competition, I have thought it best to leave this over for the present. I do not myself believe that the more important results of this work are much damaged by this omission, but that is a matter which will clearly need to be investigated in due time.

Another more important limitation is implicit in our sub-title. This is a work on Theoretical Economics, considered as the logical analysis of an economic system of private enterprise, without any inclusion of reference to institutional controls. I shall interpret this limitation pretty severely. For I consider the pure logical analysis of capitalism to be a task in itself, while the survey of economic institutions is best carried on by other methods, such as those of the economic historian (even when the institutions are contemporary institutions). It is only when both these tasks are accomplished that economics begins to near the end of its journey. But there is a good line for division of labour between them, and it is a line we do well to observe.

It must be realized, indeed, that, as the price of this austerity, the purely theoretical economist becomes unable to say that any opportunities or dangers he diagnoses are or are not present in the actual world, at any particular date. He is bound to leave that to a separate investigation. But he will at least have helped that other investigator in showing him some things to look out for.

PART I
THE THEORY OF SUBJECTIVE VALUE

Reason also is choice (*Paradise Lost*)

CHAPTER I

UTILITY AND PREFERENCE

1. THE pure theory of consumer's demand, which occupied a good deal of the attention of Marshall and his contemporaries, has received far less notice in the present century. The third book of Marshall's *Principles* still remains the last word on the subject so far as books written in English are concerned. Now Marshall's theory of demand is no doubt admirable,[1] but it is remarkable that it has remained so long upon such an unquestioned eminence. This would be explicable if there were really no more to say on the subject, and if every step in Marshall's analysis were beyond dispute. But this is clearly not the case; several writers have felt very uncomfortable about Marshall's treatment,[2] and it is actually the first step, on which everything else depends, which is the most dubious.

Let us first remind ourselves of the bare outline of Marshall's main argument.[3] A consumer with a given money income is confronted with a market for consumption goods, on which the prices of those goods are already determined; the question is, How will he divide his expenditure among the different goods? It is supposed, for convenience, that the goods are available in very small units.[4] It is assumed that the consumer derives from the goods he purchases so much 'utility', the amount of utility being a function of the quantities of goods acquired; and that he will spend his income in such a way as to bring in the maximum possible amount of utility. But utility will be maximized when the marginal unit of expenditure in each direction brings in the same increment of utility. For, if this is so, a transference of

---

[1] My own experience has been that further investigation has only increased my admiration for Marshall's theory; I hope the reader will find the same.

[2] For example, Wicksteed, *Common Sense of Political Economy*, chs. 1–3; Robbins, *Nature and Significance of Economic Science*, ch. 6.

[3] *Principles*, iii. 5. 2.

[4] This convenient assumption of continuity does, of course, always falsify the situation a little (or sometimes more than a little) as far as the individual consumer is concerned. But if our study of the individual consumer is only a step towards the study of a group of consumers on the market, these falsifications can be trusted to disappear when the individual demands are aggregated.

expenditure from one direction to another will involve a greater loss of utility in the direction where expenditure is reduced than will be compensated by the gain in utility in the direction where expenditure is increased (from the principle of diminishing marginal utility). Total utility must therefore be diminished, whatever transfer is made. Since, with small units, the differences between the marginal utilities of two successive units of a commodity may be neglected, we can express the conclusion in another way: the marginal utilities of the various commodities bought must be proportional to their prices.

Marshall's argument therefore proceeds from the notion of maximizing total utility, by way of the law of diminishing marginal utility, to the conclusion that the marginal utilities of commodities bought must be proportional to their prices.

But now what is this 'utility' which the consumer maximizes? And what is the exact basis for the law of diminishing marginal utility? Marshall leaves one uncomfortable on these subjects. However, further light on them was thrown by Pareto.

2. Pareto's *Manuel d'économie politique* (1909) has to be reckoned as the other classical treatment of the theory of consumer's demand, from which any modern investigation must begin. It is not that Pareto's book, as a whole, is at all comparable with Marshall's. The *Manuel* purports to be a sort of general *Principles*; but most problems are treated by it quite superficially, while its famous theory of General Equilibrium is nothing else but a more elegant restatement of the doctrines of Walras. However, on this particular matter of utility theory Pareto was a specialist, and his investigations well deserve attention. Since they are not very familiar to English readers, I shall summarize the relevant arguments rather carefully.

Pareto started off, originally, from the same utility theory as Marshall; the argument we have just summarized would have been quite acceptable to him also in the first stage of the development of his ideas. But instead of proceeding afterwards, as Marshall did, to concentrate attention upon the demand for a single commodity (and thus to investigate the relation between the curve of diminishing marginal utility and the demand curve), Pareto turned his attention to the problem of related—complementary and competitive—goods. Here he made an extension of the earlier analysis; or rather, something which started as an extension but ended as a revolution.

For the purpose of studying related goods, Pareto took over from Edgeworth[1] a geometrical device—the Indifference Curve. When we are concerned, like Marshall, with one commodity only, we can draw a total utility curve, measuring amounts of that commodity along one axis, and total amounts of utility derived from those various amounts of commodity along the other axis. Just in the same way, when we are interested in two commodities, we can draw a utility surface. Measuring quantities of the two commodities X and Y along two horizontal axes, we get a diagram in which any point P represents a collection of given quantities (PM and PN) of the two commodities. From every such point, we can erect an ordinate in a third dimension whose length represents the amount of utility derived from that particular collection of quantities. Joining the tops of these ordinates, we get a 'utility surface' (Fig. 1 overleaf).

In principle, this is simple enough; but three-dimensional diagrams are awkward things to handle. Fortunately, having once visited the third dimension, we need not stay there. The third dimension can be eliminated, and we can return to two.

Instead of using a three-dimensional model, we can use a map (Fig. 2). Keeping quantities of the two commodities X and Y along the two axes, we can mark off on the horizontal diagram the contour lines of the utility surface (the broken line in Fig. 1). These are the indifference curves. They join all those points which correspond to the same height in the third dimension, that is, to the same total utility. If P and P' are on the same indifference curve, that means that the total utility derived from having PM and PN is the same as that derived from having $P'M'$ and $P'N'$. If P'' is on a higher indifference curve than P (the curves will have to be numbered so as to distinguish higher from lower), then $P''M''$ and $P''N''$ will give a higher total utility than PM and PN.

What will be the shape of these indifference curves? So long as each commodity has a positive marginal utility, the indifference curves must slope downwards to the right. For if X has a positive marginal utility, an increase in the quantity of X, unaccompanied by any change in the quantity of Y (that is to say, a simple movement to the right on the diagram), must increase total utility,

[1] *Mathematical Psychics*, pp. 21–2.

and so bring us on to a higher indifference curve. Similarly, a simple movement upwards must lead on to a higher indifference curve. It is only possible to stay on the same indifference curve if these movements are compensated—X increased and Y diminished, or X diminished and Y increased. The curves must therefore slope downwards to the right.

The slope of the curve passing through any point P has indeed a very definite and important meaning. It is the amount of Y which is needed by the individual in order to compensate him for the loss of a small unit of X. Now the gain in utility got by gaining such an amount of Y equals amount of Y gained $\times$ marginal utility of Y; the loss in utility got from losing the corresponding amount of X equals amount of X lost $\times$ marginal utility of X (so long as the quantities are small). Therefore, since the gain equals the loss, the slope of the curve

$$= \frac{\text{amount of } Y \text{ gained}}{\text{amount of } X \text{ lost}} = \frac{\text{marginal utility of } X}{\text{marginal utility of } Y}.$$

The slope of the curve passing through P measures the ratio of the marginal utility of X to the marginal utility of Y, when the individual has quantities PM and PN of X and Y respectively.

Have we any further information about the shapes of the curves? There ought, it would seem, to be some way of translating into terms of this diagram the principle of diminishing marginal utility. At first sight, it looks as if such a translation were possible. As one moves along an indifference curve one gets more X and less Y. The increase in X diminishes the marginal utility of X, the diminution in Y increases the marginal utility of Y. On both grounds, therefore, the slope of the curve must diminish. Falling curves, whose slope diminishes as we move to the right, will be convex to the origin, as they have been drawn in the diagram.

But does this quite necessarily follow? As far as the direct effects just taken into account are concerned, it must; but there are other indirect effects to take into account too. The increase in X may affect not only the marginal utility of X, it may also affect the marginal utility of Y. With such related goods the above argument does not necessarily follow. Suppose that the increase in X lowers the marginal utility of Y, and the diminution in Y raises the marginal utility of X; and that these cross-effects are considerable. Then the cross-effects may actually offset the direct

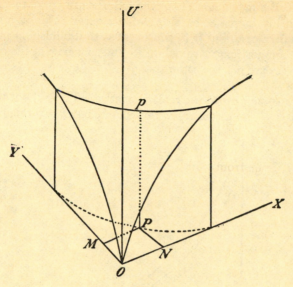

FIG. 1.

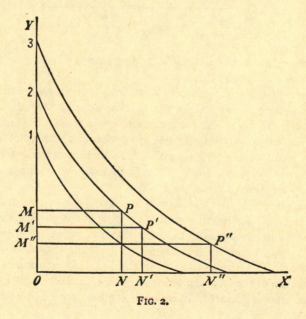

FIG. 2.

effects, and a movement along the indifference curve to the right may actually increase the slope of the curve. This is no doubt a very queer case, but it is consistent with diminishing marginal utility. Diminishing marginal utility and convexity of the indifference curves are not the same thing.

3. We come now to the really remarkable thing about indifference curves—the discovery which shunted Pareto's theory on to

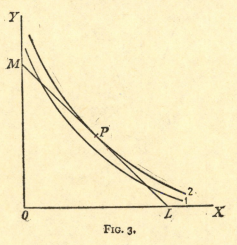

FIG. 3.

a different line from Marshall's, and opened a way to new results of wide economic significance.

Suppose that we have a consumer with a given money income, who is spending the whole of that income upon the two commodities X and Y, no others entering into the picture. Suppose that the prices of those commodities are given on the market. Then we can read off the amounts that he will buy directly from his indifference map, without any information about the amounts of utility he derives from the goods.

Mark off a length OL along the X-axis (Fig. 3), representing the amount of X which he could buy if he spent all of his income upon X; and an amount OM on the Y-axis, representing the amount of Y he could buy if he spent all his income upon Y; and join LM. Then any point on the line LM represents a pair of quantities of the two commodities which he could buy out of his income. Starting from L, in order to acquire some Y, he will have to give up X in the proportion indicated by the ratio of their prices; and the price-ratio is indicated by the slope of the line LM.

Through any point on the line LM there will pass an indifference curve; but usually the line LM will intersect the indifference curve. If this happens the point cannot be one of equilibrium. For, by moving along the line LM in one direction or the other, the consumer will always be able to get on to a higher indifference curve, which gives him greater utility. He is therefore not maximizing his utility at that particular point.

It is only when the line LM touches an indifference curve that utility will be maximized. For at a point of tangency, the consumer will get on to a lower indifference curve if he moves in either direction.

Tangency between the price-line and an indifference curve is the expression, in terms of indifference curves, of the proportionality between marginal utilities and prices.

4. Thus we can translate the marginal utility theory into terms of indifference curves; but, having done that, we have accomplished something more remarkable than a mere translation. For, in the process of translation, we have left behind some of the original data; and yet we have arrived at the desired result all the same.

In order to determine the quantities of goods which an individual will buy at given prices, Marshall's theory implies that we must know his utility surface; Pareto's theory only assumes that we must know his indifference map. And that conveys less information than the utility surface. It only tells us that the individual prefers one particular collection of goods to another particular collection; it does not tell us, as the utility surface purports to do, *by how much* the first collection is preferred to the second.

The numbers which we give to the indifference curves are indeed wholly arbitrary; it will be convenient for them to rise as we go on to higher curves, but the numbers can be 1, 2, 3, 4...., 1, 2, 4, 7...., 1, 2, 7, 10...., or any ascending series we like to take.

Pareto's little piece of geometry thus resulted in a conclusion of wide methodological importance. It is necessary, in any theory of value, to be able to define just what we mean by a consumer of 'given wants' or 'given tastes'. In Marshall's theory (like that

of Jevons, and Walras, and the Austrians) 'given wants' is interpreted as meaning a given utility function, a given intensity
of desire for any particular collection of goods. This assumption
has made many people uncomfortable, and it appears from
Pareto's work that it is not a necessary assumption at all. 'Given
wants' can be quite adequately defined as a given *scale of preferences*; we need only suppose that the consumer has a preference
for one collection of goods rather than another, not that there
is ever any sense in saying that he desires the one collection
5 per cent. more than the other, or anything like that.

Now of course this does not mean that if any one has any other
ground for supposing that there exists some suitable quantitative
measure of utility, or satisfaction, or desiredness, there is anything
in the above argument to set against it. If one is a utilitarian in
philosophy, one has a perfect right to be a utilitarian in one's
economics. But if one is not (and few people are utilitarians
nowadays), one also has the right to an economics free of utilitarian assumptions.

From this point of view, Pareto's discovery only opens a door,
which we can enter or not as we feel inclined. But from the
technical economic point of view there are strong reasons for
supposing that we ought to enter it. The quantitative concept
of utility is not necessary in order to explain market phenomena.
Therefore, on the principle of Occam's razor, it is better to do
without it. For it is not, in practice, a matter of indifference if a
theory contains unnecessary entities. Such entities are irrelevant
to the problem in hand, and their presence is likely to obscure
the vision. How important this is can only be shown by experience; I shall hope to convince the reader that it is of some
considerable importance in this case.

5. Acting on this principle, we have now to inquire whether
a full theory of consumer's demand at least as thoroughgoing as
Marshall's cannot be built up from the assumption of a *scale of
preference*. In constructing such a theory it will be necessary
every time to reject any concept which is at all dependent upon
quantitative utility, so that it cannot be derived from the indifference map alone. We start off from the indifference map
alone; nothing more can be allowed.

In undertaking this reconsideration we lose the help of Pareto;

for even after Pareto had established his great proposition, he continued to use concepts derived from the earlier set of ideas. The reason was, perhaps, that he did not take the trouble to rework his earlier conclusions in the light of a proposition which he only reached at a rather late stage of his work in economics.[1] However that may be, he missed an opportunity.

The first person to take the opportunity was the Russian economist and statistician Slutsky, in an article published in the Italian *Giornale degli Economisti* in 1915.[2] The theory to be set out in this chapter and the two following is essentially Slutsky's; although the exposition is modified by the fact that I never saw Slutsky's work until my own was very far advanced, and some time after the substance of these chapters had been published in *Economica* by R. G. D. Allen and myself.[3] Slutsky's work is highly mathematical, and he does not give much discussion about the significance of his theory. These things (and the date of its publication) perhaps explain why it remained for so long without influence, and had to be rediscovered. The present volume is the first systematic exploration of the territory which Slutsky opened up.

6. We have now to undertake a purge, rejecting all concepts which are tainted by quantitative utility, and replacing them, so far as they need to be replaced, by concepts which have no such implication.

The first victim must evidently be marginal utility itself. If total utility is arbitrary, so is marginal utility. But we can still give a precise meaning to the ratio of two marginal utilities, when the quantities possessed of both commodities are given.[4] For this

---

[1] Further, much of the energy which he had left for the subject was expended upon chasing a will-o'-the-wisp. When more than two goods are being consumed, it is possible that the differential equation of the preference system may not be integrable. This point fascinates mathematicians, but it does not seem to have any economic importance at all, the only problems to which it could conceivably be relevant being much better treated by other methods. Cf. Pareto, *Manuel*, pp. 546–57; 'Économie mathématique' (in *Encyclopédie des Sciences mathématiques*, 1911), pp. 597, 614. A recent discussion of non-integrability will be found in N. Georgescu-Roegen, 'The Pure Theory of Consumer's Behaviour' (*Q.J.E.*, Aug. 1936).

[2] E. Slutsky, 'Sulla teoria del bilancio del consumatore' (*G.d.E.*, July 1915). See also R. G. D. Allen, 'Professor Slutsky's Theory of Consumer's Choice' (*Review of Economic Studies*, 1936).

[3] 'A Reconsideration of the Theory of Value' (*Economica*, 1934).

[4] On the other hand there will be no sense in the ratio of the marginal utility

quantity is represented by the slope of an indifference curve; and that is independent of the arbitrariness in question.

In order to avoid the danger of misleading associations, let us give this quantity a new name, and call it the Marginal Rate of Substitution between the two commodities. We may define the marginal rate of substitution of X for Y as the quantity of Y which would just compensate the consumer for the loss of a marginal unit of X. This definition is entirely free from any dependence upon a quantitative measure of utility.

If an individual is to be in equilibrium with respect to a system of market prices, it is directly evident that his marginal rate of substitution between any two goods must equal the ratio of their prices. Otherwise he would clearly find an advantage in substituting some quantity of one for an equal value (at the market rate) of the other. This is therefore the form in which we must now write the condition of equilibrium on the market.

It may be observed that in this formulation we have, as yet, scarcely departed from Marshall. The marginal rate of substitution of X for Y is what he would have called the marginal utility of X in terms of Y. We may transcribe Marshall if we like, and say that the price of a commodity equals the marginal rate of substitution of that commodity for money.

7. The second victim (a more serious one this time) must be the principle of Diminishing Marginal Utility. If marginal utility has no exact sense, diminishing marginal utility can have no exact sense either. But by what shall we replace it?

By the rule that the indifference curves must be convex to the axes. This may be called, in our present terminology, the principle of Diminishing Marginal Rate of Substitution.[1] It may be expressed in the following terms: Suppose we start with a given quantity of goods, and then go on increasing the amount of X and

---

of X to that of Y, if one set of quantities is possessed when the marginal utility of X is calculated, and another set when we calculate the marginal utility of Y.

[1] I must here apologize to the reader for a tiresome change in terminology. In 'A Reconsideration' I looked at the change the other way up, and therefore talked about an Increasing Marginal Rate of Substitution where I here talk about a diminishing rate. It will be obvious why this seemed at first sight more convenient. But I have now come to think that the advantage of keeping my terminology as close as possible to the familiar Marshall terminology outweighs this slight difference in convenience.

diminishing that of Y in such a way that the consumer is left neither better off nor worse off on balance; then the amount of Y which has to be subtracted in order to set off a second unit of X will be less than that which has to be subtracted in order to set off the first unit. In other words, the more X is substituted for Y, the less will be the marginal rate of substitution of X for Y.

But what is the exact reason why we must replace diminishing marginal utility by precisely this principle—the principle of

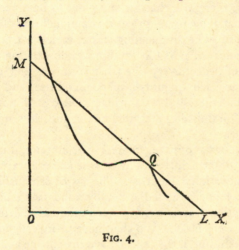

FIG. 4.

diminishing marginal rate of substitution? As we have seen already,[1] they are not exactly the same thing. The replacement is therefore not a mere translation; it is a positive change in the foundation of the theory, and requires a very definite justification.

The justification is this. We need the principle of diminishing marginal rate of substitution for the same reason as Marshall's theory needed the principle of diminishing marginal utility. Unless, at the point of equilibrium, the marginal rate of substitution is diminishing, equilibrium will not be stable. Even if the marginal rate of substitution equals the price ratio, so that the acquisition of one unit of X would not yield any appreciable advantage; nevertheless, if the marginal rate of substitution is increasing, the acquisition of a larger quantity would be advantageous. It is instructive to set this out on the indifference diagram (Fig. 4).

[1] See above, p. 16.

At the point Q on the diagram, the marginal rate of substitution equals the price-ratio, so that the price-line touches the indifference curve through Q. But the marginal rate of substitution is increasing (the indifference curve is concave to the axes), so that a movement away from Q in either direction along LM would lead the individual on to a higher indifference curve. Q is therefore a point of minimum, not maximum, utility, and cannot be a point of equilibrium.

It is clear, therefore, that for any point to be a possible rate of equilibrium at appropriate prices the marginal rate of substitution at that point must be diminishing. Since we know from experience that some points of possible equilibrium do exist on the indifference maps of nearly every one (that is to say, they do decide to buy such-and-such quantities of commodities, and do not stay hesitating indefinitely like Buridan's ass), it follows that the principle of diminishing marginal rate of substitution must sometimes be true.

However, for us to make progress in economics, it is not enough for us that the principle should be true sometimes; we require a more general validity than that. The law of diminishing marginal utility used to be assumed generally valid (with perhaps some special exceptions), and on that general validity important economic conclusions were based. We shall have to investigate those conclusions afresh; but, if they are to have any chance at all, they need as their basis a property of the indifference map which is more than *sometimes* true.

What were in fact the grounds upon which economists used to base their general principle of diminishing marginal utility? Usually an appeal to experience; though to experience of that uncomfortably vague sort which does not offer any opportunity for actual testing. Critics have not been lacking to point out that this procedure was not very scientific, and the doubts which have been thrown by our present discussion upon the intelligibility of the 'law of diminishing marginal utility' itself can only strengthen the case against the traditional procedure. If, however, we throw over diminishing marginal utility as being in any case dubious, and now certainly irrelevant, can we base upon similar 'experience' a general principle of diminishing marginal rate of substitution? Again, I suppose, we might get away without being challenged; but one would like a surer foundation.

8. We can, I think, get that surer foundation if we reflect on the purpose for which we require our principle. We want to deduce from it laws of market conduct—laws, that is, which deal with the reaction of the consumer to changes in market conditions. When market conditions change, the consumer moves from one point of equilibrium to another point of equilibrium; at each of these positions the condition of diminishing marginal rate of substitution must hold, or he could not take up such a position at all. So much is clear directly; but to proceed from this to the law of diminishing marginal rate of substitution, as we need it in economic theory, an assumption is necessary. We have to assume that the condition holds at all intermediate points, so that there are no kinks in the curves between the two positions of equilibrium. (If there are kinks in the curves, curious consequences follow, such that there will be some systems of prices at which the consumer will be unable to choose between two different ways of spending his income.) The general principle of diminishing marginal rate of substitution merely rules out these oddities; by that principle we select the simplest of the various possibilities before us.

As we go on, we shall find that most of the 'laws' of pure economic theory can be looked at in this sort of way. Pure economics has a remarkable way of producing rabbits out of a hat—apparently *a priori* propositions which apparently refer to reality. It is fascinating to try to discover how the rabbits got in; for those of us who do not believe in magic must be convinced that they got in somehow. I have become convinced myself that they get in in two ways. One is by the assumption, at the beginning of every economic argument, that the things to be dealt with in the argument are the only things that matter in some practical problem. (This is always a dangerous assumption, and nearly always more or less wrong—which is why the application of economic theory is such a ticklish matter.) That takes us much of the way, but it does not take us the whole way. The other assumption is that which we have just isolated, the assumption that kinks can be neglected, that there is a sufficient degree of regularity in the system of wants (and also, as we shall see later, in the productive system) for any set of quantities in the neighbourhood of those with which we are concerned to be a possible position of equilibrium at some system of prices. Again, this assumption may be wrong; but, being the simplest assumption possible, it is a good assumption to start with; and in fact its accordance with experience seems definitely good.

The road which lies before us now begins to be distinguishable. If this is the true foundation of the principle of diminishing marginal rate of substitution among consumption goods, other principles can be discovered whose foundation is exactly similar. These principles can be enumerated, and their consequences worked out. Some of them deal with production, and will be considered in Chapter VI below; the rest are extensions, into one field or another, of the principle elicited in this chapter. That there are a great many such extensions appears at once when we consider how wide is the variety of human choices which can be fitted into the framework of the Paretian scale of preference. What begins as an analysis of the consumer's choice among consumption goods ends as a theory of economic choice in general. We are in sight of a unifying principle for the whole of economics.

9. But this is running ahead. Before we can explore these long avenues much preparation is needed. One necessary piece of preparation may conclude this chapter.

During most of the above discussion we have made the extreme simplification that the consumer had his choice restricted to expenditure on two sorts of goods. It is high time that we abandoned this simplification, for if our theory were confined to this simple case there would not be much to be said for it. It is in fact one of the main defects of the indifference-curve technique that it encourages concentration upon this simple case, concentration that can easily prove very dangerous.

When expenditure is distributed between more than two goods, the indifference diagram loses its simplicity; for three goods we need three dimensions, and for more than three goods geometry fails us altogether. However, the principles which we have established in this chapter remain substantially unaffected. The marginal rate of substitution can be defined as before, with the added proviso that the quantities consumed of all other commodities (Z...) must remain unchanged. The consumer is only in full equilibrium if the marginal rate of substitution between any two goods equals their price-ratio. Over the principle of diminishing marginal rate of substitution there is a slight difference.

In order that equilibrium should be stable, when expenditure is distributed among many commodities, it is necessary that no possible substitution of equal market values should lead the consumer to a preferred position. This means not only that we must have a diminishing marginal rate of substitution between each pair of commodities, but also that more complicated substitutions (of some X for some Y and some Z) must be ruled out in the same way. We may express this by saying that the marginal rate of substitution must diminish for substitutions in every direction. This is a rather complicated condition, but it will appear, as we proceed, that it leads directly to conclusions of great importance.

On the same grounds as before, we shall assume that the marginal rate of substitution diminishes in every direction at every position with which we shall be concerned in our analysis. I do not think this could be established introspectively, or from 'experience', but it can be justified in the same way as we have justified the simpler condition. It becomes clear now, however, that it is a fairly drastic hypothesis, which gives us a good deal to go on, and from which we can expect to deduce some positive results.

CHAPTER II

THE LAW OF CONSUMER'S DEMAND

1. WE have now, from the conditions of equilibrium and the basic assumption of regularity, set out in the preceding chapter, to deduce laws of market conduct—to find out what can be said about the way the consumer will react when prices change. Discussion of equilibrium conditions is always a means to an end; we seek information about the conditions governing quantities bought at given prices in order that we may use them to discover how the quantities bought will be changed when prices change.

This stage of our investigation corresponds to the stage in Marshall's theory where he deduces the downward slope of the demand curve from the law of diminishing marginal utility. The particular way in which Marshall carries out that deduction is worth noting. He assumes that the marginal utility of *money* is constant.[1] Therefore, the ratio between the marginal utility of a commodity and its price is a constant ratio. If the price falls, the marginal utility must be reduced too. But, by the law of diminishing marginal utility, this implies an increase in the amount demanded. A fall in price therefore increases the amount demanded. This is the argument we have to reconsider.

What is meant by the marginal utility of money being constant? Making our translation, it would appear to mean that changes in the consumer's supply of money (that is, with respect to the problem in hand, his income) will not affect the marginal rate of substitution between money and any particular commodity X. (For the marginal rate of substitution equals the ratio of the marginal utilities or X and money.) Therefore, if his income increases, and the price of X remains constant, the price of X will still equal the marginal rate of substitution, without any change in the amount of X bought. The demand for X is therefore independent of income. His demand for any commodity is independent of his income.

---

[1] This, of course, abolishes any distinction between the diminishing marginal utility of a commodity and the diminishing marginal rate of substitution of that commodity for money. Consequently, it explains why Marshall was satisfied with diminishing marginal utility.

It will appear in what follows that this is actually what the constancy of the marginal utility of money did mean for Marshall; not that he really supposed that people's demands for commodities do not depend upon their incomes, but that in his theory of demand and price he generally neglected the income side. We shall find that he had quite good reasons for doing so, that the constancy of the marginal utility of money is in fact an ingenious simplification, which is quite harmless for most of the applications Marshall gave it himself. But it is not harmless for all applications; it is not always a good thing to be vague about the effects of changes in income on demand. There are distinct advantages to be gained from having a theory of value in which the relations of demand, price, and income are all made quite clear.

2. Let us now revert to the indifference diagram, and begin by investigating the effects of changes in income. We shall go on to investigate the effects of price-changes later, but price-changes will be easier to deal with if we examine the effects of income-changes first. Let us therefore continue to suppose, as in the last chapter, that the prices of X and Y are given, but now suppose the consumer's income to vary.

We have seen before that if his income is OL (measured in terms of X) or OM (measured in terms of Y), the point of equilibrium will be at P, where LM touches an indifference curve (Fig. 5). If now his income increases, LM will move to the right, but the new line $L'M'$ will still be parallel to LM, so long as the prices of X and Y are unchanged. (For, then, $OM'/OL' = OM/OL$, the unchanged price-ratio.) The new point of equilibrium will be at P', where $L'M'$ touches an indifference curve.

As income continues to increase, $L'M'$ continues to move to the right, and the point P' traces out a curve, which we may call the *income-consumption curve*.[1] It shows the way in which consumption varies, when income increases and prices remain unchanged. Through any point P on the diagram an income-consumption curve could be drawn; thus there will be an income-consumption curve corresponding to each possible system of prices.

What can be said about the form of the income-consumption curve? Mere experience in drawing diagrams is enough to convince

[1] In 'A Reconsideration of the Theory of Value' I called this the expenditure curve. It was clearly a bad name.

one that it will ordinarily slope upwards and to the right; but that is not enough to show that it will necessarily behave in this way. In fact, there is only one necessary restriction on its shape. An income-consumption curve cannot intersect any particular in-difference curve more than once. (For if it did so, that would mean that the indifference curve had two parallel tangents—which is impossible, if the indifference curves are always convex to the origin.) Consequently, while there is most 'room' for the income-consumption curves to slope upwards and to the right,

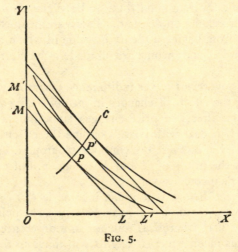

FIG. 5.

it is also possible for them to creep round to the left or downwards (PC_1 or PC_2 in Fig. 6) without ever cutting an indifference curve more than once.

And clearly that is as it should be. Curves such as PC_1 do occur. They are found whenever the commodity X is an 'inferior' good, largely consumed at low levels of income, but replaced, or partially replaced, by goods of higher quality when income rises. Margarine is obviously a case in point; its inferiority is well attested by statistical investigation.[1] But it can hardly be doubted that there are a great many others. Most of the poorer qualities of goods offered for sale are probably, in our sense, inferior goods.[2]

---

[1] Cf. Allen and Bowley, *Family Expenditure*, pp. 36, 41.

[2] It is a curious illustration of the muddle into which the theory of value was liable to fall, so long as the principle of diminishing marginal utility was not wholly abandoned, that that principle can easily be interpreted in a way which

Although the diagrammatic apparatus we have just been using is only valid for the case of two goods (X and Y), it is evident that a similar argument must hold however many are the goods among which income is being distributed. If income increases, and the increased income is spent, then there must be increased consumption in some directions, perhaps most directions or even all; but it is perfectly possible that there will be a limited number of goods whose consumption will be actually diminished. This is a very negative result and obviously needs no further elaboration.

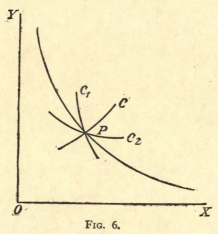

FIG. 6.

3. Let us now pass on to consider the effects of a change in price. Here again we begin with the case of two goods. Income is now to be taken as fixed, and the price of Y as fixed; but the price of X is variable. The possibilities of consumption now open are represented on the diagram (Fig. 7) by straight lines joining M (OM is income measured in terms of Y, and is therefore fixed) to points on OX which vary as the price of X varies. Each price

would exclude inferior goods from any place in economics. This interpretation was actually put forward by Pareto at one period in the development of his ideas (*Manuale di economia politica*, pp. 502–3; but cf. the later French edition, pp. 573–4). Instead of relying solely upon the *true* principle of diminishing marginal rate of substitution (that the rate will diminish when X is substituted for Y along an indifference curve), he put forward also what we may now justly regard as a false principle—that the marginal rate of substitution of X for Y will diminish when the supply of Y is reduced without any increase in the supply of X. If this were always true, it would exclude the possibility of X being an inferior good. Therefore this principle of Pareto's cannot be always satisfied.

of X will determine a line LM (OL increasing as the price falls); and the point of equilibrium corresponding to each price will be given by the point at which the line LM touches an indifference curve. The curve MPQ joining these points may be called a *price-consumption curve*. It shows the way in which consumption varies, when the price of X varies and other things remain equal.

Starting off from a particular position of LM, we have thus two

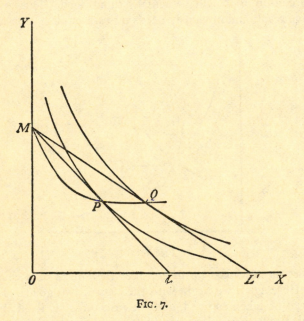

FIG. 7.

sets of straight lines, and corresponding points of contact. We have the lines parallel to LM, whose points of contact trace out the income-consumption curve. We have the lines passing through M, whose points of contact trace out the price-consumption curve. Any particular indifference curve must be touched by one line from each of these sets. Take an indifference curve I_2, which is higher than the indifference curve I_1, touched by LM. The curve I_2 is touched by a line parallel to LM at P', by a line through M at Q. Now it is at once obvious from the diagram (it follows from the convexity of the indifference curve) that Q must lie to the right of P'. This property must hold for all indifference curves which are higher than the original curve; and it therefore follows that as we go up on to higher indifference curves the price-consumption curve through P must always lie to the right of the income-consumption curve through P (Fig. 8).

This proposition, which looks like a mere piece of geometry, turns out to have much economic significance, and to be indeed quite fundamental to a large part of the theory of value. Let us try to see its implications.

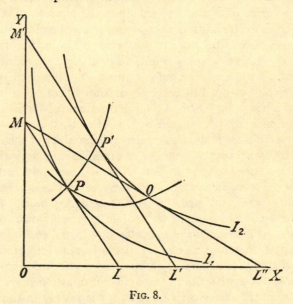

FIG. 8.

When the price of X falls, the consumer moves along the price-consumption curve from P to Q. We now see that this movement from P to Q is equivalent to a movement from P to P' along the income-consumption curve, and a movement from P' to Q along an indifference curve. We shall find it very instructive to think of the effect of price on demand as falling into these two separate parts.

A fall in the price of a commodity does actually affect the demand for that commodity in two different ways. On the one hand, it makes the consumer better off, it raises his 'real income', and its effect along this channel is similar to that of an increase in income. On the other hand, it changes relative prices; and therefore, apart from the change in real income, there will be a tendency to substitute the commodity whose price has fallen for other commodities. The total effect on demand is the sum of these two tendencies.

The relative importance of these tendencies can be further shown to depend upon the proportions in which the consumer was dividing his expenditure between this commodity (*X*) and other goods. For the extent to which he is made better off by a fall in the price of *X* will depend upon the amount of *X* which he was initially buying; if that amount was large relatively to his income, he will be made much better off, and the first effect (the Income Effect, we may call it) will be very important; but if the amount was small, the gain is small, and the income effect is likely to be swamped by the Substitution Effect.

It is this last point which is the justification of Marshall's 'constant marginal utility'. It will be observed that our two effects stand on a different footing as regards the certainty of their operation. It follows from the principle of diminishing marginal rate of substitution that the substitution effect is absolutely certain—it must always work in favour of an increase in the demand for a commodity when the price of that commodity falls. But the income effect is not so reliable; ordinarily it will work the same way, but it will work in the opposite way in the case of inferior goods. It is therefore a consideration of great importance that this unreliable income effect will be of relatively little importance in all those cases where the commodity in question plays a fairly small part in the consumer's budget; for it is only in these cases (fortunately, they are most important cases) that we have a quite unequivocal law of demand. It is only in these cases that we can be quite sure that a fall in price will necessarily lead to a rise in the amount demanded.

Marshall concentrated his attention upon these cases; and therefore he neglected the income effect. He did this by means of his assumption that the marginal utility of money could be treated as constant, which meant that he neglected the effect on demand of the changes in real income which result from changes in price. For many purposes this was a quite justifiable simplification, and it certainly did simplify his theory enormously. It is indeed one of those simplifications of genius, of which there are several instances in Marshall. Economists will continue to use these simplifications, though their path is made safer when they know exactly what it is that they are neglecting. We shall find, as we proceed, that there are other problems, not much considered by Marshall, that are made definitely easier when we are clear in our minds about the income effect.

4. The geometrical argument of the preceding section appears to apply only to the case when the consumer divides his expenditure between two commodities and no more; but it is not actually as limited as that. For suppose we regard X and Y, not as bread and potatoes, or tea and margarine (physical commodities in that sense), but as bread (some physical commodity) for one, and general purchasing power (Marshall's 'money') for the other. The choice of the consumer is a choice between spending his money on bread or keeping it available for expenditure on other things. If he decides not to spend it on bread, he will subsequently convert it into some other form by buying some other commodity or commodities with it. But even if Y were potatoes, it might still be converted into other forms, some of the potatoes being roast, some being boiled. These possibilities do not prevent us from drawing up a determinate indifference system for bread and potatoes. Similarly, so long as the terms on which money can be converted into other commodities are given, there is no reason why we should not draw up a determinate indifference system between any commodity X and money (that is to say, purchasing power in general). The distribution of purchasing power among other commodities is exactly similar to the distribution of a commodity among various uses, which may take place even if there is only one other commodity in a physical sense.

This principle is of quite general application.[1] A collection of physical things can always be treated as if they were divisible into units of a single commodity so long as their relative prices can be assumed to be unchanged, in the particular problem in hand. So long as the prices of other consumption goods are assumed to be given, they can be lumped together into one commodity 'money' or 'purchasing power in general'. Similarly, in other applications, if changes in relative wages are to be neglected,

---

[1] It is, in fact, a consequence of the principle, noted at the end of the last chapter, that the marginal rate of substitution must diminish, for substitutions in any direction. (See Appendix, § 8 (4) and § 10.)

it is quite legitimate to assume all labour homogeneous. There will be other applications still to notice as we go on.[1]

For the present, we shall only use this principle to assure ourselves that the classification of the effects of price on demand into income effects and substitution effects, and the law that the substitution effect, at least, always tends to increase demand when price falls, are valid, however the consumer is spending his income.

5. In all our discussions so far, we have been concerned with the behaviour of a single individual. But economics is not, in the end, much interested in the behaviour of single individuals. Its concern is with the behaviour of groups. A study of individual demand is only a means to the study of market demand. Fortunately, with our present methods we can make the transition very easily.

Market demand has almost exactly the same properties as individual demand. This can be seen at once if we reflect that it is the actual change in the amount demanded (brought about by a small change in price) which we can divide into two parts, due respectively to the income effect and the substitution effect. The change in the demand of a group is the sum of changes in individual demands; it is therefore also divisible into two parts, one corresponding to the sum of the individual income effects, the other to the sum of the individual substitution effects. Similar propositions to those which held about the individual effects hold about the group effects.

(1) Since all the individual substitution effects go in favour of increased consumption of the commodity whose price has fallen, the group substitution effect must do so also.

(2) Individual income effects are not quite reliable in direction; therefore group income effects cannot be quite reliable either. A good may, of course, be inferior for some members of a group, and not be inferior for the group as a whole; the negative income effects of this section being offset by positive income effects from the rest of the group.

(3) The group income effect will usually be negligible if the

---

[1] Beyond this, it does not seem necessary to worry about the definition of a 'commodity'. What collections of things we regard as composing a commodity must be allowed to vary with the problem in hand.

group as a whole spends a small proportion of its total income upon the commodity in question.

6. We are therefore in a position to sum up about the law of demand. The demand curve for a commodity must slope downwards, more being consumed when the price falls, in all cases when the commodity is not an inferior good. Even if it is an inferior good, so that the income effect is negative, the demand curve will still behave in an orthodox manner so long as the proportion of income spent upon the commodity is small, so that the income effect is small. Even if neither of these conditions is satisfied, so that the commodity is an inferior good which plays an important part in the budgets of its consumers, it still does not necessarily follow that a fall in price will diminish the amount demanded. For even a large negative income effect may be outweighed by a large substitution effect.

It is apparent what very stringent conditions need to be fulfilled before there can be any exception to the law of demand. Consumers are only likely to spend a large proportion of their incomes upon what is for them an inferior good if their standard of living is very low. The famous Giffen case, quoted by Marshall,[1] exactly fits these requirements. At a low level of income, consumers may satisfy the greater part of their need for food by one staple foodstuff (bread in the Giffen case), which will be replaced by a more varied diet if income rises. If the price of this staple falls, they have a quite considerable surplus available for expenditure, and they may spend this surplus upon more interesting foods, which then take the place of the staple, and reduce the demand for it. In such a case as this, the negative income effect may be strong enough to outweigh the substitution effect. But it is evident how rare such cases must be.

Thus, as we might expect, the simple law of demand—the downward slope of the demand curve—turns out to be almost infallible in its working. Exceptions to it are rare and unimportant. It is not in this direction that our present technique has anything new to offer.

7. But as soon as we pass beyond this standard case, we do begin to get some effective clarification.

[1] *Principles*, p. 132.

So far we have assumed the consumer's income to be fixed in terms of money. What happens if this is not so, if he comes to the market not only as a buyer but also as a seller? Suppose he comes with a fixed stock of some commodity X, of which he is prepared to hold back some for his own consumption, if price-conditions are favourable to that course of action.

It is clear that so long as the price of X remains fixed, our previous arguments are unaffected. We may suppose, if we like, that he exchanges his whole stock into money at the fixed price, when he will find himself in exactly the same position as our consumer whose income was fixed in terms of money. He can then buy back some of his X if he wants to.

But what happens if the price of X varies? The substitution effect will be the same as before. A fall in the price of X will encourage substitution of X for other goods; this must favour increased demand for X, that is to say, diminished supply. But the income effect will not be the same as before. A fall in the price of X will make a *seller* of X worse off; this will diminish his demand (increase his supply) unless X is for him an inferior good.

The significant difference between the position of the seller and that of the buyer thus comes out at once. In the case of the buyer income effect and substitution effect work in the same direction—save in the exceptional case of inferior goods. In the case of the seller, they only work in the same direction in that exceptional case. Ordinarily they work in opposite directions.

The position is made more awkward by the fact that sellers' income effects can much more rarely be neglected. Sellers usually derive large parts of their incomes from some particular thing which they sell. We shall therefore expect to find many cases in which the income effect is just as powerful as the substitution effect, or is dominant. We must conclude that a fall in the price of X may either diminish its supply or increase it.

The practical importance of such a supply curve is no doubt most evident in the case of the factors of production. Thus a fall in wages may sometimes make the wage-earner work less hard, sometimes harder; for, on the one hand, reduced piece-rates make the effort needed for a marginal unit of output seem less worth while, or would do so, if income were unchanged; but on the other, his income is reduced, and the urge to work harder in order to make up for the loss in income may counterbalance the first tendency.[1]

Such a supply curve will appear, however, whenever there is a possibility of reservation demand; that is to say, whenever the seller would prefer, other things being equal, to give up less, rather than more. The supply of agricultural products from not too

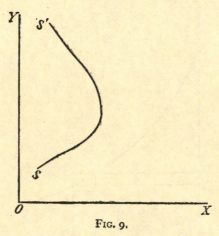

FIG. 9.

specialized farms is thus another good example. Any such supply curve, drawn on a price-quantity diagram, is likely to turn back on itself at some point. We cannot be at all confident that it will be upward-sloping (Fig. 9).

That there existed this asymmetry between supply and demand has long been familiar; it should perhaps be reckoned as one of the discoveries of Walras.[2] But so long as the reason for the asymmetry was not made clear, it was rather too easy to forget its existence. To have cleared up this matter may be regarded as the first-fruits of our new technique. It is itself a good thing to have cleared up, and, we shall find as we go on, it opens the way to some very convenient analytical methods.

[1] Robbins, 'Elasticity of Demand for Income in Terms of Effort' (*Economica*, 1930, p. 123).

[2] Walras, *Éléments d'économie politique pure* (first published 1874), leçons 5–7.

D

Note to Chapter II
CONSUMER'S SURPLUS

The doctrine of Consumer's Surplus has caused more trouble and controversy than anything else in book iii of Marshall's *Principles*; the results we have just reached throw some light upon it; consequently,

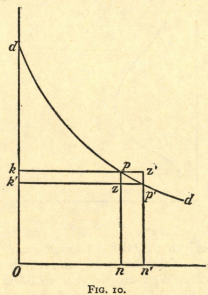

FIG. 10.

although it lies off the main track of our present inquiry, it may usefully be examined here.

Consumer's surplus is the one instance in this field where Marshall was, perhaps, just a shade too ingenious; but he was very ingenious, and we must be careful not to fall into the most common error of writers on this matter, which is to fail to give him the credit for the ingenuity he showed. We are dealing with one of those deceptive doctrines which appear to be a good deal simpler than they are. It can easily be stated in a way which is altogether fallacious; and it is easy to overlook the fact that Marshall did go to some considerable trouble in order not to state it in a fallacious way.

It is thus useful to begin by contrasting Marshall's argument with that of the original inventor of consumer's surplus—Dupuit. Dupuit, writing in 1844, gave a version that has none of Marshall's refinement.[1]

[1] Dupuit's work appeared in the *Annales des Ponts et Chaussées*, and was thus

He held straightforwardly that 'l'économie politique doit prendre pour mesure de l'utilité d'un objet le sacrifice maximum que chaque consommateur serait disposé à faire pour se le procurer' (p. 40), and therefore that the 'utility' secured by being able to purchase *on* units of a commodity at the price *pn* is given by the area *dpk* on the price-quantity demand diagram (p. 63). This without any qualification. Marshall uses the same diagram (Fig. 10) and arrives at the same result; but he

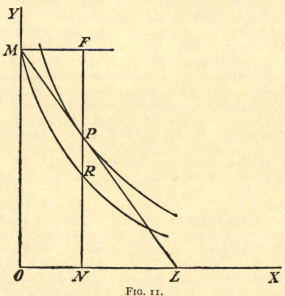

FIG. 11.

makes the significant qualification that the marginal utility of money must be supposed constant.[1]

The force of this can be readily shown on the indifference diagram, measuring, as before, the commodity X along one axis and money on the other (Fig. 11). If the consumer's income is OM, and the price of X is indicated by the slope of ML, which touches an indifference curve at P, ON will be the amount of X purchased, and PF the amount of money paid for it. Now P is on a higher indifference curve than M, and what is wanted is a money measure of this gain in 'utility'. Like Dupuit, Marshall takes 'the excess of the price which (the consumer) would be willing to pay rather than go without the thing, over that which he actually does pay'.[2] The price he actually does pay is measured on our diagram by PF, the price he would be willing to pay by RF, where

very inaccessible until M. de Bernardis' elegant reprint entitled *De l'utilité et de sa mesure* (Turin, 1933), from which I quote.

[1] Marshall, *Principles*, p. 842.   [2] Ibid., p. 124.

R lies on the same indifference curve as M (so that if he bought ON and paid RF for it, he would be no better off by making the transaction). Consumer's surplus is therefore the length of the line RP.

RP is a perfectly general representation of consumer's surplus, independent of any assumption about the marginal utility of money. But it is not necessarily equal to the area under the demand curve in Marshall's diagram, unless the marginal utility of money is constant. This can be seen as follows. If the marginal utility of money is constant, the slope of the indifference curve at R must be the same as the slope of the indifference curve at P, that is to say, the same as the slope of the line MP. A slight movement to the right along the indifference curve MR will therefore increase RF by the same amount as a slight movement along MP will increase PF. But the increment in PF is the additional amount paid for a small increment in the amount purchased at the price given by MP, an amount measured by the area $pnn'z'$ in Fig. 10. The length RF is built up out of a series of such increments, and must therefore be represented on Fig. 10 by the area built up out of increments such as $pnn'z'$. This is nothing else than $dpno$.

RP will therefore be represented on Fig. 10 by dpk—Marshall's consumer's surplus.

This is valid so long as the marginal utility of money is constant—so long as income effects can be neglected. But how legitimate is it in this case to follow Marshall in neglecting income effects? This is not a case in which they can be very safely ignored. Marshall neglects the difference between the slope of the indifference curve at P and the slope of the indifference curve at R. It is true that this difference is likely to be less important, the less important in the consumer's budget is the commodity we are considering. But the difference may still be important, even if the proportion of income spent upon the commodity is small; it will still be important, if RP itself is large, if the consumer's surplus is large, so that the loss of the opportunity of buying the commodity is equivalent to a large loss of income.

This is the weakness which remains even in Marshall's version of the consumer's surplus theory; but there is really no reason why it should be allowed to remain. We must remember that the notion of consumer's surplus is not wanted for its own sake; it is wanted as a means of demonstrating a very important proposition, which was supposed to depend upon it. However, in fact that proposition can be demonstrated without begging any questions at all.

As we have seen, the best way of looking at consumer's surplus is to regard it as a means of expressing, in terms of money income, the gain which accrues to the consumer as a result of a fall in price. Or better, it is the *compensating variation* in income, whose loss would just offset the fall in price, and leave the consumer no better off than before. Now it can be shown that this compensating variation cannot be less than a certain minimum amount, and will ordinarily be greater than that amount. This is all that is needed.

Suppose the price of oranges is 2d. each; and at this price a person buys 6 oranges. Now suppose that the price falls to 1d., and at the lower price he buys 10 oranges. What is the compensating variation in income? We cannot say exactly, but we can say that it cannot be less than 6d. For suppose again that, at the same time as the price of oranges fell, his income had been reduced by 6d. Then, in the new circumstances, he can, if he chooses, buy the same amount of oranges as before, and the same amounts of all other commodities; what had previously been his most preferred position is still open to him; so he cannot be worse off. But with the change in relative prices, it is probable that he will be able to substitute some quantity of oranges for some quantities of other things, and so make himself better off. But if he can lose 6d. and still remain better off, 6d. must be less than the compensating variation; he would have to lose more than 6d. in order to be just as well off as before.[1]

This is all that is necessary in order to establish the important consequences in the theory of taxation which follow from the consumer's surplus principle. It shows, for example, why (apart from distributional effects) a tax on commodities lays a greater burden on consumers than an income tax. If the price of oranges falls from 2d. to 1d. as the result of a reduction in taxation, then (assuming constant costs) the reduction in tax receipts from our particular consumer is 6d. If this is taken from him by an income tax, he is still left better off, and the government no worse off.

Other deductions which have been drawn from the consumer's surplus principle can presumably be tested out in a similar way.[2]

[1] The compensating variation can thus be proved to be greater than the area $kpzk'$ on Fig. 10. Can it also be proved to be less than the area $kz'p'k'$? At first sight, one might think so; but in fact it is not possible to give an equally rigorous proof on this side. This comes out clearly if we use the indifference diagram (Fig. 11). The line exhibiting opportunities of purchase, when the price of oranges falls by 1d., and income is reduced by 10d., no longer passes through the original point of equilibrium P. Thus we have no reliable information about the indifference curve it touches. We are left to infer from our earlier argument that the compensating variation will be less than the larger rectangle, so long as the marginal utility of money can be taken as constant.

[2] In an article which appeared after I had written the above ('The General Welfare in relation to Problems of Taxation and of Railway and Utility Rates', *Econometrica*, July 1938) Professor Hotelling gives a substantially similar argument and applies it to broader problems of economic welfare. It would be interesting to submit all the fundamental part of Professor Pigou's book to this sort of criticism; my impression is that most of it would come out pretty well.

CHAPTER III

COMPLEMENTARITY

1. THE definition of complementary and competitive goods given by Edgeworth and Pareto (Marshall did not go into the matter) is this.[1] Y is complementary with X in the consumer's budget if an increase in the supply of X (Y constant) raises the marginal utility of Y; Y is competitive with X (or is a substitute for X) if an increase in the supply of X (Y constant) lowers the marginal utility of Y. According to this definition, it appeared evident that the complementary-competitive relation is reversible: if Y is complementary with X, X is complementary with Y; if Y is a substitute for X, X is a substitute for Y.[2] Further, if the marginal utility of money is constant, it follows at once from this definition that a fall in the price of X, increasing the demand for X, must raise the marginal utility of Y if X and Y are complementary, and will therefore raise the demand for Y. Similarly, it will lower the demand for Y if X and Y are substitutes. So far, so good; Edgeworth and Pareto were quite satisfied.

Pareto, however, had no business to be satisfied. For when he tried to translate his definition into terms of indifference curves, he got into difficulties. He was indeed able to trace some parallelism between the case when X and Y are complementary (on the above definition) and that in which the indifference curves between X and Y (other commodities consumed taken as constant) are very bent (Fig. 12); between the case when the indifference curves are very flat (Fig. 13) and that in which X and Y are substitutes.[3] But the parallelism is not at all exact, as is made evident at once by the impossibility of discovering what degree of curvature of the indifference curves corresponds to the *distinction* between complementary and substitute goods—which ought, on the definition, to be a perfectly clear-cut distinction.

[1] Edgeworth, *Papers*, vol. i, p. 117; Pareto, *Manuel*, p. 268.
[2] With a given utility function, the order of partial differentiation is immaterial.
[3] In Fig. 12 an increase in X near the bend gives little advantage unless it is accompanied by an increase in Y. In Fig. 13 an increase in X may be accompanied by a considerable decrease in Y, and still be advantageous.

Further, the Edgeworth–Pareto definition sins against Pareto's own principle of the immeasurability of utility. If utility is not

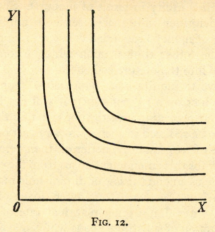

FIG. 12.

a quantity, but only an index of the consumer's scale of preferences, his definition of complementary goods has no precise meaning. The distinction between complementary and com-

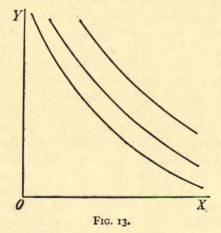

FIG. 13.

petitive goods will differ according to the arbitrary measure of utility which is adopted.[1]

2. These difficulties can be overcome in the following way.

[1] Cf. Mathematical Appendix, § 5.

We have first to replace 'marginal utility' in the Edgeworth–Pareto definition by 'marginal rate of substitution for money' (which is 'marginal utility in terms of money'). Since the Edgeworth–Pareto definition only makes sense in application if the marginal utility of money is assumed constant, it is not surprising that money—the 'other things' upon which income is spent—has got to come into the picture somehow.

Next, we have to inquire what happens to 'money' when the supply of X is increased (Y constant); it will not be surprising, in the light of our preceding investigations, to find that the supply of money has to be reduced in such a way as to set off the increase in X, and leave the consumer no better off than before.

The necessity for this amendment arises from the same reason as that which made us amend the law of diminishing marginal utility; indeed, it is a consequence of our amendment of diminishing marginal utility into diminishing marginal rate of substitution. We want a definition of substitute goods which makes it absolutely certain that an extra unit of the same physical commodity is a substitute for preceding units. Now an extra unit of X definitely lowers the marginal rate of substitution of X for money only if the extra unit is substituted for money in such a way as to leave the consumer no better off than before (our law of diminishing marginal rate of substitution). Thus we must say that *Y is a substitute for X if the marginal rate of substitution of Y for money is diminished when X is substituted for money in such a way as to leave the consumer no better off than before.* We must say that *Y is complementary with X if the marginal rate of substitution of Y for money is increased when X is substituted for money.*

This definition is free from dependence upon a quantitative measure of utility; it reduces to the Edgeworth–Pareto definition if the marginal utility of money is constant (if income effects can be neglected); and, like the Edgeworth–Pareto definition, it is reversible between X and Y. If Y is complementary with X, X is necessarily complementary with Y. If Y is a substitute for X, X is a substitute for Y.[1] And, as we shall see, it is directly

---

[1] Assume prices other than those of X and Y given, and start from the position where the consumer possesses the particular amounts of X, Y, and money in which we are interested. Let M be the maximum amount of money which the consumer would be willing to give up in order to acquire certain additional quantities x, y of X and Y. Then M is a function of x and y; and the order of partial differentiation of M with respect to x and y is immaterial—as before.

applicable to cases where the marginal utility of money cannot be assumed constant.

3. It is a very curious consequence of our new definition that the indifference diagram, which Pareto took up as a means of throwing light upon the problem of related goods, proves to be of little direct use for that particular problem.

The indifference diagram, measuring its two 'commodities' along its two axes, is only useful when the consumer can be thought of as spending his income upon two 'commodities' and two 'commodities' only; this usually means, in practice, that it must be applied to the case in which we are interested in problems of the demand for one physical commodity, and measure along the other axis all other commodities lumped together (Marshall's *money*). For these problems—Marshall's problems—the indifference diagram is very instructive, and enables us to put a keener edge on the analysis than is possible by Marshall's methods. But the problem of related goods cannot be treated on a two-dimensional indifference diagram. It needs three dimensions to represent the two related goods and *money* (the necessary background). This means that the theory is most conveniently represented either in algebra (an algebraic version will be given in the Appendix) or, as here, in ordinary words.

Let us go back to the distinction between the income effect and the substitution effect, as we developed it in the last chapter. We have seen how the income effect and the substitution effect, set up by a fall in the price of X (other prices unchanged), exert themselves on the demand for X. We have now to look at them more generally, and to see how they work themselves out in the general rearrangement of the consumer's expenditure.

The income effect causes little trouble. A fall in the price of X acts like a rise in income, and thus tends to increase the demand for every good consumed, excepting inferior goods. If the proportion of income spent on X is small, the income effect generally will be small; it will only have a small influence on the demand for X, and will have a small proportionate influence on the demand for any other commodity.

The substitution effect, as we have seen, must involve a substitution in favour of X; and therefore against something other than X. If, as on the indifference diagram, we lump together all commodities other than X into a single 'commodity' (measured along the vertical axis), the substitution effect must tend to diminish the demand for this composite 'commodity'.[1] But it is only obliged to diminish the demand for the other commodities when they are taken together; it need not diminish the demand for each one taken separately.

Suppose that Y (one of the other commodities) is complementary with X—according to our definition of complementarity. Then we know that if the amount of Y is held constant, a substitution in favour of X and against money (now 'other goods than X or Y') will raise the marginal rate of substitution of Y for money. Now the price of Y in terms of money is given and constant; so a rise in the marginal rate of substitution of Y for money must encourage a substitution of Y for money, if the marginal rate of substitution of Y for money is to be kept equal to the price of Y. Therefore, if Y is complementary with X, a substitution of X for money tends to be accompanied by a parallel substitution of Y for money. The substitution in favour of X stimulates a similar substitution in favour of Y.

On the other hand, if, on our definition, Y is a substitute for X, a substitution of X for money (Y constant) encourages a substitution in favour of money and against Y. The substitution in favour of X tends to be accompanied by a substitution against Y. It is our definition of complementarity which draws the exact line between these two situations.

4. The distinction between complementarity and substitution, when it is made in this way, incidentally clears up a point that will probably have been worrying the reader. What is the relation between this sort of substitution—the sort opposed to complementarity—and the sort of substitution we have been discussing at length in earlier chapters, before we took up the question of related goods at all? The answer is that they are the same thing.

If a consumer is dividing his income between purchases of two goods only, and cannot possibly buy any other goods than these two, then there cannot be anything else but a substitution relation between the two goods. For if he is to get more of one of them, and

---

[1] The movement from P' to Q along the indifference curve (Ch. II, Fig. 8) is to the right and *downwards*.

still be no better off than before, he must have less of the other. But when he is dividing his income between more than two goods, other kinds of relation become possible. It is still possible that all the other goods may be simply substitutes for one of the goods (say X). This will happen if, when the supply of X is increased, there has to be a reduction in the quantities of *all* other goods in order to satisfy the two conditions: (1) that the consumer is left no better off than before, (2) that the marginal rates of substitution between these other goods are left unchanged. Here the substitution in favour of X is a substitution against each of the other commodities taken separately. But it is possible that, for these two conditions to be satisfied, there must be an increase in *some* of the other commodities—the commodities complementary with X. Obviously all commodities consumed cannot be complementary with X, since the consumer cannot get more of all commodities and still be left no better off than before. Thus we see why complementarity cannot arise on the indifference diagram of two goods; for X and Y can only be complementary if there is some third thing at whose expense substitution in favour of both X and Y can take place.

Complementary groups of commodities are indeed only possible if there is something outside them for them to be substituted against. Of the three goods, X, Y, 'money', X and Y may be complementary; but if so, X must be a substitute for money, and (from considerations of what happens when there is a substitution in favour of Y, remembering that the XY complementarity relation is reversible) Y must be a substitute for money. Of the four goods, X, Y, Z, 'money', X, Y, Z may all be complementary with each other; but if so, each must be a substitute for money. Indeed, however many goods enter into the consumer's expenditure, it is possible theoretically that all but one may form a complementary group, each good in the group being a substitute for the one good left outside it. This is the maximum possible limit of complementarity; while, at the other extreme, there may be no complementarity present at all.

It seems fairly safe to assume, in practice, that we shall usually be concerned with cases nearer the minimum of complementarity than the maximum. Any particular good will have a little knot of other goods round it that are complementary with it; but its most probable relation with any other good taken at random will be one of (doubtless mild) substitutability. At least that is what one would expect to find.

5. We may now sum up our conclusions about the effect of a change in the price of one commodity X upon the consumer's expenditure. A fall in the price of X (other prices unchanged) affects both the demand for X and the demand for other commodities by means of an income effect and a substitution effect.

So far as the demand for X is concerned, the substitution effect must increase it; and the income effect will do so also, unless X is an inferior good.

So far as the demand for all other goods taken together is concerned (since their prices are given, this applies also to the total expenditure upon all other goods), the substitution effect will diminish it, and the income effect (practically speaking, always) increase it. These effects are very likely to be of comparable magnitude, so that the total demand for other goods may either increase or diminish.[1]

So far as the demand for some particular other good Y is concerned, the substitution effect will diminish it, unless Y is complementary with X; the income effect will increase it, unless Y is an inferior good. Several cases may therefore be distinguished.

(1) Y may be highly complementary with X. Here the substitution effect may easily be large enough to drown any income effect, so that the demand for Y will definitely increase. An example of this (but only an example) is the case where Y and X have to be used in fixed proportions, so that the substitution in favour of Y matches the substitution in favour of X; and is thus likely to be large relatively to the income effect in those cases when the substitution effect on the demand for X is large relatively to the income effect on the demand for X.

(2) Y may be mildly complementary with X. In this case the income effect becomes important. Ordinarily it will go in the same direction as the substitution effect, so that there will be some rise in the demand for Y. But if Y is an inferior good, the income and substitution effects may cancel out; or even, in an extreme

---

[1] From another point of view, the demand for other goods taken together will increase or diminish according as the demand for X has an elasticity less or greater than 1.

case, the (negative) income effect may be dominant, so that the demand for Y diminishes a little.[1]

(3) Y may be mildly substitutable for X. (This is doubtless a very common case indeed.) Here the income effect and the substitution effect ordinarily go in the opposite directions, thus tending to cancel out, or leave a very slight effect on the demand for Y, which may go either way. But if Y is an inferior good, the demand for it will definitely contract, though perhaps only a little.

(4) Y may be highly substitutable for X. In this case the substitution effect will be decidedly dominant, and the demand for Y must diminish. The extreme case here is that in which X and Y are *perfect substitutes*, that is to say, when a substitution in favour of X reduces the marginal rate of substitution of Y for money in exactly the same proportion as that in which the marginal rate of substitution of X is reduced. This will ordinarily happen when the consumer finds the two commodities indistinguishable, as means for satisfying his wants, whether they are physically indistinguishable or not. If Y is a perfect substitute for X, and the price of X falls, without that of Y falling, the demand for Y must fall to zero. The relation of perfect substitutability is reversible; if Y is a perfect substitute for X, X must be a perfect substitute for Y.

To conclude this classification, we may ask which are the cases in which a fall in the price of X has *no* influence on the demand for Y. This may happen, it is clear, either if both the income effect and the substitution effect on the demand for Y are negligible (less than the *minimum sensibile*); or if they are not negligible taken separately, but they go in opposite directions, and their difference is negligible. Doubtless a good many of the commodities which economists have usually treated as being 'independent' of a particular commodity X, because they do not show any sign of having their demands influenced by changes in the price of X, come under the first heading; the price of X does not affect them in any way. But one cannot resist the feeling that a fair number come under the second heading; it is hard to believe that all the substitution in favour of commodities comes about at the expense of close substitutes; one feels that a good deal of mild

[1] Compare the exception to the ordinary law of demand, when a fall in the price of X may lead to a fall in the demand for it.

substitutability must be present which is prevented from showing itself by being offset by income effects.

6. This, then, is our theory of complementary and substitute goods in the consumer's budget. It has been shown, I think, that it is a consistent and precise theory. It remains to be shown that it is a useful theory—that the classification adopted is a significant classification, which can be usefully applied to a variety of problems.

This will be our task in much of the rest of this book; there are, however, one or two preliminary points that may be dealt with here.

First of all, we may observe that the principles we have enunciated about the effect of a change in the price of X on the demand for Y are just as applicable to market demand as to the demand of the individual consumer. The effect on the demand for Y from a group of consumers is also divisible into an income effect and a substitution effect. It is possible that X and Y may be complementary for some persons, substitutes for others. If this happens, we can still regard them as complementary for the group as a whole, if the total substitution effect increases the demand for Y when the price of X falls; substitutes for the group as a whole in the reverse case. The reversibility of complementarity also holds for a group; if Y is complementary with X, X is complementary with Y; if Y is a substitute for X, X is a substitute for Y.[1]

This is one important property of our definition which makes it convenient for application. Another follows from the principle we set out in the last chapter, and have used extensively in this: that when the relative prices of a group of commodities can be assumed to remain unchanged, they can be treated as a single commodity.

We have seen that when X is a single physical commodity, and the other commodities consumed are treated as a single commodity in this way, a fall in the price of X relatively to other prices gives rise to a substitution in favour of X and against these other commodities. (Of course it gives rise to an income

---

[1] Observe that it is only the substitution effects that are reversible. If a fall in the price of X increases the demand for Y, it does not necessarily follow that a fall in the price of Y will increase the demand for X. We should, however, expect to find such a relation if the effect of the price of X on the demand for Y is at all large.

effect too, but let us leave that out of account for the present.) As a result of this substitution effect, the demand for the other commodities is diminished; that is to say, the expenditure on the other commodities taken together is diminished (although, as we have seen, there may be such a rearrangement of expenditure among these commodities, that the expenditure on some of them individually is increased).

Let us now carry this line of thought a little farther. The substitution in favour of X and against the other commodities comes about because the price of X has fallen relatively to other prices (which have maintained the same ratios among themselves). Now just the same situation would recur, causing just the same sort of substitution effect, if the price of X had remained fixed, while the prices of all other commodities had changed, but had changed in the same ratio, so that the other commodities could still be lumped together quite fairly. This suggests that we may go on to say that a fall in the prices of each of a group of goods (each falling in the same proportion) must cause a substitution in favour of the group as a whole. The deduction is perfectly justified.

We shall find, as we go on, that this proposition is a distinctly useful one; but it is important to be clear about its exact limits, about what it does not mean. It does not mean that there must be a substitution effect in favour of each commodity in the group taken separately, so that (apart from income effects) the demand for each commodity separately must increase. It is always possible that the demands for some goods in the group may diminish, since they are substituted by other goods in the group. Further, the income effect must be taken into account, and, in cases where the group is a large group, so that the consumer spends a considerable proportion of his income upon it, the income effect will be large. But negative income effects for a large group are not probable; it is unlikely that the consumer will spend less money upon a whole large group of goods when his income increases. Consequently, so far as the demand for the group itself is concerned, we should expect the income effect to pull in the same direction as the substitution effect.

7. There remains one important proposition (not noticed in the first edition of this book) which is probably the ultimate generalization of the theory of demand, since it relates, not to a particular

price-change, but to any change in the system of prices confronting a consumer. Any such price-change will set up an income effect and a substitution effect; about the income effect nothing in general can be said, but there is something to be said in general about the substitution effect. The substitution effect is concerned with the change in relative prices; we can isolate it if we consider such changes in prices as keep the consumer on the same indifference level—all other changes being reduced to a combination of this with a proportional change in all prices, which is a change in real income, so that it induces a pure income effect.

When we consider a change in prices, which is such that it leaves the consumer on the same indifference level, we can always say that the new collection of goods purchased must have a higher value in terms of the old prices than the old collection of goods had. For the old collection was the only collection of goods on this indifference level which was available to him at the old prices. Similarly the old collection of goods must have a higher value in terms of the new prices than the new collection of goods has.

It follows from the first of these inequalities that the sum of the increments in amounts purchased (due attention being paid to sign) must be positive when valued at the old prices. It follows from the second inequality that the sum of the same increments, valued at the new prices, must be negative. These two statements can only be consistent with one another if the sum of the increments, valued at the *increment* of the corresponding price in each case, is negative. This is the sense in which the most generalized change in prices must set up a change in demands in the opposite direction. It must be emphasized that it only applies to substitution effects; if there is a change in real income (or, in the case of a group of consumers, a change in the distribution of real income) then there is also an income effect to be considered, which will proceed on its own principles.[1]

---

[1] We shall not often need to use the argument of this last section in what follows. Some consequences of it, which lead in different directions from those generally pursued in this book, are discussed in Additional Note A.

PART II
GENERAL EQUILIBRIUM

A new and penetrating light descends on the spectacle,
enduing men and things with a seeming transparency, and
exhibiting as one organism the anatomy of life and movement
in all humanity and vitalized matter included in the display.
(*The Dynasts.*)

CHAPTER IV
THE GENERAL EQUILIBRIUM OF EXCHANGE

1. WE have now completed the elaboration of our theory of consumers' demand. Looked at in the most general way, what is it that we have accomplished? First of all, we have found a precise meaning for the assumption that an individual's 'wants' are given; it must mean that he has a given scale of preferences. Then we have inquired how an individual with a given scale of preferences, and given supplies of commodities, will seek to exchange those commodities for others, when the prices of both sets (the commodities he gives up and those that he acquires) are given. Next, we have inquired how these decisions to buy and sell (these demands and supplies) will be affected when prices vary. Lastly, we have aggregated these laws of demand and supply, so that they can be applied to groups of individuals, instead of to single individuals. We have discovered how the total demands and supplies of a group of persons will react to price-changes, assuming that the scale of preferences of each member of the group remains fixed.

As the discussion proceeded, we have mostly kept in mind the most obvious application of our analysis: to the ordinary consumer spending his income on the satisfaction of his immediate personal wants. This was of course the case which Marshall, upon whom we have commented so much, had almost entirely in mind. But it is not the only case to which the analysis applies. (Indeed, if it had been, I doubt if it would have been worth while pursuing it to such a degree of refinement.)

The objects bought and sold need not be consumers' goods, or they need not all be consumers' goods; the necessary condition is only that they should be objects of desire, which can be bought and sold, and which can be arranged in an order of preference (an indifference system) *which is itself independent of prices*.

There is therefore included, as well as the demand for consumption goods, the supply of labour services. As we have seen, the wage-earner (or salary-earner) can be readily thought of as choosing one way of earning an income rather than another because he prefers one size of income earned by doing so much work to another size of income earned by doing another amount of work.[1] There is also included, as Wicksteed well pointed out,[2] the purchase and sale of goods, not to satisfy one's individual wants, but in order to satisfy the wants of other people, or what one supposes those wants to be. But these do not exhaust the possible extensions, as becomes clear when we consider what it is that our criterion excludes.

It excludes one case even in the field of consumption goods. This is the Veblenesque example beloved of the text-books: the demand for an object of ostentatious expenditure (diamonds) may be reduced by a fall in its price, because the desire for diamonds (the marginal rate of substitution for money of a given quantity of diamonds) depends on the price of diamonds, and falls when the price falls. But this is a trifle compared with the important exclusions.

One is the demand and supply of goods from producers. A factor of production, to a producer, is ordinarily not something for which he has a place on his own scale of preferences. His demand for it is a derived demand, depending on the price of its product. He intends to sell the product, and then satisfy his wants with the proceeds; without any information about the price of the product, he cannot tell what it will be worth his while to pay for a unit of the factor. This is one part of the problem of economic choice which is entirely left out of account in our previous discussion. It will occupy us in the later chapters of this part.

The other case which is excluded is the case of speculative demand. It is another familiar text-book point, that a fall in price may fail to increase demand, or may even diminish it, because it creates an expectation of the price falling farther. Here the marginal rate of substitution of the commodity for money ceases to be independent of prices, because of a reaction through expectations. We shall see later on (in Part IV) how important reactions through expectations may be.

One example only may be given here. The demand for money[3] itself is necessarily and always speculative in a wide sense. There is no demand for money for its own sake, but only as a means of

---

[1] I beg the question of how to measure amounts of 'work'.

[2] *Common Sense of Political Economy*, ch. 5.

[3] Henceforward not to be understood in the special Marshallian sense used hitherto.

making purchases in the future. It is therefore always liable to be affected by expectations of the future. Every theory of money has always had to take account of this fact in one way or other.

These two exclusions—Production and Speculation—are the important exclusions. They will occupy us through many future chapters.

But observe that they are only excluded in so far as they involve a reaction of prices on the individual's scale of preferences. Any problem which does not involve such a reaction may be studied by our present technique.

2. With these things in mind, we are encouraged to proceed from our theory of consumer's choice to what may be at least a serviceable preliminary survey of the theory of Exchange.

Let us suppose that we have to deal with a world where the only objects of exchange are personal services. The demand for these services will be governed by the laws set out in the preceding chapters; so will the supplies. All the complications of production and speculation are eliminated. If we can get a clear idea of such an economic system, we shall certainly still be a long way from having a realistic model of the actual world; but we shall have a foundation on which to build, and which may be useful in itself for certain limited purposes.

In deciding to treat the general theory of exchange before dealing with production, we are following the example of Walras rather than Marshall. It was Walras who created the theory of general exchange equilibrium, as it has been known hitherto.[1] Just as we had previously to summarize Pareto's work on the theory of value, before endeavouring to carry it farther, so now we must summarize some work of Walras.

Let us begin with the elementary case where there are only two sorts of services—only two kinds of goods to be exchanged. Thus every person is either simply a buyer of X and seller of Y, or is simply a buyer of Y and seller of X. So long as we assume perfect competition, this case presents no difficulty at all. One price-ratio has to be established, the price-ratio of X to Y. One condition is available for establishing it—the condition that the demand for X must equal the supply. (If the demand for X equals the supply of X, it follows arithmetically that the demand

[1] *Éléments d'économie politique pure* (1874), leçons 5–15 (édition définitive).

for Y equals the supply of Y.) Our previous investigations have shown us how the demand and supply for X will be determined at a given price-ratio. In order for the market to be in equilibrium, it is only necessary for the price-ratio to be fixed at that level which equates demand and supply.[1]

This is universally familiar ground; but when we pass on to extend the argument to cases where more than two commodities are concerned, some new points come up, which are rather less obvious. Thus: How many prices have to be determined? For the exchange of two goods we have one price to determine; similarly for the exchange of three goods we have two prices, and so on: always one less than the number of goods. This can be seen at once if we select one of the n commodities as a standard of value; the $n-1$ prices are then the prices of the other $n-1$ goods in terms of the standard commodity. Of course the other commodities may be exchanged by direct exchange without recourse to the standard; but in equilibrium the rate of exchange between any two commodities must always equal the ratio of their prices in terms of the standard commodity. For if not, one party or the other would always be able to benefit himself by abandoning direct exchange, and splitting the transaction into two parts: first an exchange of one commodity for the standard, and then an exchange of the standard for the other commodity.

We shall find it convenient, when dealing with multiple exchange, always to take some particular commodity as a standard of value.[2] So far, this commodity is invested with some of the qualities of money. But it is not necessary to assume that our traders actually use the standard commodity as money; they may do, or they may not. If, for some purposes, we do decide to identify the standard commodity with money, then it must be clearly understood that it has not yet been given any more of the qualities of money than these—that it is an object of desire, and that it is used as a standard of value. Later on we shall be able to endow our standard commodity with other qualities, so that we can actually employ it as a means for analysing genuinely monetary problems; for the present it is very much of a shadow. But we shall find that it is

---

[1] A market is in equilibrium, statically considered, if every person is acting in such a way as to reach his most preferred position, subject to the opportunities open to him. This implies that the actions of the different persons trading must be consistent. For a further discussion of the concept of equilibrium, see Chapter X, below. [2] *Numéraire*, as Walras called it.

much more useful to have even shadow money in the early stages of our analysis than to have no money at all; for we shall then be enabled to turn out at once results that have a good prospect of being true for a monetary economy, even if they are not the whole truth.

Thus we shall assume for the present that our standard commodity is a real commodity like any other, with an ordinary place on the scale of preferences of an ordinary individual. Those people who come to the market with supplies of the standard commodity do not necessarily intend to spend the whole of their supplies. If prices are favourable to that course of action, they may decide to reserve some.

3. Once a particular set of prices is given, we know how to determine the most preferred position of any individual. This gives us the quantities he will demand of those commodities he does not possess, and the quantities he will be willing to supply in exchange for them of those commodities he does. By simple addition, we can determine the demand and supply for each commodity. If the price-system is such as to make these demands and supplies equal, we have a position of equilibrium. If not, some prices at least will be bid up or down.

The determinateness of this solution was shown by Walras to be ensured by equality between the number of equations and the number of unknowns. If there are n kinds of goods being exchanged, this gives us $n-1$ prices to be determined. It might appear at first sight that there are n equations to determine them— demand-and-supply equations on the markets for the n goods. But this is not the case. For two goods, it will be remembered, we had only one demand-and-supply equation. However many goods there are, the number of equations is always one less than the number of goods. This is because the equation of demand and supply on the market for the standard commodity follows from the rest. Once any particular individual has decided how much of each non-standard commodity he will sell or he will buy, he will automatically have decided how much of the standard commodity he will buy or sell.[1] Thus

Demand for standard = Receipts from sale of other goods
—Expenditure on purchase of others

---

[1] Lending being either left out of account or included by the device of regard-ing securities as a kind of commodity. See below, Chapter XII.

or

Supply of standard = Expenditure on purchase of others
—Receipts from sale of others

Therefore, for the whole community,

Demand for—Supply of standard commodity
= Total receipt from sale of others
—Total expenditure on purchase of others

and, once the demand for every non-standard commodity equals the supply, this must=0.

There are thus $n-1$ independent equations to determine the $n-1$ independent prices.

4. So far, this is satisfactory enough; but what does it all amount to? To some people (including, no doubt, Walras himself) the system of simultaneous equations, determining a whole price-system, seems to have vast significance. They derive intense intellectual satisfaction from the contemplation of such a system of subtly interrelated prices; and the farther the analysis can be carried (in fact it can be carried a good way) towards including not only the economics of exchange but the economics of production as well, the better are they pleased, and the profounder insight into the working of a competitive economic system they feel they get. I have myself very considerable sympathy with this point of view. I believe that we can get quite considerable insight just by extending Walrasian systems of equations; to such an extent that I shall follow Walrasian methods in considerable parts of this book, and hope to show that there are new fields where they are just as illuminating as in the old, perhaps even more so. It was a great achievement to have shown, even so schematically, the mechanism of the interrelation of markets; and there are several questions of principle which cannot be satisfactorily settled unless we stand back with Walras, and look at the price-system as a whole.

Nevertheless, in spite of these merits, it is clear that many economists (perhaps most, even of those who have studied Walras seriously) have felt in the end a certain sterility about his approach. It is true, they would say, that Walras does give one a picture of the whole system; but it is a very distant picture, and hardly amounts to more than an assurance that things will work themselves out somehow, though it is not very clear how they will work themselves out. Other economists are theoretically less ambitious, but they do at least give us results which are applicable to actual problems.

Now the reason for this sterility of the Walrasian system is largely, I believe, that he did not go on to work out the laws of change for his system of General Equilibrium. He could tell what conditions must be satisfied by the prices established with given resources and given preferences; but he did not explain what would happen if tastes or resources changed.

It is true that in the simple case of two commodities he did work things out fully, giving substantially the same analysis as Marshall gave for an application of that case (in his *Pure Theory of Foreign Trade*[1]). But he made no similar investigation of the general case.

I believe that, with the technique now at our disposal, we can make a similar investigation for the general case, and arrive, at any rate, at some results. If we can do this, the general equilibrium method will be freed from most of the reproach of sterility. For even without going farther than exchange theory we shall have a system which can be applied to the general theory of international trade, at least as far as Marshall applied his to the special case of trade in two commodities. It will also have other special applications. And, when account has been taken of production and speculation, yet more important doors will open.

[1] Walras 1874, Marshall 1879. Marshall's theory is repeated, but without gain in clarity, in *Money Credit and Commerce*, Appendix.

CHAPTER V

THE WORKING OF THE GENERAL EQUILIBRIUM SYSTEM

1. THE laws of change of the price-system, like the laws of change of individual demand, have to be derived from stability conditions. We first examine what conditions are necessary in order that a given equilibrium system should be stable; then we make an assumption of regularity, that positions in the neighbourhood of the equilibrium position will be stable also; and thence we deduce rules about the way in which the price-system will react to changes in tastes and resources.

What is meant by stability in exchange? In order that equilibrium should be stable, it is necessary that a slight movement away from the equilibrium position should set up forces tending to restore equilibrium. This means that a rise in price above the equilibrium level must set up forces tending to produce a fall in price; which implies, under perfect competition, that a rise in price makes supply greater than demand.[1] The condition of stability is that a rise in price makes supply greater than demand, a fall in price demand greater than supply.

In the theory of exchange, it is possible to do more than merely enunciate stability conditions, and deduce laws of change from them. For since the theory of exchange is based on the theory of demand, it is possible to investigate how far the stability of exchange is consistent with the theory of demand worked out in Chapters II–III above. By using this sort of check, we can learn

---

[1] It may be observed that this condition is not the same as that given in Marshall's *Principles* (p. 807 note). Marshall says that 'the equilibrium of demand and supply corresponding to the point of intersection of the demand and supply curves is stable or unstable according as the demand curve lies above or below the supply curve just to the left of that point'; that is to say, a small fall in output makes the demand price greater than the supply price. This is not identical with the condition given above, and is, indeed, nearer the stability condition appropriate to conditions of monopoly than that appropriate to conditions of perfect competition. Under monopoly, equilibrium is stable if a small fall in output makes marginal revenue greater than marginal cost. The case of a 'forward falling' supply curve (to use Mr. Kahn's phrase) which Marshall considered to be consistent with stable equilibrium is not consistent with stable equilibrium under perfect competition.

a good deal more about the working of the price-system than would otherwise be possible.

2. Let us begin with the simple exchange of two commodities. We cannot expect to get any new results in this well-worked field; but by restating the familiar theory in terms of our own analysis, we can hope to put it in a form capable of being generalized.

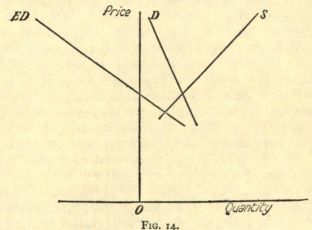

FIG. 14.

If only two goods (X and Y) are being traded, the equilibrium condition is that the supply of X equals the demand for X, and the stability condition is that a fall in the price of X in terms of Y will make the demand for X greater than the supply of X.[1] Let us call the difference between the demand and supply at any price the *excess demand*. Then the equilibrium condition is that the excess demand should be zero; and the stability condition is that a fall in price should increase the excess demand—that the excess demand curve, if we like to put it that way, should be downward sloping.[2] It is obvious from the diagram (Fig. 14) that when the demand curve slopes downwards to the right, and the supply curve

---

[1] Observe that each of these conditions is in fact symmetrical; for the equilibrium condition implies that the demand for Y equals the supply of Y, and the stability condition implies that a rise in the price of Y in terms of X will make the supply of Y greater than the demand for Y.

[2] Alternatively, we can adopt Wicksteed's device, of treating supply as the amount the sellers do not want to keep back out of some fixed amount; and drawing a demand curve consisting of demand plus reservation demand. This 'Wicksteed' demand curve will have the same properties as our excess demand curve, only differing from it by a constant.

upwards to the right, the excess demand curve must be downward sloping. But what can be said in general about the effect on excess demand of a fall in price?

Both demand and supply effects, as we have seen,[1] can be analysed into an income effect and a substitution effect; therefore excess demand can be analysed similarly. A fall in price sets up a substitution effect which increases demand and diminishes supply; this therefore must increase excess demand. It sets up an income effect through the buyers being made better off and the sellers worse off. So long as the commodity is not an inferior good for either side, this means that the income effect will tend to increase demand and *increase* supply. Thus the direction of the income effect on excess demand depends on which of these two tendencies is the stronger. If the income effect on the demand side is just as strong as the income effect on the supply side, then the income effect on excess demand will cancel out, leaving nothing but the substitution effect. In this case the excess demand curve must be downward sloping; equilibrium must be stable.

How probable is it that income effects will cancel out in this way? If the buyers and sellers are similar people, and more or less similarly situated, then it is highly probable that the income effect will cancel out. For, in equilibrium, supply equals demand; and therefore the initial effect of a fall in price (before any adjustment in supply or demand is made) is to make the buyers better off and the sellers worse off, by an exactly equal amount in terms of Y. Therefore, if buyers and sellers react to a change in income in the same way, the increased demand from the buyers (due to the income effect) will be matched by an increased supply from the sellers (due to the income effect). The income effect on excess demand will be nil.

Of course it will be very lucky if things work out exactly in this way. Generally there will be a net increase or net decrease in excess demand as a result of the redistribution of income between buyers and sellers. Still, except in cases when X is an inferior good for the buyers but not for the sellers (or an inferior good for the sellers but not for the buyers), there will be some tendency to cancel out.[2] Therefore, when dealing with problems of the

[1] Chapter II, above.
[2] If there is a great difference in the numbers of buyers and sellers, then this is perhaps a reason for supposing that the income effect on the side where numbers

stability of exchange, it is a reasonable method of approach to begin by assuming that income effects do cancel out, and then to inquire what difference it makes if there is a net income effect in one direction or the other.

If income effects cancel out, the exchange of X for Y must be stable; and it will still be stable if the income effect on excess demand goes in the same direction as the substitution effect. The only possible case of instability is when there is a strong income

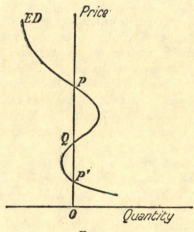

FIG. 15.

effect in the opposite direction—that is to say, *the sellers of X will have to be much more anxious to consume more X when they become better off than the buyers of X are.*[1]

In conditions of this sort, equilibrium would be unstable; but an excess demand curve which produced unstable positions (such as Q, Fig. 15) would still be able to turn round and produce stable positions (such as P or P'). The sort of difficulty which does arise in such cases is that there may be more than one position of stable equilibrium.

If (as in Fig. 14) there is only one position of stable equilibrium, then the effect of a change in demand or supply conditions on price is perfectly simple. A change in the tastes of any person trading, such that, at a given price of X in terms of Y, he desires to buy

are fewer is likely to be the more important. For, on the other side, the gain in real income for many persons may be so small as to be hardly sensible, and therefore not affect their demand at all.

[1] Observe that this is in fact a symmetrical condition.

more X or sell less X (this implies that he desires to sell more or buy less Y), must raise the price of X in terms of Y (lower the price of Y in terms of X). For such a change must move the excess demand curve to the right. The same rule holds even in Fig. 15, provided we start from a stable position; but if the stable position is placed like P', the rise in price may be sharp and discontinuous.

3. We now pass on to the case of multiple exchange (exchange of more than two commodities), where we have to break some altogether new ground. The whole question of stability in multiple exchange has, so far as I know, never been discussed before, which is a pity; for even at the threshold of the subject some questions arise of considerable interest and importance.

What do we mean by stability in multiple exchange? Clearly, as before, that a fall in the price of X in terms of the standard commodity will make the demand for X greater than the supply. But are we to suppose that it must have this effect (*a*) when the prices of other commodities are given, or (*b*) when other prices are adjusted so as to preserve equilibrium in the other markets? The answer is, I believe, that it is what happens when all other prices are adjusted that is really most important. If a small rise in price does not make supply greater than demand, when all its repercussions have been allowed for, then there will be no tendency at all for equilibrium to be restored. The market will move away from the equilibrium position rather than towards it. But if the first condition only is not satisfied,[1] the tendency to move away from equilibrium will be checked in the end, though not directly; it will be checked through repercussions in other markets, not by the working of the X-market alone. It is easy to see that in such a case as this the establishment of an equilibrium price-system is going to be a more awkward business; but once equilibrium is reached, it will still be a stable equilibrium, properly speaking. A movement away from equilibrium will set up forces tending to restore equilibrium.

[1] Strictly, we should distinguish a series of conditions: that a rise in the price of X will make supply greater than demand, (*a*) all other prices given, (*b*) allowing for the price of Y being adjusted to maintain equilibrium in the Y-market, (*c*) allowing for the prices of Y and Z being adjusted, and so on, until all prices have been adjusted. A system ceases to be unstable as soon as the last of these conditions is fulfilled; but perfect stability involves them all.

I propose to call a system in which all conditions of stability are satisfied *perfectly stable*; a system in which some of them are not satisfied, but in which supply does become greater than demand when price rises if all repercussions are allowed for, *imperfectly stable*. Thus even an imperfectly stable system is stable in the end; but its stability is only maintained by indirect repercussions.

Later on in this book I hope to show that there are some problems where imperfect stability is an interesting and important hypothesis. (Some of the most remarkable of them arise in connexion with the famous 'instability of credit'.) But that does not concern us for the present. We shall find that a pure system of multiple exchange, if it is stable at all, is likely to be perfectly stable. And wholly unstable systems, which could never rest at any determinate system of prices, are hardly interesting. The establishment of their laws of change would be a nonsense problem.

4. The general stability of a system of multiple exchange thus involves two questions: (i) Granted that the market for X is stable, taken by itself (that is to say, a fall in the price of X will raise the excess demand for X, all other prices being given), can it be rendered unstable by reactions through the markets for other commodities? (ii) Supposing that the market for X is unstable, taken by itself, can it be made stable by reactions through other markets? Let us begin with the first of these questions.

The effect on the market for X of reactions through the market for some particular other commodity Y (the prices of Z . . . being given) can be studied graphically (Fig. 16).

Measure along two axes the price of X and the price of Y. Any point on the diagram will then represent a particular pair of prices. Corresponding to any arbitrary price of Y, we can determine the price of X which will equate the supply and demand for X, and thus bring the X-market into equilibrium. (Of course the Y-market will not necessarily be in equilibrium too.) In this way, however, we can determine a pair of prices which will bring about equilibrium in the X-market. Plotting this as a point on the diagram, let us then construct a series of similar points, by starting with other arbitrary prices of Y. These points will form a curve, which we shall call XX'. What can be said about the form of this curve?

Whether or not a rise in the price of Y will raise the price of X depends upon the way in which the excess demand curve for X is affected. If it is raised, the price of X will be raised, and XX' will be positively inclined; if it is lowered, XX' will be negatively inclined.

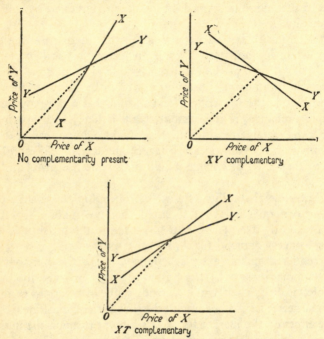

FIG. 16. All these are stable positions.

But the price of Y reacts on the excess demand curve for X through an income effect and a substitution effect, as before. There are just the same reasons as in § 2 above for supposing that the income effect on excess demand will often be small (since it consists of two parts which probably work in opposite directions). The substitution effect will raise the excess demand for X if X and Y are substitutes, lower it if they are complementary (substitution and complementarity being here understood with reference to the market as a whole, buyers and sellers together). Thus, if (as an approximation) we neglect the income effect, we can say roughly that XX' will slope upwards when X and Y are substitutes, downwards when they are complementary.

Now let us for the moment confine our attention to cases in which XX' slopes upwards. The slope of the curve depends upon the relative influence of the two prices on the excess demand for X. If the price of X has the relatively stronger influence, then a rise in the price of Y will raise the price of X less than proportionately. The curve XX' will have an elasticity less than unity. It will have an elasticity greater than unity if the price of Y has a relatively stronger influence on the excess demand for X than the price of X has.

It is possible to distinguish to some extent between the probabilities of these two cases. For this purpose, let us consider what would happen if the prices of X and Y both rose in the same proportion, so that the price-ratio of X to Y is unchanged. This, as we have seen, is exactly similar in its effects to an equal proportionate fall in the prices of all other goods than X and Y (including the standard commodity), which can thus be lumped together and treated as a single commodity T. Now (again neglecting income effects) a fall in the price of T will lower the excess demand for X unless X is complementary with T. Thus, excepting when X is complementary with T, the rise in the price of X needed to maintain equilibrium in the market for X must be less than proportional to the rise in the price of Y. The XX' curve must be inelastic.

We have thus a fairly clear idea of the properties of the curve XX'. If the income effects are neglected, we have the following precise rules. When no complementarity is present, so that X is a substitute both for Y and for T (the group of all goods other than X and Y), the curve XX' must slope upwards, and its elasticity must be less than unity. If X and Y are complementary, XX' slopes downwards. If X and T are complementary, XX' slopes upwards with an elasticity greater than unity. If income effects are important, these rules will be somewhat modified, so that exceptions to them will appear, of more or less importance.

Exactly similar results will hold for the curve YY', which represents the pairs of prices which will bring the market for Y into equilibrium. YY' will slope upwards if X and Y are substitutes, downwards if they are complementary. But when we come to consider complementarity between Y and T, we must observe that the positions of the axes are reversed. If Y and T are complementary, a rise in the price of X has to be accompanied by

F

a more than proportional rise in the price of Y in order to maintain equilibrium in the Y market. Therefore, if we are measuring the price of X along the horizontal axis, we must say that YY' will be inelastic when Y and T are complementary, elastic when Y is a substitute for both X and T.

These results can now be used to examine the stability of the system. If XX' and YY' intersect in a point P, then P represents a pair of prices at which both the X-market and the Y-market

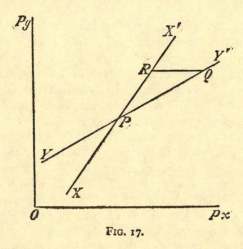

Fig. 17.

will be in equilibrium. They will be in stable equilibrium if a small rise in the price of X reacts on the price of Y, and that reacts back on the price of X in such a way as to lower it again. The condition for this is that XX' should slope upwards more steeply than YY' (or downwards more steeply than YY'). This can be seen at once by considering Fig. 17. At a price of X above the equilibrium level, the Y-market would be brought to equilibrium at a point Q on YY'. At this new price of Y, the X-market would come to equilibrium at a point R on XX', and this gives us a price of X nearer to the equilibrium position than that from which we started. The system thus tends to return to the equilibrium position, and is stable.

Using this test, we can first of all see that if there is no complementarity in the system, so that X, Y, and T are all substitutes for one another, then the system must be stable. For in this case the elasticity of XX' is less than unity, of YY' greater than unity. XX' is therefore steeper than YY', and the stability condition is necessarily satisfied.

It is further evident from the second diagram in Fig. 16 that the presence of complementarity does not necessarily mean instability. Cases in which X and Y are complementary, but in which the stability condition is still satisfied, can readily be constructed. It might however be supposed at first sight that unstable cases, in which YY' sloped downwards more steeply than XX', could be constructed also. This, however, is not so. For the most perfectly complementary relation which can exist between two goods X and Y is that in which they have to be consumed in fixed proportions. In this case there will be a set of prices of X, with corresponding prices of Y, which will make both the excess demand for X equal to zero, and the excess demand for Y equal to zero. Thus the curves XX' and YY' coincide. But if the greatest possible degree of complementarity is that which makes the curves coincide, it would appear that it would take more than this greatest possible amount to make them cut in an unstable manner. Thus in our case of three-way exchange, it is not possible for complementarity to be a source of instability. This can be proved to hold mathematically for any number of goods.

5. We may therefore conclude our long investigation into stability of multiple exchange with a tentatively negative answer to the first of the questions with which we began. If the market for X is stable, taken by itself, it is not likely to be rendered unstable by reactions through other markets. What now of the other question—supposing the market for X is unstable, taken by itself, is it likely to be rendered stable by reactions through other markets? Are imperfectly stable systems of multiple equilibrium probable?

This question will give us a good deal less trouble than its predecessor. The market for X is unstable, taken by itself, if a rise in the price of X (other prices given) raises the excess demand for X. Thus, if it is to be rendered stable by indirect reactions through other prices, these indirect reactions must lower the excess demand for X. It can be shown that they are very unlikely to do so. Take a particular other commodity Y. Then (if income effects could be neglected) it would be necessarily the case that the reactions through the Y-market must raise the excess demand for X. For if Y is a substitute for X, the rise in the price of X will raise the excess demand for Y, therefore raise the price of Y; this will again raise the excess demand for X. If Y is complementary with X, the rise in the price of X will lower the excess demand for Y, therefore the price of Y; but this will again raise the excess demand for X. Therefore in both cases the excess demand for X will be raised by the indirect reaction. If the market for X was unstable, taken alone, it must be still more unstable when indirect effects are allowed for.

This argument, however, is not conclusive. For it is subject to some slight exceptions when reactions through more than one other market are allowed for; and in any case, it is only necessarily true that the indirect reactions through another market must tend to raise the excess demand for X when the price of X rises, *if income effects are neglected*. But in this case they cannot properly be neglected. For it is only if the income effect in the X-market is large, that the X-market, taken by itself, can possibly be unstable. Now if there is a large income effect tending to increase the excess demand for X when the price of X rises, it becomes possible that there may also be such an effect when the price of Y varies. Thus it becomes possible that reactions through the markets for related commodities may sometimes go the opposite way from what we should at first have supposed. These reactions may possibly exercise a stabilizing influence on markets which, taken by themselves, are unstable.

I do not see, however, that this possibility is really of much importance. It may be noted, however, as a possible source of exceptions to the rules which we shall set out in the following section.

To sum up the negative but reassuring conclusions which we have derived from our discussions of stability. There is no doubt that the existence of stable systems of multiple exchange is entirely consistent with the laws of demand. It cannot, indeed, be proved *a priori* that a system of multiple exchange is necessarily stable. But the conditions of stability are quite easy conditions, so that it is quite reasonable to assume that they will be satisfied in almost any system with which we are likely to be concerned. The only possible ultimate source of instability is strong asymmetry in the income effects. A moderate degree of substitutability among the bulk of commodities will be sufficient to prevent this cause being effective.

Further, if a system of multiple exchange is stable at all, it is likely to be perfectly stable. It is therefore quite justifiable to proceed, as we shall now do, to investigate the ways in which a perfectly stable system of multiple exchange will react to changes in the fundamental determinants of prices. For the 'economic laws' which result are principles which we shall expect to find operating in reality, in any situation which can be reduced to a system of multiple exchange under perfect competition.

6. The precise method by which the economic laws can be deduced from the stability conditions is this. Let us suppose that a small number of the persons trading experience a certain change in their preferences. The most convenient change to take, for purposes of exposition, is an increased desire for some particular commodity, which they are prepared to satisfy by increasing their supply (or diminishing their demand) for the standard commodity, their demands and supplies for all other commodities being unaffected. What change in prices will result? The change in prices must be such as to produce an excess supply, from other persons trading, sufficient to satisfy the increased demand from the first group. Now the stability conditions have already told us what changes in prices will lead to an excess supply in the market for X, while other markets remain, as they should, in equilibrium. The stability conditions thus enable us to say what will be the effect of such an increase in demand.[1]

First of all, the price of X itself must be raised. This follows even if all secondary reactions through other markets are allowed for. The system can only be stable at all (even imperfectly stable) if a rise in the price of X (all secondary reactions considered) makes the supply of X greater than the demand.

Then there are some things which can be said about the effects on other prices. The rules on this matter can only be stated in a precise form if income effects can be neglected on balance. Since

[1] When the problem is looked at in this way, it becomes apparent that a similar analysis can be used to examine the effects of an increase in the number of persons trading. The new-comers add to the demands for some goods, the supplies of others. Prices must therefore be adjusted to the extent necessary to call forth corresponding excess supplies and excess demands from the old system.

this assumption is not likely to be wholly justified, the rules must be taken to be subject to a margin of error. It is, however, convenient to set them out with income effects neglected.

If we could assume that the reactions on other markets were confined to one particular other market, that of Y (other prices than those of X and Y being affected to a negligible extent), then the effect on the price of Y follows from § 4 above. The price of Y will rise if X and Y are substitutes, fall if they are complementary. For it is only changes of this kind which will maintain equilibrium in the market for Y.

If more than one other price is affected, then we have to allow for the way in which the markets for other goods, X, Z, and so on, may influence each other. The effect on the price of Y may be analysed as follows. First of all, if Y is a substitute for X, that tends to raise the price of Y. But the price of Y may be influenced, not only directly in this way, but also indirectly, through the change in the price of Z. If Z is a substitute for X, the price of Z will be raised; and if Y is also a substitute for Z, this in its turn will raise the price of Y. There will therefore be an indirect effect tending to raise the price of Y. Similarly, if Z is complementary with X, and complementary with Y, the price of Z will be lowered, but this will again tend to raise the price of X. On the other hand, if Z is complementary with X and a substitute for Y, the effect through the Z-market will be to lower the price of Y.

Indirect effects through third markets thus obey the rule that an increased demand for X will raise the prices of those goods which are substitutes of substitutes, or complements of complements, for X; it will lower the prices of those goods which are complements of substitutes, or substitutes of complements.

In cases where several prices are affected, it may be necessary to allow for several indirect effects of this kind, as well as the direct effect. Sometimes, perhaps often, they will all go in the same direction. X and Y may be members of a group of goods which are all substitutes for one another. The price of Y will then rise, when the price of X rises, both because of the direct substitution between them and because of the indirect substitution through the other members of the group. If, however, X and Y are members of a group of complements, things are not so straightforward. The direct effect is now to lower the price of Y, when the demand for X rises; but some of the indirect effects will raise the price of Y, in its role as complement of complement. The net effect may therefore go in either direction.

A system of multiple exchange in which no complementarity was present at all would obey a simple rule. However many indirect effects were allowed for, they would all go in the same direction. When the demand for X increased, the price of X would rise, and all other prices would rise too. Further, it can be shown that the prices of all the other goods would rise proportionately less than the price of X.[1]

Complete absence of complementarity, in this manner, is of course not at all a probable condition.[2] Nevertheless, there are several reasons why we may expect the situation which would be realized exactly in the complete absence of complementarity to be realized approximately in many actual situations. (1) There are the reasons with which we are familiar, for expecting substitution to be the dominant, and complementarity the exceptional, relation between pairs of goods taken at random. (2) There is the fact that indirect effects among groups of substitute goods work in the same direction as direct effects, while indirect effects among groups of complements may tend to neutralize the direct effects. (3) We have been supposing, hitherto, that the increased demand for X acts upon X alone, and not upon the commodities complementary with X. In practice, the demands for a group of complementary commodities will often increase simultaneously.

Taking these things into account, it does appear that an increase in demand for a particular good (or group of goods) is most likely to have an upward effect upon prices in general. Of course, the good or goods for which demand increases must be of considerable importance if this upward tendency is to be at all widespread. And it is always probable that there will be a few particular goods,

---

[1] This can be seen at once if we adopt the device of treating X (momentarily) as the standard commodity, and therefore regarding the increased demand for X as an increased supply of the old standard commodity M. It is then clear that if no complementarity is present the prices of all other commodities must fall in terms of X.

[2] One interesting example, where it may be realized approximately, is the market for foreign exchange. To the foreign-exchange dealers, bills in various currencies are probably all substitutes for one another. Thus, as we observe in practice, if there is a flight from francs into dollars, the dollar will rise in terms of francs, and all other currencies will rise too, but proportionately less than the dollar.

directly or indirectly complementary with the first, whose prices will actually fall.

7. That, I believe, is all that can be said about the effects on other prices. But one more proposition can be added to complete the laws of exchange.

We have seen that when the demand for X increases, the price of X must rise. What governs the extent of its rise? It can be shown that a given rise in demand will affect the price of X less, the more substitutability or the less complementarity there is between any pair of commodities in the system.[1]

If the commodity X possesses a large number of good substitutes, it will be much easier to satisfy an increased demand for it without any considerable rise in price. The substitutes themselves will indeed tend to rise in price; but the rise will be spread very thin over the whole group of commodities, and will thus affect each of them (including X itself) very little. If, on the other hand, it possesses a large group of complements, for which the demand has not increased, these complements will tend to fall in price (those people who provide the necessary excess supply of X will tend to dispose of goods complementary to it). This fall in the prices of the complements will in its turn increase the demand for them (and therefore for X itself); a further rise in the price of X will be necessary in order to compensate for this.

These principles can now be applied, at a second remove, to the substitutes and complements themselves. If they, in their turn, possess good substitutes, their prices will, for that reason, be less affected; and this will tend, in turn, to diminish the effect on the price of X. But if they, in their turn, are members of a group of complements, this will increase the variation in their prices, and consequently increase the necessary variation in the price of X too.

Complementarity, like imperfect substitutability, is therefore to be regarded as an element of rigidity in the system, which diminishes the elasticity of supply of any particular good. Similarly, of course, if we had begun with an increase in supply of X, we should have found the same factors diminishing the elasticity of demand.

---

[1] Once again, this proposition is only free from exceptions if income effects are neglected.

8. This concludes all I have to say on the theory of exchange. Indeed, I doubt if there is much more, on a similar plane of generality, which can be added. We might therefore proceed at once to applications; when one remembers how much of the traditional theory of international trade, for instance, has been founded on the analysis of the simple exchange of two goods, we need not be too timid in the application of our already much more general theory. However, I shall not take that course; partly because I am not much concerned in this book with the economic analysis of particular problems, but more because I do not believe it is in any way necessary to leave out of account so many aspects of the actual world as we must do if we try to reduce actual problems within the framework of the pure theory of exchange.

It is useful to have spent so much time on the theory of exchange, for quite a different reason. We shall find, when we go on to deal with production in the following chapters, and even when we come to study dynamic problems in Part IV, almost exactly the same questions coming up as those which we have examined here. They will appear at first slightly more complicated, but they can be thrown into familiar forms; and so it will turn out that we know the answers already. That is why the theory of exchange is an essential part of the study of the economic system in general.[1]

[1] In the first edition of this book, I maintained that instability of exchange equilibrium might arise from two causes, not one; in addition to the asymmetrical income effects, which we have discussed above, there was 'extreme complementarity'. Instability due to asymmetrical income effects undoubtedly makes sense; it is not difficult, as we have seen, to construct particular cases to show how it will work. But it was difficult to make sense of 'extreme complementarity', though I felt bound to retain it since it seemed to be implied by my mathematics. Some years later, when I was working on the theory of consumer's surplus ('Consumer's Surplus and Index Numbers', *Review of Economic Studies*, 1942), I found that this was an error. I had overlooked the general law of demand, now set out on p. 52 above; it is this which provides the mathematical reason why 'extreme complementarity'—such as to involve instability—is impossible. The argument is set out in full in the mathematical appendix, p. 316. So far as the present chapter is concerned, it has been possible to simplify the argument by the simple omission of a complication which never seemed to make sense. Further consequential simplifications are noted on pp. 103, 222 below.

This same correction has been made by Dr. J. L. Mosak, *General Equilibrium Theory in International Trade*, Cowles Commission Monograph, 1944, p. 42.

CHAPTER VI

THE EQUILIBRIUM OF THE FIRM

1. UNLIKE the theory of the equilibrium of the private individual, the theory of the equilibrium of the firm has been dicussed almost *ad nauseam* in contemporary literature.[1] In one sense, I have little to add to these discussions. It is, however, necessary for us to go over the ground, in order to bring out a certain parallelism which exists between the case of the firm and that of the private person. It is this parallelism which will enable us to put the laws of market conduct of the firm into a similar form to that familiar to us in the other case; and ultimately to extend the theory of exchange set out in the last chapter to take account of production as well.

The transition between value theory and production theory can be made most conveniently in the following way. Hitherto, we have assumed that our trading individuals come to the market with supplies of certain commodities or services, and that they can obtain other commodities in one way only—by exchange. We have now to take into account the fact that they can sometimes obtain new commodities in another way—by technical transformation, or production. Clearly they will not adopt this method unless it is more advantageous than simple exchange; that means that it will only be advantageous to convert one set of exchangeable goods into another set, by production, if the set acquired has a higher market value than the set given up. Therefore, under different market conditions, different opportunities for production will become profitable; and these different opportunities may be open to different people. In this way, the class of persons who acquire goods by technical transformation rather than by simple sale of their services (the class of entrepreneurs) may change.

It will usually be characteristic of an entrepreneur that he acquires some services (factors of production), not because he has any direct desire for them, but because he needs them for the full exploitation of his productive opportunities. The amount of these factors he employs may be taken to depend entirely upon the pro-

[1] See, for example, Joan Robinson, *Economics of Imperfect Competition*; Schneider, *Theorie der Produktion*; Kaldor, 'Equilibrium of the Firm' (*Econ. Jour.* 1934).

duction which they make possible; consequently, the enterprise (the conversion of factors into products) may be regarded as a separate economic unit, detached from the private account of the entrepreneur. It acquires factors, and sells products; its aim is to maximize the difference between their value.[1]

2. We may begin with an analysis exactly parallel to that of our utility theory. Assume a particular enterprise, confronted with a perfectly competitive market. What are the necessary conditions for its equilibrium?

Take first the simplest case. Technical possibilities are open to a particular enterprise, by means of which a single factor A can be converted into a single product X. The prices of both A and X are given on the market; it will therefore be to its advantage to embark upon production, so long as the total value of the product secured is greater than the total value of factor employed. Further, it will be to its advantage to produce that quantity of product which will make the excess as large as possible.

Let us look at this graphically. If we measure quantities of the factor A along the horizontal axis, and quantities of the product X along the vertical axis, a curve can be drawn showing the maximum amount of product which can be secured by the transformation of each given amount of factor. For the present we will make no particular assumptions about the shape of this *production curve* (Fig. 18).

Suppose now that an amount ON of the factor is being employed, and the amount of product secured is therefore PN. Make OM equal to PN, and let MK represent that quantity of product whose market value equals the value of ON of the factor. Then OK is the surplus product which accrues to the enterprise. The value of OK is the surplus of receipts over costs.

The conditions of equilibrium are that OK should be a maximum, and should be positive.

In the diagram as we have drawn it, the first of these conditions is not fulfilled. If P moves to the right along the curve, the line

---

[1] In addition to factors acquired on the market, an enterprise may also make use of factors provided by the entrepreneur himself. If these factors are such that they could be sold (if not employed in the business), then their market prices must be debited to the costs of the enterprise. If, however, they cannot be used in any other way than in the business, they do not give rise to costs, and need not (indeed cannot) be reckoned on the debit side of the firm's account.

PK will move upwards (keeping parallel to itself, for its slope
MK/PM equals the ratio of the prices of factor and product,
which is given by market conditions). It will continue to move
upwards, so that *OK* is increased, until it becomes a tangent to
the production curve (Fig. 19). The conditions of equilibrium
can thus be set out in full as follows:

(1) The line *PK* must touch the production curve. That is to
say, the slope of the production curve at the point of equilibrium
must equal the ratio of the price of the factor to the price of the

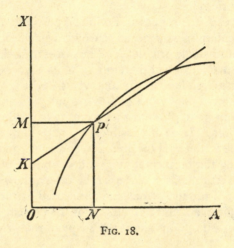

FIG. 18.

product. Now the slope of the production curve equals the
increment of product got from a small increment of factor—
that is to say, it is the marginal product. Therefore the condition
can be put in either of the two familiar forms: the price of the
factor equals the value of its marginal product, or the price of the
product equals its marginal cost.

(2) In order for *OK* to be a maximum, rather than a minimum,
it is necessary for the production curve to be convex upwards at
the point of tangency. This implies that marginal product must
be diminishing, or marginal cost increasing, at the point of equilibrium.

These two conditions, it will be observed, are closely similar in
form to those which we reached in our theory of subjective value.
The production curve, as we have drawn it, is remarkably similar
in its properties to an indifference curve. Where we had equality

between a price-ratio and a marginal rate of substitution, we now have equality between a price-ratio and a marginal product—which may be looked on, if we choose, as a *marginal rate of transformation*. As for the stability condition, diminishing marginal rate of substitution is replaced by diminishing marginal product. These two conditions are therefore substantially identical, and by their means we shall be able to construct a theory of the conduct of the firm closely similar to our theory of the conduct of the private individual.

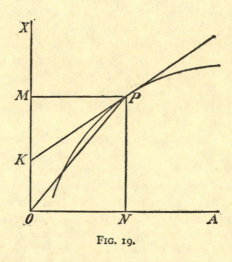

FIG. 19.

(3) But in the theory of production there is a third condition, which corresponds to nothing in the theory of subjective value. The surplus OK must be positive. Now OK can only be positive if the slope of OP is greater than that of PK; and that means that the slope of OP must be diminishing as P moves to the right. The slope of OP measures the ratio between quantity of product and quantity of factor; that is to say, it is the average product. The third condition of equilibrium is therefore that average product must be diminishing, or average cost increasing.[1]

[1] Alternatively, we may argue in the following way. If there is a positive surplus, price must be greater than average cost. But price equals marginal cost. Therefore marginal cost must be greater than average cost. Therefore the production of an additional unit must raise average cost. Therefore average cost must be increasing.

The equilibrium conditions may therefore be set out in the two alternative forms:

1. Price of factor = value of marginal product.	1. Price of product = marginal cost.
2. Marginal product diminishing.	2. Marginal cost increasing.
3. Average product diminishing.	3. Average cost increasing.

3. So far we are taken by geometry; but now it is necessary to inquire whether the equilibrium conditions thus arrived at are in fact plausible conditions. The second and third conditions relate to properties of the production curve; is it in fact probable that the relation between factor and product should have these properties? In the parallel case of the private individual, we saw no reason to doubt the plausibility of the condition of diminishing marginal rate of substitution. But here we have two conditions to deal with, not one; and altogether more serious questions to answer.

Criticism of the equilibrium conditions just set out is based upon two considerations. One is the frequent conviction of entrepreneurs themselves that they are producing under conditions of diminishing average costs. The other is of more theoretical character, and springs from the explanation of the 'laws of increasing and diminishing returns' usually accepted by modern writers. There is a tendency to increasing return (broadly, diminishing cost) due to economies of large scale, and particularly to the indivisibility of the units of certain factors, and the indivisibility of certain processes. There is a tendency to diminishing return (increasing cost) if the quantity of one kind of resources, used in making a product, increases, while some other kind (or kinds) remains unchanged, or increases more slowly. If a firm is to be producing under conditions of rising average costs, it must mean that the latter of these two tendencies is dominant— that is to say, not only must there be a scarcity of some kind of resources used, but there must be a sufficient scarcity to override any economies of large scale that may be present.[1]

A situation like that shown in our diagrams can therefore only arise if the factor A is being combined with some resources of which the firm possesses only a limited supply, and of which it

---

[1] Cf. Robinson, op. cit., Appendix; Kaldor, op. cit.

cannot procure more on the market. For short-period problems, the fixed equipment or plant of the firm, which has been built up in the past, and is likely to be to some extent unique, fits the case fairly well. For long-period problems, we have only the ultimate control, exercised by the entrepreneur himself. The only reason why marginal costs should increase is the increasing difficulty of controlling an enterprise, as its scale of production grows.[1]

We must remember, however, that we have two conditions to deal with, rising marginal costs and rising average costs. Marginal costs must rise as the firm expands, in order to ensure that its expansion stops somewhere. But it is not a sufficient condition of equilibrium that marginal cost should be rising. It is not at all an unlikely state of affairs that marginal costs should be rising a little, owing to the difficulty of control which increases as the firm expands; indeed, I think one would expect this to be the most common of all conditions for a firm to be in. But if marginal costs are only a little above their minimum, marginal cost will probably be less than average cost (at the minimum of marginal cost, average cost will be greater than marginal cost necessarily). Therefore, if the firm sells at a price equal to its marginal cost, it must sell at a loss.

4. It seems to be agreed that this situation has to be met by sacrificing the assumption of perfect competition. If we assume that the typical firm (at least in industries where the economies of large scale are important) has some influence over the prices at which it sells, and is therefore to some extent a monopolist, the above difficulties disappear. The price at which a monopolist sells is no longer equal to his marginal cost, but exceeds it by a percentage dependent upon the elasticity of demand for his product. It is therefore possible for price to be greater than average cost, even when marginal cost is less than average cost.

So far, so good; yet it has to be recognized that a general abandonment of the assumption of perfect competition, a universal adoption of the assumption of monopoly, must have very destructive consequences for economic theory. Under monopoly the stability conditions become indeterminate; and the basis on which

[1] See, however, below, pp. 199–200.

economic laws can be constructed is therefore shorn away. Not only is falling average cost consistent with monopoly; falling marginal cost is consistent with monopoly too. There must indeed be something to stop the indefinite expansion of the firm; but it can just as well be stopped by the limitation of the market as by rising marginal costs, though of course both may be in operation simultaneously.

The situation which emerges may be illustrated from the case of a rise in the demand for a monopolist's product (looking now at that market in isolation, no secondary reactions being considered). A rise in demand for the product may raise its price, or lower it; for all that we know is that the price must exceed marginal cost by a percentage—not a fixed percentage. The effect is doubly indeterminate; the percentage may vary, and marginal costs may rise or may fall with an increase in output. (It is indeed not even certain that output will rise; if the demand, as it increases, becomes less elastic, output may fall.)[1]

It is, I believe, only possible to save anything from this wreck— and it must be remembered that the threatened wreckage is that of the greater part of general equilibrium theory—if we can assume that the markets confronting most of the firms with which we shall be dealing do not differ very greatly from perfectly competitive markets. If we can suppose that the percentages by which prices exceed marginal costs are neither very large nor very variable,[2] and if we can suppose (what is largely a consequence of the first assumption) that *marginal* costs do generally increase with output at the point of equilibrium (diminishing marginal costs being rare), then the laws of an economic system working under perfect competition will not be appreciably varied in a system which contains widespread elements of monopoly. At least, this get-away

[1] It may perhaps be objected against our emphasis on this case that if the effect of a rise in demand is indeterminate, the effect of a rise in (marginal) cost is determinate. But the effect of such a rise in costs is only made determinate by the assumption of perfect competition in the factor markets; the determinate effect of a rise in costs is simply the backwash of the economic laws which are (then) still valid in those markets.

[2] In the general case, of a firm employing several factors, we have to take into account the possibility of 'monopsonistic' exploitation of factors as well as monopolistic action in the sale of the product. We may have to think of the firm gathering its (perhaps necessary) surplus from the percentage by which it squeezes the buyers of its product on the one hand, and from the percentages by which it squeezes the suppliers of factors on the other.

seems well worth trying.[1] We must be aware, however, that we are taking a dangerous step, and probably limiting to a serious extent the problems with which our subsequent analysis will be fitted to deal. Personally, however, I doubt if most of the problems we shall have to exclude for this reason are capable of much useful analysis by the methods of economic theory.

5. Let us, then, return to the case of perfect competition. Let us assume that the firm possesses a fixed supply of some productive agent (its own special productive opportunity) which is sufficiently important to cause it to produce under increasing average cost. And let us now go on to set out the conditions of equilibrium in a more general case than that of the one factor and one product which we examined above.

There is no reason, now, why we should stop short of any degree of generality. The technical opportunities which confront an enterprise are indeed usually fairly complicated. In order to produce a particular product, several factors will generally be required; very often, too, it will pay better to produce a number of joint products than to produce one product in isolation. Let us therefore think of our firm as using its productive opportunity to convert factors $A, B, C \ldots$ into products $X, Y, Z \ldots$

Just as technical conditions imposed, in our first simple case, a production curve—giving a single relation between quantity of product and quantity of factor—so now in the general case we have one relation between the various quantities of factors and the various quantities of products that can be got from them. (We can look upon it, if we like, as a surface in many dimensions.) Given this relation, and given all the quantities of factors, and all quantities of products but one, the maximum producible amount of the remaining product can be deduced. Similarly, given all the quantities of products, and all quantities of factors save one, the minimum amount needed of the remaining factor can be deduced.[2]

---

[1] It is worth observing that Cournot, the first economist to give a precise definition of perfect competition, presented it in this exact guise. Cournot certainly did not believe that competition was usually in fact perfect; but perfect competition was an immensely simplifying approximation to the facts.

[2] Obviously there will be cases when, if the amounts of other factors and products are chosen at random, no amount of a remaining factor will be sufficient to produce the given collection of products. If the amounts of products are very

Starting from any given set of consistent quantities, variations in production can take place of all degrees of complexity; but they can all be reduced to combinations of some or all of the following three types. (1) One product may be increased at the expense of another, i.e. substituted for another at the margin. (2) One factor may be substituted for another. (3) One factor and one product may be simultaneously increased (or diminished).[1]

If the prices of all products and all factors are given to the enterprise, the quantities of factors it will employ, and products it will produce, will be given by the condition that the surplus is a maximum. This implies that it cannot be increased by any type of variation. We shall thus have the following conditions of equilibrium, corresponding to the three conditions set out in the one-product one-factor case.

(1) Corresponding to the condition price = marginal cost, we have three sorts of conditions:

(a) The price-ratio between any two products must equal the marginal rate of substitution between the two products (this is now a technical rate of substitution).

(b) The price-ratio between any two factors must equal their marginal rate of substitution.

(c) The price-ratio between any factor and any product must equal the marginal rate of transformation between the factor and the product (that is to say, the marginal product of the factor in terms of this particular product).

(2) Next there are the stability conditions. For the transformation of a factor into a product we shall have the condition (already established in the one-factor one-product case) of diminishing marginal rate of transformation or diminishing marginal product.

large, and there are available only small quantities of every factor but one, even enormously large quantities of the remaining factor may not suffice to produce the products, unless the factor is very adjustable in its uses. But this difficulty does not seem to matter very much. In application, we shall always start from a position of equilibrium, i.e. from a set of consistent quantities. It is not necessary to suppose any more than that some variation from this position is possible. That, I think, will be granted.

[1] In the last analysis even this is unnecessarily complicated, for the first two types can be reduced to the third. Thus a substitution of one product X for another Y can be regarded as compounded of (1) a simultaneous increase in product X and factor A, (2) a simultaneous decrease in factor A and product Y, the quantities being adjusted in such a way that the changes in the factor cancel out. Thus we need not consider the first two types unless we wish to. I think, however, that we shall find it convenient to retain them.

For the substitution of one product for another we shall have a condition of 'increasing marginal rate of substitution', that is to say, increasing marginal cost in terms of the other product (marginal opportunity cost). For the substitution of one factor for another, 'diminishing marginal rate of substitution'.[1]

These conditions have got to hold, not only for single substitutions and transformations—of one product for one product, one factor for one factor, and one factor into one product—but also for group substitutions and transformations. The marginal rate of substitution between any pair of groups of products must increase, and between any pair of groups of factors must diminish; the marginal rate of transformation between any group of factors and group of products must diminish.[2]

One consequence of this last rule is that the marginal cost (in money terms) of producing a particular product must rise when output increases, even if the supplies of all factors (except the fixed productive opportunity) are treated as variable.

(3) Finally, instead of the single condition that there should be a positive surplus, we have a set of conditions. There must be a positive surplus, so that it does not pay to shut down production altogether. But similarly it must not pay to shut down production partially, to abandon the production of any one of the products $X, Y, Z \ldots$ or any group of these products. Therefore the average cost of producing each product must be rising, and the average cost of producing each group of products must be rising, including the whole group that includes all the products. It is only the last of these conditions (to which everything that has been said about average cost earlier in this chapter applies) that is, I believe, really likely to cause much trouble. For it is relatively easy to grant that a single product, or a sub-group,

[1] Increasing marginal rate of substitution for products, because the total value of products secured has to be *maximized*; diminishing marginal rate of substitution for factors, because the total value of factors used has to be minimized. These conditions are easily verified graphically, if the amounts of other factors and products are assumed given, and the two products (or factors) in question are measured along two axes.

[2] That is to say, if each factor out of a particular group is increased by an arbitrary increment, and a set of product-increments is found, whose production is made possible by the increase in the factors; if then a second equal increment is added to each of the factors, this second set of factor-increments will not suffice to produce a second set of product-increments equal to the first. Cf. the rule given in Chapter I, § 9.

out of a set of joint products, will generally be produced at rising average cost (sharply rising marginal cost). The production of such a sub-group will be severely limited if there is no expansion of the output of the other products.

These are the equilibrium conditions in the general case. We have now to proceed as in Part I. We shall assume that the stability conditions (2) and (3) hold in the neighbourhood of the equilibrium position; and thence we shall deduce laws of market conduct for the firm.

CHAPTER VII

TECHNICAL COMPLEMENTARITY AND TECHNICAL SUBSTITUTION

1. WE have now to ask what happens when a firm which has been in equilibrium at certain prices of products, and prices of factors, experiences a change in these prices. It will have been using certain quantities of factors, and producing certain quantities of products; in what ways will these quantities be affected?

The problem is exactly parallel to that which we discussed, in Chapters II and III, for the case of the private individual; and our analysis will proceed along exactly similar lines. However, it will not be surprising if, this time, we have to pay special attention to a rather different set of points.

Let us begin with the simplest case—that which we discussed at length in the last chapter. The entrepreneur himself possesses a productive opportunity of limited capacity; otherwise he employs only one factor, and produces only one product. His position of equilibrium is therefore that shown in Fig. 19 in the last chapter, and again by the point P in Fig. 20 overleaf. Now suppose the price of the factor falls. The immediate effect of this, before he makes any change of output, is that his surplus is increased from OK to OK_1. But since PK_1 does not touch the production curve, OK_1 is not the maximum surplus which he can secure under the new conditions. It will pay him to move along the production curve to P', where the tangent $P'K_2$ is parallel to PK_1.

Since the production curve is convex upwards (diminishing marginal product, or increasing marginal cost), the point P', where the tangent slopes upwards less steeply than at P, must lie to the right of P. The fall in the price of the factor therefore results in an increase in its employment, and in an increase in the output of the product.

A rise in the price of the product, which also involves a fall in the slope of the tangent, will have exactly the same effects.

These are elementary results; but the methods by which we have reached them yield other and more interesting conclusions. Just as with the private individual, a change in prices leads the firm to a position which can be represented as the point of contact of a new tangent with a different slope. But with the private individual the new tangent touches a different curve; with the firm it touches the same curve. Therefore, in the case of production, we do not have anything similar to the income effects which gave us so much trouble in utility theory. The only 'production effect'

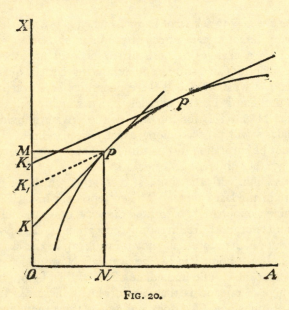

FIG. 20.

is something similar in character to the substitution effect; it is a movement along the curve (in this case a production curve, as in that case an indifference curve), the curve whose properties we know from the stability conditions.

But within the production effect, as within the substitution effect, is another complication—the complication of complementarity. This turns out to be actually more involved in production theory than it was in utility theory. For whereas in utility theory we had simply to consider the relations between commodities, commodities which could be regarded as being (in a sense) similar, here we have two sorts of commodities to consider—factors and products. Their mutual relations and their cross-relations will take a little disentangling.

2. As a first step in the disentanglement, let us construct a rather fanciful case in which we shall not be troubled by the relation between factors and products. Suppose that the output which the firm has to produce is fixed, so that it cannot be affected by ordinary changes in prices; suppose, however, that two factors are employed, A and B. The problem then is to produce the

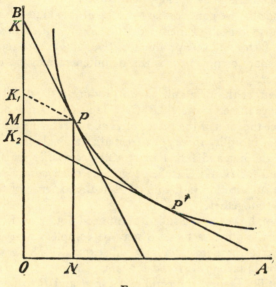

FIG. 21.

given output at a minimum cost. It can be illustrated by a diagram such as Fig. 21. The production curve will be shaped like an indifference curve, being convex downwards (diminishing marginal rate of substitution between factors). The position P, where PK touches the production curve, will be a point of equilibrium if the ratio of the prices of the factors is as MK to PM. Suppose now that the price of A falls. The amount of factor B which has an equal value to ON of A now falls from MK to MK_1; and the total cost of production (in terms of factor B) falls from OK to OK_1. But since PK_1 does not touch the production curve, costs can be reduced still farther (to OK_2) by going along the production curve to P', where $P'K_2$ is parallel to PK_1.

At the new point of equilibrium more A is employed and less

B; there has been a substitution in favour of A and against B. The result is absolutely as definite as in the case of one factor and one product. There a fall in the price of A led to an expansion in the supply of the product X; here it leads to a contraction in the demand for the factor B. Each effect is necessary.

3. Remembering the analogy with utility theory, we shall expect to find that we get necessary results of this kind in these two cases because in each of them we are working with two variables only—one factor and one product, or two factors. As soon as we go on to more complex cases the definiteness may be expected to disappear.

Suppose that the firm still has to produce a fixed output, but now employs three factors A, B, C. Suppose the price of A falls. Then, since the ratio of the prices of B and C remains unchanged, they can (as in utility theory) be treated as a single factor.[1] Consequently the demand for A must still necessarily expand; and the demand for B and C (taken together) must contract. There must be a substitution in favour of A at the expense of the other factors taken together.

As before, however, the substitution need not be at the expense of each of the other factors. B may be complementary with A, in which case the demand for B will expand. There will be a substitution in favour of A *and B* against C.

As in utility theory, the condition for A and B to be complementary is that a substitution of A for C (the amount of B being kept constant) should move the marginal rate of substitution of B for C in favour of B.

Thus, so long as output is kept constant, and we consider only the substitution among factors, exactly the same rules emerge as we found for the substitution effect in the consumer's budget. It is clear that practically the same thing would happen if we considered the case of a firm employing a constant quantity of factors, and varying its production of various joint products under the stimulus of changes in prices. Only there a rise in the price of X would lead to a substitution in favour of X against other products in general, but perhaps in favour of some complementary products.

[1] As in utility theory, this can be deduced mathematically from the stability conditions. See above, p. 33, note.

4. Now what happens when the quantities of both factors and products are variable? This is the crucial case.

Suppose the firm produces one product X, and employs two factors, A and B. Then, since the relation connecting the amounts of factors and the amount of product still has the same sorts of properties as those to which we are accustomed, the demand for A must necessarily expand when its price falls. But what will be the effects on the supply of X and on the demand for B? If we look at the effect on the product in isolation, it would appear that the supply of the product must necessarily be expanded (Fig. 20); if we look at the demand for the other factor in isolation, it would appear that it must necessarily be contracted (Fig. 21); but this is not a legitimate way of arguing. If this sort of argument had been applied to the case of three factors which we have just discussed, it would have seemed to follow that the demand for A must expand at the expense of B, *and* at the expense of C. We know that this is not necessary; *either B or C* may be complementary with A.

Applying the notion of complementarity to the case of two factors and one product, it would appear that there are three ways in which an expansion of the demand for A may be balanced:

(1) The supply of the product X may increase, and the demand for the other factor B may be reduced (here no complementarity is present).

(2) The supply of X may be increased, but the demand for B may increase as well (here the factors A and B are complementary).

(3) The demand for the factor B may be reduced, but the supply of the product X may be reduced too. Here there is a queer sort of inverted complementarity between factor and product. It is becoming evident (it is indeed directly evident from a comparison of Figs. 20 and 21 of this chapter) that the ordinary relation between factor and product, whereby the increased employment of a factor results in an increased product, has many properties in common with the relation of substitution between commodities, between factors, or between products. But if this ordinary relation corresponds to substitution, there must be something, it appears, which corresponds to complementarity. Here we have it. Let us call it 'regression'. If the factor A and the product X are regressive, a substitution of A for B will lower the marginal product of B in terms of X, and therefore (at given prices of B and X) cause the supply of X to be contracted.

I have a feeling that at this point the reader will rub his eyes, and declare that something must have gone wrong with the argument. Regression is such a peculiar relation that it is hard to reconcile it with common sense. Something, it would seem, must have been left out, which either excludes regression, or at least limits its possibility very drastically. Let us see what that can be.

5. If the third alternative (A and X regressive) seems grossly improbable, the second alternative (A and B complementary) is readily acceptable to common sense. This, we shall find, is the key to the puzzle. There are reasons why we can arrange our three alternatives in this order of probability. It is most likely that A and B will be complements, next most likely that no complementarity will be present and no regression, least likely of all that there will be regression. The reasons for this all hang together.

First of all, let us take a limiting case, in which it is possible to prove that the two factors *must* be complementary. The two factors will be complementary, we must remember, if an increase in the employment of A (with B constant), and consequent increase in the output of X, moves the marginal rate of transformation of B into X in favour of B; that is to say, raises the marginal product of B. (The criterion for the two factors being complementary is therefore nothing else but the well-established and familiar criterion for the two factors being 'co-operant'; an increase in one must raise the marginal product of the other.[1] In this case we do not need to disturb currently accepted definitions.[2])

Now consider what happens in those special conditions of production, when the contribution of the fixed 'productive opportunity' of the enterprise vanishes, so that costs do not rise with increasing output; and in which no economies of large scale are present either, so that costs do not fall with increasing output, and the situation is just consistent with perfect competition. Costs (both average and marginal) are constant; the surplus is zero; when each factor is paid a price per unit equal to its marginal

---

[1] Cf. Pigou, *Economics of Welfare*, part iv, ch. 3.

[2] However, it is only in the case of one product and two factors that my definition coincides exactly with Professor Pigou's. If there are more than two factors, my test would depend on what happened to the marginal product of B (B constant) if the supplies of other factors (C, &c.) were not kept constant, but varied in such a way as to leave their marginal products unchanged.

product, the total product is exactly exhausted.[1] Since marginal cost is constant, the increase in product due to a simultaneous proportionate increase in both factors (the marginal product of the two factors taken together) must be constant. But this joint marginal product is made up of four parts:

   (i) the marginal product of A with B constant;

   (ii) the increment (or decrement) of this marginal product due to the simultaneous increase in B. It will be an increment if A and B are complementary, a decrement if they are substitutes;

   (iii) the marginal product of B with A constant;

   (iv) the similar increment (or decrement) due to the increase in A. To this the same rule applies.

Now we know that as the amounts employed of the factors expand, the first and third of these parts decline. But we know that the whole does not decline. Therefore the decline of (i) and (iii) must be made up by *increments* under (ii) and (iv). Therefore the factors A and B must be complementary.

Thus, if the fixed 'productive opportunity' does nothing to limit the scale of production, the two factors must be complementary. As soon as it does something to limit expansion, the two factors are not, indeed, necessarily complementary. But there is still a probability in that direction if the joint marginal product of the two factors together declines slowly. When only two factors are employed in making one product, and the output of that product is variable, the two factors can only be substitutes if two conditions are fulfilled: the fixed resources of the entrepreneur must make an appreciable contribution to production, and the factors must be such that they would be *close* substitutes in the production of a *given* output.[2]

   [1] Thus the case under consideration is that in which the output of X is a linear and homogeneous function of the amounts of the factors A and B. This is sometimes called the case of 'constant returns to scale'.

   [2] Thus, in the case of constant costs and two factors, the two factors are necessarily complements in the production of a variable output, and necessarily substitutes in the production of a constant output. This is a paradoxical situation, which may easily lead to misunderstandings unless we are careful about it. If one decides to treat the case of constant costs as one's standard case, it is natural to define substitution and complementarity among factors with respect to a given output (for the important consequence of a change in factor prices is the change in the proportions of factors employed relatively to output—the effect on output itself cannot be made determinate at all without some reference to demand conditions being brought into the argument at once). This is the

We are now in a position to secure an interpretation of our queer case—regression. If A and X are regressive, A and B must be substitutes. Therefore the fixed resources of the entrepreneur must play an important part in limiting production. An increase in the employment of A must draw away these entrepreneurial resources from co-operation with B into co-operation with A. And this process must be attended with a reduction of output. The factor A must then be such that its employment is particularly suited for small-scale production of the product, and the factor B for production on a larger scale. Then it becomes just conceivable that a fall in the price of A, which must make it profitable to employ more A, can only work itself out by encouraging small-scale production; and the entrepreneurial resources are drawn away from large-scale production in co-operation with B to small-scale production in co-operation with A. Thus output may decline. Regression turns out to be a phenomenon of increasing returns; one which is just consistent with perfect competition if the fixed entrepreneurial resources are important enough. Still, it does not yet appear to be a possibility of which we need take much account.[1]

6. We are now at last in a position to have done with these special cases; we can go on to the general case of a firm which employs any number of factors, and produces any number of products. The factors must still be supposed to co-operate with a fixed productive opportunity of limited capacity, so that the condition of increasing marginal cost is satisfied.

point of view I adopted in the appendix to my *Theory of Wages*, and which was adopted by Mrs. Robinson in her discussion of the Elasticity of Substitution (*Economics of Imperfect Competition*, pp. 256 ff.). A recent and more elaborate investigation on these same lines is to be found in R. G. D. Allen, *Mathematical Analysis for Economists*, ch. xix.

After working for some time on these lines myself, I have become convinced that it is more convenient not to regard the case of constant costs as one's standard case. I prefer to treat it as the limiting case, in which the contribution to production of the entrepreneurial resources vanishes. From this point of view, it is better to define complementarity and substitution among factors with respect to a variable output—so that a pair of factors employed by a single firm ordinarily tend to be complementary.

[1] This interpretation may be tested by observing that regression, like complementarity, is a symmetrical relation. Thus, if A and X are regressive, an increase in the price of X will lead to an expansion in the output of X, an expansion in the employment of B, but a contraction in the employment of A.

Let us examine what happens (1) if the price of one factor changes, other prices (of factors and products) being given; (2) what happens when the price of a product changes, other prices being given.

(1) If there is a fall in the price of a factor A, the demand for that factor must increase. This increased employment must, somehow, be balanced; consequently either the supply of some products must expand or the demand for some other factors must contract, or both. We have seen that when there is only one other factor B, the demand for B will probably expand too (A and B complementary). The same thing can be shown to hold even when there are a number of other factors present.[1] If the fixed resources of the entrepreneur have no important effect in limiting production, the whole group of factors employed must form a single mutually complementary group, each pair of which are complements. It is only as the fixed resources become more important that the possibility of some pairs of factors being substitutes begins to appear—and ultimately also the possibility of regression in some of the factor-product relations.[2]

The typical result of a fall in the price of a factor is then this: that the supplies of products will expand, and the demand for other factors will expand too. But to each of these general rules a limited amount of exception is possible, when the fixed resources are influential enough; some factors may be substitutes for the first factor, some products may be regressive against it; the demands for substitute factors, and the supplies of regressive products, will decline.

(2) If there is a rise in the price of some product X (other prices being unchanged), the supply of X must increase. This increased supply can only be made possible by an increased employment of factors, or a diminished output of other products, or both. There are essentially the same reasons for expecting complementarity to be dominant among products as for expecting

---

[1] See below, pp. 322–3.
[2] Regression seems to be a more intelligible possibility in cases of joint production than it is when there is only one product. The factor A may play a particularly important part in the production of the product X; consequently, when the employment of A expands, the output of X must expand too. But if the entrepreneur's fixed resources are devoted more to the production of X, they will be less available for the production of Y. Thus A and Y may be regressive.

it to be dominant among factors (all the products must be complementary if the contribution to production of the entrepreneur's fixed resources is negligible). Thus, though exceptions are possible, it is likely that the outputs of most of the other products will tend to rise. A general rise in output must be matched by a general rise in the employment of factors; though once again this is not certain for every factor.

The typical situation is that an increased price of one product will induce an increased supply of other products and an increased demand for the factors. Substitute products and regressive factors will only be possible to a limited extent.

These are the principles which govern the market conduct of a firm. They differ from those governing the conduct of a private individual in two important respects: first, the income effect is absent; secondly, there is a tendency for products jointly produced in the same firm to be complementary, and for factors jointly employed in the same firm to be complementary. While substitute products and substitute factors can exist, they are unlikely to be *dominant*.

CHAPTER VIII

THE GENERAL EQUILIBRIUM OF PRODUCTION

1. WE are now in a position to attempt a provisional synthesis. We have seen (in Chapters I–III) what determines the equilibrium of the private individual, and how he may be expected to react to changes in prices. In Chapters IV–V we have used these principles to elucidate the working of an economic system which consisted only of such private individuals, so that the only economic activity possible was the exchange of goods and services. Finally, in the last two chapters, we have introduced a new kind of economic unit, the firm; and we have investigated the principles determining its market conduct. We are thus at last in a position to examine the working of an economic system containing both kinds of units, private individuals and firms; so that the price-system does not only regulate exchange, but also regulates production.

The mere fact that it does take account of production suffices to make the General Equilibrium of Production, as we shall treat it in this chapter, an hypothesis of much wider applicability than the General Equilibrium of Exchange. It is indeed already a fairly well-developed system, and includes so much of the economic problem that many of the systems of thought employed by economists during the last century fall within it, and have to be reckoned among its simplified forms. There are, I believe myself, quite a number of problems, particularly long-period problems, in such fields as Distribution and International Trade, where it is a fairly adequate hypothesis, so that its utilization is fairly safe. But there are other fields where it is most unsafe to use it; in fact the misuse of this system is one of the most fruitful sources of error in economic theory. For it still abstracts from some of the most important sides of economic life; anything which relates to those sides cannot effectively be studied by it.

Its main deficiencies may perhaps be classified as three in number. First, it pays no attention to monopoly and imperfect competition; as I have explained, I do not think the importance of this defect should be exaggerated. Secondly, it abstracts from the economic activity of the State; this is very important, but the

State is a very incalculable economic unit, so that the extent to which its actions can be allowed for in economic theory is somewhat limited. (This is, of course, a deficiency of economic theory as such, and as a whole.) Lastly, it abstracts from capital and interest, saving and investment, and all that complex of activities which, in an earlier chapter, I called 'Speculation'. This is a vital defect, which we must try to remedy in the later part of this book. However, it will appear then that we are not really going out of our way in this chapter.

2. We have now to consider a system containing two kinds of individuals, private individuals and entrepreneurs. The division between the two classes is made in this way. Every individual possesses supplies of one or both of two sorts of resources—(1) factors of production which can be disposed of on the market, (2) entrepreneurial resources which cannot be disposed of in that way, but which can be used, in combination with the other sort of factors, to produce disposable products. Given a set of market prices, for factors and products, any one who possesses entrepreneurial resources will be able to determine whether the utilization of those resources in production will yield a positive surplus. If it will do so, he becomes an entrepreneur. As entrepreneur, he has to decide what arrangement of production will make his surplus a maximum. At given prices, this most profitable arrangement is determined by the state of technique and by the extent of his entrepreneurial resources; consequently his demand for factors and supply of products (on business account) is determined; consequently the amount of his surplus is determined. This surplus now becomes part of his income on private account—that part of his account where his decisions become similar to those of the private individual.

The private individual, who only possesses factors of the first kind, or who does not find it worth while to use his entrepreneurial resources, has to decide (1) how much of his supply of factors he shall dispose of—for example, how much labour he will perform; (2) how much of the income so secured he will spend on each kind of commodity.[1] At a given system of prices, and given scale of preferences, these decisions must be made in one way.

---

[1] I say 'commodity' rather than 'product' so as to allow for the possibility that he may demand factors (services) directly.

The private individual's supply of factors and demand for commodities is therefore determined.

The entrepreneur, who possesses entrepreneurial resources as well as (or perhaps instead of) disposable factors, has to make similar decisions on his private account. His income is derived from his surplus, as well as from his supply of factors; at given prices these are both determined; therefore his income is determined, and therefore his demand for commodities is determined.

Taking entrepreneurs and private individuals together, the demands and supplies of all sorts of commodities are determined, once the system of prices is given. Strictly speaking, we have to distinguish four kinds of markets: (1) the markets for products, where demand comes from private accounts (of private individuals and entrepreneurs), supply comes from the business accounts of entrepreneurs (that is to say, from firms); (2) markets for factors, where demand comes from firms, supply from private accounts; (3) markets for direct services, where supply and demand both come from private accounts; (4) markets for intermediate products, which are products for one firm and factors for another, so that supply and demand both come from firms. In all kinds of markets, however, supply and demand are determined, once the price-system is given.

When it comes to counting equations, there is the same little complication as in the theory of exchange. One commodity must be taken as standard, and there are therefore only n-1 prices to determine, assuming n commodities in all. There are apparently n equations, but one follows from the rest. Even if the markets are not in equilibrium, accounts (whether private accounts or business accounts) must balance; this means that if n-1 markets are in equilibrium, the odd market must be in equilibrium.

3. So far, we have followed in the steps of Walras and Pareto, only adapting their arguments a little to allow for modern ideas about the equilibrium of the firm. But when we pass on to consider the stability of the system, and to examine its working, we lose their guidance.

The stability of production equilibrium has to be examined in the same way as we examined the stability of exchange equilibrium in Chapter V. Fortunately, however, it is not necessary for us to go through again anything like that complicated and rather wearisome investigation. For we are still concerned here with the stability of *markets*; the formal results of our earlier investigation can thus be taken over and applied to our present problem.

We shall find that the application proceeds quite smoothly, save on one point. Strictly speaking, we only discussed in the last chapter the effect of a change in price on the demands and supplies of a single firm. Here we need the effect on a group of firms. For the most part this effect can be got by aggregating the effects on single firms, as we found we could aggregate the effects on private individuals; so far the group must obey the same laws as the single firm. What happens, however, if the change in prices has the effect of altering the number of firms producing a particular commodity, so that firms enter or leave the 'industry'? This is a notoriously tricky matter, and it is right that we should proceed with caution; nevertheless it does not appear that for our present purposes the qualifications introduced by the possibility of new firms are likely to be serious. A rise in the price of a product X may stimulate production of X on the part of a new firm, either because it makes profitable the use of entrepreneurial resources which have not been employed before, or because it causes entrepreneurial resources, which have previously been employed in making other products, to be transferred to the production of X. In either case the same principles must apply. If the new entrepreneurial resources have not been employed before, they merely add a new source of demand for the other factors employed in the industry, and a new source of supply for X. Supplies of products and demands for factors can only be reduced, as a consequence of the entry of the new firm, through the effects which its entry has on the price-system. If, on the other hand, the new entrepreneurial resources are drawn from some other use, then the supply of other products may be directly diminished, and the demands for factors suitable to make those products may be directly diminished; but this must mean that the limited capacity of entrepreneurial resources is a significant limit to the scale of production, so that the effect is similar to that on a firm which throughout produces both products, but is led to concentrate more on one and less on the other as a result of a change in relative prices. Thus in direction of change, though not perhaps in extent, the complications due to new firms are similar in character to those we have already covered.

We may now turn to apply our analysis of exchange equilibrium to the equilibrium of production. In this case, as in that, it is still true that the only possible source of instability is strong asymmetry in income effects.[1] All we have to do now is to consider the probability of such asymmetry being strong enough to lead to actual instability under our new hypotheses.

When the demand or the supply of a commodity comes from private accounts, the effect of a change in price can be divided into an income effect and a substitution effect, as before. But when it comes from firms, then, as we saw in the last chapter, there is nothing analogous to the income effect. Thus when considering the possibility of instability through asymmetrical income effects, it is necessary to make a distinction between the four kinds of markets.

(1) In the markets for products, a fall in price will make consumers better off, entrepreneurs worse off; there is thus an income effect on both sides, which works just like that in exchange theory, and which is only likely to make for instability if the product is inferior, or if it is consumed to an important degree by the entrepreneurs who produce it. But we must remember that even so it is not enough that the net income effect should make for instability; the market will only be unstable if a net income effect making for instability is not dominated by the substitution effect. Now here we have as stabilizers, not only the substitution effects between this product and other commodities in the budgets of consumers (as we had in exchange theory), but also the effect on *production* of a change in price, which, as we have seen, works like a substitution effect, and therefore always tends towards stability.

(2) In the case of factor markets, a fall in price makes the suppliers of the factor worse off, entrepreneurs better off; in view of the specialization of individuals on the provision of particular sorts of factors (so that, for example, employees do not usually provide the same sorts of labour as their employers), this is particularly likely to leave a net income effect in the dangerous direction. Again, however, we have as stabilizers both the substitution (say between leisure and consumption) in the budgets of individuals and the production effect.

[1] Here, as in Chapter IV, the discussion of stability in the first edition of this book was complicated by the introduction of 'extreme complementarity'. Since, for the reasons explained in the note on p. 77 above, 'extreme complementarity' has turned out to be a mirage, references to it have been simply cut out.

(3) Markets for direct services, in which production plays no part, work exactly as described in our analysis of exchange.

(4) Markets for intermediate products, of which both the demand and the supply come from firms, are not troubled with any income effect on either side, and are therefore necessarily stable.[1]

It appears from all this that, so far as the question of stability is concerned, the position in the equilibrium of production is very similar to what it was in the equilibrium of exchange. We have, however, one powerful new influence (the absence of income effects in the market conduct of the firm) which makes for stability. On the other hand, it becomes evident that the danger of instability is particularly concentrated on the factor markets.

How probable is it that instability, due to this last cause, might become dominant through the system as a whole? It would seem that it is not at all likely. For we must always remember that the predominant relation on the technical side between factors and products reckons as a relation of substitution, and that it is usually a strong relation. The possibility of considerable changes in the rate of conversion of factors into products as a result of quite small changes in relative prices is a strong stabilizing element. It is this more than anything else which gives us ground for supposing that the general equilibrium of production will be stable in most ordinary circumstances.

4. There is probably more to be said on the subject of stability, but we seem to have got far enough for our purposes. We have seen enough to satisfy ourselves that a perfectly stable system of production equilibrium is a reasonable hypothesis. Let us then assume such a system and see how it will work.

The formal rules for the working of a general equilibrium system, as we found them in Chapter V, will still apply. Only we have to give them an increased variety of interpretation.

Since the system is stable, it is still true that an increase in the demand for any commodity (so that some people desire more of that commodity, and offer some of the standard commodity in exchange), must raise the price of that commodity in terms of the standard. Similarly an increase in the supply of a commodity

---

[1] Of course, entrepreneurs on the one side are better off, and on the other worse off. This has to be allowed for in considering the general effect of the change in price; but it does not ordinarily affect directly the demand or supply for the intermediate product, which (*ex hypothesi*) is not directly consumed.

(so that some people offer more of that commodity, and seek to receive some of the standard commodity in exchange) must lower the price of that commodity. These rules must hold for factors as well as products.

The extent to which the price of the commodity will be affected by a given change in demand (or supply) of this sort, depends upon the degree of substitutability in the system.[1] The greater the substitutability, or the less the complementarity, between any two products (or factors) in the system, the less will the price of any commodity be affected by a change in the demand for it. Such substitution may be on the technical side, or in the budgets of private individuals. Here, again, the normal relation between a factor and its product is to be regarded as a relation of substitution. Thus, the more elastic the marginal productivity curve of any factor in terms of its product, the less will the price of any commodity (factor or product) be affected by a change in the demand (or supply) for it.

The effects of such a change in demand (or supply) on the prices of other commodities depends primarily on whether these other commodities are substitutes or complements for the first. Of course substitution and complementarity must here be understood to have reference to the system as a whole. (If two goods are substitutes on both sides, then they are necessarily substitutes with respect to the system as a whole; similarly for complements; if they are substitutes on one side and complements on the other, then it depends on which is dominant.)

As a first approximation, we may say that a rise in the price of a commodity X will be accompanied by a rise in the prices of all those goods which are directly substitutes for X, and a fall in the prices of those goods that are complementary. But in the second place, we may have to allow for indirect effects through other prices (which obey the rule that substitutes of substitutes, and complements of complements, tend to rise in price; substitutes of complements, and complements of substitutes, tend to fall in price). If a good is such that it is at the same time a direct substitute for X, and the complement of a substitute, the direct and indirect effects will pull in opposite directions.

In the third place, we may have to allow for an income effect. Some people will be made richer, some poorer, by the change in

[1] Cf. above, p. 76.

prices; the effects of this on their demands and supplies for commodities may not cancel out. It is very difficult to say anything in general about this income effect; sometimes its working can be guessed, but very often it can only be treated as a source of random error.

5. Some simple examples of the sort of analysis which now becomes possible may next be given.

First, suppose that there is an increase in the demand for a certain product X. The price of X will rise, and this will bring with it a tendency to a general rise in prices throughout the whole system (though of course, unless X is a commodity of very great importance, the rise will only be of sensible magnitude in the cases of commodities nearly related). Among the commodities nearly related are the factors employed in the making of X; their prices will ordinarily tend to rise. The only commodities which may suffer a fall in price are those directly or indirectly complementary with X. The complements may be classified into the following groups:

(1) Commodities complementary with X in consumption. As the price of X rises, the demand for these commodities will fall off, and their prices tend to fall.[1] (This effect may frequently be masked in practice by a simultaneous rise in the demand for these complementary commodities.)

(2) Products complementary with X in production. As we have seen, any commodity jointly produced with X is very likely to fall under this heading. As the supply of X increases, the supplies of these complements will increase too, and their prices tend to fall. (This is the familiar text-book case of wool and mutton.)

(3) Factors regressive against X. In so far as any of the joint products are technically substitutes, their production will fall off, and the demands for any factors specially needed for the production of these substitute products may fall off too.

Indirect complements are either substitutes of the direct complements, or complements of the direct substitutes (whose prices rise). Under the first heading would come, for example, factors needed to produce commodities complementary in consumption with X, or products whose production is facilitated by the fall in the prices of these factors. Under the second heading might

---

[1] In the rest of this chapter I neglect income effects.

be found such things as the complements in consumption of other products whose prices had risen because they needed in their production some of the same factors as were needed for the manufacture of X.

In the cases of these remoter indirect complements, however, it is not very likely that their prices will fall on balance. For if they are indirect complements along one channel of causation, they will often be indirect substitutes along another. The general dominance of substitution throughout the system as a whole will swamp much indirect complementarity.

6. Now take the converse case—an increase in the supply of a factor A. It is clear that the price of A must fall. Effects on other prices can be worked out as above. There is, however, one type of effect which is particularly interesting. What will be the effect on the price of another factor B, employed in the same industry or industries? If B is a complementary factor (and, as we have seen, complementarity is likely to be the dominant relation among factors employed together, so that A and B will very probably be complementary, at least on the production side), the direct effect will be to raise the price of B. However, there is here one indirect effect at least that must certainly be allowed for as well—the indirect effect through the price of the product (or products). At least on the production side, their product must probably be reckoned as a close 'substitute' for both A and B. Therefore the price of B (in its role as substitute of substitute) probably tends to fall. The net effect on the price of B is thus compounded out of two contrary tendencies, a direct effect tending to raise it, an indirect effect tending to reduce it; either may be dominant. But if B is a substitute for A in production, both effects will probably tend to reduce the price of B.[1]

---

[1] Cf. J. Robinson, *Economics of Imperfect Competition*, p. 258. Mrs. Robinson, who is here dealing, like ourselves, with a case of perfect competition, only takes into account the production side, assumes only two factors, no entrepreneurial resources, no economies of large scale; hence constant costs. These assumptions enable her to divide her effects differently. She takes (1) the effect on the demand for B, when the output of the (sole) product is given; (2) the effect through variations in output. Our conclusions seem to be perfectly consistent. While Mrs. Robinson's methods have advantages for the sort of applications she wanted to make, my own can be more readily generalized to deal with problems of a whole economic system.

When the supply of a factor increases, complementary factors are perhaps the most likely of all commodities to rise in price; yet even they will only actually rise if the prices of their common products are little affected, that is to say, if the demands for the products are fairly elastic, or the products are good substitutes for other commodities.

7. In accordance with our usual convention, the increase in the supply of A (in our last paragraph) was an increase in the supply of A in terms of the standard commodity; the amount of A offered at given prices increased, and the suppliers demanded nothing but some of the standard commodity in exchange. If the standard commodity is money, this implies that they hoard all the income which they derive from the new units they supply. Similarly, in the preceding case, it is implicitly assumed that the new demand is demand in terms of the standard commodity; so that if the standard commodity is money, the new demand comes from dishoarding, not from economizing on other goods. If these assumptions are not justified, so that the increased supply of the factor A is accompanied by an increased demand for products, or the increased demand for X by a diminished demand for other products, effects along these channels must also be allowed for. Naturally they will produce an effect on general prices which goes in the opposite direction from the primary effect; so that prices in general will only move upwards as the result of an increase in demand, or downwards as the result of an increase in supply, if there is net dishoarding in the one case, or hoarding in the other.[1]

To analyse the net effect on prices of, say, an increased supply of a factor, accompanied by increased demand for certain commodities, will often be very complicated, and it is natural to seek for some other way of calculating the results. This can sometimes be achieved by the simple device of changing the standard commodity. What standard commodity we choose is, so far, entirely at our discretion; if we are dealing with an increase in the supply of a factor, the proceeds of whose disposal are to be used predominantly for the purchase of consumption goods, then it is reasonable to take as our standard commodity some representative

---

[1] It will be evident from our analysis that we should not expect this general movement to show up in *any* price-index.

consumption good, consumed by the suppliers of the factor,[1] and to work in 'real' terms. Then we have only to consider the effect of the change in the supply of the factor, and have nothing to put on the other side. Our analysis tells us directly that the price of the factor must fall in terms of this representative consumption good; while the effects on the prices of other factors may similarly be worked out in real terms.

One obstacle to the general adoption of this sort of device needs, however, to be noticed. If there are, in our system, any prices which are fixed conventionally in terms of money, no great difference will be made to our arguments, so long as we take money as the standard commodity. (The detailed adjustments necessary are examined in a note on the next page.) But if we take anything else as the standard commodity, severe intellectual contortions are needed for us to be able to make any progress.

The great importance of this consideration will emerge fully later on.[2]

[1] Cf. the 'wage-goods' of Professor Pigou (*Theory of Unemployment*, passim).
[2] See below, Chapter XXI.

Note to Chapter VIII

CONVENTIONAL OR RIGID PRICES

The exact analysis of conventional (maximum or minimum) prices is best made as follows:

Suppose all other prices to be given, and the demand curve (*D*) and supply curve (*S*) for one commodity to be drawn as in Fig. 22. If the price of that commodity were free to move, the price would be established at the intersection of the curves. But if it is fixed at, say, a

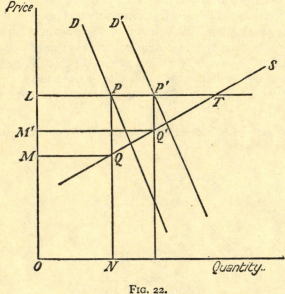

FIG. 22.

higher level than this, then only an amount *ON* (= *LP* or *MQ*) will be sold, although sellers would be willing to supply an amount *LT*. The situation is therefore identical with that which would have arisen if a price *OL* had been fixed for buyers only, a price *OM* for sellers only, the difference between these prices being handed over as a bonus to those sellers who do actually make sales. (Alternatively, we may suppose that a tax equal to *LM* per unit is laid upon the commodity, and the proceeds of that tax handed over to the sellers. A process made familiar to us by the Ministry of Agriculture!) By using this construction, we can retain the equilibrium condition that supply equals demand, though we have to sacrifice the rule that there is only one price in the market. There is a real price, which is fixed as a datum; and there is a 'shadow price', which is determined by equilibrium conditions. Since the sellers do not actually receive the shadow price, but have it made up by a bonus, the shadow price is not important for income effects; but it is important all the same, as it governs the substitution effects on the supply side.

If the demand for the commodity increases (the demand curve moving from D to D'), it cannot result in a change in the fixed price. But since the amount bought will increase, the shadow price will rise from OM to OM'. The bonus will be changed from $LPQM$ to $LP'Q'M'$; but this is not likely to be of much importance. What is important is that supply will increase in just the same way (apart from the income effect) as it would have done if the actual price had risen from OM to OM'. That is why the shadow price is important. All reactions on other markets which start from the supply side in this market will proceed just as if there had been a real change in price; it is only reactions on the demand side which are cut off by the price-fixation.

Take as an illustration the effects of a minimum price for wheat, combined with just sufficient restriction of supply to make the minimum price effective. If demand from some particular source expands, this may have no effect on the price, and therefore no effect on the demand for wheat from other sources. But nevertheless it may still affect the supply, which may expand, perhaps at the expense of other crops. The prices of these may then rise, just as they would have done if the price of wheat itself had risen.

The significance of this proposition (which is equally valid for maximum prices, when all terms are reversed) is self-evident. Price control can damp down a general rise in prices; but, unless it is absolutely complete, it cannot prevent it altogether.

We shall have to return to this proposition in a different connexion. (See Chapter XXI below.)

PART III

THE FOUNDATIONS OF DYNAMIC ECONOMICS

O God! that it were possible
To undo things done, to call back yesterday;
That time might turn up his swift sandy glass,
To untell the days, and to redeem these hours.
(*A Woman killed with Kindness.*)

CHAPTER IX
THE METHOD OF ANALYSIS

1. THE definition of economic dynamics (that much controverted term) which I have in mind here is this. I call Economic Statics those parts of economic theory where we do not trouble about dating; Economic Dynamics those parts where every quantity must be dated. For example, in economic statics we think of an entrepreneur employing such-and-such quantities of factors and producing by their aid such-and-such quantities of products; but we do not ask when the factors are employed and when the products come to be ready. In economic dynamics we do ask such questions; and we even pay special attention to the way changes in these dates affect the relations between factors and products.[1]

We have therefore been concerned, up to the present, with economic statics; and very strictly so concerned, for we have maintained a rigid rule to abstain from any suggestion of dating. Most economists who have dealt with similar problems have not been so strict; and, indeed, it was only because I had a dynamic theory in preparation that I could dare to make my static theory so static. I shall try to show that in these circumstances there were great advantages in our procedure. It is true that if one follows the usual course of economists in the past (at least of the vast majority of nineteenth-century economists) and gives one's static theory some slight dynamic flavouring, it can be made to look much more directly applicable to the real world. It can contain most of the staple diet of traditional economics, from the theory of rent and the theory of comparative cost to the theory of monopolistic exploitation; all of which can be established without any consideration of time ever coming into the argument. It can be decked out with illustrations and institutional qualifications, until the skeleton takes on the form of a standard work.

[1] The distinction between economic statics and economic dynamics has thus not much in common with the distinction between statics and dynamics in the physical sciences. One's justification for using the terms lies in the fact that they have a fairly well-established place in economic terminology; and if they have not acquired precise meanings, they have at least a series of meanings which seem to be converging upon something useful.

But it will still be quite incompetent to deal properly with capital, or interest, or trade fluctuations, or even money—problems where the dating of economic quantities is of the first importance.[1]

If, on the contrary, the theory of economic statics is presented in its barest and starkest form, as we have presented it, then the dynamic problem is thrown up as a challenge. The economic system has now to be conceived of, not merely as a network of interdependent markets, but as a process in time. Is it possible to use the same methods of analysis in this dynamic field? Or must we have recourse to wholly different methods? It is not obvious that anything like the same methods will do. Nevertheless, we shall find, as we proceed, that there is a way of reducing the dynamic problem into terms where it becomes formally identical with that of statics. Thus the results of static theory can be used after all; though almost all of them need drastic reinterpretation.

2. When economists first embarked upon the study of dynamics, it was natural for them to try out at first a much less drastic readjustment. This was reached in the following way. Static theory gives us the system of prices as depending on the preferences of the individuals composing the economy, on the productive resources (or factors) under their control, and on the state of technique (the production functions). Now we should be able to apply static analysis with the maximum of convenience if, when it comes to dating, we could date all these things to the same moment; if we could say that the system of prices existing at any moment depends upon the preferences and resources existing at that moment and upon nothing else. This is clearly not true (at least, not in the sense needed); but is there not some way by which it could be made to be true?

The main reason why it is not true is that the adjustments needed to bring about equilibrium take time. A rise in the price of a commodity exercises, at once, only a small influence upon

---

[1] Of course, people used to be able to content themselves with the static apparatus, only because they were imperfectly aware of its limitations. Thus they would often introduce into their static theory a 'factor of production' capital and its 'price' interest, supposing that capital could be treated like the static factors. (Cf. J. B. Clark's 'free capital' and Cassel's 'capital disposal'.) That some error was involved in this procedure would not have been denied; but the absence of a general dynamic theory, in which all quantities were properly dated, made it easy to underestimate how great the error was.

the supply of that commodity; but it sets entrepreneurs guessing whether the higher price will continue. If they decide that it probably will continue, they may start upon the production of a considerably increased supply for a future date. This decision will affect their current demand for factors; the current position in the factor markets will thus be governed by the way entrepreneurs interpret the rise in the price of the product.

Similarly, the current supply of a commodity depends not so much upon what the current price is as upon what entrepreneurs have expected it to be in the past. It will be those past expectations, whether right or wrong, which mainly govern current output; the actual current price has a relatively small influence.

This is the first main crux of dynamic theory; and it marks the first parting of the ways. Either we have to face up to the difficulty, and allow deliberately for the fact that supplies (and ultimately demands too) are governed by expected prices quite as much as by current prices; or we have to evade the issue by concentrating on the case where these difficulties are at a minimum. The first is the method of Marshall; the second (broadly speaking) is the method of the Austrians.[1] Its hall-mark is concentration on the case of a Stationary State.

Although it is my firm belief that the stationary state is, in the end, nothing but an evasion, nevertheless it has played so large a part in modern economic thought that we must give it some attention. The stationary state is that special case of a dynamic system where tastes, technique, and resources remain constant through time. We can reasonably assume that experience of these constant conditions will lead entrepreneurs to expect their continuance; so that it is not necessary to distinguish between price-expectations and current prices, for they are all the same. We can assume, too, that entrepreneurs did expect in the past that to-day's prices would be what they now turn out to be; so that the supplies of commodities are fully adjusted to their prices. Then it can be shown that the price-system established in such a stationary state is substantially identical with that static price-system whose properties we already know.

[1] The classical exposition of Austrian capital theory is, of course, Böhm-Bawerk's *Positive Theory of Capital*; but an even more refined version of what is fundamentally the same theory is to be found in the first volume of Wicksell's *Lectures*. (Wicksell was a Walrasian on Value, but an Austrian on Capital.)

This can be seen in the following way. It is true that factors are actually employed in processes which will only result in future output, and that it is the expectation of future vendibility which provides the stimulus to their employment. But, nevertheless, in a stationary state the factors currently employed do seem to produce the current output; for they make it possible to produce that output, subject to the condition that the stock of intermediate products (fixed and working capital generally) shall not be diminished in consequence. As in Professor Pigou's famous illustration,[1] the stock of intermediate products is a 'lake' fed by the input of current services, drained by the output of current products. Although the water generally remains in the lake a certain length of time, nevertheless, if we impose the condition that the total amount of water in the lake should be kept constant, there is a direct relation between current input and current output. So long as we make the 'stationary' assumption that capital is maintained intact, the technical production function becomes a relation between current input and current output—we are back in the 'static' world.

One thing, however, is evident when we look at this stationary economy, which was not evident in the static theory when time was left out of account altogether. This is the dependence of the input–output relations (the production functions) on the quantity of intermediate products carried by the system. How will the quantity of intermediate products—the quantity of capital—be determined?

It turns out to be determined through the rate of interest. A fall in the rate of interest would encourage the adoption of longer processes, requiring the use (at any moment) of larger quantities of intermediate products. But since we are in a stationary state, there can be no tendency for the stock of capital to increase or diminish; constancy of the stock thus gives us one relation between its size and the rate of interest. Also, if entrepreneurs do not desire to increase or diminish their stock, their net borrowing must be nil. If the demand and supply for loans are to be in equilibrium, net saving must therefore also be nil. The rate of interest must therefore be fixed at a level which offers no incentive for net saving or dis-saving. What this level is depends partly upon the propensities to save of the individuals composing the

---

[1] *Economics of Welfare*, 4th ed., p. 43.

community, partly upon their real incomes—and these depend again upon the size of the stock of intermediate products. We therefore have two equations to determine the size of the stock of capital goods and the rate of interest; consequently both are determined.

The theory thus baldly summarized is a plausible theory of a stationary state; unfortunately it is only a theory of a stationary state. It is only in very special conditions that saving and investment will both = o, for every unit in the economy; and it is only if they do that we can separate out the equations concerning capital and interest, leaving the rest of the price-system to be determined as in statics. Once we leave that special case, a crowd of new complications need to be considered, which are simply eliminated in the stationary economy. It is because preoccupation with stationary conditions has encouraged the neglect of these complications (many of which are supremely important) that it has had such a baneful influence on the minds of economists.

It is only in a stationary state that actual prices do not need to be distinguished from expected prices; that income does not need to be distinguished from product; that money rates of interest do not need to be distinguished from real rates of interest, and interest rates for one period of lending from interest rates for another. The stationary state has positively impeded the development of the theory of interest, by leaving out so many vital aspects. Further, although it would always be recognized that the actual state of any real economy is never in fact stationary, nevertheless stationary-state theorists naturally regarded reality as 'tending' towards stationariness; though the existence of such a tendency is more than questionable. Of course, the stationary theory itself gives no indication that reality does tend to move in any such direction. It tells us that if we got to a stationary state, then (other things being equal) we should stick; but it gives us no indication that we are in fact aiming for such a position; for it can tell us nothing about anything actual at all.

3. Our own approach to the dynamic problem must be entirely different. It will have more in common with the method of Marshall; though since, in the relevant part of Marshall's work (the great fifth book on 'General Relations of Demand, Supply, and Value'), he is concerned with the determination of the value of

one commodity only, considered as much as possible in isolation, while we are concerned with the determination of the whole system of values, we cannot follow him in all respects.[1]

Marshall's analysis starts off on a particular day (let us call it Day I). He does not make the unreal 'stationary' assumption that the demand-and-supply conditions which actually exist on Day I were foreseen by producers in the past. Instead, he goes so far as to regard the finished supply, coming forward for sale on Day I, as wholly determined by past expectations, and therefore already a datum; nothing that is done now can alter it. The demands of the buyers, however, and perhaps also the reservation demands of the sellers, will be determined by the preferences and income conditions that actually exist on Day I; they may also be affected by the expectations which exist on Day I, particularly if the commodity is durable, and some persons expect an increased demand (or diminished supply) in the future.

To what extent is the price fixed on Day I determinate? The price at which trading opens is clearly not determinate; for traders do not know exactly what supplies will be coming forward to-day, nor what buyers will be demanding to-day. They are obliged to begin by fixing prices through trial and error (though of course the less present market conditions differ from what they had expected, the easier the adjustment will be). But Marshall has an ingenious argument by which he seeks to show that the price at which the market will finish up is nevertheless determinate; in the end supply and demand must be equated—in the sense that buyers buy what they desire to buy on Day I at the market price of Day I, and sellers sell what they desire to sell. We shall come back to this argument later.[2]

Next he goes on to Day II, or perhaps some 'days' later. The supplies of goods coming forward will, after a time, cease to be influenced solely by decisions taken before the beginning of Day I; the price arrived at on Day I will begin to affect supply. But

---

[1] Although Marshall raises at least a part of the general dynamic problem, it is curious to observe how reluctant he is to abandon static conceptions even in his dynamic analysis. Statics and dynamics are very little separated in his work; his dynamics are not made easier by running in terms of a very static 'equilibrium', and by the fact that their central passage leads up to the introduction of that 'famous fiction', the stationary state.

[2] Marshall, *Principles*, v. 2; see the 'Note on Formation of Prices' at the end of this chapter.

it will affect it in a different way according as we go forward for a 'short period' or a 'long period'. In a short period 'the supply of specialized skill and ability, of suitable machinery and other material capital, and of the appropriate industrial organization has not time to be fully adapted to demand; but producers have to adjust their supply to the demand as best they can with the appliances already at their disposal'.[1] 'In long periods, on the other hand, all investments of capital and effort in providing the material plant and the organization of a business, and in acquiring trade knowledge and specialized ability, have time to be adjusted to the incomes which are expected to be earned by them.'[2] As we shall find, the 'long period' in its strict sense (of a 'full adaptation' of supply to demand) is not a concept that fits very well into a general dynamic theory; but the substance of Marshall's famous distinction will need our full attention.

If we assume that producers base their expectations of future prices upon the prices actually realized on Day I (Marshall generally appears to make this assumption), then we can say that when the price of Day I is above a certain level ('short period normal supply price'), producers will begin to plan, for future dates a short period ahead, a larger output than the output they actually produced for sale on Day I. If the price of Day I is above 'long period normal supply price', they will seek to expand their equipment, and will begin to plan an increased future output along this route.

Strictly speaking, we can start from Day I, and inquire what output producers will plan to produce on Day N, if they expect the price on Day N to be such and such; we can then draw up a curve giving the planned output for every possible expected price. Such a curve could be drawn up for each particular future date; Marshall's short and long period curves are samples taken out of this potentially large collection.[3]

4. The way in which Marshall proceeds to work out his theory will be familiar; the above summary may suffice to recall to the reader's mind those parts of his analysis which are most relevant to our purposes. What we have to do now is to generalize his

---

[1] Marshall, p. 376.   [2] Ibid., p. 377.

[3] It should be observed that these curves are only determinate if something is known about the prices expected to rule on other days than N; a complete theory will need to take this complication into account.

framework, so that it can be used for the discussion of the problems of a whole economic system.

First of all, there are some parts of his model that we shall hardly find it worth our while to retain. The rigid tripartite division (Temporary Equilibrium on the first 'Day', Short Period, and Long Period) is the most important of these. These categories are suitable enough for Marshall's isolated market, but they hardly fit the analysis of the whole system. There is scarcely any period of time so short that it can give us temporary equilibrium (in Marshall's sense) for all commodities; there will nearly always be some products whose supply can be increased within the period. There is scarcely any nameable period of time so long that the supply of all commodities can be 'fully adjusted' within it; the extension of the long period to involve perfect equilibrium of the whole economy can, moreover, easily involve us in begging questions about a tendency to stationary equilibrium. Thus I shall not employ Marshall's tripartite classification—while endeavouring to keep the truth it embodies (the time taken in adjustment) clearly in mind.

Even if we decide to admit some small variability of output into our shortest period, nevertheless that shortest period (which I shall call a Week, to distinguish it from Marshall's Day) still needs to be clearly conceived and clearly defined. I shall define a week as that period of time during which variations in prices can be neglected. For theoretical purposes this means that prices will be supposed to change, not continuously, but at short intervals. The calendar length of the week is of course quite arbitrary; by taking it to be very short, our theoretical scheme can be fitted as closely as we like to that ceaseless oscillation which is a characteristic of prices in certain markets. I think we shall find, however, that when the week is supposed to be very short, our theory becomes rather uninformative; I believe it is better to think of it as being fairly long, though that means we have to be content with a fairly loose approximation to reality.

A convenient way of visualizing this assumption of constant prices during the week is to suppose that there is only one day in the week (say Monday) when markets are open, so that it is only on Mondays that contracts can be made. Contracts can, indeed, be carried out during the week (goods can be delivered, and so on); but no new contracts can be made until Monday week. Monday's prices will therefore rule during the week, and they will govern the disposition of resources during the week.

Now it is not hard to see that prices will remain constant during the week, when the markets are not open, and when there is therefore no opportunity for prices to change. But we need also to try and bring ourselves to suppose that price-changes are negligible during market hours on the Monday, when the market is open and dealers have to fix market prices by higgling and bargaining, trial and error. This implies that the market (indeed, all markets) proceeds quickly and smoothly to a position of temporary equilibrium—in Marshall's sense. Marshall gave certain grounds for supposing this to be a reasonable assumption under the conditions of his model; I shall examine in the note at the end of this chapter how far these grounds are available to us. For the present, I must ask the reader to accept the assumption of an easy passage to temporary equilibrium as one kind of 'perfection' which we may assume into market conditions; just as we shall assume perfect contemporaneous knowledge—that every one knows the current prices in all those markets which concern him. As far as I can see, these simplifications do not make very much difference to the sort of results we may expect to obtain by our analysis.[1]

5. A second property of the week follows from this first, or rather follows from the way we have interpreted the first property. We assume that the week is the planning interval—that is to say, all decisions about the disposition of resources for the future are made on Mondays. Since almost any new decision will involve the making of new contracts, and new contracts can only be made on Mondays, we can very reasonably assume that Mondays are the planning dates too.

It is fundamentally important to realize that the decisions of entrepreneurs to buy and sell (and to some extent also the similar decisions of private persons) nearly always form part of a system of decisions which is not bounded by the present, but has some reference to future events. The current activities of a firm are part of a plan, which includes not only the decision to make immediate purchases and sales, but also the intention to make sales (at any rate, and usually purchases as well) in the more or less distant future.

[1] See, however, Additional Note C for further remarks on this point.

A realistic description of the economic process would no doubt show us firms making plans at irregular intervals. During the time which must elapse between the plan-making dates, the last plan is carried out more or less as laid down, though some power will generally be delegated to subordinates to make minor changes. When the next plan-making date arrives, the whole position is reconsidered in the light of new information, and a plan drawn up.

It is perhaps one of the most important issues of business management, how frequently the whole situation is examined with an eye to the possible necessity of major alterations in plan. Willingness to make major alterations is one of the surest signs of first-rate business enterprise; an inefficient firm will make major plans as rarely as possible, and do all its planning by small adjustments of detail, which take only a few elements of the situation into account, and do not need much thinking. Nevertheless, in spite of the importance of this distinction, we shall pay little attention to it here. We shall assume that every firm more or less reconsiders the whole situation every Monday; though this means that we shall tend to impute to the system a higher degree of efficiency than it is in fact likely to possess. But I do not think this much matters, for it is fairly easy to make allowances for inertia at a late stage of the argument.

Let us then assume that firms (and private persons) draw up or revise their plans on Mondays in the light of the market situation which is disclosing itself; and that any minor adjustments made during the week can be neglected. This means, in combination with our other assumptions, that when markets close on Monday evenings, they have reached the fullest equilibrium which is possible on that date; not only have prices settled down, but every one has made the purchases and sales which seem advantageous to him at those prices. The making of these purchases and sales indicates that plans have been adjusted to these prices— or, if we prefer to allow for inefficiency, that they are as well adjusted as is consistent with imperfect efficiency of the planners.

6. The plans which are adopted in any given week depend not only upon current prices but also upon the planner's expectations of future prices. We shall generally interpret these expectations in a strict and rigid way, assuming that every individual has a definite idea of what he expects any price which concerns him

to be in any future week. This assumption is of course excessively rigid, and actually errs in two different ways. For one thing, people's expectations are often not expectations of prices given to them from outside, but expectations of market conditions, demand schedules for example. This must always be so to some extent in the case of monopoly, so that the assumption of precise *price*-expectations is really one aspect of the assumption of perfect competition, which we have maintained throughout, and shall continue to maintain here.

Secondly, and perhaps more importantly, people rarely have *precise* expectations at all. They do not expect that the price at which they will be able to sell a particular output in a particular future week will be just so-and-so much; there will be a certain figure, or range of figures, which they consider most probable, but deviations from this most probable value on either side are considered to be more or less possible. This is a complication which deserves very serious attention.

For some purposes, as when an estimate is being made of the Capital value of a person's assets (or, as we shall see, of his Income), it is sufficient to concentrate attention on the most probable value, and leave the rest of the frequency distribution out of account. But for most purposes the dispersion has a very real importance.

When we are considering what determines the plan finally adopted, we have to think of the individual as choosing between various lines of conduct whose outcome is not equally certain. Even if the most probable price expected to rule at some future date remains unchanged, a person's readiness to adopt a plan which involves buying or selling at that date may be affected, if he becomes less certain about the probability of that price, if the dispersion of possible prices is increased.[1] Generally, one would suppose, an increased dispersion would make him less willing to make plans which involve buying or selling on the date affected. If this is so, an increased dispersion will have the same effect as a reduction of the expected price, in cases where the individual plans to sell, as an increase of the expected price, in cases where he plans to buy. If we are to allow for uncertainty of expectations,

[1] To be quite accurate, some attention ought also to be paid to the skewness of the distribution. (Cf. a paper of my own summarized in *Econometrica*, 1934, p. 195.)

in these problems of the determination of plans, we must not take the most probable price as the representative expected price, but the most probable price $\pm$ an allowance for the uncertainty of the expectation, that is to say, an allowance for risk.

An analysis such as that which follows, in which we suppose people to have precise expectations of prices, is therefore not altogether incompetent for dealing with a world in which risk is supremely important. When we are concerned with the determination of plans, we must suppose the expectations of the planners to be adjusted for risk. This is not an absolutely satisfactory way of dealing with risk—I feel myself that there ought to be an Economics of Risk on beyond the Dynamic Economics we shall work out here—but it does suffice to show that the investigations we are about to make are not devoid of applicability.

It is important to realize that the allowance for risk, the percentage by which the representative expected price falls short of or exceeds the most probable price, is not determined solely by the *opinion* of the planner about the degree of uncertainty. It is also influenced by his *willingness* to bear risks, by an element which in the last analysis depends upon his scale of preferences. An increased willingness to bear risks will therefore be represented in our analysis by a change in expected prices in favour of the planner.

Further (and this is the most serious weakness of our treatment), the willingness to bear any particular risk (to plan to buy or sell at any particular future date for which expected prices are uncertain, and to act on that plan) will be appreciably affected by the riskiness involved in the rest of the plan. I can do very little about this on present methods, though some consequences of the interrelations of risks will come to our notice now and then.

Thus we shall formally assume that people expect particular definite prices, that they have *certain* price-expectations. But we shall be prepared on occasion to interpret these certain expectations as being those particular figures which best represent the uncertain expectations of reality.[1]

7. These three notions—the week, the plan, the definite ex-

---

[1] What plan a firm decides to adopt will depend not only on its price-expectations, but also on technical expectations, such as expectations of the yield of crops. We shall generally assume that these expectations too are definite, subject to the same qualifications as above.

pectations—are fundamental for the inquiry which lies before us. By employing them we do a certain amount of violence to the phenomena of the actual world, but not more than seems necessary, if we are to make any headway in dynamic theory. I have tried to show that the rather excessive rigidity of our model need not have very serious consequences.

By using the week, we become able to treat a process of change as consisting of a series of temporary equilibria; this enables us still to use equilibrium analysis in the dynamic field. By using the plan, we become able to bring out the relation between those actions devoted to present ends, and those actions which are directed to the future. By supposing plans to unroll themselves during the week, we find ourselves able to conceive of the situation at the end of the week being different from the situation at the beginning; thus the new temporary equilibrium which is established in a second week must be different from that which was established in the first; going on in like manner, we have a process under way.

By the device of definite expectations, we are enabled to use the same analysis as we used in statics to set out the equilibrium of the private individual and the firm, to determine the dependence of plans on current prices *and* expected prices. Taking this together with the fact that we have preserved the concept of market equilibrium, the essentials of static analysis are still available to us.

Thus, without abandoning our model to stationariness, we have preserved the essentials of the static machinery. Let us proceed to see how it all works out.

Note to Chapter IX

THE FORMATION OF PRICES

1. In the second chapter of his fifth book, and in his Appendix on Barter, Marshall has an ingenious argument designed to show that the process of fixing prices by trial and error, necessary when market conditions are changing, need not have any appreciable effect upon the prices ultimately fixed. Since the matter is of some importance for our analysis also, this argument of Marshall's deserves examination here.

Since, in general, traders cannot be expected to know just what total supplies are available on any market, nor what total demands will be forthcoming at particular prices, any price which is fixed initially can be only a guess. It is not probable that demand and supply will actually be found to be equated at such a guessed price; if they are not, then in the course of trading the price will move up or down. Now if there is a change of price in the midst of trading, the situation appears to elude the ordinary apparatus of demand-and-supply analysis; for, strictly speaking, demand curves and supply curves give us the amounts which buyers and sellers will demand and supply respectively at any particular price, if that price is fixed at the start and adhered to throughout. Earlier writers, such as Walras and Edgeworth,[1] had therefore supposed that demand-and-supply analysis ought strictly to be confined to such markets as permitted of 'recontract'; i.e. markets such that if a transaction was put through at a 'false' price (we shall find it convenient to have a term to mark prices other than the equilibrium price), it could be revised when the equilibrium price was reached. Since such markets are highly exceptional, their solution of the problem (if it can be called one) was not very convincing.

Marshall's argument is stated in terms of his 'Constant Marginal Utility of Money'; it will be convenient for our purposes if we restate it in the corresponding terminology with which we have now become familiar. The essential is to show that a change in price in the midst of trading has the same sort of effect as a redistribution of wealth. Suppose that the equilibrium price is 6d. per lb.; but at the beginning of trading a false price is fixed at 10d., the price being afterwards dropped to 6d. Suppose a person buys 3 lb. at the false price; then his position is ultimately exactly the same as if the price had been kept at 6d. throughout, but this buyer had been compelled to hand over $3 \times (10-6)d$. to a seller. His total demand, and the seller's total supply, will be exactly the same as if such a direct transference had taken place.

Now the effects of such transferences are income effects, as we have termed them here; and, as we have repeatedly found, income effects can be very frequently neglected. In the particular case considered by Marshall, it may be supposed that the individual buyer is spending only a small part of his resources upon the commodity in question; if that is so, a change in price will affect the real value of his resources to a small extent only. This, it is clear, was the basis of Marshall's proposition. The assumption 'is justifiable with respect to most of the market dealings with which we are practically concerned. When a person buys anything for his own consumption, he generally spends on it a small part only of his total resources.'[2] The buyer is made better (or worse) off by the early 'false' trading; but if his total expenditure

---

[1] Walras, *Éléments*, p. 44; Edgeworth, *Mathematical Psychics*, p. 17.
[2] Marshall, p. 335.

on the commodity is small, this gain (or loss) must be small, and his demand for the commodity will be very little affected. Consequently the market must finish up very close to the equilibrium price.

2. This, then, is what Marshall's argument comes to. It is clearly quite valid for the sort of 'fish market' case Marshall had in mind. In Marshall's theory of temporary equilibrium, supply is fixed, demand comes from a multitude of final consumers, and interactions between markets are neglected. For our purposes, it is desirable, if we can, to remove these limitations. Can we remove them without the whole structure falling to the ground?

It remains true in the general case, just as in Marshall's special case, that gains and losses due to false trading only give rise to income effects —effects, that is, which are the same in kind as the income effects which may have to be considered even when we suppose equilibrium prices to be fixed straight away. We have seen again and again that a certain degree of indeterminateness is nearly always imparted by income effects to the laws of economic theory. All that happens as a result of false trading is that this indeterminateness is somewhat intensified. How much intensified depends, of course, upon the extent of the false trading; if very extensive transactions take place at prices very different from equilibrium prices, the disturbance will be serious. But I think we may reasonably suppose that the transactions which take place at 'very false' prices are limited in volume. If any intelligence is shown in price-fixing, they will be.

Just as in statics, we may expect some damping down of these disturbing effects from the fact that gains to the buyers mean losses to the sellers, and vice versa. Thus, whenever the two sides are at all similar in their distribution of increments of expenditure among different goods, a shift in demand will be partially offset by a corresponding shift in supply.[1]

The effect of false prices is limited to the income effect by our assumption of markets being only open on Mondays; the equilibrium prices are therefore taken to be used as indicators for the production and consumption plans carried out for the rest of the week. If the calendar length of the week is supposed long, this device does indeed imply some arbitrariness in the practical application of our results; but if we are particularly interested in reducing that arbitrariness, we can always do so by shortening the length of the week.

[1] See above, p. 64.

CHAPTER X

EQUILIBRIUM AND DISEQUILIBRIUM

1. THE general method we have to pursue will by now be clear. We must first concentrate attention on some particular Monday, and ask what determines the price-system then set up. In this inquiry, we must treat everything that has gone before that Monday as a datum; no decision now made can alter it. 'Not heaven itself upon the past hath power.' In particular, this means that the whole material equipment of the community, as it exists when the market opens on Monday morning, including the finished goods now ready for sale, the half-finished goods and raw materials, the fixed plant of all sorts and the durable consumers' goods, must be taken as given. From now on, the economic problem consists in the allotment of these resources, inherited from the past, among the satisfaction of present wants and future wants.

On the basis of these inherited resources, entrepreneurs (and even private individuals as well) may be supposed to draw up plans, which determine their current conduct and their intended conduct in future weeks. An entrepreneur's plan includes decisions about the quantities of products he will sell in the current week and in future weeks, and about the quantities of inputs (services, materials, perhaps even new acquisitions of plant), which he will purchase or hire in current and future weeks. A private person's plan includes decisions about the quantities of commodities he will buy (and perhaps also the quantities of services he will supply) in current and future weeks. Thus, as part of the plans, the current demands and supplies of all goods and services are determined; though they are determined jointly with people's intentions to demand and supply at future dates.

The plans which people adopt depend upon current prices and on their expectations of future prices; but current prices are themselves determined by current demands and supplies, which are part of the plans. Thus, if a set of prices is fixed on the first Monday which does not equate demand and supply in all markets, there will have to be an adjustment of prices; prices will fall in those markets where supply exceeds demand, rise in those markets where demand exceeds supply. This change of current prices will induce an alteration of plans, and consequently of supplies and demands; through the alteration of plans supplies and demands are brought into equilibrium.

We are supposing that trading continues, on the Monday, until supplies and demands are brought into equilibrium; this is essential in order for us to be able to use the equilibrium method in dynamic theory. Since we shall not pay much attention to the process of equilibration which must precede the formation of the equilibrium prices,[1] our method seems to imply that we conceive of the economic system as being always in equilibrium. We work out the equilibrium prices of one week, and the equilibrium prices of another week, and leave it at that.

2. So far as this limited sense of equilibrium is concerned, it is quite true that we assume the economic system to be always in equilibrium. Nor is it unreasonable to do so. There is a sense in which current supplies and current demands are always equated in competitive conditions. Stocks may indeed be left in the shops unsold; but they are unsold because people prefer to take the chance of being able to sell them at a future date rather than cut prices in order to sell them now. The tendency for the current price to fall leads to a shift in supply from present to future. An excess of supply over demand which means more than this is only possible if the price falls to zero, or if the commodity is monopolized, or if the price is conventionally fixed. (We shall again return to conventional prices at a later stage in our dynamic theory.[2])

In this (analytically important) sense the economic system (or at least all those systems with which we shall be concerned) can be taken to be always in equilibrium; but there is another wider sense in which it is usually out of equilibrium, to a greater or less extent. Some such sense of the word is familiar in modern discussions of applied problems; we can use our apparatus to give it a precise meaning.

In determining the system of prices established on the first Monday, we shall also have determined with it the system of plans which will govern the distribution of resources during the

---

[1] See note to preceding chapter.
[2] See below, p. 265.

following week. If we suppose these plans to be carried out, then they determine the quantity of resources which will be left over at the end of the week, to serve as the basis for the decisions which have to be taken on the second Monday. On that second Monday a new system of prices has to be set up, which may differ more or less from the system of prices which was established on the first.

The wider sense of Equilibrium—Equilibrium over Time, as we may call it, to distinguish it from the Temporary Equilibrium which must rule within any current week—suggests itself when we start to compare the price-situations at any two dates. A stationary state is in full equilibrium, not merely when demands equal supplies at the currently established prices, but also when the same prices continue to rule at all dates—when prices are constant over time. It might be thought at first that the same criterion (constancy of prices) would be applicable to a changing economy as well; but this is clearly not the case.[1] For there is a more important test than mere arithmetical sameness or difference, which does imply constant prices in a stationary economy, but does not necessarily imply constant prices in an economy subject to change. This is the condition that the prices realized on the second Monday are the same as those which were previously *expected* to rule at that date.

Of course, even in a changing economy, people may still expect constant prices, but if they do their expectations are very unlikely to be realized. It will generally be expectations of *changing* prices which can be realized. In equilibrium, the change in prices which occurs is that which was expected. If tastes and resources also remain what they were expected to remain, then in equilibrium nothing has occurred to disturb the plans laid down on the first Monday. So far as can be seen, no one has made any mistakes, and plans can continue to be executed without any revision. An economy in perfect equilibrium over time is like the sun in *Faust*:

ihre *vorgeschrieb'ne* Reise
vollendet sie mit Donnergang.

The degree of disequilibrium marks the extent to which expectations are cheated, and plans go astray.

---

[1] It is not so even if we relax the condition, and demand only some sort of constant price-level.

No economic system ever does exhibit perfect equilibrium over time; nevertheless the ideal is approached more nearly at some times than at others. Doubtless it is usually approached most nearly when conditions are most nearly stationary: when people expect prices to remain steady, and they do remain steady. However, when we remember that the expectations of entrepreneurs are in fact not precise expectations of particular prices, but partake more of the character of probability distributions, then it becomes evident that the realized prices can depart to some extent from those prices expected as most probable, without causing any acute sense of disequilibrium. For practical purposes, the ideal condition of equilibrium over time can be interpreted quite loosely. Whenever prices are fairly steady, the system is likely to be quite adequately in equilibrium. It is chiefly in times of rapid price-movement that acute disequilibrium is likely to occur.

In spite of this latitude in the practical application of the concept, it is the strict interpretation—divergence between expected and realized prices—which is of central importance theoretically. Whenever such a divergence occurs, it means (retrospectively) that there has been malinvestment and consequent waste. Resources have been used in a way in which they would not have been used, if the future had been foreseen more accurately; wants, which could have been met if they had been foreseen, will not be satisfied or will be satisfied imperfectly. Thus disequilibrium is a mark of waste, and imperfect efficiency of production. Now how does disequilibrium arise?

3. Our analysis suggests several possible causes of disequilibrium. One (perhaps the least important) arises when different people's price-expectations are inconsistent. If one person expects the price of a particular commodity to fall between this Monday and the next, and another person expects it to rise; then they cannot both be right. But, excepting when expectations are very definite, the disequilibrium so caused is unlikely to be very serious.

Secondly, though price-expectations are consistent, plans may be inconsistent. Even if all buyers and sellers of a commodity expect the same price, nevertheless the total quantity all buyers together plan to buy in the second week may fail to equal the total quantity all sellers together plan to sell. If the planned supply is greater than the planned demand, then, when the second Monday comes, the price will be lower than it was expected to be. This is evidently a potent cause of disequilibrium; it is perhaps the most interesting cause of all.

Thirdly, even if price-expectations are consistent, and plans are also consistent, still people may foresee their own wants incorrectly, or make wrong estimates of the results of the technical processes of production. If this happens, then, on the second Monday, they will find themselves unwilling or unable to buy or sell those quantities of goods they had planned to buy or sell. Thus, once again, realized prices will be different from expected prices. And the imperfect foresight of some persons will put others too into disequilibrium.

These are the only sorts of disequilibrium which could arise in an economy where all expectations were definite; but in the actual world, where people only expect 'probably', there is a fourth kind which may arise on occasion. Since it depends upon the ambiguity in the notion of price-expectations which we discussed in the last chapter, it is best reckoned as a type of Imperfect Equilibrium rather than of disequilibrium. We saw, in our first discussion of the nature of expectations, that when risk is present, people will generally act, not upon the price which they expect as most probable, but as if that price had been shifted a little in a direction unfavourable to them. Now this means that even if no disequilibrium in any of the above senses is present, even if price-expectations are consistent, and plans are consistent, and there are no unforeseen changes in tastes and no unforeseen results of technical processes, still the most perfect adjustment of resources to wants may not be reached. The system may be in equilibrium, in the sense that the realized prices are those which were expected as most probable. Nevertheless, their sense of risk may have prevented entrepreneurs from producing those quantities of output, or those sorts of output, which they would have produced if they had been more confident that their anticipations were right. In this way the efficiency of the system may be very seriously damaged, without any of the types of disequilibrium mentioned above coming into question.

This is a possible source of waste; but of course lack of confidence in one's foresight is not necessarily a source of waste. The loss only accrues if the expectations would have been right after all. Putting insufficient faith in good judgements is a source of inefficiency; but scepticism about bad judgements may be better than implicit trust. However, we shall find as we go on that there are reasons for suspecting that the economic system loses more by mistrust than by over-confidence.

4. This classification of the causes of disequilibrium has a distinct bearing upon the great dispute about the relative efficiency of different types of economic organization. The third and fourth sources of waste must be found in every conceivable economic system, Capitalist or Socialist, Liberal or Authoritarian. Even Robinson Crusoe would not be free of them; he could not foresee when he might be ill, or when his crops might fail; and he would be troubled in his search for the most perfect adjustment of means to ends by the uncertainty of such events in the future. Even the most perfectly organized economic system (whatever that may be) will be thrown out of its stride by harvest fluctuations, inventions, or political upheavals. It would appear at first sight, on the other hand, that the first and second sources are peculiar to a system of private enterprise. In a completely centralized system they would be removed. But a completely centralized system is a mere figment of the imagination; every government delegates its authority to some extent. Thus in practice the different parts of a State machine can get out of step, just as entrepreneurs can get out of step. Whether capitalism is less or more efficient than socialism depends very much upon the efficiency of socialism. That is still rather an open question.

It is often supposed that capitalism is entirely devoid of any organization for the co-ordination of plans; but that is not altogether the case. A way does exist, within the orbit of private enterprise, whereby expectations and plans can be (at least partially) co-ordinated. This is the device of forward trading (including not only dealings in forward markets, commonly so called, but also all orders given in advance, and all long-term contracts). It is very instructive, even at this stage, to pay some attention to the working of this sort of co-ordination, and to examine why it is not more efficient, and its range more extensive, than it is in fact.

A system of private enterprise is perfectly conceivable, in which there would be no forward trading, all transactions being for immediate delivery ('Spot'). In such a 'Spot Economy', nothing would be fixed up in advance, and co-ordination would be left very much to chance. Only current demands and supplies would be matched on the market; people would have to base their expectations of future prices, as best they were able, upon these current prices, and any other information available. Of course, even so, the amount of disequilibrium likely to arise need not be very considerable. If plans are mostly of a fairly stationary type, so that most people are planning to buy and sell much the same quantities in future periods as in the current period, not much disequilibrium due to inconsistency will arise, so long as they merely expect a continuance of current prices. Even if plans are not stationary, but the quantities people plan to buy or sell have some tendency to increase or diminish with futurity, this will not necessarily lead to inconsistency disequilibrium, if people can make good guesses at the relevant plans of other people. This is a good deal more to ask, but still observation of the current conduct of business men does give some clue to their plans, so that something of this sort probably does take place to some extent. When firms are planning a large extension of their operations, it is impossible to keep it dark altogether. Yet this is not much to go on. When conditions are at all disturbed, a spot economy must be expected to get out of equilibrium to a considerable extent.

It is possible, at the other extreme, to conceive of an economy in which, for a considerable period ahead, everything was fixed up in advance. If all goods were bought and sold forward, not only would current demands and supplies be matched, but also planned demands and supplies. In such a 'Futures Economy', the first two kinds of disequilibrium would be absent. Plans would be co-ordinated; and, for practical purposes, expectations would be co-ordinated too. (The price which would govern a firm's planned output for a particular future week would be the futures price, and not its own individual price-expectation.) Thus inconsistency disequilibrium would be removed; but the possibility of disequilibrium due to unexpected changes in wants or resources would not be removed. People would be under contract to buy or sell certain goods on the second Monday. But when the second Monday arrived, they might be unwilling or unable to buy or sell the amounts of goods contracted for. They would then be obliged to make additional spot sales or purchases, or to offset their contracts by spot transactions. Thus a spot market would come into existence, and the spot price established in that market would probably be different from the futures price which had previously been established for that Monday.

Now people know that they cannot escape the third kind of disequilibrium by forward trading; and this it is, in the end, which limits the extent to which forward trading can be carried on in practice. They know that the demands and supplies which can be fixed up in advance for any particular date may have little relation to the demands and supplies which will actually be forthcoming at that date; and, in particular, they know that they cannot foretell at all exactly what quantities they will themselves desire to buy or sell at a future period. Consequently the ordinary business man only enters into a forward contract if by so doing he can 'hedge'—that is to say, if the forward transaction lessens the riskiness of his position. And this will only happen in those cases where he is somehow otherwise committed to making a sale or purchase at the date in question; if he has already planned such a sale or purchase, and if he has already done something which will make it difficult for him to alter his plan. Now there are quite sufficient technical rigidities in the process of production to make it certain that a number of entrepreneurs will want to hedge their sales for this reason; supplies in the near future are largely governed by decisions taken in the past, so that if these planned supplies can be covered by forward sales, risk is reduced. But although the same thing sometimes happens with planned purchases as well, it is almost inevitably rarer; technical conditions give the entrepreneur a much freer hand about the acquisition of inputs (which are largely needed to start new processes) than about the completion of outputs (whose process of production—in the ordinary business sense—may be already begun). Thus, while there is likely to be some desire to hedge planned purchases, it tends to be less insistent than the desire to hedge planned sales. If forward markets consisted entirely of hedgers, there would always be a tendency for a relative weakness on the demand side; a smaller proportion of planned purchases than of planned sales would be covered by forward contracts.[1]

---

[1] This congenital weakness of the demand side of course applies only to forward markets in commodities, and will not apply (for instance) to forward

But for this very reason forward markets rarely consist entirely of hedgers. The futures price (say, for one month's delivery) which would be made by the transactions of hedgers alone would be determined by causes that have nothing to do with the causes ordinarily determining market price; it would therefore be widely different from the spot price which any sensible person would expect to rule in a month's time, and would ordinarily be much below that expected price. Futures prices are therefore nearly always made partly by *speculators*, who seek a profit by buying futures when the futures price is below the spot price they expect to rule on the corresponding date; their action tends to raise the futures price to a more reasonable level. But it is of the essence of speculation, as opposed to hedging, that the speculator puts himself into a more risky position as a result of his forward trading —he need not have ventured into forward dealing at all, and would have been safer if he had not done so. He will therefore only be willing to go on buying futures so long as the futures price remains definitely below the spot price he expects; for it is the difference between these prices which he can expect to receive as a return for his risk-bearing, and it will not be worth his while to undertake the risk if the prospective return is too small.

Mr. Keynes has pointed out the consequences of this in an important passage of his *Treatise on Money*. In 'normal' conditions, when demand and supply conditions are expected to remain unchanged, and therefore the spot price is expected to be about the same in a month's time as it is to-day, the futures price for one month's delivery is bound to be below the spot price now ruling. The difference between these two prices (the current spot price and the currently fixed futures price) is called by Mr. Keynes 'normal backwardation'.[1] It measures the amount which hedgers have to hand over to speculators in order to persuade the speculators to take over the risks of the price-fluctuations in question. Ultimately, therefore, it measures the cost of the co-ordination

markets in foreign exchange. However, in all forward markets there is likely to be a tendency for hedgers to predominate on one side or the other over long periods. No forward market can do without the speculative element.

[1] Keynes, *Treatise on Money*, vol. ii, pp. 142–4. In market language, there is said to be a 'backwardation' if the futures price is below the spot price, a 'contango' in the reverse case. It will be evident that a contango can only arise when spot prices are expected to rise sharply in the future; this usually means that spot prices are *abnormally* low.

achieved by forward trading; if the cost is very heavy, potential hedgers will prefer not to hedge.

The same sorts of considerations limit those other kinds of transactions which we have classified as types of forward trading, although they are not usually so regarded. For example, it is usually to the interest of an employee to 'hedge' future sales of his labour—as he would do, if he could secure engagement for a long period. But it is not to the interest of his employer to make such contracts, unless he derives some particular advantage from so doing—as he would do, if this particular employee were difficult to replace. In this way we can fit into our analysis that particular type of long-term contract which distinguishes (more or less) the salary-earner from the wage-earner.[1]

5. Generally, then, it is uncertainty of the future, and the desire to keep one's hands free to meet that uncertainty, which limit the extent of forward trading under capitalism; the ultimate cause why the first two kinds of disequilibrium cannot be met more efficiently reduces itself to the unavoidable presence of the third and fourth kinds. But these are the kinds which may be present in any type of society; in any type of society uncertainty is likely to produce 'planlessness'. When the ends of society are certain, socialist organization, paying little attention to the need for allowing a margin of error, and co-ordinating plans as firmly and directly as possible, has a strong case on grounds of efficiency; but in the ordinary pursuit of peace-time economic welfare, immediate ends are likely to be much less certain, the natural method of economic policy being trial and error. In this situation, the wise socialist dictator, finding himself afflicted by those same sorts of uncertainty which impede co-ordination under capitalism, may well come to prefer a loose and decentralized organization, itself open to the charge of planlessness, and not clearly superior in its power of adjusting means to ends.

With these remarks we may turn away from the great debate; its further examination would lead us away from those matters

---

[1] Both in this case of labour contracts, and in the case of ordinary forward markets in commodities, there is another kind of uncertainty which limits forward dealing. This is uncertainty about the exact quality of the goods promised to be supplied at the future date. Organized produce markets adopt elaborate devices to mitigate this uncertainty, but all such devices are costly, and the cost easily becomes prohibitive.

which are our present concern. I think it may have been useful
to show that there is a relation between the problems of planning
under capitalism and under socialism; no doubt the acute phases
are different in the two cases, but parallel questions come up in each.

For our own purposes, the things discussed in the present chapter have a different significance. We shall find, as we go on, that
it is very important to bear in mind the distinction between spot
and forward dealing, in the general sense of each term. A certain
proportion of the transactions which take place in reality have to
be reckoned (in whole or in part) as forward transactions; their
place in the sort of analysis we have decided to undertake is bound
to be different from that of spot transactions. That being so, we
find it naturally suggested to us as a convenient procedure to begin
by neglecting forward transactions—to begin by studying the
economics of a world where only spot transactions have to be
taken into account. We have already made the acquaintance of
such a model—it is our 'Spot Economy'. Owing to the limitations
of forward trading, this model is not really a very drastic simplification of reality. But we need not stop at this model unless we want
to; we have learnt quite enough about forward markets to be
able to take them into account on occasion.

At the other extreme from our pure 'Spot Economy' we had
another model—our pure 'Futures Economy'. This can have no
claims to be a good approximation to reality, for it would only be
in a world where uncertainty was absent and all expectations
definite, that everything could be fixed up in advance.[1] Nevertheless, the pure 'Futures Economy' may have some theoretical
uses. By examining what system of prices would be fixed up in a
futures economy, we can find out what system of prices would
maintain equilibrium over time under a given set of changing
conditions. Economists have often toyed with the idea of a system
where all persons trading have 'perfect foresight'. This leads to
awkward logical difficulties,[2] but the purpose for which they have
invented such systems can be met by our futures economy. Whenever the question is asked: What movement of prices, if it had been
expected, could have been carried through without disequilibrium?
this is the sort of way it can be tackled.

---

[1] Even subject to the condition that contracts could be *de facto* voided by
the subsequent buying and selling of futures.

[2] Cf. Knight, *Risk, Uncertainty and Profit*, chs. 5–6.

CHAPTER XI

INTEREST

1. A FUNDAMENTAL approach to the problem of interest suggests itself naturally, after the discussions of the preceding chapter. We have learnt to distinguish transactions according to the date at which they are due to be executed. Spot transactions are due to be executed currently—that is to say, in the current week in which they are drawn up. Forward transactions are due to be executed entirely at a future date—both sides of the bargain in the same future week. But there is no reason why the two sides of a bargain should be due to be executed at the same date. Thus we get a third type, loan transactions, which are such that only one side of the bargain is executed currently, the other side being due to be executed at some future date, or perhaps a series of future dates. The essential characteristic of a loan transaction is that its execution is divided in time.

Any exchange of present goods or services for a promise to deliver goods or services in the future has the economic character of a loan; but in practice the whole class of loan transactions is dominated by a particular sub-species: the type where both sides of the transaction are in money form. It is not that this is the only kind of loan practised. Direct exchange of present real goods for future real goods is rare, for the same reason as the exchange of one sort of real goods in the present for another sort of real goods in the present is rare: the inconvenience of barter. But people do not infrequently exchange present commodities for promises to pay money in the future (deferred payment); or, vice versa, they exchange ready money for promises to deliver goods in the future (payment in advance). It is not that these transactions are not practised, but that they are naturally thought of as reducible to a money loan *plus* a spot transaction (or a forward transaction). In fact any loan transaction can be reduced in that way.

Even a pure barter of present commodities for future commodities (say an exchange of coffee now for coffee a year hence) can be similarly reduced to a spot transaction, a forward transaction, and a money loan. Where forward markets exist, rates of interest in real terms are always implicitly established. Suppose the money rate of interest for a year's loan is 5 per cent., and the futures price of coffee for twelve months' delivery is 3 per cent. above the spot price; then it is possible to lend coffee for one year by selling coffee spot, lending the money proceeds, and covering the sale by a purchase on the forward market. The whole chain of transactions establishes an absolutely definite rate of interest in coffee terms. One unit of coffee now is exchanged for 105/103 units of coffee to be delivered in a year's time, so that the rate of interest fixed is approximately 2 per cent. in terms of coffee.[1] (The coffee rate will only be the same as the money rate if the spot price of coffee and the forward price are equal.)[2]

Commodity rates of interest are thus of little direct importance for us; they are parts of the system we do not emphasize, just as we do not emphasize the rate of exchange between two commodities in spot transactions, when neither of the two commodities is the standard of value. Without assuming any more of the properties of money than we have assumed up to the present (that it is a commodity selected as the standard of value) we are entitled to assume that all loans are in money terms; for any loan transaction which takes place otherwise is always capable of being reduced to a money loan combined with a spot transaction and a forward transaction.

2. We can thus confine ourselves to the study of money rates of interest; but even within that field we have to face a somewhat bewildering complexity. The money rates of interest paid for different loans at the same date differ from one another for two main reasons: (1) because of differences in the length of time for which the loans are to run, and in the way repayment is to be

---

[1] Cf. Keynes, *General Theory*, pp. 222–3. The formula which thus emerges —that a commodity rate of interest approximately equals the money rate of interest *minus* the contango (percentage excess of futures price over spot)— is worth noting.

[2] In the case of foreign exchange dealing, we do have an example of what happens when there is a loan market in each of two commodities (currencies) and also spot and forward trading between them. If all four markets are free, not even temporary equilibrium is possible unless the above relation holds— unless, say, the discount on forward francs equals the difference between interest rates in Paris and London for the relevant period. If this relation ceases to hold altogether, it is an indication that dealings are being restricted in one at least of the four markets. (It should be emphasized that the four markets are mutually interdependent, and any or all of them may be affected in the process of equilibration.)

distributed over time; (2) because of differences in the risk of default by the borrower. Other differences in the terms of the loan may sometimes reckon for something, but these are the main things that have to be considered.

Questions of risk come up in the discussion of both these reasons for divergence, but it is the second which is responsible for the element of 'risk-premium' in interest rates as generally understood. When a borrower's credit is poor, people will not be prepared to pay the same price for his promise to pay certain sums in the future as they would do if his credit were good. There are two reasons for this which can be distinguished. First, a completely trustworthy borrower gives complete assurance that the promised sums will be paid; the lender thus receives a practically certain prospect, as against the uncertain prospect he receives in the other case. Secondly, even if the supposedly untrustworthy borrower does discharge his obligations, he will not pay more than he is obliged; that sets a maximum to the receipts which can be expected by the lender; all the possible variations from it are in one direction. This means that the mean value of the probable outcomes is less than in the case of the sound borrower; and the other consideration means that the dispersion of probable outcomes is greater. Both of these things may be expected to deter the lender; so that he will only be induced to lend to the less sound borrower if he is offered better terms.

The full analysis of the working of this risk factor in the market for loans would be very complicated; we shall not attempt to pursue it very far here. One thing to be considered is the fact that a borrower's creditworthiness is a matter for the individual estimate of lenders; and these individual estimates are likely to differ. Thus, if a business requires to raise only a small amount of capital, it can do so by appealing only to that inner circle of potential lenders with which it has a good standing, and who may thus be expected to be willing to lend to it on relatively favourable terms. If it desires to raise more, it must either apply directly to a less trusting section of the market (to whom it will have to offer better terms), or it must get some of the inner circle to stand surety for it (either by borrowing themselves and re-lending the proceeds to it, or by some method of guarantee or acceptance). But if they are persuaded to this, they will be involving themselves in an additional risk, for which they will require compensation.

The amount which a particular borrower can raise from any particular lender is limited partly by the limitation of that lender's resources, but perhaps more immediately limited by the risk a lender incurs by investing too much of his resources in one direction—by 'putting all his eggs in one basket'. By offering better terms (which may be taken to amount to a higher rate of interest, but need not necessarily take that overt form), it may be possible to extract more from individual lenders; and, for the reasons we have just seen, it will usually be possible to extract more from the market as a whole, by persuading new lenders to come in. Each particular borrower thus finds himself confronted with a sort of 'supply curve for loan capital', analogous to the supply curves of other factors of production which confront a producer when he is in a 'monopsonistic' (or monopoly buyer) position. There is no reason to suppose that this curve will be perfectly elastic, at least for large variations in the amount of capital to be raised. This consideration introduces into the theory of interest questions analogous to those which have been discussed by writers on Imperfect Competition, and there is no doubt that a complete theory of interest ought to take them formally into account.[1] I cannot undertake that here, but we must not allow these matters to slip our minds altogether.

3. Rather more can be said on our present methods about the differences between rates of interest which arise from differences in the duration of loans. These also turn out to be partly a matter of risk; but they are also influenced by other considerations.

There is a distinct analogy between long-period loan contracts and those long-period contracts for the delivery of goods or services which, as we saw in the last chapter, can be reduced to a combination of spot and forward trading. A contract to deliver goods at monthly intervals over a period of six months is equivalent to a spot transaction and a series of forward transactions; similarly, a loan for six months is equivalent to a loan for one month, combined with a series of forward loan transactions, each renewing the loan (re-lending the principal, or principal and interest) for a successive month. If we decide upon some minimum period of time, loans for less than which time we shall be prepared to dis-

---

[1] Thus the complications of the financial structure of firms seem to be largely due to attempts at discrimination on the capital market.

regard, every loan of every duration can be reduced to a standard pattern—a loan for the minimum period, combined with a given number of renewals for subsequent periods of the same length, contracted forward. It is clearly most in accordance with our general method if we take as the minimum period one 'week'.

Looking at it in this way, the rate of interest for loans of two weeks, running from our first Monday, is compounded out of the 'spot' rate of interest for loans of one week and the 'forward' rate of interest, also for one-week loans, but for loans to be executed in the second week. If no interest is to be paid until the conclusion of the whole transaction, then the same capital sum must be arrived at by accumulating for two weeks at the two-weeks rate of interest, or alternatively by accumulating for one week at the one-week rate, and then accumulating for a second week at the 'forward' rate. The two transactions are ultimately identical. Thus, if we write R_2, R_3,... for the current two-weeks, three-weeks,... rates (the 'long' rates), r_2, r_3,... for the 'forward' short rates, r_1 (or R_1) for the current short rate (it belongs to both systems), we shall have[1]

$$1+R_1 = 1+r_1,$$
$$(1+R_2)^2 = (1+r_1)(1+r_2),$$
$$(1+R_3)^3 = (1+r_1)(1+r_2)(1+r_3).$$

If, as a first approximation, we allow ourselves to assume simple interest, these relations are much simplified. They become

$$R_1 = r_1,$$
$$2R_2 = r_1+r_2,$$
$$3R_3 = r_1+r_2+r_3.$$

The long rate is the arithmetic average between the current short rate and the relevant forward short rates.[2]

4. The system of interest rates for loans of various durations can thus be reduced to a standard type of short rate (the rate of interest for a loan of one week) combined with a series of forward

---

[1] All rates taken per week, and measured in fractions rather than percentages; a rate of $\frac{1}{10}$ per cent. per week is thus written 0·001.

[2] If the long loan involves a promise to pay interest at regular intervals instead of all together at the conclusion of the transaction, the general formulae are more complicated, but the simple interest formulae are naturally unaffected.

short rates: rates for loans of one week, to be executed not in the current week, but in some future week. These latter rates are strictly analogous to the futures prices we discussed in the last chapter, and are determined in almost exactly the same way.

It is not usual to think of the market for long-term loans in terms of hedgers and speculators; but that distinction does in fact continue to be relevant here. Other things being equal, a person engaging in a long-term loan contract puts himself into a more risky position than he would be in if he refrained from making it; but there are some persons (and concerns) for whom this will not be true, because they are already committed to needing loan capital over extensive future periods. They may be embarking on operations which take a considerable time to come to fruition; or they may merely be laying down plans for continuous production, in the form of a long series of planned inputs and outputs, which it will not be easy to break off at any particular point. These persons will want to hedge their future supplies of loan capital, just as they will want to hedge their future supplies of raw materials. They will have a strong propensity to borrow long.

On the other side of the market there does not seem to be any similar propensity, though there is an important circumstance which demands attention. The actual making of any transaction involves some time and trouble, and loan transactions are no exception to the rule. But the amount of gain which can be expected to accrue from making a very short loan is very small, so that it will not counterbalance the trouble of arranging the loan unless the lender is well placed for operating in the short-term market. This difficulty has been largely overcome in modern times by the development of banks, whose offer of interest on deposit accounts provides what is in substance a 'short' market for the small investor. (That it really is a short market is proved by the maintenance of the bank's right to alter the rate of interest it pays.) Nevertheless, the difficulty of short lending may sometimes have the effect of driving lenders into the long market.[1]

Taking these things together, it still appears that the forward market for loans (like the forward market for commodities) may be expected to have a constitutional weakness on one side, a weakness which offers an opportunity for speculation. If no extra return is offered for long lending, most people (and institutions)

---

[1] We shall be returning at length to this important matter. See below, Ch. XIII.

would prefer to lend short, at least in the sense that they would prefer to hold their money on deposit in some way or other. But this situation would leave a large excess of demands to borrow long which would not be met. Borrowers would thus tend to offer better terms in order to persuade lenders to switch over into the long market (that is to say, enter the forward market). A lender who did this would be in a position exactly analogous to that of a speculator in a commodity market. He would only come into the long market because he expected to gain by so doing, and to gain sufficiently to offset the risk incurred.

The forward rate of interest for any particular future week (which we have seen to be the unit from which long-term rates are built up) is thus determined, like the futures price of a commodity, at that level which just tempts a sufficient number of 'speculators' to undertake the forward contract. It will have to be higher than the short rate expected by these speculators to rule in that week, since otherwise they would get no compensation for the risk they are incurring; it will, indeed, have to exceed it by a sufficient amount to induce the marginal speculator to undertake the risk. The forward short rate will thus exceed the expected short rate by a risk-premium which corresponds exactly to the 'normal backwardation' of the commodity markets. If short rates are not expected to change in the future, the forward rate will exceed the current short rate by the extent of this premium; if short rates are expected to rise, the excess will be greater than this normal level; it is only if short rates are expected to fall that the forward rate can lie below the current rate.

The same rules must apply to the long rates themselves, which, as we saw in the last section, are effectively an average of the forward rates. If short rates are not expected to change, the long rate will exceed the short rate by a normal risk-premium; if the current short rate is regarded as abnormally low, the long rate will lie decidedly above it; the short rate can only exceed the long rate if the current short rate is regarded as abnormally high.[1]

5. This analysis of the relation between short and long rates of interest has a distinct bearing upon the decision of policy we took

---

[1] One practical consequence of this, whose implications we shall examine at length later, is that short rates are bound to be liable to much greater fluctuations than long rates. See below, pp. 260–1.

at the end of the preceding chapter; in that connexion it is, indeed, rather disconcerting. It seemed then to be a convenient simplification which might be of use in further analysis, if we began by concentrating attention on a pure 'Spot Economy', defined as one in which all goods and services are sold *spot*, no forward trading taking place. So far as commodity trading is concerned, this simplification seemed quite legitimate; forward markets in commodities are not, in fact, of such great importance that we do much violence to reality by leaving them out. But now long lending turns out to be a concealed form of forward trading; and so it would seem that a pure spot economy ought to exclude long lending as well. That is a much more drastic abstraction. Let us try to visualize it.

In a pure spot economy where only short lending is allowed no goods are bought and sold forward, and all loans are made for the minimum period—one week. Consequently, when the markets open on the first Monday, all debts carried over from the preceding week must be supposed to be paid off, so that there are no outstanding contracts at all. On the other hand, since no forward contracts can be made now, entrepreneurs (and every one else) have to draw up their plans on the basis of their own individual expectations of future prices (including the future course of the short rate of interest). In both these ways—the complete clearing of decks every Monday, and the absence of the security given to enterprise by long-term borrowing—this model looks very unrealistic. Although we could probably adjust it subsequently to allow for its deficiencies, there would be much to be gained if we could find an equally simple model which would give a closer approximation to actual conditions.

The great advantage of this first model, which we should desire to retain, is its reduction of the complex system of interest rates for various maturities, which exists in practice, to a single rate. (If default risks are neglected, only one rate has to be considered altogether.) Economists, in their discussions of interest problems, often talk about the determination of *the* rate of interest. It would seem that they must have some such reduction as this in mind; yet *the* rate of interest which they discuss is more usually the long rate.[1]

Consider the working of an economic system in which there is

[1] *The* rate of interest in Mr. Keynes's *General Theory* is the long rate.

still no forward trading in goods and services, and in which there is still only one type of lending. But now, instead of that one type of lending being lending for one week only (the type which characterized our previous 'Spot Economy'), suppose that it is lending for an indefinite period. In each system there is only one type of security. But whereas, in the spot economy with short lending previously discussed, that one security was the bill (a promise to pay such-and-such a capital sum at the end of the week), in our new model—the spot economy with long lending—it is the undated debenture (a promise to pay such-and-such a sum in perpetuity at regular intervals, as interest on the loan).

If the only rate of interest established on the market is a rate for loans of indefinite duration, the rate which must be paid in this economy for loans of *any* finite length is always a matter for conjecture. Even the rate of interest for loans of one week (the one rate which was determinate in our first model) becomes a matter for personal anticipation in the spot economy with long lending. For if a person desires to borrow money for one week, he can now only do it in one way. He must issue a loan of indefinite duration at the current rate of interest R, and then plan to redeem the loan at the end of the week, at the market price then ruling, which will depend upon the rate of interest R', which rules in the second week. The effective rate for a loan of one week thus depends upon the borrower's expectation of the future rate of interest R'. The capital value of the loan will change in the course of the week in the proportion R/R'. Thus the effective rate he will have to pay will be

$$R + \frac{R}{R'} - 1,$$

which is less than R if $R' > R$. Thus the rate at which people can expect to borrow or lend for short periods will depend upon their anticipations of the future course of market rates; it will be less than the current market rate if the market rate is expected to rise, greater than the market rate if the market rate is expected to fall.

In a spot economy with long lending, loans are not necessarily paid back at the beginning of the week; so we must suppose a typical individual to find himself on the first Monday in the possession of certain securities, debts due from other persons issued at certain dates in the past, or with certain debts due to other persons which he has acquired in the past. If, during the week, he decides to borrow, he can do so either by selling some old securities which he possesses, or by issuing new securities. Similarly, the acquisition both of old securities and of new securities will reckon as lending. The prices of old securities will have to adjust themselves to the rate of interest established on new securities (or, if we like to put it that way, the rate of interest on new securities will have to adjust itself to the prices of old securities); since, for an equal degree of default risk, it will be indifferent to an individual whether he buys or sells new securities or old securities. Since there is this purely arithmetical relation between the prices of old securities and the rate of interest, the prices of old securities need not be reckoned among the prices that have to be determined. Effectively, there is only one market rate of interest in the system.

6. There are thus two possible ways of constructing an economy with only one market rate of interest; each of them has its uses. We shall find, as we go on, that it is a distinct convenience to possess these alternative lines of approach; some things come out more clearly if we use the one route, some more clearly by the other. We shall therefore try to drive them for a while in double harness.

We have seen that it is possible to build up the whole system of interest rates, using the short rate as unit; if the spot economy with long lending is also to be a useful tool, it will have to be possible to build up the whole system in a parallel manner from the long rate. Can this be done? We saw that a system of nothing but short lending would break down in practice because many borrowers would desire the additional security that comes of borrowing for longer periods, and lenders would be prepared to grant them this security in return for a concession of rather higher rates of interest. How would it fare with a system of nothing but indefinitely long lending?

Such a system would be quite satisfactory to a certain class of borrowers—those who are embarking on continuous production; and even those borrowers who would prefer not to borrow quite indefinitely may not be ill content with doing so, if the length of time for which they would prefer to borrow would in any case extend into the distant future. These two classes probably cover a large proportion of industrial borrowing (roughly speaking, that borrowing which is for investment in fixed capital). On the other side, there may be a certain class of lenders who would be content with indefinite lending—those whose object is simply to derive a regular income from their capital, and have no thought of anything else. How large this class is can be disputed (broad historical movements may well have changed its size very drastically); nevertheless, in any circumstances the qualification—*they have no thought of anything else*—is important. As soon as a lender begins to envisage the possibility that he may want his capital back in conceivable cases—and it is hard to believe that this idea is ever wholly absent—the drawback of indefinitely long lending begins to be evident. As we have seen, the rate of interest which can be earned on a loan of any finite duration, by investing in undated debentures, is always highly conjectural. If there is a serious rise in the long-term rate of interest, the effective yield may be completely wiped out. But this is much less likely to happen if the security acquired has a definite maturity, even if it is disposed of at a different date from that at which it falls due.

Thus lenders will always tend to reduce the risks to which they are subject if they can substitute shorter lending for longer lending, although the extent to which they are conscious of this advantage may differ at different times. In general, we may suppose that they will be willing to make some sacrifice of interest (which may be large or small) in order to achieve greater security. Now we have seen how to determine the most probable rate of interest which can be earned on a loan of finite length through investing in undated debentures; lenders may be expected to accept something less than this in order to get the greater security of lending short. In this way short (and medium-term) rates of interest will be determined. They will lie below the most probable yield of undated debentures over the period of the loan—differing from it, once again, by some sort of 'normal' risk-premium, whose size will depend upon the estimate put upon the gain in security.

As we have seen, the most probable yield, over a finite period, of investment in undated debentures will lie below the current (long-term) market rate when that rate is expected to rise in the future, above it in the contrary case. Thus, in stable conditions, when the long rate is expected to remain steady, the short rate will lie below it to the extent of the normal risk-premium; when the long rate is expected to rise, the short rate will lie below it still further; it is only when the long rate is expected to fall that the short rate may lie above the long rate.

These conclusions, it will be seen, are perfectly consistent with those reached by our earlier method. The only difference between them is that while we there explained the span of interest rates in terms of expectations about the future course of the short rate, here we explain in terms of expectations about the future course of the long rate. In practice, the relevant expectations are no doubt expectations about the course of the whole system of rates; but (provided that they are fairly consistent) they can be reduced to either terms. The short rate can only lie above the long rate if the short rate is regarded as abnormally high, and if the long rate is regarded as abnormally high; but these phenomena are in fact mutually consistent, and do indeed tend to produce one another. A position of temporary equilibrium in which the long rate is expected to fall appreciably in the near future can only exist if speculators are prevented from buying securities at once in order to profit from the expected rise in their value—as they will be prevented if the short rate is high enough to offset this anticipated profit. But at the same time (looking at it the other way) this high short rate tends to raise the long rate rather above normal; for the long rate is an average of current and forward short rates, and this average is somewhat raised. From either point of view, there is a tendency for short and long rates to move in the same direction, but for the movement of short rates to have the larger amplitude.

CHAPTER XII

THE DETERMINATION OF THE RATE OF INTEREST

1. WE now approach one of those questions which has been in the forefront of discussion in modern monetary theory. What is it that determines the Rate of Interest? Until very lately, economists would have replied unanimously that it is determined by the demand and supply for 'capital'; but since they were not very certain exactly what they meant by 'capital', their unanimity was more apparent than real. Does capital mean 'real capital' in the sense of concrete goods and the power to dispose over a given quantity of them? If this interpretation is taken, the forces governing the rate of interest are naturally reduced to those technical and psychological factors influencing the relative urgency of wants for present and future goods—that is to say, we get a theory such as that worked out elaborately by Böhm-Bawerk. Or does 'capital' mean 'money capital' in the sense of loanable funds —power to dispose over a given quantity of money? It makes a great deal of difference which interpretation we take.

This first division of opinion is serious; it is a real dispute, in which one side must be right and the other wrong, even if the rightness or wrongness may ultimately turn out not to be absolute, but only relative to particular problems. But the real dispute has lately been complicated by a sham dispute within the ranks of those who adhere to the monetary approach.[1] Is the rate of interest determined by the supply and demand for loanable funds (that is to say, by borrowing and lending); or is it determined by the supply and demand for money itself? This last view is put forward by Mr. Keynes in his *General Theory*. I shall hope to show that it makes no difference whether we follow his way of putting it, or whether we follow those writers who adopt what appears at present to be a rival view. Properly followed up, the two approaches lead to exactly the same results.

[1] Keynes, 'Alternative Theories of the Rate of Interest' (*E.J.*, June 1937); rejoinders by Ohlin, Robertson, Hawtrey (*E.J.*, Sept. 1937); Keynes, "The "Ex-Ante" Theory of the Rate of Interest' (*E.J.*, Dec. 1937); Robertson and Keynes on 'Finance' (*E.J.*, June 1938).

2. Two difficulties, which would otherwise cause us a lot of trouble, have already been cleared out of the way by our previous analysis. First of all, it is evident that any treatment which pretends to deal with the economic system as a whole (and it is with such general analysis that the whole controversy has been concerned) cannot possibly regard the rate of interest in isolation. It is a price, like other prices, and must be determined with them as part of a mutually interdependent system. The problem is not one of determining a rate of interest *in vacuo*, but is really the general problem of price-determination in an economy where borrowing and lending are practised, and in which the rate of interest is therefore a constituent part of the general price-system. This way of looking at it appears to complicate the problem; but actually it makes it a good deal easier to understand.

Secondly, we cannot determine *the* rate of interest excepting in an economic system where there is only *one* rate of interest; in any other case we have to deal with a whole system of interest rates. Now we have already become acquainted with two different simplified models in which there is only one rate of interest— the spot economy with short lending, and the spot economy with long lending, described in the previous chapter. The problem we have to consider here reduces itself to a consideration of these simplified cases; for we have already gone a good deal of the way towards learning how to determine the system of interest rates, once one or other of the basic rates—*the* short rate or *the* long rate—is determined.

Thus the particular problem left for us to discuss here is the determination of the system of spot prices established on a particular Monday; and it divides into two sub-problems, according as we assume short lending, or long lending, to be the only kind of lending practised. Let us take these two questions in turn.

3. In a spot economy with short lending, the decks are cleared of all past contracts as soon as the market opens. The only prices which have to be determined are the spot prices of goods and services, and the rate of interest on one-week loans, loans from this Monday to next Monday. These are determined by current demands and supplies. On the basis of any set of current prices (including the current rate of interest), entrepreneurs and private persons alike will draw up plans, though these plans will be governed not only by current prices and the current interest rate, but also by their expectations of the future movements of prices and of the rate of interest. Current demands and supplies are simply facets of these plans, for the plans include decisions about current policy and provisional decisions about future policy as well. But, in a spot economy, it is only the decisions about current policy which are executed; thus it is only current demands and supplies which are matched on the market. If the system of prices first proposed does not induce a set of plans which equate current demands and supplies, it will have to be adjusted until temporary equilibrium is reached. Temporary equilibrium implies that current demands and supplies have been rendered equal.

In order to satisfy ourselves of the internal consistency of this system, it is necessary to check up the number of prices which have to be determined, and the number of demand and supply equations we have available to determine them, as we did when dealing with static systems.[1] Suppose that there are n kinds of exchangeable goods and services; then there are in all n prices to be determined.[2] For among the 'goods' must be reckoned that good which is taken as a standard of value (money). This leaves us $n-1$ prices of the other goods and services in terms of the standard, and one rate of interest (here the rate on loans for one week). This makes n prices in all. To determine the n prices, we have $n-1$ equations of supply and demand for the $n-1$ commodities (excluding money), one equation of supply and demand for loans, and one for money. This makes $n+1$ in all. However, as in the Walrasian systems with which we are previously acquainted, one of these $n+1$ equations follows from the rest. This leaves us n equations to determine the n prices. The system is neither over- nor under-determined.

It will be as well to check through carefully the way in which the $(n+1)$th equation can be eliminated. Since all trading is an exchange of money values for equal money values, a private individual can only spend more than he receives if he borrows or reduces his cash balance; he can only spend less than he receives

[1] Cf. Chapters IV and VIII above.
[2] It may be, of course, that some of these goods, though exchangeable, do not change hands at all during the current week. In spite of that, it will be convenient to think of them as having a market price, fixed (or roughly fixed) in such a way that their demand = supply = 0.

if he lends or increases his cash balance. Thus we can write, for any private individual,   .

Acquisition of cash by trading = Receipts—Expenditure—Lending

(bearing in mind that some of these items may be negative). The same equation will hold for entrepreneurs on their private accounts; therefore it will also hold for the private accounts of all individuals (including entrepreneurs) taken together.

The case of a firm is more complicated. It will, initially, deplete its cash balance by repaying last week's loans; but it may be expected to cover this to some extent (or perhaps more than cover it) by re-borrowing. It will reduce its cash balance by any acquisition it makes of factors of production, increase it by any sales of products. Finally, it will diminish its cash balance by any dividend it pays out to entrepreneurs.

Thus, for a firm,

> Acquisition of cash by trading
> = Value of output—Value of input
> —Repayment of old loans+New borrowing
> —Dividends.

The same equation holds for all firms taken together. Further, when the equation is used for industry as a whole, all those unfinished goods which are sold to other firms may be excluded. Once the demand and supply equations for these goods have been established they can be taken to cancel out. The input to be reckoned is simply the input of labour and material property provided by private persons; the output is simply the output of finished goods sold to private persons.

In the same way, a part of the receipts of private persons is due to the expenditure of other private persons; this, too, can be taken to cancel out when all private accounts are taken together. The *net* receipts of private persons are then derived from the inputs of firms, from their repayments of old loans, and from their dividend payments. If demands equal supplies in the input markets, these totals are equal in value. (Repayments are given in advance, and dividends are arbitrary.) Similarly, if demands equal supplies in the output markets, the value of the output of industry equals the net expenditure of private persons. If demand equals supply in the loan market, borrowing equals lending.

Therefore, for the community as a whole,

Net acquisition of cash by trading

= (Value of output—Net expenditure by private persons)
  +(Net receipts of private persons—Value of input
  +(Borrowing—Lending) —Dividends—Repayment of old loans)
= 0.

To say that the net acquisition of money by trading is zero, taken over the whole community, is the same thing as to say that the demand for money equals the supply of money. Consequently, if there is equilibrium in the markets for goods and services, and in the market for loans, there must also be equilibrium in the market for money. There are only n independent equations to determine the n prices; so the system is perfectly consistent.

4. Before going on to consider the implications of this, let us turn aside to work out our other model in a similar way. In a spot economy with long lending there are, as before, n prices (the $n-1$ prices of goods and services, and the one current rate of interest on undated debentures). We could, if we liked, add to these the prices of all old securities; but it seems simpler to suppose them directly adjusted to the new rate of interest by the ordinary rule. Any security, old or new, is in this world a promise to pay sums of money of given amount in a perpetual series; by regarding the promise to pay (say) £1 per annum as a unit of 'security', we can reduce them all to an homogeneous commodity, whose price is the reciprocal of the current interest rate. (It is, of course, immaterial whether we take, as the price to be determined, this reciprocal or the actual current rate of interest itself.)

As before, we have $n+1$ demand and supply equations—given by the $n-1$ goods and services, by securities, and by money. As before, one equation can be eliminated. But the elimination will proceed a little differently in this case, since on the one hand there is now no repayment of loans when the market opens, and on the other hand, borrowing may take the form of selling old securities as well as that of issuing new ones. The general layout of the elimination is as follows:

For any private individual,

Acquisition of cash

= Receipts (including interest on securities owned)
  —Expenditure—Value of securities acquired.

For any firm,

> Acquisition of cash = Value of output — Value of input
> — Interest on debts — Dividends
> + Value of securities issued (or sold).

For the community as a whole,

Net Expenditure by private persons = Value of net output,

Net Receipts by private persons = Value of net input
+ Dividends + Interest payments,

> Value of securities bought = Value of securities sold (or issued).

Therefore, as before, net acquisition of cash by trading = 0. As before, the system is determined with n unknowns and n independent equations.

5. It is time for us to consider just what this elimination of the odd equation signifies. It means that if a system of prices is established which equates the demand and supply for each of the $n-1$ goods and services, and equates the demand and supply for securities (or loans), then the demand and supply for money must be equal, so that that equation has nothing further to tell us. But it must be observed that the argument merely enables us to eliminate *one* out of the $n+1$ equations; it does not matter in the least which equation we choose to eliminate. If we decide to eliminate the money equation, then we can think of prices and interest being determined on the markets for goods and services, and the market for loans; the money equation becomes completely otiose, having nothing to tell us. But we have only to put the argument another way round, and we can eliminate any other single equation we choose. If we choose to eliminate another equation, the money equation comes back into its rights; the other equation becomes otiose, while the money equation plays an effective part in the determination of the price-system.

Thus, whenever the money equation is used as an effective part of the mechanism of price-determination it must be implied that some other equation has been selected for elimination. In the more developed versions of the quantity theory of money, where the money equation is used to determine the *price-level*, it must be supposed that the relative values of other goods and services are independently determined, the money equation being needed to determine their money values only. However, it is impossible to determine even relative prices except in terms of some standard. Thus the prices of goods and services must first be fixed in terms of some auxiliary standard commodity (unskilled labour in the classics, a representative consumption good in more modern writers); and the money equation then used to determine the money value of the auxiliary standard, that is to say, the value of money. There is still a superfluous equation, but it is the equation for the supply and demand of the auxiliary standard, not of money.

In itself, this is a perfectly legitimate line of approach; but it is subject to one great danger, which is, indeed, the source of most of the trouble which has occurred about this whole matter. If the equation chosen for elimination is that of an auxiliary standard commodity, then it appears that the whole system of relative prices can be worked out in 'real' terms, and the question of the value of money only introduced afterwards. The (relative) values of commodities and the value of money become entirely separate questions, even entirely separate subjects; they can be, and have been, handed over to separate specialists to study and even to teach. But if this dichotomy is maintained what happens to the rate of interest?

The monetary specialist, intent upon the determination of the price-level by means of the money equation, refines upon that equation; and in refining upon it, he cannot help stumbling upon interest, for example in the form of bank rate. But he regards this interest as a factor controlling the quantity of money (in some sense), and may not relate it to the general interest problem. The specialist in 'real' economics, on the other hand, considers the determination of the rate of interest to fall within his province; for it is only the money equation which has been handed over to the monetary specialist—all the other *live* equations (on this plan the equation of demand and supply for loan capital is a *live* equation) are the 'real' economist's business. But the 'real' economist, working with his auxiliary standard, only determining values in terms of that, and paying no attention to the value of money, cannot get to grips with the rate of interest. Unless he looks very carefully where he is going, he will find himself determining, not the true rate of interest, which (as we have seen) is a money rate, but the only rate of interest which is contained within his limited system—a rate indicating the value of future deliveries of the auxiliary standard commodity in terms of current deliveries of the same auxiliary standard.

Now there is no reason why this 'natural' rate (as we may call it, following Wicksell[1]) should be the same as the true *money* rate of interest. As we have seen, they will be identical only if futures prices of the auxiliary commodity are the same as spot prices.[2] This condition will be fulfilled if the value of money (or the money value of the auxiliary standard commodity) is not expected to change at all, *and* if this expectation is absolutely certain, so that risk is absent. (It will also be fulfilled in certain other special conditions, but these are obviously not relevant.) The assumption of constant value of money is a severe limitation on the argument; but the assumption of no risk is more than a limitation—it is a source of actual error.

We need not of course deny the possibility of overcoming this difficulty; once it is realized clearly that a rate of interest in terms of the auxiliary standard is not likely to be the same thing as the money rate of interest, the general method of working in real terms can still be used. But it ceases to have much to be said for it as an approach to the problem of interest. It looks as if it will be better to eliminate a different equation.

6. In his *General Theory of Employment* Mr. Keynes has much to say against the dichotomy of real and monetary economics, partly on the ground of its falsification of the rate of interest, partly because of the difficulty to which it is exposed when allowance has to be made for the existence of conventional prices, fixed in money terms.[3] It should be observed that these objections are quite independent; whatever one's view about the rigidity of money wages, the interest objection holds. It is quite sufficient in itself to justify Mr. Keynes in his refusal to hand over the determination of the rate of interest to 'real' economics.

But it is not sufficient in itself to decide how it is best to regard the determination of the rate of interest. Even if we abandon

---

[1] Wicksell's *Geldzins und Güterpreise* may be regarded as a first attempt to meet this difficulty, by confronting the *money* rate of interest (which arises in the work of *monetary* economists) with the *natural* rate (which arises in the work of *real* economists). We shall return to Wicksell's argument later; see below, pp. 251–3.

[2] See above, p. 142.

[3] See Note to Chapter VIII above.

the auxiliary standard, there is still a choice about the equation we shall choose to eliminate. If we choose, we can eliminate the money equation, thus determining the prices of commodities by the demands and supplies of commodities, and the rate of interest by the demand and supply of loan funds; this is the most natural course to pursue, and there does not seem to be anything against it. Or alternatively we can follow Mr. Keynes in eliminating the other equation which stands out from the rest as being peculiar—the equation of borrowing and lending, or purchase and sale of securities. If this is done, the $n-1$ ordinary prices and the one rate of interest are determined by the n equations of supply and demand for the n commodities, including money. Of course, as always, each equation plays its part in the determination of all prices; but since it is natural to 'match' the price of each commodity with the demand and supply equation for that same commodity, the rate of interest is bound to be 'matched' with the equation for the demand and supply of money.

It seems to me that either of these methods is perfectly legitimate; the choice between them is purely a matter of convenience. Against the background of the way in which economic theory has developed, Mr. Keynes's method has the advantage that it retains the services of the monetary specialists; instead of compelling them to become general economists, as the other method would do, it merely diverts their attention from the determination of the price-level to the determination of the rate of interest. If we use the other method, we have got to be prepared to keep monetary factors in our minds all the time. On the other hand, Mr. Keynes's method loses something in convenience when we leave the spot economy, with its one rate of interest, and begin to concern ourselves with the system of interest rates. Securities are not in fact a 'homogeneous commodity', so that if they are eliminated wholesale from the determining equations, their differences are rather likely to receive insufficient attention. (This is not a very serious objection, so far as securities of different maturity are concerned; we saw in the last chapter that the determination of relative rates of interest on loans of different maturity could be reduced to speculation on the future course of the rate of interest. Differences due to default risk are more serious, but ways can probably be found for dealing with these after a fashion.) However, all these advantages and disadvantages are matters of opinion; there is no reason why we should commit ourselves to the regular use of one method or the other. It is indeed very useful to have two methods to serve as a check.

The important advantage which Mr. Keynes himself derives from his way of putting it is that it gives him an excellent opportunity of stressing the closeness of the connexion between money and interest. That is a matter to which it is high time for us to turn.[1]

[1] It appears that my earlier attempt to convince Mr. Keynes that the above is a valid way of approaching his theory was not very successful. (Keynes, 'Alternative Theories of Interest', *E.J.*, June 1937, quoting my review article, 'Mr. Keynes's Theory of Employment', *E.J.*, June 1936.) I think the obscurity in this article of mine arose mainly from the fact that I was not clear when I wrote about the different properties of a spot economy with short lending and a spot economy with long lending. Mr. Keynes habitually works with the latter model; I was already, before the appearance of his book, beginning to work out the properties of the former. The device of eliminating the loans (or securities) equation can be used with either model; I had discovered its convenience for my model before Mr. Keynes's book came out. (See my 'Wages and Interest', *E.J.*, Sept. 1935, p. 467.) I hope the present chapter will clear up the matter.

CHAPTER XIII
INTEREST AND MONEY

1. EVERY kind of fixed-interest bearing security (bill, bond, or debenture) is a promise to pay certain sums of money in the future; but there are certain kinds of promissory documents, usually not reckoned as securities, but included as types of money itself, which in fact fall under the same classification. Bank deposits, commonly reckoned as money nowadays, are promises to pay money in the future; even bank-notes are promises to pay money. This character of bank-notes is plain and agreeable to common sense, when the bank-note is a promise to pay some other money (gold or the notes of some superior bank); when the superior money has disappeared, the situation becomes very paradoxical. Yet that paradox reflects an essential part of the problem, and is not at all an accident; it is good to have a perpetual reminder of it in our pockets, in the inscription on the £1 note of the Bank of England: 'Promise to pay the Bearer on Demand the sum of One Pound'.

Those kinds of securities which are money differ from those which are not money by the fact that they bear no interest; that is to say, their present value equals their face value, instead of falling below their face value, as is the case with bills. Looked at in this way, money appears simply as the most perfect type of security; other securities are less perfect, and command a lower price because of their imperfection. The rate of interest on these securities is a measure of their imperfection—of their imperfect 'moneyness'. The nature of money and the nature of interest are therefore very nearly the same problem. When we have decided what it is which makes people give more for those securities which are reckoned as money than for those securities which are not, we shall have discovered also why interest is paid.

We have already seen, in our earlier chapter on interest, that a part of the interest paid on actual securities is to be attributed to default risk; and a part of the interest paid, at least on long-term securities, is to be attributed to uncertainty of the future course of interest rates. Both of these elements are purely risk-elements; if these were the only elements in interest, it would be true to say that all interest is, in the end, nothing but a risk-premium. That is, I take it, the view of Mr. Keynes; his doctrine of 'Liquidity Preference' appears to reduce all interest into terms of these two risk factors.[1] But to say that the rate of interest on perfectly safe securities is determined by nothing else but uncertainty of future interest rates seems to leave interest hanging by its own boot-straps; one feels an obstinate conviction that there must be more in it than that. Let us try to discover what that something more can be.

2. We shall get nearest to the true nature of interest if we consider the relation between money and that type of security which comes nearest to being money, without quite being money. This is to be found in the very short bill, a bill payable in the very near future, when that bill is regarded as perfectly safe from risk of default. If we can find a reason why such a bill should stand at less than its face value, at less, that is to say, than money of the same face value, we have found a reason for the existence of pure interest.

Let us begin by considering this problem in the light of the model system we have been using hitherto. (Actually, it is not one of those questions which can be discussed wholly in terms of our model system; still that system will give us a good start.)

If markets are only open every Monday, and the shortest currency of any bill is from one Monday to the next, is it possible for such a bill to stand at a discount relatively to money? (We have hitherto assumed that it is possible, but we now see that we ought to call that assumption into question.) If bills stand at a discount, and consequently earn interest, is there anything to stop any individual from investing all his surplus funds in bills, and holding them during the week in that form? If there is nothing to stop him, then money has no superiority over bills, and therefore cannot stand at a premium relatively to bills. The rate of interest must be nil.

The only possible incentive to hold money is one which we have already touched on in an earlier chapter, but must now explore more fully. If people receive payment for the things they sell in the form of money, to convert this money into bills requires a separate transaction, and the trouble of making that transaction

_____
[1] Keynes, *General Theory*, ch. 13.

may offset the gain in interest. It is only if this obstacle were removed, if safe bills could be acquired without any trouble at all, that people would become willing to convert all their money into bills, so long as any interest whatever was offered. Under the conditions of our model, it must be the trouble of making transactions which explains the short rate of interest.

The level of that rate of interest measures the trouble involved in investing funds, not in general, but to the marginal lender. There is no reason to suppose that the cost of such investment will be the same to different lenders. Relatively large transactions can usually be made with very little more trouble than small transactions, but the total interest offered on a large sum is much larger than on a small sum; thus large capitalists will be tempted to buy bills much more easily than small capitalists. If the demand for loans of one week was low enough for it to be capable of being satisfied entirely by the largest capitalists, the rate of interest on these loans would be very low indeed, practically zero. But if it became necessary to call upon the funds of smaller capitalists, the rate might be expected to rise sharply after a point.

This is one way of looking at the determination of the short rate of interest, but it is not wholly satisfying, even in terms of our model system. For the cost of investing funds to be an effective barrier to the acquisition of bills it is necessary for people to have to make a separate transaction, in order to acquire bills. But they only have to make such a transaction if they are paid for the things they sell in something else, namely money. Now if bills are perfectly safe (and we assumed that we were dealing with bills on which there was no risk of default), why should not people be paid in the form of bills, and not in the form of money? If this were to happen generally, there would be no cost of investment, and therefore, so it would appear, no reason for the bills to fall to a discount.

This is not at all a fanciful hypothesis; it is what does actually happen with a certain class of bills. As we saw at the beginning of this chapter, bank-notes (and even bank-deposits) are bills, which do not stand at a discount, and are therefore reckoned as a kind of money. If default risk is so generally ruled out, that all traders reckon, and are known to reckon, a particular bill as perfectly safe, then there is no reason why that bill should stand at a discount, for the obstacle of cost of investment can be circumvented. But this general acceptability is something different from

M

the mere absence of default risk, which we assumed previously. A class of bills may be regarded as perfectly safe by those who actually take them up, and yet these persons may be different from those to whom the borrower has to make payments. These latter would not accept his bills, so he has to pay *cash*; the former are perfectly willing to lend, but require interest to compensate for their cost of investment.

Thus the imperfect 'moneyness' of those bills which are not money is due to their lack of general acceptability; it is this lack of general acceptability which causes the trouble of investing in them, and that causes them to stand at a discount.

3. So far as our model economy is concerned, that is really all that needs to be said about the relation between money and interest. We have now seen how there comes to be a short rate of interest; long rates have been explained in Chapter XI in terms of speculation on the future course of the short rate. But since, in reality, there is no minimum period of borrowing and lending, and no division of trading into discontinuous 'market days' (as we have conveniently supposed), those influences which we have described as working on the short rate become entangled with the speculative elements discussed previously. In practice, there is no rate so short that it may not be affected by speculative elements; there is no rate so long that it may not be affected by the advantages of the alternative use of funds in holding cash.

Any one purchasing a bill whose currency is for more than the minimum period (this means in practice any bill whatever) has to take into account the possibility that he may want the use of his funds again before the bill matures. If this should happen, he would have to rediscount his bill; rediscounting will necessarily involve trouble, equal to (or even greater than) that of the original act of investment; it may also involve a further risk, that if rates of interest have risen between the date of the original investment and the date of rediscounting, he may only be able to rediscount on unfavourable terms. The longer the time before the maturity of the bill, the more serious this latter risk is likely to be; and thus, as we saw in our previous discussions of the long-term rate of interest, the long rate is *normally* likely to exceed the short rate by a risk-premium, whose function it is to compensate for the risk of an adverse movement of interest rates. This sort of risk-premium is fundamental to the difference between long and short rates; but the shorter the period for which a bill is to run, the less important this risk is likely to be. The main loss involved, if the bill has to be rediscounted, will generally be nothing else but the sheer trouble of rediscounting; it is the risk of being involved in this trouble which is the main risk to be taken into account.

To sum up these conclusions. Securities which are not generally acceptable in payment of debts bear some interest because they are imperfectly 'money'. Even if the possibility of default is ruled out by the actual lenders, nevertheless costs and risks are involved when funds are held in the form of securities rather than money, for which the lenders require some compensation. (1) For a bill so short that the possibility of having to rediscount is ruled out, the only inferiority of the bill is the cost of investment; so the rate of interest on the bill corresponds to the cost of investment to the marginal lender. (2) For a bill of rather longer maturity than this, the possibility of having to rediscount the bill has also to be considered. The rate of interest on such a bill will have further to offset the risk of such rediscounting being necessary, to offer some compensation for the trouble which would be incurred in that eventuality. (3) For bills of still longer maturity, for long-term securities in general, and (sometimes) even for short bills, there has to be considered the additional risk that, if rediscounting becomes necessary, it will only be to be had on unfavourable terms. But this additional risk, though it is always important for long-term securities, only becomes important for short-term securities as well, if the first risk (of having to rediscount at all) is already serious; thus it is essentially in conditions of great strain—more or less crisis conditions—that it may be expected to influence short rates of interest.

4. The various sorts of securities we have been considering—including money—behave in very much the same sort of way as a chain of substitute commodities, say different qualities of wheat or sugar. Money is naturally the highest grade, and that is why other grades ordinarily stand at a discount relatively to money.[1] It is

---

[1] The only exceptions to this rule will be found in those cases when the holding of money is not regarded as perfectly safe, stocks of money being exposed to depreciation (in money terms) through theft or confiscation. This is the reason why people are prepared to pay bank charges for the keeping of small sums— that is to say, they accept a negative rate of interest.

because money and securities are a chain of substitutes that rates of interest are ordinarily positive; and for the same reason (except when default risk is very heavy) they are generally small—only a few points per cent. per annum.

In early stages of society, the 'money' which stood alone in the highest grade was usually some sort of durable material commodity; as long as this was the case, it was not easy to distinguish the demand for the commodity as money from the demand for it as durable consumption good—or even to see what the demand for it as money could mean. But when some sorts of promises to pay money began to be so generally acceptable as to become perfect substitutes for the original money—and thus to stand with the original money in the highest grade—it became clear that the pure monetary demand had acquired an independent existence. Money had left its chrysalis stage of durable consumption good, and had developed into pure money—which is nothing else but the most perfect type of security.

Bills of short maturity form the next grade, being not quite perfect money, but still very close substitutes for it. How close can be seen in an impressive way if we compare the sort of fluctuations which take place (on an organized market) in the money value of good three months' bills, with the variations which take place in the relative values of different grades of the same physical commodity. £100 is an impossibly high price, and £98 an exceedingly low price for a £100 bill; we should regard two material commodities as very good substitutes even if their relative values were subject to much greater fluctuations than that.

Longer term securities form a yet lower grade, worth less and —from the fluctuations which take place in their values—obviously much less perfect substitutes. (The rate of interest per annum on long-term securities, free from default risk, may be less liable to fluctuate than the rate of interest per annum on short-term securities; but the capital value of long-term securities is much more liable to fluctuate.) Still, substitution between money and long-term securities does take place. It may be useful to follow out some of its different forms.

First, there is the case of the ordinary small investor, who buys long-term securities in order to live upon the interest from them. He will have to accumulate a money balance before he can invest it, since he is deterred from investing too small sums by the cost and trouble of investing. From his point of view, the cost of investment is the really important thing; it is probably the main determinant of the date at which he converts his money into securities. Thus there cannot be very much direct substitution here; a change in the rate of interest may sometimes affect the date at which he makes his purchase; but one would suppose that it would need a large change in the rate of interest to have much effect on this sort of margin.

Secondly, there is the more speculative investor. If he is not sufficiently in touch with the money market to have ready access to short-term issues, he will use the long-term security market as a repository for funds only temporarily idle. This class includes all private investors who have to pay much attention to the capital value of their securities, because they want to sell them for the acquisition of property (houses and so on); those concerns and institutions which invest a portion of their assets in securities (a very important group nowadays); and finally also speculative investors in the narrow sense, who are out to make capital gains by speculation, and who have, as a consequence, to be prepared to meet capital losses. For all these, the margin between money and securities is a very sensitive margin; the more conscious they are of the importance of capital losses, the more easily they will switch about when the rate of interest varies.

Nevertheless, for most of this second class, at least one form of short-term security is available; they can place their funds on deposit account at a bank. Thus the second class melts imperceptibly into the third. Banks themselves, financial houses, public institutions, large industrial and commercial firms, all of these have at their disposal a whole gamut of securities of different maturity. Therefore their substitution between money and long-term securities probably takes place mainly through the mediation of shorter-term securities and bills; if the long rate is too low to compensate for the risk of capital loss, they begin to go into shorts; if the short rate is too low to compensate for the risks involved even there, they hold cash; it does not take much to induce them to make these changes. It is these professional investors, operating upon the whole gamut, and paying close attention to small differences in rates, who provide most of the logic of the interest system (just as it is the professional arbitrageurs who provide most of the logic of the system of foreign exchange rates). It is not necessary to suppose that the small investor has to do much in that direction; the specialists can do it quite sufficiently by themselves.[1]

The whole working of the system of interest rates is an example of the working of the general rule of substitution: if two commodities are close substitutes for an important section of a market, they will behave as close substitutes for the market as a whole.

5. No attempt has been made in this chapter to give a complete theory of the demand for money; still less to give a complete theory of the working of interest rates. Both these matters must be held over for the more systematic analysis of Part IV. But I have felt that some preliminary indication of the point of view from which we intend to approach monetary problems had to be given here— and some preliminary survey of the relation between money and interest. The fact that money and securities are close substitutes is absolutely fundamental to dynamic economics; we should waste our time if we did not bring ourselves to realize it as soon as possible.

This close substitutability is much the most important property of actual money which we shall need in our further inquiries. For the rest, it will do little harm if we continue to think of money in the same light as we have considered it in earlier chapters—as standard commodity, a commodity selected from the rest to serve as standard of value. Since one of the properties of actual money is that it is used as a standard of value, the various propositions which we established in earlier chapters about the standard commodity are true of actual money; but they are not only true of actual money, they would also be true of any other commodity we might like to take as standard of value for purposes of argument. (That this is so has been made clear by the ease with which we could change our standard commodity when we chose.) Actual money has the property of being a standard of value, but it has also other properties—the familiar properties of being a 'medium of exchange' and a 'store of value'. These properties we have considered for the first time in the present chapter. Their important consequence for the working of the price system is simply this: they explain why there is such a close relation of substitution between money and securities, that is to say, they explain the phenomenon of interest—*money interest*.

[1] The important part played by banks and public authorities in determining the system of interest rates has, of course, a great bearing upon the possibility of controlling that system; a possibility much exploited in recent years.

CHAPTER XIV

INCOME

1. WE have now concluded our discussion of interest; and, by so doing, we have also concluded all that it is absolutely necessary to say about the foundations of dynamic economics. If we chose, we could thus proceed at once to analyse the working of the dynamic system, proceeding on parallel lines to those on which we analysed the working of a static system in Part II. That is what we shall do, ultimately; but meanwhile the reader has the right to raise an objection. Nothing has been said in the foregoing about any of a series of concepts which have usually been regarded in the past as fundamental for dynamic theory. Nothing has been said about Income, about Saving, about Depreciation, or about Investment (with a capital I). These are the terms in which one has been used to think; how do they fit here?

My decision to abstain from using these concepts in the last five chapters was, of course, quite deliberate. In spite of their familiarity, I do not believe that they are suitable tools for any analysis which aims at logical precision. There is far too much equivocation in their meaning, equivocation which cannot be removed by the most painstaking effort. At bottom, they are not logical categories at all; they are rough approximations, used by the business man to steer himself through the bewildering changes of situation which confront him. For this purpose, strict logical categories are not what is needed; something rougher is actually better. But if we try to work with terms of this sort in the investigations we are here concerned with, we are putting upon them a weight of refinement they cannot bear.

I do not think that any one who has followed the theoretical controversies of recent years will be very surprised at my putting forward this view. We have seen eminent authorities confusing each other and even themselves, by adopting different definitions of saving and income, none quite consistent, none quite satisfactory. When this sort of thing happens, there is usually some reason for the confusion; and that reason needs to be brought out before any further progress can be made.

2. Although we have refrained from using the term income in our dynamic theory, the reader will remember that we had no such inhibition when we were concerned with statics. In statics the difficulty about income does not arise. A person's income can be taken without qualification as equal to his receipts (earnings of labour, or rent from property). Sleeping dogs can be left to lie. The same is true in the economics of the stationary state, a branch of dynamic economics, but one which (as we have seen) blacks out some of the most important of dynamic problems. If a person expects no change in economic conditions, and expects to receive a constant flow of receipts, the same amount in every future week as he receives this week, it is reasonable to say that that amount is his income. But suppose he expects to receive a smaller amount in future weeks than this week (this week's receipts may include wages for several weeks' work, or perhaps a bonus on shares), then we should not regard the whole of his current receipts as income; some part would be reckoned to capital account. Similarly, if it so happened that he was entirely dependent on a salary paid every fourth week, and the present week was one in which his salary was not paid, we should not regard his income this week as being zero. How much would it be? We cannot give an exact answer without having a clear idea about the nature of income in general.

The purpose of income calculations in practical affairs is to give people an indication of the amount which they can consume without impoverishing themselves. Following out this idea, it would seem that we ought to define a man's income as the maximum value which he can consume during a week, and still expect to be as well off at the end of the week as he was at the beginning. Thus, when a person saves, he plans to be better off in the future; when he lives beyond his income, he plans to be worse off. Remembering that the practical purpose of income is to serve as a guide for prudent conduct, I think it is fairly clear that this is what the central meaning must be.

However, business men and economists alike are usually content to employ one or other of a series of approximations to the central meaning. Let us consider some of these approximations in turn.

3. The first approximation would make everything depend on the capitalized money value of the individual's prospective receipts.

Suppose that the stream of receipts expected by an individual at the beginning of the week is the same as that which would be yielded by investing in securities a sum of £M. Then, if he spends nothing in the current week, reinvesting any receipts which he gets, and leaving to accumulate those that have not yet fallen due, he can expect that the stream which will be in prospect at the end of the week will be £M plus a week's interest on £M. But if he spends something, the expected value of his prospect at the end of the week will be less than this. There will be a certain particular amount of expenditure which will reduce the expected value of his prospect to exactly £M. On this interpretation, that amount is his income.

This definition is obviously sensible in the case when receipts are derived entirely from property—securities, land, buildings, and so on. Suppose that at the beginning of the week, our individual possesses property worth £10,010, and no other source of income. Then if the rate of interest were $\frac{1}{10}$ per cent. per week, income would be £10 for the week. For if £10 were spent, £10,000 would be left to be reinvested; and in one week this would have accumulated to £10,010—the original sum.

In the case of incomes from work, the definition is less obviously sensible, but it is still quite consistent with ordinary practice. Not having to do with a slave market, we are not in the habit of capitalizing incomes from work; but in the sorts of cases which generally arise this makes no difference. Fluctuations in receipts from work are not usually easy to foresee in advance; and any one who expects a constant stream of receipts (and does not expect any change in interest rates) will reckon that constant amount as his income, on this definition. If fluctuations are foreseen, they are nearly always so near ahead that interest on the variations is negligible. With interest neglected, calculation by capitalization reduces to mere arithmetical division over time. £20 per month of four weeks can be taken as equivalent to £5 per week.

Income No. 1 is thus the maximum amount which can be spent during a period if there is to be an expectation of maintaining intact the capital value of prospective receipts (in money terms). This is probably the definition which most people do implicitly use in their private affairs; but it is far from being in all circumstances a good approximation to the central concept.

4. For consider what happens, first, if interest rates are expected to change. If the rate of interest for a week's loan which is expected to rule in one future week is not the same as that which is expected to rule in another future week, then a definition based upon constancy of money capital becomes unsatisfactory. For (reverting to the numerical example we used above), suppose that the rate of interest per week for a loan of one week is $\frac{1}{10}$ per cent.; but that the corresponding rate expected to rule in the second week from now is $\frac{1}{5}$ per cent., and that this higher rate is expected to continue indefinitely afterwards. Then the individual is bound to spend no more than £10 in the current week, if he is to expect to have £10,010 again at his disposal at the end of the week; but if he desires to have the same sum available at the end of the second week, he will be able to spend nearly £20 in the second week, not £10 only. The same sum (£10,010) available at the beginning of the first week makes possible a stream of expenditures

$$£10, \ £20, \ £20, \ £20,...,$$

while if it is available at the beginning of the second week it makes possible a stream

$$£20, \ £20, \ £20, \ £20,... \ .$$

It will ordinarily be reasonable to say that a person with the latter prospect is better off than one with the former.

This leads us to the definition of Income No. 2. We now define income as the maximum amount the individual can spend this week, and still expect to be able to spend the same amount in each ensuing week. So long as the rate of interest is not expected to change, this definition comes to the same thing as the first; but when the rate of interest is expected to change, they cease to be identical. Income No. 2 is then a closer approximation to the central concept than Income No. 1 is.

5. Now what happens if prices are expected to change? The correction which must be introduced suggests itself almost immediately. Income No. 3 must be defined as the maximum amount of money which the individual can spend this week, and still expect to be able to spend the same amount *in real terms* in each ensuing week. If prices are expected to rise, then an individual who plans to spend £10 in the present and each ensuing week must expect to be less well off at the end of the week than he is at the beginning. At each date he can look forward to the opportunity of spending £10 in each future week; but at the first date one of the £10's will be spent in a week when prices are relatively low. An opportunity of spending on favourable terms is present in the first case, but absent in the second.

Thus, if £10 is to be his income for this week, according to definition No. 3, he will have to expect to be able to spend in each future week, not £10, but a sum greater or less than £10 by the extent to which prices have risen or fallen in that week above or below their level in the first week.

Some correction of this sort is obviously desirable. But what do we mean by 'in real terms'? What is the appropriate index-number of prices to take? To this question there is, I believe, no completely satisfactory answer. Even when prices are expected to change, there is, indeed, still available a very laborious criterion which would enable us to say, for any given set of planned expenditures, whether it is such that the planner is living within his income or not.[1] If the application of this test were to show that the individual's expenditure equalled his income, then of course it would determine his income; but in all other cases it does not suffice to show by how much he is living within his income, that is to say, exactly how much his income is.

Income No. 3 is thus already subject to some indeterminateness; but that is not the end of the difficulty. For Income No. 3 is still only an approximation to the central meaning of the concept of income; it is not that central meaning itself. One point is still left out of consideration; by its failure to consider this even Income No. 3 falls short of being a perfect definition.

[1] If he is living within his income he must be able to plan for the second Monday the same stream of purchases as for the first, and still have something left over. Suppose he plans to purchase of commodity X quantities $X_0, X_1, X_2,...$ in successive weeks; of commodity Y quantities $Y_0, Y_1, Y_2,...$; and so on. The condition for him to live within his income in the first week is that the stream of purchases actually planned for later weeks,

$$X_1 Y_1 Z_1..., \qquad X_2 Y_2 Z_2..., \qquad X_3 Y_3 Z_3...,$$

valued at the prices at which each is actually expected to be made (those of the 2nd, 3rd, 4th,... weeks respectively), should have a greater value than the original stream

$$X_0 Y_0 Z_0..., \qquad X_1 Y_1 Z_1..., \qquad X_2 Y_2 Z_2...,$$

valued, not at the first, but at the second, Monday, and valued at the same prices as that of the other stream (those of the 2nd, 3rd, 4th weeks, &c.), that is to say, valued at prices expected to rule one week later in each case than the dates at which these purchases are expected to be made in fact.

This is the matter of durable consumption goods. Strictly speaking, saving is not the difference between income and expenditure, it is the difference between income and consumption. Income is not the maximum amount the individual can *spend* while expecting to be as well off as before at the end of the week; it is the maximum amount he can *consume*. If some part of his expenditure goes on durable consumption goods, that will tend to make his expenditure exceed his consumption; if some part of his consumption is consumption of durable consumption goods, already bought in the past, that tends to make consumption exceed expenditure. It is only if these two things match, if the acquisition of new consumption goods just matches the using up of old ones, that we can equate consumption to spending, and proceed as before.

But what is to be done if these things do not match? And worse, how are we to tell if they do match? If there is a perfect second-hand market for the goods in question, so that a market value can be assessed for them with precision, corresponding to each particular degree of wear, then the value-loss due to consumption can be exactly measured; but if not there is nothing for it but to revert to the central concept itself. If the individual is using up his existing stock of durable consumption goods, and not acquiring new ones, he will be worse off at the end of the week if he can then only plan the same stream of purchases as he could at the beginning. If he is to live within his income, he must in this case take steps to be able to plan a larger stream at the end of the week; but how much larger can be told from nothing else but the central criterion itself.

6. We are thus forced back on the central criterion, that a person's income is what he can consume during the week and still expect to be as well off at the end of the week as he was at the beginning. By considering the approximations to this criterion, we have come to see how very complex it is, how unattractive it looks when subjected to detailed analysis. We may now allow a doubt to escape us whether it does, in the last resort, stand up to analysis at all, whether we have not been chasing a will-o'-the-wisp.

At the beginning of the week the individual possesses a stock of consumption goods, and expects a stream of receipts which will enable him to acquire in the future other consumption goods, perishable or durable. Call this Prospect I. At the end of the week he knows that one week out of that prospect will have disappeared; the new prospect which he expects to emerge will have a new first week which is the old second week, a new second week which is the old third week, and so on. Call this Prospect II. Now if Prospect II were available on the first Monday, we may assume that the individual would know whether he preferred I to II at that date; similarly, if Prospect I were available on the second Monday, he would know if he preferred I to II then. But to inquire whether I on the first Monday is preferred to II on the second Monday is a nonsense question; the choice between them could never be actual at all; the terms of comparison are not *in pari materia*.

This point is of course exceedingly academic; yet it has the same sort of significance as the point we made at a much earlier stage of our investigations, about the immeasurability of utility.[1] In order to get clear-cut results in economic theory, we must work with concepts which are directly dependent on the individual's scale of preferences, not on any vaguer properties of his psychology. By eschewing *utility* we were able to sharpen the edge of our conclusions in economic statics; for the same reason, we shall be well advised to eschew *income* and *saving* in economic dynamics. They are bad tools, which break in our hands.

7. These considerations are much fortified by another, which emerges when we pass from the consideration of individual income (with which we have been wholly concerned hitherto) to the consideration of social income. Even if we content ourselves with one of the approximations to the concept of individual income (say Income No. 1, which is good enough for most purposes), it remains true that income is a subjective concept, dependent on the particular expectations of the individual in question. Now, as we have seen, there is no reason why the expectations of different individuals should be consistent; one of the main causes of disequilibrium in the economic system is a lack of consistency in expectations and plans.[2] If A's income is based on A's expectations, and B's income upon B's expectations, and these expectations are inconsistent (because they expect different prices for the same commodity at

---

[1] Cf. above, p. 18.   [2] Cf. above, p. 133.

particular future dates, or plan supplies and demands that will not match on the market), then an aggregate of their incomes has little meaning. It has no more to its credit than its obedience to the laws of arithmetic.

This conclusion seems unavoidable, but it is very upsetting, perhaps even more upsetting than our doubts about the ultimate intelligibility of the concept of individual income itself. Social income plays so large a part in modern economics, not only in the dynamic and monetary theory with which we are here concerned, but also in the economics of welfare, that it is hard to imagine ourselves doing without it. It is hard to believe that the social income which economists discuss so much can be nothing else but a mere aggregate of possibly inconsistent expectations. But if it is not that, what is it?

In order to answer this question, we must begin by making a further distinction within the field of individual income. All the definitions of income we have hitherto discussed are *ex ante* definitions[1]—they are concerned with what a person can consume during a week and still *expect* to be as well off as he was. Nothing is said about the realization of this expectation. If it is not realized exactly, the value of his prospect at the end of the week will be greater or less than it was expected to be, so that he makes a 'windfall' profit or loss.[2] If we add this windfall gain to any of our preceding definitions of income (or subtract the loss), we get a new set of definitions, definitions of 'income including windfalls' or 'income *ex post*'. There is a definition of income *ex post* corresponding to each of our previous definitions of income *ex ante*; but for most purposes it is that corresponding to Income No. 1 which is the most important. Income No. 1 *ex post* equals the value of the individual's consumption *plus* the increment in the money value of his prospect which has accrued during the week; it equals Consumption *plus* Capital accumulation.

This last very special sort of 'income' has one supremely important property. So long as we confine our attention to income from property, and leave out of account any increment or decrement in the value of prospects due to changes in people's own earning power (accumulation or decumulation of 'Human Capital'), Income

[1] To use a term invented by Professor Myrdal, and exported by other Swedish economists.
[2] To use a term of Mr. Keynes's.

No. 1 *ex post* is not a subjective affair, like other kinds of income; it is almost completely objective. The capital value of the individual's property at the beginning of the week is an assessable figure; so is the capital value of his property at the end of the week; thus, if we assume that we can measure his consumption, his income *ex post* can be directly calculated. Since the income *ex post* of any individual is thus an objective magnitude, the incomes *ex post* of all individuals composing the community can be aggregated without difficulty; and the same rule, that Income No. 1 *ex post* equals Consumption *plus* Capital accumulation, will hold for the community as a whole.

This is a very convenient property, but unfortunately it does not justify an extensive use of the concept in economic theory. *Ex post* calculations of capital accumulation have their place in economic and statistical *history*; they are a useful measuring-rod for economic progress; but they are of no use to theoretical economists, who are trying to find out how the economic system works, because they have no significance for conduct. The income *ex post* of any particular week cannot be calculated until the end of the week, and then it involves a comparison between present values and values which belong wholly to the past. On the general principle of 'bygones are bygones', it can have no relevance to present decisions. The income which is relevant to conduct must always exclude windfall gains; if they occur, they have to be thought of as raising income for future weeks (by the interest on them) rather than as entering into any effective sort of income for the current week. Theoretical confusion between income *ex post* and *ex ante* corresponds to practical confusion between income and capital.

8. It seems to follow that any one who seeks to make a statistical calculation of social income is confronted with a dilemma. The income he can calculate is not the true income he seeks; the income he seeks cannot be calculated. From this dilemma there is only one way out; it is of course the way that has to be taken in practice. He must take his objective magnitude, the Social Income *ex post*, and proceed to adjust it, in some way that seems plausible or reasonable, for those changes in capital values which look as if they have had the character of windfalls. This sort of estimation is normal statistical procedure, and on its own ground it is wholly justified. But it can only result in a statistical estimate; by its very nature, it is not the measurement of an economic quantity.[1]

For purposes of welfare economics it is generally the *real* social income which we desire to measure; this means that an estimate has to be made which will correspond to Income No. 3 in the same way as the above estimate corresponds to Income No. 1. Here we have the additional difficulty that it is impossible to get an objective measurement of Income No. 3, even *ex post*; since Income No. 3 always depends upon expectations of prices of consumption goods. But something with the same sort of correspondence can be constructed. Variations in prices can be excluded from the calculation of capital values, in one way or another; one of the best ways theoretically conceivable would be to take the actual capital goods existing at the end of the period, and to value them at the prices which any similar goods would have had at the beginning; any accumulation of capital which survives this test will be an accumulation in *real* terms. By adding the amount of consumption during the period, we get at least one sense of real income *ex post*; by then correcting for windfalls, we get a useful measure of real social income.[2] But it is just the same sort of estimate as the measure of social money income.

I hope that this chapter will have made it clear how it is possible for individual income calculations to have an important influence on individual economic conduct; for calculations of social income to play such an important part in social statistics, and in welfare economics; and yet, at the same time, for the concept of income to be one which the positive theoretical economist only employs in his arguments at his peril. For him, income is a very dangerous term, and it can be avoided; as we shall see, a whole general theory of economic dynamics can be worked out without using it. Or rather, it only becomes necessary to use it at a very late stage in our investigations, when we shall wish to examine the effect of

---

[1] Since the statistician must adopt this line, it is not surprising to find him turning for assistance to those other seekers after objective income—the Commissioners for Inland Revenue. The best thing he can do is to follow the practice of the Income Tax authorities. But it is the business of the theoretical economist to be able to criticize the practice of such authorities; he has no right to be found in their company himself!

[2] The process of correcting for windfalls will usually be less important in this case of real income, since all windfalls due to mere changes in money values have already been excluded; only such things as windfall losses due to natural catastrophes and wars are left to be allowed for.

the practical precept of 'living within one's income' upon the course of economic development.[1] For that purpose, it is not necessary to have an exact definition of income; something quite rough, suitable to a rough practical precept, will do quite well.

Notes to Chapter XIV

There are two matters arising out of the theory of income which I feel ought to be discussed in this book, although, for the reasons just stated, I am anxious not to allow myself to be drawn into them too deeply. One is the question of the relation between Saving and Investment; I think the reader has a right to demand some expression of opinion on that controversial topic. The other concerns the effect of interest changes on the calculation of Depreciation, and hence of Income; this is a matter of some importance in itself, and its consideration here will have the advantage of throwing up one or two ideas which it will be rather useful for us to have in our minds later on.

A. SAVING AND INVESTMENT.

The principal difficulty in this matter of saving and investment evidently arises from the multiplicity of ways in which the terms can be defined. Without involving ourselves in any of the more recondite definitions which have been put forward, it is directly obvious that there is a definition of saving to correspond with each of the definitions of income set out in the preceding chapter. Saving can be defined *ex ante* or *ex post*; it can be defined to match definitions of Income Nos. 1, 2, or 3. To each of these definitions of saving there corresponds a definition of investment. This provides a good many ways in which arguments may get at cross-purposes!

As soon as we have these different definitions spread out before us it becomes clear that there is no reason, in general, for expecting any sort of significant correspondence between the saving that relates to one definition of income, and the investment that relates to another. The different definitions of income move on quite different planes, and take different things into account. It is only between those sorts of saving and investment which spring from the same definition of income that we can expect to find a correspondence worth studying.

This first remark clears out a good many of the possible issues, but it still leaves us with quite a wide choice. We have still to decide whether to concern ourselves with the saving and investment which correspond to Income No. 1, No. 2, or No. 3; and whether to consider them *ex ante*

[1] See below, Chapter XXIII.

N

or *ex post*. Now I do not believe that the first decision is a very important one; we can start with any sort of approximation to the concept of
income, and we shall find things working out very similarly. But the
ex ante-ex post distinction is of course very important.

For brevity I shall confine myself here to those definitions of saving
and investment which correspond to Income No. 1. If we were to
start with, say, Income No. 3, the whole argument would be exactly
duplicated; but I think I may leave the reader to test this for himself.
If we start from Income No. 1, we define a person's saving (*ex ante*) as
the difference between his actual consumption during the week and
that level of consumption which would leave the money value of the
prospect he can expect to have at the end of the week the same as it
actually was at the beginning. If we take the week to be short enough
in length for the accretion of interest during the week to be negligible,
we may say that his saving is the increment in the money value of his
prospect planned to accrue during the week. Further, if we neglect
any changes in his prospect due to changes in his own personal earning
power, his saving may also be written as the planned increment in the
value of his property. All this is saving *ex ante*; saving *ex post* will be
the realized increment in the value of his property.

Savings *ex post* may be aggregated for all members of the community.
Their sum total will equal the total increment in the money value of
all persons' property which accrues during the week. Now property
has three forms: it may consist of physical goods (real capital), or securities, or money. But money, as we have seen, is either a physical good,
like gold, or a security, like notes or bank deposits. Our three categories
thus reduce to two. Further, securities are simply debts of various sorts
from one person (or concern) to another; and therefore, when all property is aggregated, they cancel out. Total savings *ex post* therefore
reduce to nothing else but the increment in the value of physical
capital; which is what seems to be meant by investment—of course
investment *ex post*.

Equality between saving *ex post* and investment *ex post* is thus
necessarily assured, for the community taken as a whole. But this
equality is a mere truism—it expresses nothing else but the mere fact
that all the capital goods in the economy belong to somebody. And that
is not a consideration of very profound theoretical significance.

The relation between saving *ex ante* and investment *ex ante* is more
interesting. By analogy, investment *ex ante* must equal the planned
increment in the value of physical capital, including both producers'
goods and durable consumers' goods. Now, following out this definition,
a particular person (or concern) can plan to save more than he plans
to invest, only if he plans to acquire, during the week, property of the

non-material kind—property in securities. Similarly, he can only plan to invest more than he plans to save if he intends to diminish his holding of securities; which, as we have seen, includes issuing securities, creating securities against himself. Thus the difference between planned saving and planned investment is the difference between the planned demand and planned supply for securities in general—including money.

Now it will be remembered that, under the special assumptions of the model with which we are working throughout, the 'week' is a period of temporary equilibrium, characterized by the condition that all demands and corresponding supplies are equal during the week. This rule applies to the demand and supply for securities. The planned demands and supplies for securities are supposed to be at once made actual on the market on 'Monday'. They are therefore necessarily equal for the community as a whole. Therefore, during the week, not only does saving *ex post* equal investment *ex post*; saving *ex ante* also equals investment *ex ante*.[1]

This equality between the *ex ante* magnitudes is not, however, a mere truism, like the equality between the *ex post* magnitudes. It is an expression of the equation of supply and demand for securities; and that, as we have seen, forms part of the system of equations determining the price-system. I do not think, however, that we ought to admit any particular connexion between this savings-investment equation and the rate of interest. There is, as we have seen,[2] a sense in which the rate of interest is particularly determined by the equation of supply and demand for securities—excluding money; but the equation here is one including money, and that has no special connexion with the rate of interest. Since the equation of supply and demand for securities, including money, is the same thing as the equation of supply and demand for real goods in general (producers' goods *plus* consumers' goods *plus* factors of production);[3] if we are to allow ourselves to connect the savings-investment equation with the determination of any particular part or aspect of the price-system, it is the general price-level which ought to be chosen. Still, when we remember how the whole system is interconnected, this relating of particular equations to particular prices becomes rather idle.

Thus, during the week, savings *ex ante* equal investment *ex ante*; but this is a property of the week, and not of any longer period. The *ex post* magnitudes will be equal whatever period we take, but the *ex ante* magnitudes will only be necessarily equal if plans are consistent. Equality between savings *ex ante* and investment *ex ante* is then one of the conditions of equilibrium over time. In conditions

---

[1] At the same time, there is of course no necessity for the *ex ante* magnitudes and the *ex post* magnitudes to be equal to one another.

[2] Cf. Chapter XII, above.

[3] Ibid.

of disequilibrium, it is perfectly possible for planned saving to exceed planned investment, if we look forward for a longer period than a week. And it is through the working of this inequality that the disequilibrium is likely to show itself. If an attempt is made to carry through the plans without readjustment, supplies of commodities will begin to exceed demands, and (so far as we can see at present) prices will tend to fall. Similarly, if planned investment exceeds planned saving, there will be a tendency for prices to rise.

What a tricky business this all is! In his *Treatise on Money*, Mr. Keynes told the world that savings and investment are only equal in conditions of equilibrium; that an excess of investment over saving means rising prices, and vice versa. In his *General Theory*, he told us that savings and investment are always equal, and that this is a mere identity or truism, without significance for the determination of prices. As far as I can make out, there are relevant and important senses in which all these four statements are each of them right and each of them wrong.

B. Interest and the Calculation of Income.

1. Whichever of the three 'approximations' to the concept of Income we choose to use, the calculation of income consists in finding some sort of *standard* stream of values whose present capitalized value equals the present value of the stream of receipts which is actually in prospect. It is a standard stream in that it maintains some sort of constancy, as against the actual expected stream of receipts, which may fluctuate in any manner whatsoever. But the sorts of constancy involved in the three approximations are different. The standard stream corresponding to Income No. 2 is a constant stream in the arithmetical sense; it imputes identically the same sum of money value to each successive week. The standard stream corresponding to Income No. 3 is constant in real terms, so that the money values imputed to successive weeks will vary as the price-level is expected to vary. The standard stream corresponding to Income No. 1 will also vary in money terms if the rate of interest is not expected to be constant; it will be calculated in such a way as to make the capitalized money value of all future values (in the standard stream) constant from week to week.

But in each case we are broadly doing the same thing. We are replacing the actual expected stream of receipts by a standard stream, whose distribution over time has some definite standard shape. We ask, not how much a person actually does receive in the current week, but how much he would be receiving if he were getting a standard stream of the same present value as his actual expected receipts. That amount is his income.

If there is a rise in his expectation of some future receipts, the present value of his prospect will be raised, and it will become greater than the present value of his old standard stream. In order to restore equality it will be necessary to raise the standard stream, still keeping it to its old standard shape, but raising it throughout. Income will thus be increased.

When rates of interest vary, things are more complicated. For not only will the present value of the actual expected stream of receipts be changed, but the present value of the old standard stream will be changed too. In order to discover the effect on income we have to find which of these two present values is affected the more. A fall in interest rates will raise income if it raises the present value of actually expected receipts more than it raises the present value of the standard stream; a rise in interest rates will raise income if it lowers the present value of the standard stream more than that of the actually expected stream.

If we confine our attention to cases where the rate of interest is the same for loans of all durations (a simplification which is often or even usually legitimate in income calculations), this relation can be studied further graphically.

2. Any stream of values whatsoever has a capitalized value, which may now be regarded as a function of the rate of interest; this function may then be drawn out in the form of a curve. As it turns out, it proves most convenient to draw this curve in a slightly different form from that which would seem most natural at first sight. We shall measure the capitalized values along the horizontal axis,[1] but along the vertical we shall measure, not the rate of interest, but what may be called the *discount ratio*—the proportion in which a sum of money has to be reduced in order to discount it for one week. (If the rate of interest per week is i, then β, the discount ratio, equals $1/(1+i)$.)

Corresponding to the given expected stream of receipts, we have a capital-value curve RR, which will slope upwards because a rise in the discount ratio (a fall in the rate of interest) raises capitalized value. Corresponding to any particular level of income, we have a capital-value curve (dotted in the diagram) which shows the present value of the standard stream corresponding to that particular level of income (according to the definition of income we are using) at various discount ratios. Such a curve can be drawn for any level of income. If the discount ratio is OH, the present value of the prospective receipts is HA, and the level of income is that represented by the dotted curve SS, which passes through A.

---

[1] Adopting the convention, usual in economics, of putting the dependent variable on the horizontal axis.

If the discount ratio rises, A will move to the right along RR; and it will be evident from the diagram that this means moving on to a dotted curve representing a higher income, if, as we have drawn them, SS is more steeply inclined than RR—or, what comes to the same thing, SS is less elastic than RR. Everything thus depends upon the relative elasticities of the RR and SS curves.

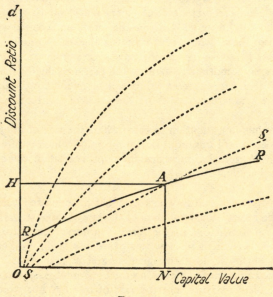

FIG. 23.

The capital value of a stream of payments $(x_0, x_1, x_2,..., x_\nu)$ is $x_0+\beta x_1+\beta^2 x_2+...+\beta^\nu x_\nu$. The elasticity of this capital value with respect to the discount ratio β is

$$\frac{\beta x_1+2\beta^2 x_2+3\beta^3 x_3+...+\nu\beta^\nu x_\nu}{x_0+\beta x_1+\beta^2 x_2+\beta^3 x_3+...+\beta^\nu x_\nu}$$

(for the elasticity of a sum is the *average* of the elasticities of its parts). Now when we look at the form of this elasticity we see that it may be very properly described as the *Average Period* of the stream; for it is the *average length of time for which the various payments are deferred from the present, when the times of deferment are weighted by the discounted values of the payments.* (The reader may perhaps be angry with me for appropriating the term 'Average Period' to this quantity, since he may have in his head what appears to be a very different meaning of the term. I hope to show at a later stage, however, that the meaning I am giving it is a fair extension of the traditional meaning.)[1]

It follows at once from all this that if the average period of the stream of receipts is greater than the average period of the standard stream with which we are comparing it, a fall in the rate of interest will raise the capital value of the receipts stream more than that of the standard stream, and will therefore increase income. But if the average period of the stream of receipts is less than that of the standard stream, it is a rise in the rate of interest which will increase income.

3. This test by average periods seems valid enough mathematically; but it looks curiously different from the common-sense test we should commonly employ. If a person's receipts are derived from the exploitation of a wasting asset, liable to give out at some future date, we should say that his receipts are in excess of his income, the difference between them being reckoned as an allowance for depreciation. In this case, if he is to consume no more than his income, he must re-lend some part of his receipts; and the lower the rate of interest is, the greater the sum he will have to re-lend in order for the interest on it to make up for the expected failure of receipts from his wasting asset in the future. Thus, if receipts are expected to decline in the future, income will be lower the lower the rate of interest; while in the opposite case of a person whose receipts are expected to expand in the future (who will have to borrow, or sell securities, if he is to live up to his income), income will be higher the lower the rate of interest.

Is it possible to reinterpret the test by average periods so that it shall agree with this common-sense test? It can be done in the following way.

Let us confine attention to the case where neither interest rates nor prices are expected to change, so that all three 'approximations' to the concept of income coincide, and the standard stream corresponding to any of them is a standard stream constant in money terms from week to week.

Remembering that the prospective stream of receipts and the standard stream from which income is calculated must have the same capitalized value, it follows that if the average period of receipts is greater than the standard average period, then the prospective stream must tend to be *below standard* in the near future, while somewhere in the more distant future it must compensate by being *above standard*. Looked at as a whole, it must have a rising tendency; as we may say, a *crescendo*. The

---

[1] See below, Chapter XVII. The reader may also find it rather surprising that an elasticity, usually supposed to be a pure number, independent of units, turns out to be equal to a length of time. This is a consequence of compound interest. The rate of interest for two years is not double that for one; so that time cannot be eliminated by considering proportional changes.

average period turns out to be nothing else but an exact method of measuring the *crescendo* (or *diminuendo*) of a stream of values.

What is in fact the average period of a stream of constant size and indefinite length, discounted throughout at the same rate of interest? It can easily be shown that it is equal to the reciprocal of the rate of interest, i.e. to the number of 'years' purchase'.[1] If the rate of interest is 5 per cent. per annum, the average period of a standard stream is 20 years. If the average period of any other stream comes out at more than 20 years, this means nothing else than that the stream has a *crescendo*; if it comes out at less than 20 years, the stream has a *diminuendo*. That is all the average period means.[2]

This way of measuring the trend of a stream of values can be used for any stream whatsoever; it seems to have more significance than any other from the point of view of economic theory. We shall come back to it again when we consider the effects of interest changes on the organization of production.

[1] For
$$\frac{\beta + 2\beta^2 + 3\beta^3 + \ldots}{1 + \beta + \beta^2 + \beta^3 + \ldots} = \frac{\beta}{(1-\beta)^2}\bigg/\frac{1}{1-\beta} = \frac{\beta}{1-\beta} = \frac{1}{i}.$$

[2] The best numerical definition for the *crescendo* of a stream of values is the rate of expansion of a stream, continuously expanding by the same proportion in every period, which has the same average period as the original stream. This rate of expansion is related to the average period by a simple formula. If P is the average period of a stream, i the rate of interest, and c the *crescendo*, so defined, then
$$c = i - \frac{1}{P}.$$

PART IV

THE WORKING OF THE DYNAMIC SYSTEM

Uncertainty and Expectation are the joys of life.
(CONGREVE, *Love for Love*.)

CHAPTER XV

THE PLANNING OF PRODUCTION

1. THE programme we have to carry out in this fourth and final part has been already decided. We have to take the dynamic system, whose general properties we studied in Part III, and put it through the same sort of analysis as we applied to the static system in Part II. The series of problems we have to discuss is therefore exactly parallel to the series we discussed in the earlier parts of this book. We have to consider again the position of the private individual, and to investigate the laws of his behaviour; only we have now more things to take into account. We have to consider the ways in which his conduct may be affected, not only by present prices, but also by interest rates, and also by price- and interest-expectations; we have to examine, not only his demands and supplies of commodities, as before, but also his demand or supply of securities (including that particular kind of security, which is money). We have to make a similar investigation for the case of the firm. Then, having established the laws of supply and demand for commodities, securities, and money, we have to bring these laws together, to give us laws for the working of the whole price-system. The only laws we can expect to find, in the first place, are the laws of the working of the price-system in any particular 'week'; and that is only the beginning of what we should like a dynamic theory to tell us. (However, even temporary equilibrium analysis of this sort yields several important and rather surprising conclusions when it is carefully carried out.) To penetrate beyond this point is very difficult; but we shall make an effort before concluding to see what can be said about the laws of development of the price-system through time.

The first thing to be done is to study the behaviour of the individual person and the individual firm; now there is something to be said for reversing the order of discussion we adopted in statics, and beginning with the firm. In practice, firms probably work out their production plans a good deal more fully than private individuals work out their expenditure plans; since we shall want, on one occasion or the other, to give a formal cut-and-dried analysis of the determination of a plan, it is better to give it for the case of a firm, where it is fairly realistic, than for the case of a private individual, where it is not very realistic. Having once become acquainted with the general principles of plan-determination from our analysis of the firm, we can then, when we come to the deal with the private person, take into account as much or as little of these general principles as seems fitting. The advantages of this procedure will become clearer as we go on.

2. Like other branches of economic dynamics, the dynamic theory of production has been the occasion of great controversy. Indeed, perhaps more than any others, the issues which here arise are the classical debatable issues; they are the great questions in the theory of capital which vexed economists in the past. To-day they have been overshadowed by other questions—probably more important questions. But, though overshadowed, they have not been settled; if it lies in our power to settle them, we ought not to refuse the task.

Even to-day, the great name in this department of economics is the name of Böhm-Bawerk. This is so, not because his doctrine is generally accepted (it was not generally accepted even in his own time, and it has still fewer supporters in ours), but because it is a challenge that has somehow to be met. Nearly every one who comes to the study of capital falls a victim to Böhm-Bawerk's theory at some stage or other.[1] The definition of capitalistic production as time-using production; of the amount of capital employed as an indicator of the amount of time employed; of the effect of a fall in interest on the structure of production as consisting in an increase in the amount of time employed; all these ideas give to the subject an apparent clarity which is, at first sight, irresistible. The theory stands up very well to the more obvious objections which can be made against it; yet, as one goes on, difficulties mount up. The definition of the 'time taken in production' gets harder and harder; and so most people find themselves driven, in the end, to abandon the theory, even if they have nothing much to put in its place.

The objections to this 'Austrian' theory have been forcefully

[1] The classical statement of Böhm-Bawerk's theory is of course his *Positive Theorie des Kapitales* (1889). It was translated into English by Smart, and, as I write, a revised translation by H. N. Gaitskell is announced to appear shortly. The section on capital in Wicksell's *Lectures* (vol. i) takes the same sort of treatment to a higher degree of refinement.

and repeatedly stated in a recent series of articles by Professor Knight. These articles have provoked a remarkable recrudescence of the old Böhm-Bawerkian controversy;[1] but the main issue is still left unsettled. The reader rises from a perusal of these papers with the feeling: 'Clearly Böhm-Bawerk was wrong; but there must have been something in what he said; you cannot construct such an elaborate theory as that out of nothing.' The core of truth in the Austrian theory needs to be discovered before we can really claim to have a satisfactory theory of capital.

The trouble is, I hope to show, that when we transcend the artificially simple cases (with which capital theory naturally began, but, even with Wicksell, never quite outgrew), the central propositions change their character rather markedly. The Austrian theory remains valid as a limiting case, though not a very important case. The general theory differs from Böhm-Bawerk's in some important respects.

3. As we have repeatedly seen, the decision which confronts any particular entrepreneur at any date (say on our 'first Monday') may be regarded as the establishment of a *production plan*. Written out in full, a production plan would look like this:

$$A_0, A_1, A_2, A_3, ..., A_n$$
$$B_0, B_1, B_2, B_3, ..., B_n$$
$$\cdot \quad \cdot \quad \cdot \quad \cdot \quad \cdot \quad \cdot$$
$$X_0, X_1, X_2, X_3, ..., X_n$$
$$Y_0, Y_1, Y_2, Y_3, ..., Y_n$$
$$\cdot \quad \cdot \quad \cdot \quad \cdot \quad \cdot \quad \cdot$$

$A, B,...$ are different kinds of inputs, $X, Y,...$ are different kinds of outputs, and the entrepreneur is supposed to make his plan for a period of n future weeks. An input is merely something which is bought for the enterprise, an output something which is sold. Thus, if the whole concern were to be wound up, and all its equipment sold off, this equipment could be regarded as an 'output' of the date at which the sale took place—all subsequent outputs being

---

[1] Of Professor Knight's articles, see particularly 'The Quantity of Capital and the Rate of Interest' (*Journal of Political Economy*, 1936). A general bibliography of the controversy is given in Kaldor, 'Annual Survey of Economic Theory' (*Econometrica*, 1937). It has been further continued by Knight and Kaldor in *Econometrica*, 1938.

zero. This idea allows us to think of the entrepreneur as planning ahead for a limited period (n weeks); for we regard the plant he plans to have left over at the end of that time as a particular kind of output (say Z_n), a kind which is only produced in the last week.

It will be observed that even if there is only one physical kind of output (say X), the production plan nevertheless includes a number of different outputs (X at different dates) which have now to be distinguished. The reader may now begin to understand why, in our static theory of the firm, we decided to pay such unusual attention to the case of a firm producing many kinds of products.

Just as the static problem of the enterprise is the selection of a certain set of quantities of factors and products, so the dynamic problem is the selection of a certain production plan from among the alternatives that are open. As in statics, the limitation on the choice of the entrepreneur is technical. There are a certain number of alternative production plans that are technically possible. If all inputs, and all outputs but one, are given in magnitude, this technical limitation (or production function) will give the maximum output possible on the remaining date; if all outputs, and all inputs but one, are given in magnitude, it will give the minimum input necessary on the remaining date.[1] Since he works under this limitation, the entrepreneur can only change from one production plan to another either (1) by substituting some amount of one output for some amount of another, (2) by substituting one input for another, (3) by increasing or diminishing one input and one output simultaneously. All changes in the production plan must be reducible to one or other of these 'elementary variations' or to some combination of them. All this exactly as in statics.

4. But now which will be the preferred production plan? In statics, we were content to think of the entrepreneur maximizing his surplus of receipts over costs; this caused no special difficulty. But when the problem is looked at dynamically, it becomes clear

---

[1] Once again, it is necessary that the given inputs and outputs should be consistent. Otherwise the odd output will not be positive, or even zero, and the odd input would have to be infinite. We have discussed all this before; see above, p. 85 note.

that the entrepreneur can expect, not a single surplus, but a stream of surpluses, going on from week to week. If two streams were such that every surplus in the one stream was greater than the corresponding surplus in the other stream, then there would be no question which stream was the larger. But if this condition is not fulfilled (and there is no reason why it should be fulfilled always, or even often), we need some criterion to enable us to judge whether one stream is to be reckoned larger than another.

The establishment of this criterion in general terms seems to have caused some economists a little difficulty; though there is really no reason why it should have done so. The criterion can be stated in several forms; but, properly considered, they all reduce down to the same thing.

The most fundamental way of stating the criterion is in terms of the capitalized value of the stream of surpluses—what we may call the capitalized value of the production plan. If we assume that the entrepreneur can borrow and lend freely at given market rates, and that he is only in business in order to get an income from it, then the preferred production plan must be that whose present capitalized value is the greatest.

We define the surplus of any week as the amount by which the value of output in that week exceeds the value of input in that week.[1] Thus, if prices and price-expectations are given, this surplus is determined as soon as the production plan is determined. And its present value is also determined if interest rates and interest-expectations are given.

The prospective net receipts of the entrepreneur in any future week may be defined as his anticipated surplus *minus* any charges (such as interest on debentures) which he may have to meet as a result of contracts entered into in the past. Since these charges are independent of his present decisions, they cannot be modified by any change in the plan. The capital value of these charges is a given magnitude, as soon as interest is given; thus the capital value of his prospective net receipts only differs from the capital value of his prospective surpluses by a constant, and will be maximized when that is maximized.

---

[1] It is, of course, perfectly possible that, in any particular week, the value of input will exceed that of output, so that the surplus becomes a deficit. This need not necessarily spell bankruptcy; it may only mean that investment is taking place, so that the deficit is expected to be matched by surpluses later on.

Now it is easy to show that any increase in the capital value of his prospective net receipts must always take the entrepreneur to a preferred position. If he is the head of a private business, so that his business receipts go directly into his private pocket, this is evident directly; any increase in that capital value will enable him to plan the same expenditures as before (on his private account) and still to have something left over. If he is the administrator of a company, it is perhaps less directly evident; but it is still true that any increase in the present value of the company's prospective net receipts will enable him to plan the same stream of dividends as before, and still have something left over—so that he will be able to pay a higher dividend at some date or other, whatever date seems convenient.

The same matter can be looked at another way—perhaps a more obviously realistic way—by making use of the concept of income. We have seen[1] that a person's *income* can be regarded as the level of a standard stream whose present value is the same as the present value of his prospective receipts. The same applies to a firm. Its income (or profit) is the level of a standard stream whose present value is the same as the present value of its prospective net receipts. Thus we have the relations

Net receipts = Surplus — Charges arising out of past contracts

Profit (or income) = Net receipts — Depreciation (or + Appreciation)

Once price- and interest-expectations are given, and the type of standard stream (i.e. definition of income) to be used is decided on, all these things are perfectly determinate. Now we know that when these things are given, any increase in the present value of a stream must raise the level of the standard stream corresponding to it.[2] Thus any increase of the present value of the stream of prospective net receipts must raise profits. We can either say that the entrepreneur maximizes his profits, or that he maximizes the present value of his prospective net receipts, or that he maximizes the present value of his prospective surpluses. All these tests come to the same thing; but it is the last of them (what we have called the present value of the plan) which is the most convenient analytically.

5. The problem of maximizing the present value of the production plan is formally identical with the problem of maximizing

---

[1] Above, p. 184.   [2] Ibid.

the surplus of receipts over costs in the static problem of the firm. Outputs of different dates are to be regarded as different outputs; inputs of different dates as different inputs; and beyond that there is only one little difference. If, in static conditions, an entrepreneur employed one extra unit of a factor, that began by reducing his surplus (the thing we supposed him trying to maximize) by an amount equal to the price of the factor. But if, in our new problem, we suppose an entrepreneur deciding to employ an extra unit of a factor at some particular date, it does not reduce the capitalized value of his surpluses (the thing he is now effectively trying to maximize) by the full price of the factor, not even by the full expected price of the factor. Future costs only enter into the present value of the plan at their *discounted* values; and the same is true of future receipts. Consequently, when we are adapting our static analysis, we must always replace the 'prices' of statics by discounted prices, in order to fit the dynamic problem. With these adjustments, the whole static theory of the firm still holds. We have nothing to do but translate.

The same conditions of equilibrium hold as in the static case. There are three kinds, corresponding to the three 'elementary' forms of variation. (1) The marginal rate of substitution between outputs of any two dates must equal the ratio of their discounted prices. (2) The marginal rate of substitution between inputs of any two dates must equal the ratio of their discounted prices. (3) The marginal rate of transformation of any input into any output must equal the ratio of their discounted prices.

The various equilibrium conditions which have been stated by earlier writers are all special cases of these general conditions. For example, (1) the often stated rule that the current rate of wages equals the discounted value of the marginal product of current labour is a special case of our third condition. Whenever the labour in question is engaged upon processes which take a definite (technically given) time to come to fruition, this condition is sufficient by itself to determine the demand price for labour. But it should be observed that this is not true generally.

(2) Wicksell's rule that the rate of interest equals the *relative* marginal productivity of waiting[1] appears as a special case of our first condition. It follows from that first condition that if the price of a product is not expected to change in two successive weeks,

---

[1] *Lectures,* i, pp. 172–84.

the marginal rate of substitution between outputs of these dates must equal the ratio in which money is expected to be discounted over the period between them. Consequently the expected rate of interest must equal the *proportion* in which a marginal unit of product is expected to be increased if it is deferred from one of these weeks to the next.

(3) Mr. Keynes's rule that 'short-period supply price is the sum of marginal factor cost and marginal user cost'[1] is a combination of our first and third conditions. Mr. Keynes assumes that it is only possible to increase current output by increasing current input (factor cost) and substituting current output for future output (user cost) in certain fixed proportions.

(4) Again, when dealing with what he calls the 'marginal efficiency of capital',[2] Mr. Keynes assumes that the increase in output made possible by a certain increase in input has to be divided in some given manner among future periods. Therefore the cost of increasing input by one unit has to equal the present value of the stream of output-increments made possible by the increase in input. This is what he means by equality between the rate of interest and the marginal efficiency of capital.

Cases of fixed proportions, such as these of Mr. Keynes's, are no doubt extremely common. There will very often be groups of outputs, and groups of inputs, within which no substitution is possible at all; and there will be input–output pairs which will be quite unrelated, in the sense that a small increase in input at date t_1 will not facilitate any increase in output at date t_2, while a small decrease in input at t_1 could not leave all other outputs unchanged, even if output at t_2 were abandoned altogether. Since such pairs have no marginal rates of substitution or transformation, they give rise to no equilibrium conditions by themselves, but only in combination.

However, as we found when we were concerned with statics, there is little to be gained by paying a great deal of attention to these cases of fixed proportions at this stage of our inquiry. At a later stage they will fit in quite easily, merely appearing as cases of complementarity.

6. The three sorts of conditions of equilibrium must be satisfied, for all the marginal substitutions and transformations that are

---

[1] *General Theory*, p. 67.   [2] Ibid., p. 135.

technically possible, if the production plan selected is to be that which is most profitable. They are *necessary* conditions, that is; in order that the present value of the plan should be a true maximum, stability conditions have to be satisfied too.

The stability conditions are the same in form as those we found for the static equilibrium of the firm. There must be (1) an *increasing marginal rate of substitution* between outputs; (2) a *diminishing marginal rate of substitution* between inputs; (3) a *diminishing marginal rate of transformation* of an input into an output. Further, corresponding to the static conditions that the surplus must be positive, we have a dynamic condition that the present value of the stream of surpluses must be positive.

Now these stability conditions necessarily cause all the same difficulties as the static conditions of which they are an extension. I do not think they cause any additional difficulties; but the old difficulties are not removed when we spread the production plan out through time. There is still a question about the size of the firm.

It will be remembered that in static analysis we were only able to get the sort of diminishing returns necessary for stable equilibrium under perfect competition, by postulating the existence of some fixed resources, not capable of being increased when variable factors are increased, the limitation of whose capacity should be capable of calling forth sufficiently diminishing returns to other factors. This was admittedly not very convincing; how does the situation look in dynamic terms?

It seems first of all necessary to distinguish between the cases (1) where the entrepreneur, at the date in question, has an already established business, (2) where he is a potential entrepreneur considering whether to set up a business, and, if so, what sort of a business to set up. In the first case, the necessary fixed resources seem to lie ready to our hand. The entrepreneur already has under his control a complex of goods, the equipment of the firm. Equipment includes land, buildings, machinery, tools, raw materials, goods in process, goods technically finished but not yet sold. Now it does seem reasonable to assume that this equipment will have acquired some organic unity, so that it cannot be exactly reduplicated at a moment's notice. It is the firm's legacy from the past, and, as such, does seem to constitute a block of 'fixed resources' in the relevant sense. We had best not reckon it among the inputs listed in the production plan; it is better to regard the various alternative production plans as alternative streams of (net) output which can be derived from this initial equipment. The fixity of initial equipment may thus provide the necessary diminishing returns, which will limit, if not the ultimate size of the firm, at least the rate at which it can expand. That, however, is sufficient for our immediate purpose.

This is all very well; but what about the case of the new firm? Here there is no legacy from the past to check expansion; is there anything to stop new firms from being planned on an indefinitely large scale—anything, that is, other than the imperfection of competition and the limitation of the market? Common sense replies that there must be something; even in industries which seem to approximate to the perfectly competitive type, we do not observe new firms starting up at once on a mammoth scale, but rather the opposite. There must be some obstacles still present, even obstacles which are particularly present in the case of new firms.

One of these obstacles is of course that which we have already mentioned when dealing with the static problem—the increasing difficulty of management and control as the firm gets larger. In a new firm, where everything has to be arranged from the start, and there is no possibility of proceeding by standing rules, this difficulty is particularly intense; so it does something to explain why firms usually start on a small scale.

Another obstacle, also present generally, but particularly present with new firms, is the element of risk. As the planned size of the firm increases, the possible losses become steadily greater; and people will usually become less and less willing to expose themselves to the chance of such losses. Now we have shown[1] that this increasing risk-factor may be represented as a shift in expected prices to the disadvantage of the entrepreneur (as the actual rate at which he can borrow may shift to his disadvantage in fact); evidently it is quite capable of bringing expansion to a stop.

On the whole, then, we need have rather less compunction about using the assumption of perfect competition in dynamic conditions than we had in statics. The elements which limit the size of firms in practice are very largely dynamic elements; it is therefore not surprising that static theory has had so much trouble over the matter.[2]

[1] Above, p. 125.
[2] This is not the place to pursue further the question of the relation between

7. One other characteristic of the production plan—which ought perhaps to be reckoned among the stability conditions—may be noted in conclusion. Not only is it necessary for the present value of the plan to be positive, but the entrepreneur must also expect the remainder of his plan to have a positive capitalized value at all future dates within the period for which he is planning. Clearly, it would not be worth his while to continue the plan after a date at which its capitalized value became negative, and he may be supposed to foresee this.

The importance of this condition will emerge fully at a later stage. If we write out an auxiliary stream of values equal to the expected capitalized values of the production plan at the ends of the 1st, 2nd, 3rd,... weeks from the planning date, and then calculate the present value of this auxiliary stream, the ratio of the present value of this stream to the present value of the plan itself is what we have called the average period of the stream of surpluses.[1] The characteristic just noted therefore implies that the average period of the stream of surpluses must be positive. The significance of this average period will come out when we discuss the effect of changes in interest on the production plan.

the restriction of production due to imperfect competition and the restriction of production due to risk; but I should like to express my opinion that there are several very important things to be said on that subject. (See Kaldor, 'Market Imperfection and Excess Capacity', *Economica*, 1935.)

[1] See above, p. 186.

CHAPTER XVI

PRICES AND THE PRODUCTION PLAN

1. THE equilibrium conditions and the stability conditions, which we worked out in the preceding chapter, have of course identically the same role as the parallel conditions in static theory. We have now discovered what are the principles which determine the character of the production plan adopted when prices, and price-expectations, and interest, and interest-expectations, are all given; the next thing to do is to use those principles to show what difference is made to the production plan when some of these stimuli are varied. It should be emphasized that the variations we shall be considering are still purely hypothetical variations; we are still on our 'first Monday'; we are inquiring into the difference between the actual production plan of a firm (including, as part of the plan, its actual current behaviour) and the plan which would have been adopted if the stimuli had been different.

Enough has already been said about the dynamic problem of the production plan to show that it is a mere translation of the corresponding static problem; this exact parallelism will spare us the trouble of working through the purely formal properties of technical substitution and technical complementarity all over again. We can take these formal properties for granted, and simply content ourselves with seeing how they look in dynamic terms. Even so, there are a good many things to discuss; the introduction of interest, in particular, presents a new and rather formidable complication; so I think we had better proceed rather circumspectly. I shall devote this chapter to discussing the effect on the production plan of changes in prices and changes in price-expectations; the effect of interest changes will be left over to the next chapter.

2. In order to convert the static theory of the firm into a dynamic theory of the production plan, we have found two amendments only to be necessary. Outputs and inputs due to be sold (or acquired) at different dates have to be treated as if they were different products or factors; actual prices have to be replaced, not merely by expected prices (when that is necessary) but by the discounted values of those expected prices. However, so long as we are neglecting the problems of interest changes, this second amendment need not trouble us greatly. If rates of interest can be taken as given, any change in an expected price will change its discounted value in the same proportion. The two of them will always move together; so for the present we can leave the whole matter of discounting out of account.

The standard propositions, which define the behaviour of a firm in static conditions, were most conveniently stated by supposing the price of one product to rise a little, and examining the effects of this on its general policy. These standard propositions would be directly translated into dynamic terms, if we supposed the expected price of some particular product at some particular future date to rise a little, say the price of commodity X expected to rule in the week starting t weeks from now. We can reckon this as a rise in the price of the product X_t. Applying our static rules, we learn, first, that there must be an increase in the planned output X_t. This may come about either through an increase of inputs, or a diminution of other outputs, or both. The inputs may be current or only planned; the diminished outputs may be of the same kind but differently dated $(X_{t'})$, or of a different kind physically (Y_t or $Y_{t'}$). Further, it is always possible that there may be some outputs which are complementary with X_t, so that they will be expanded with it; and it is possible (though less likely) that there may be some inputs which are regressive against X_t, so that they will be contracted.

This is all very well; nevertheless, the problem of what happens when there is a change in the price expected to rule for a particular commodity at a particular future date is not one we should much care to study. Cases do arise where the above analysis fits exactly; one sees it working on a large scale on such occasions as the announcement of a coronation; but these are not at all typical cases. We should prefer to be able to use our theory another way.

The changes in prices whose effects we analysed in statics were changes in real prices, real market prices; here too we should much prefer to be able to study the effects of changes in real prices instead of merely studying the effects of changes in expectations. Now there is one sort of change in market prices which can be studied by direct application of the standard propositions; current output is a particular output of a particular date, so that the effect of a change in the price of current output can be worked out by the same rules. But it should be observed that the change we can work out in this way is a change in the current price, *ceteris paribus;* that means, in the present context, a change with given price-expectations. The change in the current price must not be allowed to disturb price-expectations, not even expectations of what this same price will be in the future. That is to say, the change must be treated as a purely temporary change.

Thus, if we stick to direct translation of the main static rules, we are inhibited from considering any sorts of changes in market prices excepting those which are expected to be temporary. We are unable to make any allowance for the effect of the current situation on people's expectations. And yet, if our theory is to lead to useful results, we must take that effect into account.

3. It seems possible to classify three sorts of influences to which price-expectations may be subject. One sort is entirely non-economic: the weather, the political news, people's state of health, their 'psychology'. Another is economic, but still not closely connected with actual price-movements; it will include mere market superstitions, at the one extreme, and news bearing on future movements of demand or supply (e.g. crop reports), at the other. The third consists of actual experience of prices, experience in the past and experience in the present; it is this last about which we can find most to say.

For the purpose of our inquiry, changes in price-expectations which result from either of the first two sorts of influence have to be treated as autonomous changes. The current economic situation may perhaps react along these channels in mysterious and indirect ways; but we cannot hope to do anything about it. We must never forget that price-expectations are liable to be influenced by autonomous causes; otherwise we must leave it at that.

The effect of actual prices on price-expectations is capable of further analysis; but even here we can give no simple rule. Even if autonomous variations are left out of account, there are still two things to consider: the influence of present prices and the influence of past prices. These act in very different ways, and so it makes a great deal of difference which influence is the stronger.

Since past prices are past, they are, with respect to the current situation, simply data ; if their influence is completely dominant.

price-expectations can be treated as data too. This is the case we began by considering; the change in the current price does not disturb price-expectations, it is treated as quite temporary. But as soon as past prices cease to be completely dominant, we have to allow for some influence of current prices on expectations. Even so, that influence may have various degrees of intensity, and work in various different ways.

It does not seem possible to carry general economic analysis of this matter any farther; all we can do here is to list a number of possible cases. A list will be more useful if it is systematic; let us therefore introduce a measure for the reaction we are studying. If we neglect the possibility that a change in the current price of X may affect to a different extent the prices of X expected to rule at different future dates, and if we also neglect the possibility that it may affect the expected future prices of other commodities or factors (both of these are serious omissions), then we may classify cases according to the *elasticity of expectations*. I define the elasticity of a particular person's expectations of the price of commodity X as the ratio of the proportional rise in expected future prices of X to the proportional rise in its current price. Thus if expectations are rigidly inelastic (elasticity 0), we get the case of given expectations, the case we have been considering. If the elasticity of expectations is unity, a change in current prices will change expected prices in the same direction and in the same proportion; if prices were previously expected to be constant at the old level, they are now expected to be constant at the new level; changes in price are expected to be permanent. Obviously these two are the pivotal cases. But it is also useful to be able to distinguish the intermediate case of an elasticity of expectations less than 1 and greater than 0; and the two extreme cases, of an elasticity greater than 1 and a negative elasticity. The elasticity of expectations will be greater than unity, if a change in current prices makes people feel that they can recognize a trend, so that they try to extrapolate; it will be negative if they make the opposite kind of guess, interpreting the change as the culminating point of a fluctuation.

Although it is desirable for us to have all these possibilities in mind, it will clearly be impossible (and unnecessary) for us to work through all of them for every one of the various dynamic problems with which we shall be confronted. The principles which can be used for working out each case will soon become very evident. However, the second pivotal case (that in which the elasticity of expectations is unity) is of such obvious importance that we ought to make a practice of working out that case, whenever it is relevant. Let us begin by working it out with reference to the problem in hand.

4. If the entrepreneur's elasticity of expectations for commodity X is unity (changes in price are taken to be permanent), a rise in the current price of X will raise all expected prices of X in the same proportion. Now we discovered in statics that when the prices of a set of commodities change all in the same proportion, the set can be treated as a single commodity, and all rules of economic behaviour can be applied to it as if it were a single commodity. So here. If the elasticity of expectations is unity, a rise in the price of X currently quoted on the market must raise the planned output of X taken as a whole; there is no opportunity for substitution over time, and so, from one point of view, the time factor can be neglected. The rules for the working of the production plan are exactly the same as the rules for a firm's behaviour in static conditions; there must be an increase in the output of X, brought about either by increased inputs of one sort or another, at one time or another, or by substitution at the expense of other products (now other products in the physical sense, not outputs of the same physical product at different dates).[1]

The planned output of X must increase, when it is taken as a whole; but there is of course no reason why this increased output should be spread at all evenly over all periods. There are indeed special reasons for supposing the contrary. The additional output which can be produced in the current week, or planned for weeks in the near future, will usually be quite small. The initial equipment, which the entrepreneur possesses at the planning date, will generally contain, in a nearly finished form, most of the output which can be produced in the present and near future; since there can only exist a limited amount of these nearly finished goods, the flexibility of such output in response to any change of price will necessarily be small. But there is no such check on the expansion of distant future outputs; or rather the check gets less and less strong as the output recedes into the future.

[1] This proposition is of course the main justification for holding that there are some practical problems which can be adequately treated by static methods. The precise range of these problems will become clearer as we proceed.

There is, of course, nothing else but Marshall's doctrine of the
'short' and 'long' periods. It may be of some interest if we try to
explore it a little further.

5. The standard Marshall case can be put on a diagram in the
following way. Measuring future time along the horizontal axis,
and outputs along the vertical, suppose first of all that prices are

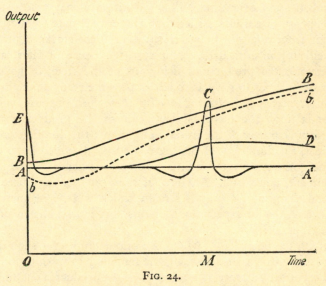

FIG. 24.

such that the entrepreneur plans a steady stream of output AA'.
Then if the price of his product were to rise, and to be considered
to have risen permanently, he would (so it appears) plan a stream
such as BB, which would rise while equipment was being adjusted
to the new conditions, but would probably settle down in the end
to a new 'equilibrium'.

In order to see whether this distribution over time of the
increments of output is a necessary distribution, let us consider
how the effect of a 'permanent' rise in price is made up. Elasticity
of expectations unity means that the current price of the commodity
and all its expected future prices rise in the same proportion; so
the total effect of the rise in price is compounded out of the effect
of a rise in the current price (expected prices unchanged) and of
the effects of a rise in each particular expected price (the current

price and other expected prices remaining unchanged). Let us consider, on the same diagram, what effect each of these partial changes has on the production plan.

Suppose first of all that there is an increase in the price of the commodity expected to rule at date *M* (other prices unchanged). The consequences of this may take one or other of two forms:

(1) It may be possible to meet the situation—at least in part—by substitution over time. This substitution may take place at the expense of outputs earlier than the critical date (reduction of output from now on, in order to accumulate stocks which can be sold at the critical date), or at the expense of later output (acceleration of production, using up of the stock of goods in process, in order to have as much as possible ready at the critical date), or perhaps of both. How far these methods are available depends upon the technical character of the product and the technical character of the initial equipment: the durability of the product, the durability of the unfinished goods which go to make it, the quantity of such unfinished goods available in the initial equipment, and so on. Anyhow, if these methods are used, the general shape of the output stream which will be planned as a result of a rise in expectations of this sort is that shown on the diagram as *ACA'*.

(2) On the other hand, where the opportunities for such direct substitution over time are small, the tendency to substitution may be overborne by a contrary tendency. If the product is not durable, and the materials which go to make it are not durable, there cannot be much substitution over time. Nevertheless, it is still quite possible that some durable equipment may be needed as an instrument in its production; production at any particular date will then be limited by the amount of that durable equipment which then exists. If the expected rise in price is large enough, it may become worth while to install more of this durable equipment in order to increase output at the critical date; but the existence of the equipment will then facilitate increased output at other dates as well. This is the case of complementarity over time. If outputs of different dates are complementary, the stream of planned outputs (induced by an expectation of a higher price at date *M*) will take the form *AD*.

The same distinction as holds for the effects of a rise in the price expected to rule at date *M* (*ceteris paribus*) holds also for the effects of a rise in the current price which is not expected to last. But when we proceed to work it out, it becomes evident why the effects of such a rise are often very small. In the complementarity case, the effects are almost necessarily nil. There will not be time to install the additional equipment before the price has relapsed to normal, and thus there will be no inducement to install it. In the substitution case, the effect is not so negligible; nevertheless, it is important to observe that substitution can now take place only one way. From the nature of the case, there can be no substitution in favour of current output at the expense of output earlier in date than itself; that is to say, there can be no piling up of stocks in anticipation of demand when no notice of that demand is given in advance. We are left with the possibility of accelerating production, of substituting current output for future (of course, some additional input may be required in order to enable production to be accelerated); consequently, either the effect on the output stream is nil, or the new stream takes the form EA'.

6. The total effect on the stream of planned outputs, which occurs when the rise in price is expected to be permanent, can be calculated by summing these partial effects. In the complementarity case, when the effect of the rise in the current price (*ceteris paribus*) is practically nil, and the rise in expected future prices induces a set of streams of output increments such as AD, it is easy to see that the total effect must be of the form BB—the curve we drew for Marshall's case. Each of the components is more or less of this form; consequently the resultant must be of this form too. In this case no exceptions can arise.[1]

In the substitution case, on the other hand, the constituent effects are much less simple in character; and the result of aggregating them is far from being so certain. The total effect on the output of any given date is made up out of things tending to

---

[1] It is indeed true that a rise in price expected to occur in some particular future 'week', and in that alone, may be insufficient to induce the laying down of the necessary equipment; while a rise expected to last some considerable time may be sufficient. If this occurs (doubtless it often will) the total effect may be greater than the sum of the constituent effects. But, though greater, it will still be of the same kind—as can be seen at once when we recollect that the length of our 'week' is arbitrary; by increasing its length we can diminish the importance of this discrepancy, without damaging the essentials of our argument.

increase that output, and things tending to diminish it. There is no reason why the resultant should follow any simple pattern, or even why the influences making for an increase in output should be dominant at every date. It is still likely, on the whole, that the main increase in output will come at dates in the further future; so that a resultant such as *BB* is still the most probable. But variations from the standard pattern are much more possible; thus the adoption of a production plan such as *bb*, with some outputs actually less than the corresponding outputs in the original stream, is not ruled out.

There is, however, one further property, which we discovered in our static theory of production, and which is relevant here. If the fixed resources of the enterprise are not very important, there is a tendency for the products it produces, and the factors it employs, to fall apart into two separate groups, within each of which complementarity is the dominant relation, though it is balanced by a high degree of transformability (which reckons as a kind of substitution) of one into the other.[1] As with other static propositions, the significance of this property transcends the static assumptions. If the 'initial equipment' of the firm does not play a very large part in limiting its possible production plans, complementarity among outputs (even complementarity over time) is a more probable relation than high substitutability. Therefore such abnormal effects as are represented in the curve *bb* are only likely to occur in those cases where the character of the initial equipment dominates the whole situation.

An instance which would seem to fit these requirements is to be found in the history of South African gold-mining in 1934–5. 'With higher prices, production on the Rand fell slightly, because it paid better to use existing plant to crush ores of a lower gold content rather than to extract the lower but richer ores. Meantime, new plant which has been erected will shortly enter into production.'[2] Whether this is a true explanation of what happened, is a disputed question into which I shall not enter. I am only concerned to point out that there is no theoretical reason why it should not have happened like that.

7. The general principles which govern the effects of changes in input prices are, of course, the exact counterparts of those which

---

[1] See above, p. 97.   [2] *World Economic Survey*, 1935–6, p. 246.

govern the effects of changes in output prices. If the price of a particular factor A rises, and is expected to remain constant at the higher level, the total planned input of that factor must be reduced. Once again there is no necessity for the reduction in input to be spread at all evenly over different future periods; and once again there are reasons (less powerful reasons than on the output side, but still reasons worth attending to) for supposing that the effect on the inputs planned for the more remote future will be greater than the effect on current input and input of the near future.

The main reason for this is still, as before, the specific character of the initial equipment. Initial equipment will consist, to a large extent, of goods at the intermediate stage of production; work has already been done on them with the object of converting them in the end into a certain kind of product; if this process is at all far advanced, the degree to which its ultimate object can be changed will be limited. We have seen how this characteristic puts a limitation upon the nature, and perhaps also the timing, of the nearer parts of the output stream which can be got from the given equipment; since further inputs will generally be needed in order to complete these particular outputs, it puts a limitation on the nearer parts of the prospective input stream as well. Even if input prices rise unexpectedly, it will pay to finish processes which have been started but not finished, so long as the rise in input prices is not very large; even though it may sometimes be possible to find a middle way between pure continuance of the preceding plan and complete cessation of processes, it will take some time before the entrepreneur has a really free hand to deal with the new situation.

When the change under consideration is a fall in the price of a factor, the same thing holds, in general; but there is now a new possibility. An entirely new process of production may be started (either through a new firm being set up, or perhaps through a new process being started by an old firm—we may reckon it as a new process if it is not very intimately connected with the preceding operations). But even a brand-new process of this sort is liable to be affected by technical rigidities—which are, indeed, nothing else but an expression of that complementarity over time, the tendency towards which we previously noted. It is not that the time-shape of the new input stream is a pure technical datum; but the technical factors in its make-up are likely to be very important. Now it is, of course, quite possible for technical factors to induce input streams of any conceivable shape; the amounts of inputs needed at first may be very large, and they may then fall off; or they may be very small at first, and then increase. But, as a matter of general experience, there is generally a peak rate of input at some stage or another, and the peak rate generally occurs after the first beginning of the process. (We mark this in common speech by saying that most processes require a stage of 'preparation' before they can get going.) The point is really technological in character, rather than economic; but its economic consequences are so important that a good economic theory needs to find a place for it.

Marshall's doctrine of the short and long periods has familiarized us with the notion of lags on the output side; it is a pity that the corresponding lags on the input side have not received more attention. They are closely connected with some of the major social problems that concern the economist—unemployment and the intractability of unemployment; in this direction above all a theory which leaves out the probability of input lags is likely to be gravely misleading.

CHAPTER XVII

INTEREST AND THE PRODUCTION PLAN

1. WE now approach the really controversial question. So far as the effects of price-changes on the production plan were concerned we had no new major principles to enunciate; the important things in that field have been familiar since the time of Marshall, at least. In the theory of interest-changes, on the other hand, there is no such body of doctrine which is settled and easily acceptable; there is a 'classical' theory (that of Böhm-Bawerk), but its validity is widely questioned; there is a sketch of an opposition theory (put forward by Professor Knight and his followers), but the opposition is largely unresolved; the field is therefore open for us to try to discover a new theory, which shall fit these jarring elements into their places.

I believe I have discovered such a theory, and I propose to set it out in this chapter. Some inkling of that theory may be present to the reader's mind already, since the investigations we have lately been engaged on have been set out in such a way as to lead up to this culmination. For example, the effects of price-changes on the plan were set out with such elaboration, not for their own sake (the really important results in that field being already familiar), but in order to lead up to the analysis of interest-changes. We have only to apply the same method to interest-changes, and we shall find the solution in our hands.

The reason why the theory of interest-changes is so much more difficult than the theory of price-changes is this. When we are dealing with prices it is possible to proceed directly to the most interesting case—the case of a change in prices which is expected to be permanent. (We saw why this is: a permanent change in prices is equivalent to a proportional change in current prices and price-expectations, so that we become entitled to use the *static* convention of treating commodities due to be bought or sold at different dates as the same commodity.) When we are dealing with interest rates, however, we cannot employ the same convenient simplification. A change in interest rates which is expected to be permanent implies a proportionate change in the discount ratio *per week* for loans of all durations; and this does not lead to a proportionate change in discounted prices—the prices which are

P

relevant to the determination of the plan. It is true that there is a systematic change in discounted prices, but it is not a proportionate change; the discounted prices of the outputs and inputs further ahead in time are regularly affected *more* than the discounted prices of the nearer outputs and inputs. As a consequence of this property, we cannot proceed directly to the important propositions in interest theory by the application of any static principles which are known to us. The only possible line of approach is to proceed by splitting up the general change in interest rates into a number of particular changes in particular rates (just as we split up the general change in prices and price-expectations into a number of particular changes in expectations). When we were dealing with prices we got some illumination from this splitting-up, even though it was not strictly necessary; here it is the only line of attack which we have open.

2. Let us begin by supposing that a different rate of interest is fixed on the market for loans of each relevant duration; and let us inquire, first of all, what happens when *one* of these rates is varied. All other rates of interest are to be supposed unchanged, and (of course) all prices and price-expectations to be unchanged.

If it is the rate of interest for loans of t weeks which varies, this will affect the discounted prices of all outputs due to be sold in the $(t+1)$th week from the planning date, and the discounted prices of all inputs due to be acquired in that week. All the other discounted prices will be unaffected.

A fall in the rate of interest for loans of t weeks will thus raise the discounted prices of X_t, Y_t,... A_t, B_t,... (the outputs and inputs planned for the week starting t weeks ahead). The most natural effect of this would be to increase the planned outputs X_t, Y_t,..., and to diminish the planned inputs A_t, B_t,.... This would involve, as a counterpart, either an increase in the inputs planned for other weeks, or a decrease in the outputs, or both.

Since, however, the increase in the output of X_t (due to the rise in its discounted price) may take place at the expense of Y_t, or may stimulate an increased demand for the contemporaneous inputs A_t, B_t,... (and similarly for other outputs and inputs), it is not absolutely certain that the direct effect in favour of a particular output (or against a particular input) may not be offset by an indirect effect working in the opposite direction. Consequently it is not absolutely certain that any particular output of the date in question will be increased, nor that any particular input will be diminished. Cases are conceivable in which the reaction on a particular output or particular input may go the opposite way. But since all the outputs and inputs of the group we are considering are contemporaneous, a change in the rate of interest will change all their discounted prices in the same proportion; and the familiar rule about treating commodities whose prices change in the same proportion as a single commodity will hold here. It is true that when we try to lump together a set of inputs and outputs, so as to treat them as a single commodity, we must remember that inputs and outputs have what amounts to a different *sign* (the rules applying to inputs are the reverse of the rules applying to outputs). This does not prevent the rule of treating them as a single commodity from applying just the same; only it is to the *difference* between the value of the outputs and the value of the inputs that the rule applies. The absolutely definite rule, which gives without any exception the effect of a fall in the rate of interest for loans of t weeks, is simply this: the surplus planned for the $(t+1)$th week must be increased.

This principle holds quite generally; it offers us a convenient shorthand which will be of use in our further investigations. So long as price-expectations are given, any change in rates of interest will change the discounted prices of *contemporaneous* outputs and inputs in the same proportion. Consequently, throughout our whole discussion of interest-changes, we can lump contemporaneous outputs and inputs together, whenever we choose to do so. We can simplify down the problem of the production plan, and regard it merely as the problem of choosing the most profitable stream out of a set of possible streams of surpluses; the list of possible streams being given by technical conditions, and converted into value terms by the assumption of given prices and given price-expectations. The effect of interest-changes can then be regarded as consisting in substitution among surpluses, using this as a shorthand expression for substitution and transformation among the outputs and inputs, from which the surpluses are built up. The discount ratio for t weeks (the proportion in which money has to be reduced in order to discount it for t weeks) has then to be regarded as the 'price' of the surplus accruing in the $(t+1)$th week. If this discount ratio rises, that is to be treated as a rise in the 'price' of the corresponding surplus. Thus the case we have been discussing can be summed up by saying that there must be a rise in the surplus planned for the $(t+1)$th week; that this must take place by substitution at the expense of other surpluses (it is only possible for one surplus to be expanded if others are contracted);[1] though it is possible for a limited number of other surpluses to be complementary with the $(t+1)$th surplus, in which case they will expand too.

3. When the theory of the effect of a particular change in interest is set out in this way, it is fairly easy to generalize it so as to give the effect of a general shift in interest rates. If rates of interest per week fall for loans of all periods, the discount ratios (that is to say, the 'prices') corresponding to all future surpluses will be raised; and this in itself induces a direct tendency for substitution in favour of future surpluses, against the current surplus. Nevertheless, the change in question is not a mere proportional shift in all the 'prices' of future surpluses; each 'price' is affected more than any of the 'prices' earlier in the series than itself, less than any later 'price'. Each surplus experiences a double pull; the rise in its own 'price' causes substitution in its favour, the rise in other 'prices' usually causes substitution against it. However, the later it comes in the series, the stronger is the pull working in favour of expansion, and the less strong is it possible for the pull making for contraction to be. Thus we should expect to find the greatest expansion in those surpluses which are farthest away in time, and the greatest contraction in those surpluses nearest in time. The whole effect on the stream of surpluses may be expressed by saying that it is given a tilt; it is lowered at one end and raised at the other; it is rotated, as it were, about some point in the middle.

Since a surplus can be expanded, either by an expansion of the corresponding outputs or by a contraction of the corresponding inputs, the effect of this tilt on the output and input streams which compose the plan would be as follows. Output streams will be tilted upwards to the right, like this

$$X_0, X_1, X_2, X_3, ..., X_n$$

(just in the same way as the stream of surpluses itself would be

---

[1] Expansion of a deficit to be regarded as contraction of a surplus.

tilted). But input streams would be tilted in the opposite direction

$$\overset{\uparrow}{A_0}, A_1, A_2, A_3, ..., \underset{\downarrow}{A_n}.$$

The way in which the tilting of the surpluses would be divided between output streams and input streams would depend upon technical conditions.

Now it will be remembered that we have encountered this phenomenon of tilting, in output streams, before. The effect of a rise in the price of a particular output, when that rise was expected to be permanent, was also to tilt the output stream upwards (compare the curve *BB* in the diagram on p. 207). But that tilt was due to a very different cause from this. In itself, an expected permanent rise in the price of output gives an equal stimulus to output at all periods; only the response to the stimulus is likely to be greater in the farther future than in the nearer, owing to technical rigidities and the specificity of initial equipment. Here, the fall in the rate of interest gives a greater stimulus to the increase of output at more distant future dates; it is not the technical rigidities that cause the tilt; it is the very nature of interest itself.

However, technical rigidities and complementarities will play their part here too. Although there is a stimulus to the reduction of current output, it is not very likely that that stimulus will be effective, since current output is largely predetermined. Even the stimulus towards increasing current input may be rather ineffective, for the similar reasons which we set out in the last chapter; the main weight of the increase in planned input may well come in the *middle* future. The precise distribution over time of the new production plan depends upon technical conditions, for they decide when it will be possible to increase the futurity of output, and diminish the futurity of input. It is not possible to lay down any hard and fast rule about the output or input of any given date (or even the surplus of any given date); all we can say is that there must be an upward tilt to the stream of surpluses, in some broad sense or other.

Can we give that broad sense an exact definition?

4. What we want to find is a numerical index to the character of the plan, which can be relied upon to change in a given direction when the rate of interest varies; though we may perhaps allow ourselves to be content with an index whose direction of change is almost reliable (in most of these matters we cannot hope to exclude rare exceptions, similar to the case of the backward-sloping demand curve).

It was the search for such an index which led Böhm-Bawerk and his followers to put forward their 'average period of production' or 'average period of investment'. In the simple cases they dealt with it seemed natural to think of a particular unit of current input giving rise to a finite stream of future outputs at determinate dates in the future. After a certain time the 'intermediate products' (or, as we might say, equipment) which result directly from the initial input will be worn right out or have passed finally into finished output. By averaging the lengths of time for which it is necessary to wait for the finished outputs due to the initial input, we get the Austrian 'average period of production'.

But what sort of an average is it? What are the weights? It might have been thought that this matter would have received some attention, yet it has received surprisingly little. So far as one can judge, the weights appear to be taken as quantities of output, or, at the furthest, values of output.

When the 'average period' is understood in either of these senses it has to meet crushing objections. Professor Knight has shown how impossible it is to identify a finite series of outputs of this sort, which can be imputed to any particular current input. It is ordinarily intended that current input shall be succeeded by an indefinite stream of future inputs, giving rise to an indefinite stream of future outputs. It is not possible to distinguish particular outputs out of this stream as being 'due' to current input. If current input were withdrawn, there would have to be some reduction of future output (provided future inputs are not to be increased); but this reduction might take place at one time, or at another, or be spread in different ways over different future dates.

Nor is it possible to evade this difficulty by abandoning the attempt to isolate a stream of outputs which can be imputed to any particular input, and concentrating attention on the production plan of the firm as a whole. There is no reason why that production plan should have any sort of end which is significant for this purpose; inputs are planned to succeed inputs, outputs outputs, just as far ahead as the entrepreneur cares to look.

Therefore the Austrian 'period' will not do; nevertheless, Böhm-Bawerk was not talking complete nonsense. His theory was valid enough for the cases he was considering; it ought to be possible to find a generalized concept which will meet Professor Knight's objections, and will yet include Böhm-Bawerk's argument as a special case.

We ourselves need not go far to find such a concept; we have it in our hands already. We have already, in the course of our argument, come across an average period which is proof against these objections. We shall proceed to show that it was this which the Austrians were looking for.

If we take the expected stream of surpluses and deficits (the differences between value of output and value of input in successive periods), and calculate its average period by *our* rule for calculating the average period of a stream—weighting by discounted values— we have something which at once looks more promising than the Austrian 'period'. On this definition, even a stream of indefinite length will have a finite average period; therefore we need not trouble ourselves with attempting to discover the future outputs imputable to current input. We can concentrate attention on the average period of the stream of surpluses—that is to say, the average period of the plan as a whole.

Further, it will have become evident, throughout our investigations of this chapter, that it is always discounted values, and never undiscounted values, which are relevant to the decisions of entrepreneurs. Undiscounted values of outputs or inputs at different dates are never compared by an entrepreneur when he makes his decisions; consequently any measure into which these quantities enter cannot be expected to behave in a determinate manner, or indeed to lead anywhere at all.

But, so it will appear, our own measure has to meet one apparently fatal objection. When the rate of interest changes, even if the production plan is not changed at all, our average period will be changed. A fall in the rate of interest will raise the discounted values of the more distant future surpluses; it must therefore almost necessarily raise the average period, even if no inputs or outputs are varied. Since we want to use the average period as a measure of changes in the plan, this sort of change in the period is entirely irrelevant for our purposes.

The average period of a stream (so, it will be remembered, we discovered at an earlier stage of our work)[1] is a satisfactory index of the time-shape of the stream, only when it is calculated at a *given* rate of interest. The same stream will have a whole series of different average periods, arrived at by using different rates of interest in the calculation. If the average period changes, without the rate of interest having changed, it must indicate a change in the stream; but if it changes, when the rate of interest changes, this need not indicate any change in the stream at all.

Consequently, even when we are considering the effect of changes in the rate of interest on the production plan, we must not allow the rate of interest which we use in the *calculation* of the average period to be changed.[2] What we must do is to start with a certain rate of interest, a certain production plan drawn up in view of that rate, and an average period calculated from this production plan at this rate of interest. Then we must suppose the rate of interest to fall, and the production plan to be varied in consequence. Finally, we must calculate the average period of the new plan, using the same rate of interest in its calculation as before—that is to say, the old rate of interest. Then our proposition is that the new average period, calculated in this way, must be longer than the old. A fall in the rate of interest lengthens the average period.

5. I do not know any very simple way of proving this proposition; the easiest I have been able to discover is the following. If we take the stream of surpluses which would be planned at the old rate of interest $(S_0, S_1, S_2,..., S_n)$, and compare it with the stream which would be planned at the new rate $(S_0', S_1', S_2',..., S_n')$, we can identify a *marginal stream*

$$S_0'-S_0, \ S_1'-S_1, \ S_2'-S_2, \ ..., \ S_n'-S_n$$

consisting of the differences between the corresponding surpluses,

[1] See above, p. 186.
[2] This rather curious procedure may be made clearer by an analogy. If we want to measure the effect of a rise in prices on the output of an industry, we have in practice (since the industry's output is not homogeneous) to weight the various sorts of products by their prices. But if we do this, then, although prices will have changed in the second situation, we must still continue to use the same price-weights; otherwise our calculation will merely register the change in receipts (which would have risen even if there had been no change in output), not the change in output at all.

proper attention being paid to sign. The new stream can then be thought of as being formed by adding the marginal stream to the old stream. It can easily be shown from the formula for an average period[1] that so long as they are calculated at the same rate of interest, the average period of the new stream is the average of the average period of the old stream and the average period of the marginal stream. More precisely, if P is the average period of the old stream and C its capital value at the planning date; if p, c are the average period and capital value of the marginal stream; then the average period of the new stream $= \dfrac{CP+cp}{C+c}$. This method of compounding average periods holds quite generally.

Now consider the nature of the particular marginal stream which is planned when there is a small fall in the rate of interest. It is such that at the old rate of interest it would just not have paid to undertake it; but when the rate of interest falls a little, it just does pay to undertake it.[2] Its capital value must therefore be negative at the higher rate, and positive at the lower rate. But since the fall in the rate of interest may be made as small as we like, these two values can be brought as near together as we like. c, the capital value of the marginal stream, can thus be made as near as we like to o.

The quantity cp, on the other hand, is definitely positive, and definitely finite. We saw in an earlier chapter that the product of the average period of a stream by its capital value equals the capital value of an auxiliary stream formed by capitalizing, in each successive week, the items in the stream of surpluses which remain over after that week.[3] We saw too that every item in this auxiliary stream must be positive (otherwise it would never pay to go through with the production plan implied in the stream); consequently the capital value of the auxiliary stream must be positive.

Thus, when we apply the formula given above to the calculation of the average period of the new stream, we can neglect the term c,

---

[1] See above, p. 186.

[2] Our *marginal stream* has something in common with the 'marginal unit of investment', familiar in the works of other writers. But it should be observed that there is no theoretical necessity for the marginal adjustment to involve any decrement or increment in the *current surplus*; the adjustment in the plan may relate entirely to the future.

[3] See above, p. 201.

but the term cp must not be neglected. The new average period therefore becomes

$$\frac{CP+cp}{C} = P+\frac{cp}{C}$$

and this is necessarily greater than P.

I think this is a satisfactory proof of the proposition; an alternative mathematical proof, in which I should myself place rather more reliance, is, however, given in the Appendix.[1]

6. We can now see just where it was that Böhm-Bawerk went wrong. He was quite right to conceive of the process of capitalistic production as being essentially a process in time, a process in which outputs are characteristically produced at later dates than those at which the inputs which give rise to them are utilized. Starting from this conception, and wishing to bring out as clearly as possible the fundamental nature of this production, he naturally concentrated attention on what seemed to be its simplest case: the case where all the input is utilized at one given date, and all the output comes to fruition at another given date. There is no objection to this. For purposes of elucidating the nature of capitalistic production, the standard Austrian cases (storing wine and planting trees) are distinctly illuminating. But when he proceeded to work out the theory of this simple case, he reached a result which is valid in that case, but does not generalize in the sort of way in which it might have been expected to generalize. If an entrepreneur possesses a quantity of wine already laid down, or a quantity of trees already planted, it is quite true that a fall in the rate of interest may induce him to postpone the completion of the process to a later date than that which he would otherwise have planned. There is nothing the matter with the Austrian theory here. Nevertheless, consideration of this case very naturally suggested conclusions which look as if they ought to be true generally, though in fact they are not true generally. In this simple case there is only one term in the anticipated stream of surpluses—the value of the product at the date of fruition; therefore it does not

---

[1] In the first edition of this book, I was worried by a slight discrepancy between the above argument and the corresponding mathematical proof. I have since discovered the reason for the discrepancy, which was another consequence of my error about 'extreme complementarity'. It has accordingly been removed in the version given on p. 328 below.

matter what weights are used in calculating the 'average period';
on any system of calculation, the 'average period' of this rudi-
mentary 'stream' must equal the actual period of production, the
actual length of time which must elapse before the process is
completed. Having got to this point (and there is no error in the
argument we are discussing up to this point), it was almost inevitable that an error should be made. It was too tempting to jump
to the conclusion: that because, in the first case considered, the
effect of a change in interest was to change the actual length of
time elapsing between input and output, so something of the same
kind must be generally true. In this way, arguing from analogy,
the Austrians built up their 'average period'—a real length of time,
a technical characteristic of the productive system, assembled out
of the year of agriculture, the five-year life of a machine, the twenty-
year life of a ship, and so on. But the argument from analogy was
treacherous; they argued, not from a representative case, but from
an exceptional case; save in this exceptional case, the true average
period (there must be a true average period, or the original Austrian
argument could not have been valid, as it is valid) is a mere index
of the tilting of the plan; it is not a real length of time at all.

The absolute length of the true average period has no significance
whatsoever; it depends only in part upon the character of the
production plan; it will be lengthened and shortened in an entirely
arbitrary manner according as we calculate the average period of
the same plan at different rates of interest. Change in the average
period is important, but not the length of the period itself. The
average period measures nothing else but the *crescendo* of the plan;
and that has nothing to do with the technical methods of production employed.

This complete lack of connexion between the average period of
the plan (when it is properly defined) and the technical methods of
production follows at once from the way in which we have
established our fundamental proposition; but it may still be useful
to press the point home by working out a particular illustration.[1]
Suppose that the production undertaken by a particular firm consists simply in the simultaneous carrying out of a number of quite

[1] I borrow this illustration from Kalecki, 'The Principle of Increasing Risk'
(*Economica*, 1937). Mr. Kalecki seems to regard the situation in question as
being more typical of the nature of the general productive process than I should
regard it myself; however, we need not quarrel about that, since my theory
covers his case perfectly well.

separate processes, each of which takes n weeks from first to last. Suppose (initially) that the firm is in stationary equilibrium, with mn of these processes being carried on together; m new processes are started every week, to replace the m processes which are finished at the beginning of the week; thus the streams of total inputs and total outputs are both constant over time. The firm contents itself with no more than mn processes for reasons of risk; risk-coefficients increase as the scale of output expands; the entrepreneur declines to undertake extra processes, because their capitalized value (allowance being made for risk) would be negative. Now suppose that the rate of interest falls; the capitalized value of a new process will then be raised; and it may become profitable to undertake some of these extra processes, which were not profitable previously. Now there is absolutely no reason why the new processes should not have identically the same technical character as the old; nevertheless, in spite of that, just because they are new processes, undertaken only because the rate of interest has fallen, their inception must raise the average period of the plan. Previously to the fall in the rate of interest, the planned stream of surpluses was expected to remain constant through time; when the rate of interest falls, the current surplus is diminished, some later surpluses are increased; the stream is given a *crescendo*.

7. We have been very much occupied in this chapter with purely formal properties; looking back over what I have written, I cannot help feeling a little apologetic about it, since I fear I may have laid myself open to the charge of having done nothing but state simple things in a complicated way. However, the justification for what we have been doing (even if it is a little pointless in itself) lies in the present state of capital theory; we cannot hope to banish the spectre of Böhm-Bawerk (so far as it needs to be banished) until we have explained where he went wrong. I do not think it is possible to do this with less elaboration, if we are to do justice to the perfectly sound elements in his theory, and to recognize what a nasty trap it was into which the poor man fell!

Still, once the Austrian theory is put behind us, the only important thing which emerges is the general conclusion (which can be stated clearly enough for nearly all purposes without any of this rigmarole about average periods) that changes in the rate of interest affect the 'tilt' or *crescendo* of the production plan. All possible effects of the rate of interest on the production plan can be summed up in this way; and, as a matter of formal theory, that is all that need be said.

Yet there is one further point we ought to make in conclusion: a point of much greater practical importance than those with which we have been labouring. So long as we are concerned with movements in rates of interest which fall within the ordinary range of such movements (say between 2 per cent. and 7 per cent. per annum), the effects of such changes on the discounted prices of outputs or inputs due for dates in the near future will be very slight. Very often they will be slight enough for the business man to be able to neglect them altogether; and it is only in special cases that they are likely to have much appreciable effect on business policy. But this same principle holds at the other extreme; when an output or input is planned for a date very far in the future, its discounted price becomes extremely sensitive to changes in the rate of interest. Consequently, the more of these distant outputs or inputs the plan contains, the more sensitive to interest it will be; if entrepreneurs' plans only extend into the near future (they are 'living from hand to mouth'), the interest rate will have little effect on them; if they are looking forward a long way, interest becomes very important.

The length of time for which an entrepreneur will be prepared to plan ahead depends partly upon technical conditions (in some kinds of business it is more necessary to plan ahead than in others), but it also depends, in a very important way, on risk. As we have often seen, the effective 'expected price' of a future output—the price at which it has to be estimated for purposes of the plan— is not the most probable price, but the most probable price *minus* an allowance for risk. Now the farther ahead the future output is, the larger this risk-allowance is likely to become, just because the uncertainty of the future price increases; after a certain point, therefore, the risk-allowance will become so large as to wipe out any possible gains, and the effective 'expected price' will become nil. This is what brings the plan to an end, and prevents it extending into the indefinite future; but the plan is not merely cut short after a certain length of time; even those only relatively distant outputs whose 'expected prices' are not quite abolished by risk, are nevertheless gravely weakened in their influence on the plan by this writing-down due to risk (anticipated obsolescence of the equipment which might be installed to produce them). But it is these very outputs upon whose *pull* interest must mainly rely, if it is to cause large adjustments in the plan; we now see that their *pull* is likely to be much less strong than we might have expected.

Interest is too weak for it to have much influence on the near future; risk is too strong to enable interest to have much influence on the far future; what place is left for interest between these opposing perils? How far it can find a place depends upon the strength of the risk factor; and that, as we have seen, is largely a psychological question. In a state of grave mistrust, people will 'live from hand to mouth'; if they do so, changes in the rate of interest (the moderate changes we are talking about) can have little influence on their conduct. In a state of confidence, on the other hand, risk-allowances are much smaller; and a space will probably be left between the extremes where interest is ineffective, within which it can have a significant influence, of the kind we have analysed in this chapter.

The bearing of all this upon the whole question of interest policy during trade fluctuations is obvious; but we shall be in a better position to discuss that at a later stage.

CHAPTER XVIII

SPENDING AND LENDING

1. WE now pass on to the dynamic problem of the private individual. If we are content to pursue our usual method of attack, the line we have to take in dealing with this is obvious. The static problem of the firm consisted in maximizing the surplus of receipts over costs which could be earned by exploiting a given productive opportunity in given technical conditions; the corresponding dynamic problem consisted in maximizing the capital value of the stream of surpluses which could be expected to accrue, in the present and in the future, from the exploitation of such an opportunity. The static problem of the private individual consisted in choosing the most preferred collection of commodities which could be purchased out of a given sum of money. Working out the parallel in the same way, it appears that the dynamic problem of the private individual ought to be conceived as the choice of a most preferred collection of streams of commodities, out of the various collections of streams which the individual could expect to be able to purchase out of a given expected stream of receipts. The firm has to choose the most profitable production plan; the individual has to choose the most preferred expenditure plan; the transition from statics to dynamics is exactly similar in the two cases.

We seem to be committed to this sort of approach; but all the same one cannot help feeling considerable qualms about it. When we are considering the case of a firm, which is only concerned to draw the maximum profit from a given situation, it is reasonable enough to suppose that the firm will have to draw up a fairly definite 'plan' to attain that end. There are of course various uncertainties in the situation—uncertainties of future technical conditions, uncertainties of future market conditions—but these are not sufficient to deprive the idea of the 'plan' of all meaning and all usefulness. They can be allowed for, quite sufficiently, without sacrificing the idea of planning altogether. But when we turn to the case of the private individual, whose 'plan' (if he has a plan) must be directed solely to the satisfaction of his wants in the present and in the future, then the fact that he will ordinarily not know what his future wants are going to be (and will know that he does not know) becomes very upsetting. It is possible to plan ahead when one's plan is directed towards a given end (such as profit), but it is not possible to plan ahead when the object of planning is unknown. For this reason the whole method of analysis threatens to break down.

However, it would be a mistake to take this objection too seriously. Even although people are well aware that they are ignorant of the details of their own future wants, they do not behave as if they were ignorant of their future wants altogether. At the very least, they take into account the high probability that they will have *some* wants in the future, and usually they go a good deal farther than this. When they buy durable consumption goods, they usually do so, not merely because they have a desire for these goods in the present, but also because they expect that desire to recur in the future; this means that they are acting on an expectation of future wants—indeed, on a quite definite expectation. Further, a person is always aware, in a general sort of way, that the more he spends now, the less he will have available to be spent in the future; this consideration could not influence his conduct if he was not intending to have certain sums available for expenditure in the future, any inroad upon those sums being felt as a sacrifice. Now what these things mean, when one thinks them out, is that although no definite planning of future expenditure as a whole takes place, nevertheless whenever any piece of current expenditure has a definite bearing upon the satisfactions which will be attainable in the future, the relevant part of future policy is made more or less explicit. People do not plan their future expenditure as a whole; but they do plan, more or less consciously, and more or less definitely, those parts of future expenditure which are relevant to current expenditure. These include, on the one hand, some particular items of future expenditure, which are closely related to particular items of current expenditure; and on the other hand, that general notion about the size of future resources as a whole, which is relevant to the determination of the total amount of current expenditure.[1]

[1] The formation of this general notion about the size of future resources as a whole is considerably facilitated in practice by the use of the concept of income. The sacrifice of future resources involved in an increase in current expenditure is thought of as a sacrifice of future income; but this is only a form of shorthand, and does not give us a convenient model with which to work.

2. If this view is correct (as it appears to be), we are relieved of the greater part of our difficulty. If we assume the individual to have a complete plan of expenditure, extending over a considerable future period, and complete in every detail, we are falsifying his actual behaviour quite absurdly; but if we merely use this assumption, not to determine the details of the purchases which may (or may not) be planned to be made in the future, but to determine the details of current expenditure alone, we are not involved in anything which is at all absurd. The determination of current expenditure will proceed just as if there was such a complete plan; if we assume the existence of a complete plan we can proceed to determine current expenditure with the minimum of trouble.

Suppose then that we are dealing with an individual who possesses, at the planning date, a certain stock of durable consumption goods; who is receiving a sum of money R_0 in the current week (as earnings of his labour, or as interest or dividends on securities in his possession); and who expects to receive a series of sums $R_1, R_2, R_3,...$ in the same way in the following weeks. The prices of consumption goods and his expectations of their future prices being given, he plans to make certain purchases of the commodities $X, Y, Z,...$ in the current and following weeks; these purchases will involve him in a series of expenditures (in money terms) $E_0, E_1, E_2, E_3,....$. The difference between these receipts and expenditures must be made up either by changes in his holding of money, or by changes in his holding of securities; I shall assume for the present that they all take the latter form (the whole question of the demand for money being left over for consideration in the next chapter). The stream

$$R_0 - E_0, \ R_1 - E_1, \ R_2 - E_2,...;$$

may thus be regarded as a stream of *lendings*.

Let us assume that our individual carries forward his expenditure plan for a limited period of time—say n weeks. The stream of receipts, the stream of expenditures, and the stream of lendings are thus all regarded as coming to an end after n weeks. If, during these n weeks, he plans to lend on balance, then at the end of that time he can expect to have acquired, as a result of his lending, a capital sum C_n in securities, which will be available as an addition to his resources in the remoter future.[1] The more he spends

---

[1] C_n is the value of the securities expected to have been acquired as a result

during the currency of his plan, the smaller will this capital sum be; there is therefore a real choice between expenditure during the n weeks and the possession of such a capital sum at the end. The choice is exactly similar to that between expenditure at one date and expenditure at another; consequently, for purpose of analysis, it is convenient to assimilate this capital sum to expenditure of the last week. If we regard the provision of such a capital sum as one of the things to which expenditure can be devoted in the last week of the plan, we have an accounting device which enables us to reduce the whole problem to one of distributing expenditure between the n weeks.

The stream of lendings, adjusted in this way, becomes

$$R_0 - E_0,\ R_1 - E_1,\ R_2 - E_2, ...,\ R_n - E_n - C_n.$$

In this stream the borrowings and lendings cancel out, since if the above amount were really spent in the last week, nothing would be left over as a result of all these operations. Consequently, the capital value of this stream, taken at any point of time, must be zero. In particular, its *present value* (its capital value at the planning date) must be zero. Therefore the present value of the adjusted stream of expenditures

$$E_0,\ E_1,\ E_2.\ E_3, ...,\ E_n + C_n$$

must equal the present value of the stream of receipts

$$R_0,\ R_1,\ R_2,\ R_3, ...,\ R_n.$$

This is the clue which enables us to reduce the planning of expenditure (just as we reduced the planning of production) into terms of a problem we have already solved in static theory.

3. Just as in the case of production, we have only to make a distinction between transactions due to be made at different dates, and to replace actual prices by discounted prices; when we have made these changes, the whole static theory of value becomes directly applicable. Neither equilibrium conditions nor stability conditions need here give us any trouble. The marginal rate of substitution between two commodities planned to be bought at given future dates must equal the ratio of their discounted prices.

of the lending which is to take place during the period of the plan. It will only equal the increment in value of all securities held, if the securities initially held are expected to retain the same value at the end as they possessed at the beginning.

This marginal rate of substitution must be diminishing, in the same sense as in statics. That is all that need be said.

As in the static theory of value, the effects of changes in prices (including, here, changes in interest rates) have to be divided up into two parts. There is a substitution effect, due to the change in the relative discounted prices of different planned purchases; there is an effect, corresponding to the 'income effect' of statics, due to the extent to which the individual is made better or worse off by the change in question. The test for being made better or worse off must now be taken with reference to the whole expenditure plan. An individual will be made worse off if he is unable to expect, under the new conditions, to be able to purchase the same quantities as before of all goods at all dates, but must retrench somewhere; he will be better off if he has something left over, after planning the same purchases as before. The effect in question therefore depends upon the relative movements in the capital values of his previously planned stream of expenditures and of his expected stream of receipts. Looking at it in this way, it appears that it would be more logical to call it a 'capital effect', or something of that sort, rather than an 'income effect'. However, such consistency would be troublesome, and I do not think that it is necessary. I do not think that we shall involve ourselves in any difficulties if we continue to speak of an 'income effect', as we are accustomed to do. But we must remember the precise meaning which has to be given to it from now on.

4. If there is a rise in the price of some commodity X, and that rise is expected to be permanent, then (as we have seen) the current price and all expected future prices of X all rise in the same proportion. If the rate of interest is unchanged, all discounted prices also rise in the same proportion. Therefore, in this case, there is no need to distinguish between the purchases of X made at different dates; the laws of demand run exactly as in statics. There will be a substitution effect against X in favour of other goods; and there will be an income effect, which must also run against X, save in the exceptional case where X is an inferior good. As we have seen when dealing with production, it is the practical justification of the static model that its rules do hold exactly in these cases of permanent changes in price. But, as we also saw there, there is no definite rule about the way in which the reduction in demand will be spread over time. There may be a reduction in the *current* demand for X, but there may not.

If the price of X rises, and the rise is not expected to be permanent, the income effect will usually be very slight or indeed quite negligible. The substitution effect, however, may well be much more considerable than in the preceding case. For substitution may now proceed, not only in favour of other commodities, but also in favour of future purchases of X itself. The main effect of such a temporary rise may well consist in the postponement of expenditure.

If the price of X rises, and this rise is interpreted to mean that the price will rise still further in the future (elasticity of expectations greater than unity), then we have to deal with a rise in expected prices more than proportionate to the rise in the current price. The substitution against buying X now, which follows from the rise in the current price, may then be overmatched by the substitution in favour of present purchase, induced by the greater rise in expected prices. If the elasticity of expectations is large enough, the income effect too may be outweighed; and the final result may be that current demand is increased. This is the familiar case of speculative demand.

5. Changes in rates of interest can now be dealt with in a substantially similar way. Their effects also divide up into income effects and substitution effects (since, on the one hand, they make the individual better or worse off, and, on the other hand, they change relative discounted prices). A general rise in the rate of interest, for example, lowers the discounted prices of future purchases relatively to present purchases, and of more distant future purchases relatively to less distant future purchases; this will cause a general substitution all along the line, exactly similar to that we have already encountered in the theory of production. The net effect of this systematic shift in discounted prices is undoubtedly in the direction of a general postponement of expenditure; it will therefore usually tend to lower present expenditure; but there is plenty of opportunity for all sorts of cross-effects, and all sorts of complementarity to muddle things up.

The direction of the income effect depends upon the way in which the capitalized value of the originally planned stream of expenditures (including the capital sum C which is to be left over at the

end) is affected relatively to the capitalized value of the stream of
receipts. If the rate of interest is raised, both of these capitalized
values will be reduced; but which of them will be reduced the
more? This problem is formally identical with one which we
have discussed previously, when we were dealing with the calculation of income.[1] We found then that the relative movement of the
capitalized values of two streams (previously of the same capitalized value), when the rate of interest varies, depends upon their
relative average periods. The individual will be made better off
when there is a general rise in the rate of interest, if the average
period of his receipts stream is less than the average period of his
stream of expenditures.

If an individual's average period of expenditure is greater than
his average period of receipts, this means that he plans to spend
less than he receives in the present and near future, to 'spend'
more than he receives in the remoter future. (It must be remembered that 'spending' in the remoter future includes the
accumulation of a capital sum C at the end of the period of planning.) He may therefore be described as 'planning to be a lender'.
Such persons are made better off by a rise in the rate of interest;
the income effect thus tends to increase their expenditure, including (probably) their present expenditure. Thus for such persons
the income effect and the substitution effect go in opposite directions, and either may be dominant. We cannot say whether their
present expenditure will be increased or diminished by a rise in
the rate of interest.

This is of course the same proposition as that which is advanced
in elementary text-books, where we are told that a rise in the
rate of interest will make some people 'save' more (those who are
tempted by a higher rate of return, and so substitute future
expenditure for present); some people 'save' less (those who desire
to secure a fixed income as a result of their saving, and so take out
the improvement in their position by increasing their present
expenditure). As a result of our investigations we have been able
to define these tendencies a little more strictly. We can see that
their indecisiveness arises from the same cause as in the case of
the effect of changes in wages on the supply of labour, or of changes
in the price for one commodity on the demand for another. But
the most important thing which emerges is the way in which this

[1] Cf. above, pp. 185–6.

indecisiveness depends upon the assumption that the individual 'plans to be a lender'. What happens in the contrary case?

If an individual's average period of expenditure is less than his average period of receipts, he will be made worse off by a rise in the rate of interest. Income effect and substitution effect will therefore both work in the same direction, both of them tending to reduce current expenditure. When the rate of interest rises, such a person's expenditure must almost infallibly be reduced.

Who are these people who 'plan to be borrowers'? Apart from the mere spendthrifts, who may be left out of account, they consist simply of those entrepreneurs who are undertaking real investment. Receipts derived from borrowing must not be reckoned as receipts for the present purpose, so that the entrepreneur's receipts consist simply of the surplus he derives from production *minus* charges arising out of past contracts.[1] These receipts will very often be negative in the current period. But the entrepreneur's current expenditure (on private account) will not be negative; he will expect to make up the excess of expenditure over receipts by an excess in the other direction in later periods. His average period of expenditure will thus be less than his average period of receipts.

In our investigations into static theory, we have been accustomed to find that income effects, even when they are important on one side of a market, always have something to offset them (more or less) on the other side. When we are interested in the things making for differences between market demand and supply (and it is these differences which are significant for price changes), there is always an income effect on each side, and these income effects ordinarily go in opposite directions. So it is here.

While those persons who plan to be lenders have an income effect increasing their present expenditure when the rate of interest rises, those who plan to be borrowers have an income effect reducing it. If these income effects cancel out, then there is nothing left but the two substitution effects, each of which tends to *reduce* current expenditure.

Are the income effects likely to cancel out? There is one broad reason why they should tend to do so, but it is subject to two sorts of exceptions. The broad reason why they should tend to cancel out is that, for equilibrium on the market for securities, it

[1] Cf. above, p. 195.

is necessary that current borrowing and current lending should be equal. But that is not enough to show that borrowers and lenders are made worse off and better off, to an exactly equivalent extent, by a rise in the rate of interest. For the effect on their general prospects depends upon the relation between their average periods; that is to say, upon the relation between planned borrowing and lending as well as current borrowing and lending. And planned borrowing and lending, being mainly inside people's heads (and not very definite even there), are not matched on the market. There may be an excess on one side or on the other; though, if there is, it spells inconsistency between plans, and consequent potential disequilibrium.[1]

This is doubtless less important than the other kind of exception—due to the possibility that borrowers and lenders may adjust their present expenditure to changes in their wealth in appreciably different ways. This is essentially a matter of the speed with which they adjust their expenditure to new conditions. If borrowers are quicker to adapt themselves than lenders (I should judge that in practice this is probably the case), the income effect on the borrowers' side is likely to be stronger than the income effect on the lenders' side. This would make the net income effect work in the same direction as the total substitution effect, and reinforce the conclusion that, for the market as a whole, *a rise in the rate of interest will reduce current expenditure, a fall in the rate of interest increase it.*

6. Although this conclusion looks rather different from the sort of thing to which the reader will have become accustomed in most modern writings, we are (of course) not really introducing any new principle; we are merely taking up familiar reactions in an unfamiliar way. That is rather a tiresome thing to do, in itself; but in this case it is necessary. We are all the time preparing the ground for an attempt to apply to the general dynamic problem the same sort of reasoning as we used in statics. For that purpose it is necessary to group the relevant forces in a particular way; and we cannot expect that it will always be the same as the way in which we have been accustomed to group them.

The traditional way of answering the question 'How does a change in the rate of interest affect present expenditure?' would be

---

[1] Cf. above, p. 133.

(i) to inquire how the amount spent out of a given income would be affected; and (ii) (if the supplementary question was not forgotten) to inquire how the level of income would be affected. Now the effect on the level of income is not at all a simple effect, but is actually compounded out of two different stages. There is (ii *a*) the effect on the incomes of entrepreneurs which would accrue even if they kept their production plans entirely unchanged; and (ii *b*) the effect on their incomes and on those of other people as well which results from any changes they may make in their production plans. The traditional answer under (i) would be that expenditure might be reduced by a rise in the rate of interest, though there are forces working in the other direction; and under (ii), not distinguishing much between (*a*) and (*b*), that income would certainly be reduced, and this would certainly reduce expenditure.

We ourselves have learnt to mistrust the concept of income; and, in any case, the distinction between (i) and (ii), income constant and income variable, is not relevant for our sort of analysis. The distinction between (ii *a*) and (ii *b*) is, however, of great importance to us; we do want to distinguish between those changes in expenditure which would arise even if production plans were unchanged, and those which depend upon the change in production plans. Thus we take (i) and (ii *a*) together—which is what we have done in the preceding section. When we do that, we cease to be dependent upon the concept of income. We get the result that, with given production plans and given prices, a change in the rate of interest will affect the volume of current expenditure in the opposite direction.

It is, of course, quite another matter to say how large this effect may be; there are much the same reasons for distrusting the effectiveness of interest changes as in the case of production. However, the direction of the effect seems fairly clear.

CHAPTER XIX
THE DEMAND FOR MONEY

1. As the reader will no doubt have noticed, our discussion of the individual's expenditure plan has been deficient in one serious and important respect. We have been assuming that the difference between the value of his receipts in any week and his expenditure in that week is made up by a change in his holding of securities (that is to say, by lending or borrowing) and has to be made up in that way. Though this assumption was convenient enough for the moment, it would let us down badly in the applications we want to make later on. It is not justifiable save for very special purposes.

An excess of receipts over expenditure may be made up either by the acquisition of securities or by the acquisition of money. An excess of expenditure over receipts may be made up either by selling securities (including the creation of securities against oneself) or by parting with money. It is a matter of considerable importance which form the balancing takes; we need to find some way, within the formal structure of our theory, of distinguishing between the two methods.

If it were permissible to regard money as a particular sort of durable consumers' good, then money could be fitted into our previous analysis with no trouble at all. It is a condition of equilibrium for the individual that the marginal rate of substitution between acquisitions of any commodities at given dates must equal the ratio of their discounted prices; this rule could be taken as applying to money as well. The marginal rate of substitution between money now and any other commodity now would equal the current price of that commodity (just the same rule as we found for the standard commodity in statics); the marginal rate of substitution between the acquisition of money now and the acquisition of money at a later date would equal the discount ratio over the period of deferment. This implies that the interest charge over a period would measure the sacrifice involved in postponing the acquisition of a marginal unit of money to the end of the period; just as (apart from the risk of price-changes) it measures the sacrifice involved in postponing the purchase of any other durable good to the end of the period. In other words, the rate of interest would measure the impatience to possess money now instead of money in the future.

As we have seen, a rise in the rate of interest (prices being supposed constant) tends to diminish the demand for present commodities in general; the same applies to any particular present commodity, so long as there is no reason to suppose that it is complementary with the future commodities, planned purchases of which will be increased. The same would apply here to the demand for money in the present. A rise in the rate of interest may be expected to diminish the demand for money. Again, a general rise in the prices of commodities (whether or not it is expected to continue permanently) is equivalent to a fall in the value of money in terms of those commodities, and it would appear that this must increase the demand for money.

These are the rules for the behaviour of money which one would expect to apply if it were possible to treat money as being no more than a particular kind of durable consumption good. They are very reasonable rules; it would be surprising if more careful attention to the true nature of money were to make it necessary to alter them very considerably.

2. Money (or, at the least, modern money) is, as we saw in our earlier discussion of the subject,[1] not a durable consumers' good, but a kind of security. It is desired, not as an end in itself, but as securities are desired, in order that it should be available as a means of meeting future expenses. The right way to conceive of the demand for money is not to assimilate it to the rest of expenditure (as we have just been doing), but to assimilate it to the demand for securities. People can devote current receipts to the satisfaction of future wants either by acquiring securities or by acquiring money. When the matter is looked at in this way, we are at once led to ask how it is possible for people to prefer to hold money rather than securities, since securities yield interest, and money does not. We have seen how this question ought to be answered. Even the safest and most negotiable securities, which are not money, involve some risks to their holders, and some costs of acquisition and disposal, from which money is free. Only when there is an expectation (and a confident expectation) that

[1] Chapter XIII, above.

funds will not be needed for at least some minimum length of time in the future, will the expected return more than cover these costs and risks, so that it will be worth while to hold the funds in a form that bears interest. Otherwise it will actually be better to hold them in money form.

One of the most important consequences of this we have already examined: the close dependence of the demand for money upon the rate of interest (or rather on the system of interest rates). There is no need to suppose that money and securities behave as particularly close substitutes from the point of view of every single person trading; but we must expect to find an appreciable number of persons or concerns for whom money and the various different sorts of securities form a chain of very close substitutes indeed. This is sufficient to cause money and securities to behave as very close substitutes, from the point of view of the economy as a whole. As we have seen, even if money could be regarded as a durable consumers' good, a rise in the rate of interest would probably diminish the demand for money; better appreciation of the nature of money only modifies our previous theory in this case to the extent of preparing us to lay greater stress upon this reaction than we should otherwise have been likely to do.[1]

If rates of interest are given, what determines the way in which an individual will distribute his funds between money and securities? This is the main question which remains to be discussed. We can approach it most easily if we consider a number of special cases.

3. First of all, as a standard of reference, let us try to construct a case in which the individual's demand for money will be nil— in which he will be content to keep all his funds in the form of

---

[1] The treatment of money as a kind of security also obliges us to make some amendment to the argument of the preceding chapter. We there assumed that all funds transferred from present expenditure to future expenditure bore interest; we now see that this may not be the case. Some funds will be held in money form, and bear no interest; and (to generalize completely, while we are at it) some funds may be held in forms that bear low rates of interest, some in forms that bear higher rates. But all this seems to make very little substantial difference; we have already seen that it is only the more distant planned expenditures whose discounted values will be much affected by a change in interest rates; the fact that some of the (nearer) expenditures ought not to be discounted at all therefore makes hardly any difference. The correction involved is simply not worth examining in detail.

securities. Suppose that the interest on the securities he possesses at the planning date, together with any other kinds of revenue which may be due to him, is expected to yield a constant flow of receipts, the same amount in every future week. Suppose, further, that he plans to spend, in every future week, the same amount as he receives, no more and no less. Then, if he is perfectly confident that he can carry out his plan, his demand for money will be nil. All the money he receives will be paid out again at once; he will need to keep over from one week to another no money balance at all to finance his transactions.

Such a situation as this practically never occurs—for two different reasons. One is that this exact balancing between receipts and expenditures practically never happens. Receipts do not come in at exactly the same moments as expenditures are required to be made; receipts come in rather irregularly, and expenditures are made very irregularly. A closer representation of the actual situation could be made in terms of our model if we supposed receipts to come in, not every week, but, say, every fourth week; then, even if receipts and expenditures balanced over the four weeks taken together, the money balance could only fall to zero in the week just before the month's receipts were due to come in. At other times an appreciable money balance would be held, since it would probably not pay to invest it in securities if it was expected to be wanted in a week or two's time.

Mere periodicity of receipts and expenditures is thus responsible for the holding of a certain amount of money—probably, for the community as a whole, a fairly constant amount of money, only liable to some quite regular fluctuations at quarter-days and Christmas and so on. Apart from these regular fluctuations, it is only liable to be affected by a change in people's habits about the dating of payments, or by a general change in the volume of expenditure in money terms. (It should be observed that the demand for money from this source cannot be much influenced by changes in interest.)

There is, however, another reason why money is held, even in the case when receipts and expenditures are broadly expected to balance. An individual's expenditure plan is never definite; there is always the possibility that he will desire, at any moment, to make some unforeseen expenditure. The costs of realizing securities to meet this unforeseen expenditure would be considerable, so that the mere risk of having to do this would be sufficient to offset a moderate gain in interest. Some portion of possible (not merely probable) expenditures is therefore likely to be covered by holding money; how large a portion depending upon the individual's attitude to the risk and upon the size of the gain offered by investment in securities. This part of the demand for money is therefore liable to be affected by interest rates, but it is also very susceptible to changes in the risk factor. Apart from these, it probably bears a fairly constant relation to the aggregate volume of expenditure.

One sort of possible expenditure which is very important in this connexion is that arising out of liabilities incurred in the past. Every business has, at any moment, a certain amount of claims outstanding against it, which it may be called upon to meet at dates which cannot be quite certainly predicted. The clearest case of this is, of course, the case of banks, which live by acquiring such liabilities, and therefore have an exceptional amount of them. Nevertheless, the cash reserve a bank keeps against its liabilities is simply a special case of the holding of money against uncertain future expenditures, which is practised to some extent by all businesses, and by many private individuals as well.

4. These are the main reasons for holding money which would persist even in stationary conditions, where a general balancing of receipts and expenditures was the rule. When conditions are not stationary, two further reasons have to be added. They are, in a sense, extensions of the reasons already noted; but it seems best to classify them separately.

If a person is definitely planning some considerable increase in his expenditure in the near future, he is extremely likely to add to his money balance in order to prepare for it. He will generally not know exactly at what date his funds will have to be disbursed; and even if he does, the disbursement may well take some time, and it will be easier to prepare for it by transferring all the funds that will be needed into money form in a single transaction. Consequently, we may lay it down as a fairly general rule that a rise in the expenditure planned for the near future usually increases the demand for money in the present.[1]

The same thing evidently holds if he is spending less than his current receipts in order to be able to spend more than his receipts

[1] Cf. Keynes, 'The "Ex-ante" Theory of Interest', *E.J.*, 1937.

in the near future. (This is, in fact, the same as the first case we discussed in the preceding section.) But it may also hold—and this is the other new point we have to take into account in non-stationary conditions—if he is spending less than he receives in the present, in order to add to his stock of securities (and so to be able to spend more than he receives at some distant and probably conjectural future date). This may happen because of the costs of investing in securities, which become less onerous if they can be spread over larger sums. The ultimate object of holding cash in this case is not to spend it in the near future, but to invest it in securities in the near future; it is not invested at once because it will be cheaper to convert the 'savings' of a number of 'weeks' into securities in a single transaction, instead of investing them week by week as they are made.

These are the main reasons for holding money. They are rather heterogeneous, and not very easy to fit into a convenient formula. Yet we require such a formula for our further investigations, since we cannot repeat the whole analysis of this chapter every time we want to make use of it. Apart from this last point (accumulation of money in the process of saving), we should not go far wrong if we said that the demand for money depends upon the rate of interest, and upon the volume of planned expenditure in the near future (in money terms), some attention being paid to the confidence with which it is expected that this expenditure and no more will be carried out. That covers all our reasons for holding money, except the last. We can only take the last point into account, if we add that the demand for money may sometimes be increased, not by an increase in planned expenditure in the near future, but by an increase in the amount of securities which the individual plans to buy in the near future. This is an awkward exception, but I do not see any convenient way of reformulating the rule by which it can be avoided.

5. It will be evident, from the examples we have given, that *expenditure*, in the above formula, must be taken to include expenditure on inputs, needed for the continuance or expansion of a productive process, as well as expenditure on consumption goods. We have in fact slipped over, in a way that could not easily be avoided, from considering the disposal of resources by the private individual alone, to the consideration of matters which are relevant both to the problem of the private individual and to that of the firm. It will be useful if, in conclusion, we consider a moment just how this happened.

The firm, as we analysed its operations in Chapters XV–XVII, was regarded as a purely technical unit; it absorbed certain inputs, sold certain outputs; its net receipts (difference between value of output and value of input in any particular week, after deduction of any fixed charges) were supposed to be transferred to the private account of the entrepreneur. If these net receipts were positive, they could then be allotted by the entrepreneur, in his private capacity, to his personal expenditure, or to building up his cash balance, or to the acquisition of securities; if they were negative, he would be obliged to borrow (or sell securities) or allow his cash balance to run down, in order to have anything available for his private expenditure at all.

What this amounts to is that the whole financial side of the firm's operations was supposed transferred to the private account of the entrepreneur; though there is some theoretical convenience in that supposition, it is obviously a most unrealistic approach. Even in a private firm, when the entrepreneur is a real individual, not a legal fiction, he does usually in practice keep two accounts. (It is true that in the private firm the separation is very artificial and very arbitrary, so that it is probably justifiable to neglect it for theoretical purposes.) But when the typical firm becomes a joint-stock company, the separation ceases to be artificial. There is a real line of division; the financial side of the firm's operations has an existence of its own quite separate from the private accounts of the shareholders—a separation maintained by the legal principle of limited liability.

But although the division ceases to be artificial, it does not cease to be rather arbitrary. The natural way of dealing with the situation is to treat the financial account of the firm as a special kind of private account (there is no necessary reason which binds us to regard as 'private individuals' only separate human beings); the 'receipts' of this account being the net receipts of the firm, its 'expenditure' consisting in the payment of dividends. To this account the analysis of the present chapter would apply perfectly well (though we should have to be clear that what we should now be calling negative receipts must reckon as a kind of expenditure from the point of view of the demand for money—it is the total volume of the firm's planned disbursements, not merely of its planned distribution of dividends, which is relevant to the size of its cash balance). All this can be perfectly well worked out by using the device of regarding the financial account of the firm as an independent 'private' account. But there is still one difficulty.

No clear principle is left to determine on what scale dividends should be paid—that is to say, how much should be paid out in dividends in the current period and how much should be 'ploughed back into the business'. Nor does there seem to be any theoretical device by which this arbitrariness can be removed; it is a real arbitrariness, a real peculiarity of the joint-stock company. Its implications are very considerable, but we cannot go into them here; the only implication for the general dynamic theory, on which we have now to embark, is that we must be prepared sometimes to treat dividend policy as an independent variable.

CHAPTER XX

THE TEMPORARY EQUILIBRIUM OF
THE WHOLE SYSTEM

I. *Its Imperfect Stability*

1. It is one of the most exciting characteristics of the method of analysis we are pursuing in this book that it enables us to pass over, with scarcely any transition, from the little problems involved in detailed study of the behaviour of a single firm, or single individual, to the great issues of the prosperity or adversity, even life or death, of a whole economic system. The transition is made by using the simple principle, already familiar to us in statics, that the behaviour of a group of individuals, or group of firms, obeys the same laws as the behaviour of a single unit. If a particular change in price (other prices being constant) can be shown to increase the demand for a certain commodity on the part of a representative individual, then it must increase the demand for that commodity on the part of all individuals similarly situated. (We have learnt to mark out, by our 'income effects', the differences in the situations of those persons who appear as buyers, and those who appear as sellers, in the relevant markets.) The laws of market behaviour, which we have laboriously elaborated for those tenuous creatures, the representative individual and the representative firm, thus become revealed 'in their own dimensions like themselves' as laws of the behaviour of great groups of economic units, from which we can readily evolve the laws of their interconnexions, the laws of the behaviour of prices, the laws of the working of the whole system.

The general conditions for the equilibrium (temporary equilibrium) of a whole economic system during a particular 'week' were set out at an earlier stage of our inquiry.[1] They are nothing else but equations of supply and demand for goods and services of every sort, for securities, and for money. Since it was possible to write down these equilibrium equations before any investigation had been made into the behaviour of representative economic units, it seemed best to take the opportunity of doing so (and of

---

[1] Chapter XII, above.

showing how *one* of the equations can be regarded as being super-fluous) as early as possible, in order to have the equations available for reference when we wanted them. But it is only now that we can really begin to set the equations to work. The equilibrium equations determine the prices which will be established in *given* conditions (that is to say, in the present context, with given tastes, resources, and expectations); we have now to discuss what happens when some of these data are changed.

In so doing, we have to follow out a programme exactly parallel to that which we previously followed when dealing with a static price-system. But there is one important difference between our present situation and the corresponding situation in statics which needs to be noticed at once. In statics, the ultimate aim of all our endeavours is the discovery of the laws of the working of a static price system; but in dynamics, the parallel laws—the laws of the working of a temporary equilibrium system—cannot claim so ulti-mate a place. It must be emphasized that the changes in data we have to consider are purely hypothetical changes. We seek to compare the system of prices actually established in a particular week with that system which would have been established in the same week if the data (tastes, resources, or expectations) had been rather different. This is an important problem, but it is not the ultimate dynamic problem. Even when we have mastered the 'working' of the temporary equilibrium system, we are even yet not in a position to give an account of the process of price-change, nor to examine the ulterior consequences of changes in data. These are the ultimate things we want to know about, though we may have to face the disappointing conclusion that there is not much which can be said about them in general. Still, nothing can be done about these further problems until after we have investi-gated the working of the economy during a particular week.

The theory of temporary equilibrium does not include the ultimate dynamic problems, but it is not therefore devoid of direct practical application. For many purposes, what we want to know is exactly what the theory of temporary equilibrium tells us—what immediate alteration in the course of events will follow from a particular change in data. Further, when we remember that the length of our 'week' is fairly arbitrary (that it can be made shorter or longer according as we desire more or less exact con-clusions), it becomes evident that the word 'immediate' can be interpreted more or less strictly as we prefer. It may often be legitimate to spin it out into something like a Marshallian 'short period'—the time during which existing equipment (in a broad or narrow sense) can be taken as given. The main problems where it is necessary to consider more than one 'week' are those where we are specially interested in the consequences of accumulation or decumulation of capital. These have to be held over for later consideration; they belong to a part of dynamics which falls outside temporary equilibrium theory.

In accordance with our usual procedure, we shall continue to assume that the length of time necessary for entrepreneurs (and others) to wake up and change their plans, in consequence of price-changes, can be neglected. Since in fact many people are fairly slow at such reactions, this assumption necessarily extends the length of time to which our 'week' corresponds in practice; all repercussions which result from people's (perhaps belated) apprehension of the original change being reckoned as occurring within the 'week'. Of course, in practice important effects upon the accumulation of capital may be visible before quite a number of people have 'woken up'. We must be aware of this defect in our methods. We shall be treating as successive two kinds of effects which may in fact go on concurrently. But, though it is a defect, it is not without countervailing advantages. It is rather useful to be able to distinguish, on the one hand, those consequences of the initial change which result simply from people's awareness of the initial effects (which may thus take place more or less quickly according as they are more or less alert); and, on the other, those effects which depend on capital accumulation, and whose dating is thus more or less strictly determined by the technically given duration of the processes needed to bring about changes in productive equipment. Our method consists in supposing the first sort of effect to go through with the maximum of rapidity; even if in ordinary times it does actually go through as slowly as the other, it is always possible that it may be speeded up considerably, and it is desirable to be able to take account of this. The fact that it naturally proceeds more slowly will not really cause any great difficulty.

2. The particular problems which have to be considered under the heading of temporary equilibrium analysis are again, to a large

extent, topically interesting problems. They include such highly controversial issues as the effects of saving and investment on the rate of interest, and the effects of general changes in money wages. I hope that these issues will be considerably cleared up as a result of the inquiries we have now to make. For I hope to show, not only what are the right answers to these questions, but also the reason why it is so difficult to give the right answers. If that reason had to be expressed in a phrase, it is that phrase which I have set at the head of this chapter: the temporary equilibrium system is liable to be *imperfectly stable*.

In order to grasp the significance of this it is necessary to cast our minds back to our original discussion of stability in exchange.[1] In order for a system of multiple exchange to be perfectly stable (and the temporary equilibrium system is simply an extended system of multiple exchange), the following conditions must be satisfied. A rise in the price of any commodity must make the supply of that commodity exceed the demand (*a*) if all other prices are given, (*b*) if some other prices are adjusted so as to preserve equality between demand and supply in their respective markets, (*c*) if all other prices are so adjusted. If the last of these conditions is not satisfied the system is not stable at all, but will break down at the slightest disturbance. If some of the stability conditions are not satisfied, though others (including the indispensable last condition) are satisfied, then the system will be imperfectly stable. It is stable in the end, so it does not break down; but we have to be prepared for its working to show queer anomalies.

When we applied these tests to the systems we had to consider in statics—the system of multiple exchange and the system of exchange with production—we found no significant reason to suppose that they gave any particular trouble. We therefore proceeded, with fair confidence, to treat these static systems as being perfectly stable; and it was from their perfect stability that we deduced the economic laws they could be expected to obey. What happens when we apply the same tests to the dynamic system—or rather to the system of temporary equilibrium?

The easiest way of answering this question is to begin by seeing whether it is possible to construct a particular case of the temporary equilibrium system which has the same formal properties

[1] Chapter V, above.

as the static systems already known to be stable. If it is possible to do this, then in this particular case the temporary equilibrium system will be perfectly stable. By comparing the particular case with the general case, we can then see whether there is anything in the general case likely to upset its stability—and if so, what the disturbing element is.

3. The most obvious difference between any static system of exchange and production, and any dynamic system, consists in the absence of borrowing and lending in the one case and its presence in the other. In statics, an individual's receipts and expenditure can only differ to the extent of the change in his money balance; in dynamics, the difference can also be made up by a change in his (net) holding of securities. We have seen at great length how important this introduction of borrowing and lending can be; nevertheless, it is not *necessarily* significant in the sense relevant here. Securities are something which is bought and sold; therefore they are a kind of commodity; therefore their introduction only changes the formal properties of the system in so far as this special kind of commodity fails to observe the static rules of behaviour.

As we noticed on a previous occasion, these static rules hold so long as the individual's scale of preferences is independent of the prices fixed on the market.[1] This condition will continue to hold, even in a dynamic system, so long as elasticities of expectations are zero, that is to say, so long as all price-expectations and interest-expectations are given. If these expectations are given, the demand for securities can be taken as being formally equivalent to a demand for given quantities of physical commodities to be supplied in the future; the price of these commodities (the only part of their price which can vary) being the rate of interest.[2] The fact that the commodities in question are only to be enjoyed at a future date is irrelevant to the determination of prices in the current week; the individual behaves exactly as if he were buying the commodities now. Similarly, when a firm borrows, it behaves exactly as if it were selling commodities to be delivered in the future, selling them at a price also determined by the rate of interest. Thus securities behave exactly like ordinary commodities; the replacement

---

[1] See above, p. 55.

[2] More precisely, the discount ratio, which has a definite and constant arithmetical relation with the rate of interest.

of one of the commodities of static theory by this peculiar sort of commodity does nothing to change the fundamental character of the system.

The matter can be put more precisely in this way. Suppose that we are dealing with a spot economy with short lending,[1] in which all loans are made for the minimum period—one week. Then the only rate of interest established on the market is a rate of interest for one week; though of course people's expenditure and production plans depend upon the rates of interest which they expect to rule in future weeks. If these expected rates of interest are given, and the expected prices of all commodities in all future weeks are given as well, then the discounted prices of all future commodities are given, when the discounting is taken, not to the current week, but to the next week, to that week which commences when all the current loans fall due. In order to discount these prices to the current week we have only to multiply each of them by the discount ratio for the current week (which is not given, since it depends upon the current rate of interest); this must, however, leave their ratios unaffected. But when the ratios of the discounted prices of a number of commodities are given, we know that they can be treated as one homogeneous commodity. All we are doing is to call that commodity 'securities' We are entitled to fit it in to the static system on the same footing as any ordinary commodity. It is just a commodity whose price is the discount ratio for one week.

It is fairly obvious that the same principle will hold outside the special conditions of the spot economy with short lending. If long lending also is practised, then rates of interest for loans of different lengths will have to be adjusted to conform to the change in the rate for one-week loans; and there will also be a new set of income effects to allow for, arising out of past contracts. But there is no reason to suppose that these will be seriously destabilizing.

We may therefore sum up the first step in our argument. So long as elasticities of expectations are zero, the temporary equilibrium system works exactly like a static system and is as stable as that is. This is an eminently sensible conclusion, as appears at once when it is checked up from another point of view. So long as all changes in current prices are regarded as being temporary changes, any change in current prices will induce very large

[1] See above, p. 148.

substitution effects in a large number of markets. A rise in price will make people postpone expenditure, entrepreneurs postpone input and accelerate output; a fall in price will work the opposite way. This substitution over time will be strongly stabilizing; small rises in price will produce large excesses of supply over demand; indeed the forces making for stability are likely to be so potent that it will take a very violent disturbance of data to have any considerable effect on the price-system at all.

4. When once we have seen that, in this perfectly stable case, stability is chiefly maintained by substitution over time, it becomes natural to ask whether the system will still be stable if the opportunity for substitution over time is withdrawn. Opportunities for substitution over time still remain so long as a change in current prices changes expected prices in less than the same proportion— so long, that is to say, as elasticities of expectations are less than 1. When elasticities of expectations become all equal to 1, there is no longer any opportunity left for substitution over time. This is therefore the critical case.

When the matter is approached from our present standpoint, it does not appear at all surprising that the case of unity elasticities of expectations should be very tricky. Yet it is certainly extremely upsetting that this should be so. It looks an extremely plausible thing to take as one's standard assumption that elasticities of expectations are unity, that any change in current prices is expected to be a permanent change. It is so plausible that it has been simply taken for granted by the majority of economists, being assumed implicitly far more often than it is assumed explicitly.[1] Just for this reason, it has caused an immense amount of trouble. The most natural assumption which one can make for dealing with dynamic problems is one of the most dangerous assumptions, for it involves treading on the very borderland between stability and instability. The fact that the first explorations of economists in the field of dynamics were conducted on this shaking soil explains much of the bewilderment of 'monetary theory' during the present century.

It was, in fact, just before the beginning of this century that Wicksell gave the first indication that something was wrong.[2]

[1] The habit of working in real terms no doubt encouraged this.
[2] *Geldzins und Güterpreise* (1898); Mr. Kahn's English translation is entitled *Interest and Prices*.

His comparison of the money rate of interest with a 'natural rate' conceived in real terms (whatever one may think of the mysterious process of lending 'real capital *in natura*') betrays that he is thinking of the case where elasticities of expectations are unity. Roughly, what his central argument amounts to is this. In equilibrium, there corresponds to a particular rate of interest a particular relation between current prices in general and expected prices in general. If the rate of interest is lowered, current prices will rise; if expected prices had remained unchanged, this process would restore equilibrium with current prices bearing a higher ratio to expected prices. But if expected prices rise *pari passu*, the equilibrium tendency is defeated; current prices can never catch up. The system is involved in the famous 'cumulative process'.

However, let us look at the matter more closely. It is a central feature of Wicksell's analysis that he assumes a pure credit system, rather than a monetary system.[1] He assumes that all transactions are financed by credit, that is to say, by interest-bearing bills; there is no place in his system for a money that does not bear interest; it is neither demanded nor supplied. Consequently, as compared with our system of temporary equilibrium, Wicksell has one equation less. Supposing that there are $n-1$ sorts of commodities (real goods and services not including securities or money), then we have each of us n prices to determine (the money prices of the $n-1$ commodities, and one rate of interest). In our system of temporary equilibrium, we had $n+1$ equations to determine them (supply-and-demand equations for the $n-1$ commodities, for securities, and for money). Of these equations one followed from the rest; so that in the end there were n equations and n unknowns, as there should be.

Wicksell, on the other hand, dropped the money equation. No genuine money circulates in his system, and therefore there can be no supply and demand for it. He is left with n equations, of which one follows from the rest as before (since accounts must still balance); thus $n-1$ equations net. But $n-1$ equations are insufficient to determine n unknowns.

Subject to the condition that the elasticities of expectation are unity, what Wicksell's $n-1$ equations do determine are the *relative* prices of the $n-1$ commodities ($n-2$ in number, if they

[1] *Interest and Prices*, pp. 62–75.

are measured in terms of one of the commodities taken as a provisional standard) and the one rate of interest. The general level of money prices (the value of money) is left indeterminate. This can be seen if we reflect that a general increase of 5 per cent. in *all* prices (*all* must be emphasized[1]), involving a general increase of 5 per cent. in all expected prices, will leave every one's position unchanged, so long as the rate of interest does not vary. The prices of the things a person buys are up 5 per cent., but his income is up 5 per cent., too. The prices of the factors an entrepreneur employs are up 5 per cent., but his expected selling prices are up 5 per cent., too. There is no incentive to substitute between present and future. Therefore the demands and supplies of all commodities will be unchanged; being equal before, they will be equal still. The system can come to equilibrium at any level of money prices.

Wicksell's price-system consists of a perfectly determinate core —the relative prices of commodities and the rate of interest— floating in a perfectly indeterminate aether of money values. Since the money price-level is so utterly arbitrary, any slight and temporary disturbance of data may shift it about to a large extent. *The* rate of interest is determined as part of the core, by 'real' causes; but over periods of time so short that they are insignificant for the establishment of equilibrium (that is to say, in our terminology, periods less than a week), there may be a slight difference between this determinate *natural rate* and the momentary *money rate*. Such slight divergencies are sufficient to set up large changes in the price-level.

It is a rather unfortunate thing that Wicksell and his immediate followers remained for so long under the delusion that the possibility of discrepancy between the *money rate* and the *natural rate* was the keystone of his theory. If the theory is interpreted strictly, the possible discrepancy is only a *virtual* discrepancy; as soon as the discrepancy becomes actual, the theory breaks down. For this reason, the theory is of very little use as a guide to banking policy, the field in which it was thought to have direct applicability. Further, the true significance of Wicksell's construction was only

[1] There must be no contracts fixed up in advance which have still to be executed under the new conditions; and there must be no conventional prices, such as conventionally fixed money wages. I shall return to these points in the next chapter.

obscured by preoccupation with the discrepancy; this true significance comes out much better if we look at the whole matter in
another way, which incidentally enables us to dispense with
Wicksell's assumption of a Pure Credit Economy.

5. Let us therefore revert to our earlier assumptions. Let
us suppose that there does circulate a genuine money, which does
not bear interest. We have seen that in this case the whole system
of prices and interest rates is determinate, the number of equations
equalling the number of unknowns.

Let us now suppose that all elasticities of expectations are
unity; and let us test the system for one particular condition out
of the set of stability conditions which it ought to satisfy. Suppose
that the rate of interest (or, better, the whole system of interest
rates) is taken as given, while the price of one commodity (X) rises
by 5 per cent. If the system is to be perfectly stable, this rise
should induce an excess supply of X, however many (or however
few) repercussions through other markets we allow for. Now
what are the changes in prices which will restore equality between
supply and demand in the markets for other commodities? If
we consider *some* other markets only, we get results which do not
differ very much from those to which we have been accustomed;
the stability of the system survives these tests without difficulty.
But when we consider the repercussions on *all* other markets
(but not the market for securities, since the rate of interest is
taken as given, and not the market for money, since it is not
independent from the rest), then we seem to move into a different
world. Equilibrium can only be restored in the other commodity
markets if the prices of the other commodities all rise by 5 per
cent. too. For if the price-ratios between all commodities are
unchanged, and the price-ratios between all current prices and
all expected prices are unchanged (since elasticities of expectation
are unity), and (*ex hypothesi*) rates of interest are unchanged—
then there is no opportunity for substitution anywhere. The
demands and supplies for all goods and services will be unchanged.
Being equal before, they will be equal still. It is a general proportional rise in prices which restores equilibrium in the other
commodity markets; but *it fails to produce an excess of supply
over demand in the market for the first commodity X.* So far as
the commodity markets taken alone are concerned, the system

behaves like Wicksell's system. It is in 'neutral equilibrium'; that is to say, it can be in equilibrium at any level of money prices.[1]

If elasticities of expectations are generally greater than unity, so that people interpret a change in prices, not merely as an indication that the new prices will go on, but as an indication that they will go on changing in the same direction, then a rise in all prices by so much *per cent.* (with constant rate of interest) will make demands generally greater than supplies, so that the rise in prices will continue. A system with elasticities of expectations greater than unity, and constant rate of interest, is definitely unstable.

Technically, then, the case where elasticities of expectations are equal to unity marks the dividing line between stability and instability. But its own stability is a very questionable sort. A slight disturbance will be sufficient to make it pass over into instability. Suppose that the demand for X increases in terms of money, while rates of interest are kept constant as before. Then the price of X will rise, and other prices rise with it; but that will fail to induce the excess supply of X, which is needed to satisfy the increased demand.[2] The price of X will thus rise again, and prices in general rise again; there is nothing to stop this going on indefinitely. Even when elasticities of expectations are equal to unity, the system is liable to break down at the slightest disturbance.

6. The proposition which we have thus established is perhaps the most important proposition in economic dynamics. It is important, of course, not because the sort of break-down it describes is a break-down which does normally occur; the assumptions necessary for the break-down to occur are not, in every respect, realistic assumptions. But they are not so very unrealistic as to be irrelevant to actual conditions; they are a quite plausible simplification of reality, being, indeed, just the sort of simplifica-

---

[1] The reader will have noticed that this argument depends upon the assumption that the system of *relative* prices is *uniquely* determined. I do not feel many qualms about this assumption myself. If it is not justified anything may happen.

[2] For this method of deducing laws of change from stability conditions, see above, p. 73. It may be objected that the increased demand itself will be checked by the higher price, but this is not a valid objection. The new buyers themselves will find their incomes gone up; so they will still be anxious to buy the same increased amount of X as at the lower prices.

tion economists generally use when they wish to construct a convenient model with which to work. Our proposition shows that this model is a highly inconvenient model; once you begin to shape your assumptions that way you are nearing a whirlpool. This has a strong bearing on the sort of analytical methods it is wise to use in dynamic theory; and it has a strong bearing upon one's whole conception of the economic system, considered as a process in time.

So long as economists were content to regard the economic system in static fashion, it was reasonable to treat it as a self-righting mechanism. A static economy is inherently stable; small causes produce small effects; the system is therefore not liable to large disturbances, excepting those which originate definitely outside itself. But this appearance of stability was only achieved by leaving out part of the problem. As soon as we take expectations into account (or rather, as soon as we take the elasticity of expectations into account), the stability of the system is seriously weakened. Special reasons may indeed give it a sufficient amount of stability to enable it to carry on (we shall examine these special reasons in the next chapter), but it is not inherently and necessarily stable. It is henceforth not at all surprising that the economic system of reality should be subject to large fluctuations, nor that these fluctuations should be so very dangerous.

As has been made evident from the line of approach we have chosen, our proposition is an extension of the famous proposition of Wicksell about the 'cumulative process'. One naturally associates it, however, with the name of Mr. Keynes, as well as with that of Wicksell. In *The General Theory of Employment* the proposition is turned the right way round; but the proof of it which Mr. Keynes gives is more limited than ours. He assumes a unity elasticity of expectations only for prices expected to rule in the near future; for prices expected in the further future he assumes that they move with money wages. (In his terminology, the Marginal Efficiency of Capital is given in terms of *wage-units*.) Consequently, the instability of the system is regarded as being in abeyance so long as money wages are kept constant (for then the more distant prices have a zero elasticity of expectations, and this acts as a stabilizer). It is only when money wages move that instability (or imperfect stability) declares itself. I think my proof is more general. It is true that the formal statement of my proof depends upon the assumption that expected prices of commodity *X* are only affected by the current price of that same commodity, not by other current prices.[1] If this had to be taken strictly, it would make my proof as limited as Mr. Keynes's. But there is no need to take it strictly. Expected prices can depend on current prices in any way whatsoever—so long as a proportionate rise in *all* current prices raises *all* expected prices in the same proportion —and my proof holds.

When the argument is stated as Mr. Keynes states it, it looks possible to maintain that the instability (alleged to occur when money wages are flexible) is due simply to the special assumption about the nature of expectations which he has made. My proof shows this to be wrong. In itself, the instability has nothing to do with wages; although, as we shall see, there are reasons for supposing that a special importance has to be attributed to wage-policy when it is a question of working out the practical consequences of the instability. The instability is not a property of wages; it is a property of money and of securities, those awkward things which are not demanded for their own sake, but as a means to the purchase of commodities at future dates.[2]

[1] Cf. the definition of 'elasticity of expectations', p. 205, above.

[2] Some time after the original publication of this book, the argument of the above chapter was submitted to a close scrutiny by Professor Lange in his *Price Flexibility and Employment* (Cowles Commission, 1944) and also by Dr. Mosak in his *General Equilibrium Theory in International Trade* (also Cowles Commission, 1944). As a result of their work, I feel that my treatment should be somewhat modified, though not in a way which substantially affects the argument. It is not a case where the necessary amendments can be easily incorporated into the text, as I have done with some of the amendments I have introduced into this revised edition; consequently I have left the text of this chapter unaltered, and have set out the qualifications I should now desire to make in an additional note at the end of the volume (Additional Note B, p. 333).

Another line of inquiry which has thrown new light upon these matters is the 'process analysis' of Professor Samuelson. When I was writing my original text, the form of process analysis which I had mainly in mind was that of Professor D. H. Robertson, and some reference to his work was made in this place (in a footnote now suppressed). Later work has shown that process analysis has a closer relevance to the issues I was discussing than I then supposed. I am still not convinced that it has a very close relevance, but it deserves more discussion than I gave it in 1938. I have therefore included a further note on this subject (Additional Note C, p. 335).

CHAPTER XXI

THE TEMPORARY EQUILIBRIUM OF THE WHOLE SYSTEM

II. *Possible Stabilizers*

1. WE are now in the position of having constructed a model economy, which we have found to lie upon the verge of instability. It is not a realistic model; it is a very much simplified model; yet it appears to have some relevance to actual situations. The kind of instability it exhibits is recognizable as being akin to the instability we seem to detect in the economic systems of reality— the instability which makes them liable to fluctuations; nevertheless, though they show this instability, they do not seem to be unstable to such an exaggerated degree. Consequently, somewhere among the modifications which would have to be introduced if our model is to be made more realistic, we should expect to find possible stabilizers—elements which limit the fluctuations of the economy, though they do not prevent it from fluctuating altogether.

Let us proceed to relax some of the special assumptions under which our model was constructed; and see what the consequences of such relaxation are likely to be. This will involve us in a series of separate investigations, which had better be conducted under separate heads.

2. *The rate of interest.* The first possible stabilizer is the rate of interest. It will have been observed that the system we have been discussing is not wholly unstable (at least we have not shown it to be wholly unstable); it is imperfectly stable, being unstable if all secondary price-reactions *save one* are taken into account, but not necessarily unstable if *all* reactions are taken into account, including that on the rate of interest. While general prices swing up and down in this uncontrolled manner, what will have been happening to the rate of interest?

As often happens, the rate of interest can be most conveniently thought of as being determined, not on the market for loans, but on the market for money. The demand for money must continue to equal the supply, if the rate of interest is to remain unchanged.

Now we have seen that the main factors governing the demand for money can be taken as being (1) the rate of interest, (2) people's planned rate of expenditure in the near future (in money terms). The first is supposed unaffected, but the second must be affected when there is a general change in prices. If prices rise by so much *per cent.* (being expected, *ex hypothesi*, to remain at the higher level), and the goods and services people plan to buy are unaltered in quantity, then the demand for money must rise. Consequently, the rate of interest can only remain unaffected—our provisional assumption can only be a valid assumption—if the supply of money is increased to match the increased demand. Otherwise, the rate of interest will rise, and this will check the rise in prices.

This is all very well; but when we turn to the converse case of a fall in prices, a new difficulty presents itself. It is now necessary for the rate of interest to fall, in order for equilibrium to be restored. If the rate of interest was reasonably high to begin with, it seems possible that this reaction may take place without difficulty. But if the rate of interest is very low to begin with, it may be impossible for it to fall farther—since, as we have seen, securities are inferior substitutes for money, and can never command a higher price than money. In this case, the system does not merely suffer from imperfect stability; it is absolutely unstable. Adequate control over the supply of money can always prevent prices rising indefinitely, but it cannot necessarily prevent them from falling indefinitely. Trade slumps are more dangerous (not merely more unpleasant) than trade booms.

The discovery of this dangerous possibility is due to Mr. Keynes. From some points of view it is the most important thing in his *General Theory*, since it finally explodes the comfortable belief (still retained by Wicksell, and inherited by many contemporary economists) that in the last resort monetary control (that is to say, interest control) can do everything. But although that is where Mr. Keynes's doctrine leads, he himself expresses more faith in the rate of interest than one feels he ought to do on his own principles; consequently, I think the matter will stand a little further investigation here.

3. So far we have talked about reactions through *the* rate of interest, without specifying what rate of interest—a thing which it is only legitimate to do if one is dealing with a simplified model in which there is only one rate of interest, or alternatively, if one is assuming the system of interest rates to be bound together in some given way. As we discovered in Chapter XI above, the mutual relations of different interest rates depend partly upon risk-factors, and partly upon the expected course of interest rates in the future. These interest-expectations can be regarded either as expectations of future short rates, or as expectations of future long rates—the same theory can be expressed in either set of terms. If we take interest-expectations as being expectations of short rates, then we should say that the current long rate is compounded out of the current short rate and the future short rates that are expected to rule during the currency of the loan; if we take them as expectations of long rates, then the current short rate is determined at that level which just makes it preferable to borrow or lend short, instead of borrowing or lending long and then cancelling the loan by another transaction of the same kind in the contrary direction at the end of a short period.

Let us begin by working out our argument on the assumption that interest-expectations mean expectations of short rates. Then the effect of a general fall in prices on the system of interest rates depends on whether these interest-expectations are elastic or inelastic. (In all our discussion of the elasticity of price-expectations, we have had no cause hitherto to pay any attention to the elasticity of interest-expectations; but we had to come to it sooner or later.) If interest-expectations are rigidly inelastic, a change in the short rate can have very little influence upon long rates of interest; long rates can therefore be taken as given (or nearly so). The rate of interest whose changes we have been discussing must be almost solely a short rate. In this case, where the whole burden of adjustment is thrown upon the short rate, any considerable alteration in the price-level must lead to very considerable changes in this (short) rate of interest, if the supply of money is not adjusted. It becomes very easily conceivable that downward adjustments may be necessary on a scale which would involve a negative rate of interest, if interest changes are to restore equilibrium. Consequently, the system may very easily be absolutely unstable.

If, however, interest-expectations are elastic, a reduction in short rates will be accompanied by a significant reduction in long rates. Since reductions in long rates presumably have some additional tendency to increase the demand for current commodities, and hence to check the fall in prices, a smaller movement of the short rate will be necessary to restore equilibrium when interest-expectations are elastic than when they are inelastic. It becomes less likely that the short rate will have to be reduced to an impossible extent in order to preserve equilibrium.

Substantially the same argument may be stated in terms of expectations of long rates. If these expectations are inelastic, the current long rate cannot possibly fall by more than a very slight extent. For example, if the current long rate is 4 per cent., and it is expected to be 4 per cent. in a year's time, then 4 per cent. is the yield which can be earned by investing money now, rather than holding it in money form and only investing it in securities at the end of the year. But if the expected rate remains at 4 per cent., and the current rate falls to $3\frac{7}{8}$ per cent., the net amount which can be earned on a year's loan (allowing for the expected capital loss) is only $\frac{3}{4}$ per cent. If the current rate falls only a little farther, the net yield on a year's loan becomes negative. When allowance is made for the riskiness of investing in long-term securities,[1] it becomes clear that a very slight fall in the long rate of interest will be sufficient to make people postpone the purchase of securities, so long as they are under the impression that the fall is only temporary, and that the rate will soon be back at its old level.[2]

Thus, whether the matter is looked at in terms of expectations of long rates, or in terms of expectations of short rates, it seems to come out in the same way. Even a large fall in the demand for money is not sufficient in itself to bring about a general fall in interest rates; it will certainly be effective in reducing short rates as far as they can be reduced, but it will only exert an appreciable influence upon long rates if interest-expectations are fairly elastic. The long rate of interest is not a thing which it is possible to reduce temporarily (or what appears to be temporarily); if people do not

---

[1] Cf. Chapter XI above.

[2] Since (above, p. 149) the net yield obtainable by investing in long-term securities for a given period is $R+(R/R')-1$ (where R is the current long-term rate, and R' is the rate expected to rule at the end of the period), the maximum possible fall in the rate is easily calculated. Since $R+(R/R')-1$ must be > 0, R must be $> R'/(1+R')$; approximately, $R > R'(1-R')$. If the rate at the end of a year is expected to be 4 per cent., the current rate cannot fall below it by more than 4 per cent. of 4 per cent.; and so on. This is the maximum fall possible under any conceivable conditions; since it neglects risk, it exaggerates the fall which is possible practically. Cf. Keynes, *General Theory*, p. 202.

believe that the decline is fairly permanent, the rate will fail to come down to an appreciable extent.

4. While a high elasticity of price-expectations is a destabilizer, a high elasticity of interest-expectations thus appears to be a stabilizing influence. If there were the same prospect of interest-expectations being elastic as there is of price-expectations being elastic (and particularly if the two things were likely to occur together), the prospect of the whole system being effectively stabilized by interest changes would be fairly bright. Unfortunately it does not seem likely that highly elastic interest-expectations are as common as highly elastic price-expectations. Price-levels can move up and down to any extent whatever, and quiet times can be enjoyed at all sorts of levels of prices. However much the price-level rises or falls, the mere fact of its having risen or fallen gives no necessary presumption that it will return to its old level, or anywhere near it.[1] But the sort of variations in interest rates which are consistent with quiet times and with the maintenance of organized markets are quite small; for, as we have seen, the level of interest rates ultimately measures the intensity of a certain set of risk factors, and this intensity is unlikely to remain for long outside certain broad limits. Consequently, when the rate of interest (any rate of interest) rises or falls very far, there is a real presumption that it will come back to a 'normal' level. This consideration would seem to prevent interest-expectations from being very elastic.[2]

The effectiveness of the rate of interest as a stabilizer depends not only upon the extent to which changes in short rates are transmitted to long rates (a point about which we cannot be very optimistic), but also upon the extent to which we can rely upon interest changes affecting prices. Here, too, the situation does not

---

[1] But see below, pp. 270–1.

[2] The existing long rate discounts the sort of changes in short rates which are expected to occur, not only in the near future, but in the more remote future as well. A sharp fall in the short rate may therefore be expected to push down the long rate in time, if the short rate goes on being maintained at the new level, and this creates an expectation that high short rates are less likely in the future than they were in the past; but it will only react quickly upon the long rate if there is immediately apparent some significant reason why this should be so— as happened, on a rare occasion, in England in 1932, when a period of high short rates, necessitated by an awkward clinging to the gold standard, was brought to a definite close.

look very favourable. As we saw in a previous chapter, the long rate ought, theoretically, to be more effective than the short rate, because the discounted prices of distant outputs are influenced by interest much more than the discounted prices of outputs due for the near future.[1] But the long rate itself can only be effective if people are planning far ahead, otherwise there are no distant outputs to be affected. Now when prices are falling, a psychological condition of depression seems to be induced, which is very unpropitious to distant planning.[2] So once again, for this reason, interest changes are likely to be effective for stopping an upward movement of prices, but much less effective for stopping a downward movement.

All the relevant considerations point in this same direction. If prices are moving upwards, and the supply of money is not (at least after a point) increased proportionately, the short rate of interest will certainly rise. There is no limit to its possible rise, and this in itself can be quite sufficient to stop any rise in prices. But how far the short rate will have to rise depends upon the effect upon long rates (which depends on the elasticity of interest-expectations). If the long rate does rise too, this also may be expected to be an effective brake; so it will diminish the extent of the rise in the short rate which will be necessary. Nevertheless, even if the long rate does not rise, the short rate can be quite effective by itself—though of course a larger rise in the short rate will be necessary in that case.

On the other hand, if prices are moving downward, the extent of the fall in short rates which is possible is very limited, and such a limited fall may be insufficient to check the fall in prices unless long rates fall too. But in this case, even if long rates do fall, the situation is still not certainly cleared up; for this is the case when the effect on prices of a fall in long rates may well be at a minimum. Taking all these things together, we may say that interest policy—which is monetary policy—gets very high marks as a means of checking booms, but very low marks as a means of checking slumps. It can set a point beyond which prices shall not rise; but it cannot ensure that they do rise to that point.

We have had to occupy ourselves for some time with the rate of interest; it looked such a hopeful stabilizer, and turns out to be such a broken reed. Let us now turn to some of the other modifications which are needed to make our model more realistic. We begin with the least hopeful.

5. *Past contracts*. So far we have left out of account the fact that in any actual economy the transactions of any given short period take place against a background of contracts inherited from the past. These contracts have ordinarily been made in money terms; thus if all prices change in the same proportion, and the rate of interest is unchanged, every one is not in fact left in the same situation, as we have been supposing hitherto. Those people who are due to receive money payments arising out of past contracts are made worse off when prices rise; debtors are made better off. This change in the distribution of wealth will have some effect on the demands for different goods, and may have some effect on the total demand in terms of money for goods in general.

This effect is evidently an *income effect*, in the sense in which we have been using that term; as usual, nothing can be said *a priori* about its direction. In practice, one may guess that the debtor class will perhaps spend a larger proportion of an increment of income than the creditor class would. If this is so, the aggregate demand for consumers' goods would tend to increase when prices rise; and the existence of contracts fixed up in the past turns out to be a destabilizing influence, rather than a stabilizer. But it may always work the other way.

There is, however, another more important point to be considered. When there occurs a general fall in prices (or at least a fall of any magnitude), a new influence comes in which must cause these fixed contracts to be destabilizing. As the real value of debts increases, it becomes more and more difficult for debtors to meet their obligations. The first result is that the *fear* of bankruptcy spreads wider and wider through the debtor class; with this risk hanging over them, they become less and less willing to expose themselves to other risks; they become disinclined to start new processes of production, and try to convert their assets into the most liquid form possible.[1] Next, when bankruptcy or default actually occurs, there is generally a further period during which arrangements for a composition are made; during this period, when the ownership of assets is uncertain, initiative is

---

[1] This will be recognized as the 'depression psychology' which diminishes the effectiveness of the interest rate.

paralysed. Taking all these things together, the fall in prices tends to reduce inputs, therefore lowers the demand for goods, therefore lowers prices yet further. The burden of debts is a potent agent of deflation.[1]

6. *Price rigidities.* The next point we have to consider offers a prospect which is, in a sense, more hopeful. So far we have been assuming that prices are perfectly flexible, so that it is possible for *all* prices to move together, under the free play of supply and demand, in the course of a single week's trading. This assumption too must now be dropped, for it is of course highly unrealistic. In most communities there are a large number of prices which, for one reason or another, are fairly insensitive to economic forces, at least over short periods. This rigidity may be due to legislative control, or to monopolistic action (of the sleepy sort which does not strain after every gnat of profit, but prefers a quiet life).[2] It may be due to lingering notions of a 'just price'. The most important class of prices subject to such rigidities are wage-rates; they are affected by rigidity from all three causes. They are particularly likely to be affected by ethical notions, since the wage-contract is very much a personal contract, and will only proceed smoothly if it is regarded as 'fair' by both parties. But, for whatever cause rigidity occurs, it means that some prices do not move upward or downward in sympathy with the rest—they may consequently exercise a stabilizing influence.

[1] The increased demand for money, which accompanies debt deflation, will not necessarily raise the rate of interest. If the rate of interest has already fallen to a minimum, so that there is much 'idle money', it can be met without causing any strain on the money supply. Thus a spate of bankruptcies is quite compatible with low interest rates in the later stages of trade depression. On the other hand, the high rates of interest which often prevail during a crisis are largely to be explained on these lines.

[2] This particular sort of monopolistic action is simply a kind of price rigidity, and has just the same chances of being a stabilizer as any other kind of price rigidity. Otherwise, there is no particular reason to suppose that monopolistic action is stabilizing. If the general equilibrium system under conditions of monopoly could be assumed to be determinate, the Wicksell–Keynes proposition (discussed in the preceding chapter) would apparently hold even under monopoly; a general proportional change in prices would reproduce the same *real* situation as before, and would therefore leave equilibrium undisturbed. But I must admit to having grave doubts whether the general monopoly system is determinate in the relevant sense. If it is not determinate, anything may happen; but I do not see any reason to suppose that this 'anything' is bound to be stabilizing.

Even apart from their function as stabilizers, these rigidities are undoubtedly phenomena of great economic importance; for their existence explains why disturbances of the sort we are considering produce not only large changes in prices, but also large changes in production and employment. Mr. Keynes goes so far as to make the rigidity of wage-rates the corner-stone of his system. While his way of putting it has many advantages for practical application, it seems to me that the more fundamental sociological implications are brought out better if we treat rigid wage-rates as merely one sort of rigid prices. It is hard to exaggerate the immediate practical importance of the unemployment of labour, but its bearing on the nature of capitalism comes out better if we look at it alongside the unemployment (and even the misemployment) of other things.[1]

A method by which the existence of a rigid price for some particular commodity can be allowed for within the framework of our analysis has already been worked out at an earlier stage of this book.[2] We suppose that all other prices are given, and under this assumption we draw a demand curve (DD) and a supply curve (SS) for the commodity in question. If the price of that commodity were free to move, it would be determined at the intersection of these curves. But if it is fixed at (say) a higher level, only an amount ON ($=LP$ or MQ) will be sold, although sellers would be willing to supply an amount LT. The situation is therefore identical with that which would have arisen if a price OL had been fixed for buyers only, a price OM for sellers only, the difference between these prices being handed over as a bonus to those sellers who do actually make sales. We have already found the convenience of this device in other connexions; it can be used for the present problem as well.

Suppose that all prices, except the rigid price and the 'shadow' sellers' price, rise in the same proportion. If elasticities of expectations are unity, the demand and supply curves retain their original shape, but move upwards. The resulting position can be best exhibited if we simply change the scale on which prices are measured on the vertical axis, so that the new demand and supply

[1] Mrs. Robinson has done something to extend Mr. Keynes's doctrine in her theory of 'Disguised Unemployment' (*Essays in the Theory of Employment*). But she has not shown what are the exact limits to which the extension is possible.   [2] See the note to Chapter VIII, above.

curves occupy the same positions as the old ones, and we can use
the old diagram. Only, since the scale of prices is changed, the
rigid buyers' price will now be represented, not by *OL*, but by
OL', which is less than *OL*. The amount bought will be *ON'*,
and the sellers' price which would make supply equal to demand
will be *OM'*, ordinarily greater than *OM*.[1] The bonus handed

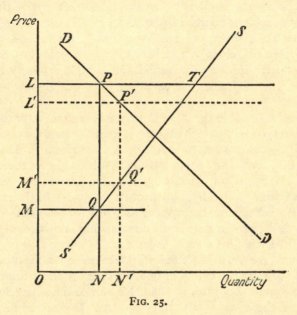

FIG. 25.

over to sellers is changed from *LPQM* to *L'P'Q'M'*; it is uncertain
which of these areas is the larger. The net effect of the general
rise in prices is thus (1) to increase the sales of the commodity,
(2) to leave the buyers' price constant, thus lowering it relatively
to other prices, (3) to raise the sellers' price relatively to other
prices, (4) to change the size of the bonus, but whether to raise it
or to lower it in real terms is uncertain.

The change in the size of the bonus produces an income effect,
indeterminate as usual. The changes in the buyers' and sellers'
prices will have some influence on the demands and supplies of
other commodities. Whether or not this influence is in the
direction of stability depends on whether the ordinary effect on

[1] It may be less than *OM* if the supply curve slopes backwards.

other prices is to raise them or to lower them. Since we began with the case of a general rise in prices, the existence of a rigid price will make for stability if these changes in the buyers' price and in the sellers' price relatively to the general price-level tend to lower the price-level.

7. The effects on other prices can be worked out in the usual way by considering substitution and complementarity relations. Since we are assuming unity elasticities of expectations, we need not concern ourselves with substitution over time, but can confine our attention to substitution and complementarity between sorts of commodities, just as if we were dealing with a static problem.

The relative fall in the buyers' price will tend to lower the prices of all those goods for which the buyers can substitute the commodity with rigid price, or into which they can transform it. It will also lower the prices of any goods which are substitutes for these goods, and so on; but it will raise the prices of complements. Since, as we have seen repeatedly, substitution is always likely to be the dominant relation in the system as a whole, the relative fall in the buyers' price is likely to be a stabilizing influence. This is of course just what we should expect.

The relative rise in the 'shadow' sellers' price, on the other hand, is likely to raise the prices of goods which are substitutes for the original commodity through the behaviour of the sellers, lower the prices of those which are complements. Owing to the general dominance of substitution, this is most likely to be a destabilizing influence. The direct effect of the rigid price is stabilizing, but the rigid price has a 'shadow' price opposed to it on the other side of the market, which is not rigid, and whose influence is likely to be destabilizing.[1]

It follows that the existence of rigid prices only makes for stability if the direct influence of the rigid price outweighs the indirect influence through the shadow price; and this is only certain

---

[1] In the converse but less important case, where the rigid price is fixed at a level which makes supply greater than demand, it is still true that the rigid price is stabilizing, the shadow price destabilizing. But it is now the sellers' price which is rigid, the buyers' price which is the shadow. A general upward movement in the prices of other goods will diminish sales of the fixed-price commodity, produce a relative fall in sellers' price, and a relative rise in buyers' price.

to happen if the movement in the shadow price (relatively to the general price-level) is small. This always *may* happen; but there is only one case in which it is certain to happen. That is the case where the rigid price is the price of a factor of production, and the units which are excluded from sale by the rigid price are wholly unemployed.

When the rigid price is the price of a product, the fact that this price does not rise when other prices rise checks the rise in price of those goods which are substitutes for the product on the demand side; but it stimulates the rise in prices of those goods which are substitutes for it on the supply side (and of factors which can be transformed into it). When the rigid price is the price of a factor, its failure to rise may still stimulate a rise in the prices of those products the factor was driven to make because it could not gain access to this industry. But if the excluded units were wholly unemployed, then the shadow price is zero, and remains zero; the existence of unemployment almost necessarily makes for stability.

The existence of unemployed labour, particularly when the unemployment extends to a good many sorts of labour, is particularly important as a stabilizer. On the one hand, there is no reaction through the shadow price; and on the other hand, such generalized labour has strong substitution (or transformation) relations with most sorts of goods. Indirectly it probably has such relations with nearly all goods, since it can be used for the production of substitutes for nearly any good. Unemployment is the best stabilizer we have yet found.

8. This is a profoundly distressing conclusion, yet it does not seem to be avoidable, so long as we assume unity elasticities of expectations. It is, of course, the conclusion of Mr. Keynes, who stresses it so much as to make his *General Theory* a *General Theory of Employment*. The upward instability of the price-system can be checked by movements of the rate of interest, but instability downwards cannot necessarily be checked in that way. The only reliable check within the system is the rigidity of wage-rates; though the operation of this check to downward instability is necessarily attended by a contraction of total output below the maximum technically possible and by the existence of unemployed labour. If the rigid wage-rates give way, then, broadly speaking, the effect is that of a fall in prices without any checking rigidity; so that general wage-reductions only involve a further fall in prices, and fail to expand employment.[1]

These conclusions follow inevitably so long as we stick to the assumption that elasticities of expectations are unity. But though we have followed that assumption through thick and thin, we are, after all, not bound to it; it is time for us to call it in question. If people believe that existing prices will continue indefinitely, and if, when prices change, they simply shift over and believe that the new prices will continue indefinitely, it means that the influence of past prices in the formation of expectations is at a minimum. This is not a general case; it is a very special case; and our investigation of its properties does not conduce to the view that it is likely to be a special case of very frequent occurrence.

If all elasticities of expectations are unity, the stability of the system can only be maintained by the existence of rigid wage-rates; but if all elasticities of expectations are unity, why should wage-rates be rigid? It cannot be maintained that wage-rates are fixed at a particular level in money terms because wage-earners want so much money for its own sake; the reason why money wages are rigid must be because those people who fix wages have some degree of confidence in a stable value of money—that is to say, because they have fairly *inelastic* price-expectations. So long as they retain the view that a certain level of prices is 'normal', it is perfectly rational for them to fix wage-rates in money terms at a level which seems to them 'fair' in relation to this 'normal' price-level. But that gives us no justification for assuming that money wages would remain rigid if the sense of normality was lost.

In order to explain the rigidity of wages, we have to assume in the parties to the wage-bargain some sense of normal prices, hardly distinguished (perhaps) from 'just' prices. The rigidity of wages extends over precisely that time—it may be quite a long time—during which the parties concerned persuade themselves that changes in related prices (whether prices of the products of labour, or of the things labour buys) are temporary changes. Once they become convinced that these changes are permanent changes, there *is* a tendency for wages to change; in situations of

[1] In practice, there is another repercussion to be taken into account, that through public finance. It is not by any means inevitable that this should work in a stabilizing direction, though there is some probability that it will do so in the end, at least in countries where there is strong pressure to relieve unemployment and not too strong a pressure to balance the budget.

extreme instability, when they have lost their sense of normal prices, negotiators have recourse to automatic sliding scales and the rigidity of money wages ceases altogether.

9. *Normal prices.* When we take this last consideration into account, the assumptions which ought to be made in order to get a reasonably realistic model of the economic system begin to define themselves. We must give the system sufficient factors of stability to enable it to work; but we must not assume that these forces are so powerful as to prevent the system from being liable to fluctuations. There must be a tendency to rigidity of certain prices, particularly wage-rates; but there must also be a tendency to rigidity of certain price-expectations as well, in order to provide an explanation for the rigidity of these prices. There is no reason to suppose that all price-expectations are inelastic. Indeed, we should do better to assume a good deal of variation in different people's elasticities of expectations. Some people's expectations do usually seem to be in fact fairly steady; they do not easily lose confidence in the maintenance of a steady level in the prices with which they are concerned; so that, when these prices vary, their natural interpretation of the situation is that the current price has become abnormally low, or abnormally high. But there are other people whose expectations are much more sensitive, who easily persuade themselves that any change in prices which they experience is a permanent change, or even that prices will go on changing in the same direction. (This difference in sensitivity between the price-expectations of different people betrays itself in a difference in the behaviour of those prices with which these people are specially concerned; sensitive traders make sensitive prices, insensitive traders sticky prices. The most sensitive prices are found in those markets which are marked out in common parlance as 'speculative markets'.)[1]

Of course the way in which a population is divided with respect to this sort of sensitivity will vary very much in different circum-

---

[1] More strictly, we ought to take into account the fact that a change in current prices may not affect people's expectations of all future prices to the same extent. Even if a person expects prices to revert to normal after some interval of time, he will still behave *sensitively* if his conduct is much influenced by the prices he expects in the near future; while the same prospect will cause a person whose current conduct is only influenced by expectations of the farther future to behave *insensitively*.

stances. People who have been accustomed to steady prices, or to very gradual price-movements, are likely to be insensitive in their expectations; people who have been accustomed to violent change will be sensitive. We have to be prepared to deal with a range of possible cases, varying from that of a settled community, which has been accustomed to steady conditions in the past (and which, for that very reason, is not easily disturbed in the present), to that of a community which has been exposed to violent disturbances of prices (and which may have to be regarded, in consequence, as being economically neurotic).

The distinction of different cases according to sensitivity depends, however, not only on the psychological condition of the individuals trading, but also on the length of time our analysis is taken to cover. We must never forget that our 'week' is arbitrary in length; this is of great importance in the formation of expectations. The elasticity of expectations depends upon the relative weight which is given to experience of the past and experience of the present; now if the 'present' is taken to cover a longer period of time, 'present experience' will necessarily weigh more heavily, and (even in the same psychological condition) expectations will tend to become more elastic. It takes a very neurotic community indeed to show much sensitivity in total over a very short period of actual time; people do not usually expect to be able to foresee the actual prices ruling on any particular day with complete accuracy, so that an appreciable variation from what they had thought to be the most probable price may fail to disturb their expectations at all. But if the average price realized over a longer period fails to agree with what had been expected, it is likely to disturb the further expectations of the most stolid. Thus it is reasonable to assume that sensitivity will increase with the length of the 'week'.

Does this mean that while any system (excepting the most neurotic) is stable in the short period, it is bound to become unstable in the long period? I do not think we need be afraid of falling into that conclusion. For the longer the period over which our 'week' is taken to extend, the less satisfactory an approximation to reality we know it becomes. There are things which lie outside Temporary Equilibrium analysis, and some of those things ought to be taken into account before we can make any generalization about long periods.

CHAPTER XXII

THE TEMPORARY EQUILIBRIUM OF THE WHOLE SYSTEM

III. *The Laws of Its Working*

1. BEFORE we leave the temporary equilibrium system, we ought to make an attempt to sum up the formal rules of its behaviour. This was the last step in our analysis of the parallel problem in statics; but here it turns out to be a great deal more complicated than it was in statics. For we have to consider not only all the same questions we considered there, but also questions of interest rates, and also the different cases of more or less elastic expectations. These complications are not merely additive but multiplicative; so when one tries to set out the results schematically, it becomes apparent that there is a perfect labyrinth of possible questions and possible answers. In these circumstances, I have decided to abandon the attempt to give a complete system of rules, and to content myself with something more modest. I shall give one fundamental proposition, on which the rules for all particular cases must be based; and afterwards I shall simply give a few illustrations of the ways in which this proposition can be applied.

The principal things we want to know about are the effects of those broad changes commonly known as hoarding, saving, and investment, upon prices and production and interest rates. These broad changes can be expressed in terms more suitable to our present discussion if they are described as shifts in demand between commodities and money, or money and securities, or commodities and securities. Our static theory has given us a technique for studying the effects of shifts in demand; so it would appear that what we have to do is to translate the static rules into terms of the triad—Commodities, Securities, Money.

Unfortunately, things are not so simple as this. It is only in one special case that there is an exact correspondence between the static system (whose rules we know) and the temporary equilibrium system (whose rules we want to discover). This is the case where all expectations are rigidly inelastic. In all other cases, there is no reason to suppose that the rules will correspond at all closely. Yet, from many points of view, it is the cases of elastic expectations (at least, fairly elastic expectations) which are the more important.

The best way of overcoming this difficulty is to split up the effect of a change with elastic expectations into steps. First of all, consider what would happen if expectations were inelastic. This will involve a certain (primary) shift in prices and interest rates. Next, suppose that price-expectations, or interest-expectations, or both, are shifted in the same direction as current prices or interest rates are shifted initially. This shift in expectations will result in a further shift in demand, similar in character to the first shift. The effects of this secondary shift can then be worked out in the same way as those of the primary shift.

One advantage of this method of analysis is that it gives us a logical sequence which is not unlikely to correspond fairly well with the actual temporal sequence of cause and effect. We have seen that expectations usually become more elastic, the more time is allowed for adjustment.[1] Thus the primary effects of changes, as we shall work them out, bear at least some relation to the impact effects; the secondary effects of our sequence may well be the same as those effects which are deferred in time.

2. The first thing to be done, then, is to work out the rules for a system with inelastic expectations. It will be sufficient, for the purpose of working out formal rules, if we reduce the system to a triangle, consisting of three 'goods'—commodities, securities, money. Three 'goods' gives us two 'prices'—the price-level of commodities and the price of securities, which is an expression for the rate of interest. How will these 'prices' be affected when there is a shift in demand?

The behaviour of such a triangle as this was worked out in detail in Chapter V above. In a system which can be reduced to the exchange of three goods X, Y, Z, an increase in the demand for X in terms of Z must raise the price of X in terms of Z. The effect on the price of Y was divided into an income effect and a substitution effect. The substitution effect tends to raise the price of Y in terms of Z if X and Y are substitutes, lower it if they are complements. It will lower the price of Y in terms of X if Y and Z are substitutes, raise it if they are complements. So far as the income effect is concerned, it is best dealt with by taking the initial price-change due to the substitution effect, and considering whether the change in the distribution of wealth brought about by this initial price-change will have any important effect on the relative demand for the different 'goods' (the same device as we are using for dealing with expectations). If there is an important change in relative demand, it will have to be allowed for in calculating the final issue.

When we apply this reasoning to the triad—commodities, securities, money—it is evident that there is little which can be said *in general* about the income effect, though care must be taken to allow for it when making particular applications. Quite a good deal can be said about the substitution effect, however; on that we may proceed to concentrate attention.

First of all, is there likely to be any complementarity between any pair of the triad? This is a matter which we have not properly settled. However, we have seen reason to suppose that money and securities are likely to be *close* substitutes;[1] if that is so, it is unlikely that the relations between money and commodities on the one hand, and securities and commodities on the other, can be very different. This would mean that all the three pairs composing the triad must be substitutes. For at most only one pair out of the three can be complementary (according to the usual rule), so that either money–commodities must be complementary, while securities–commodities is not, or vice versa. If these possibilities are ruled out, the only alternative left is that all three pairs are substitutes.

We know how the system works in that case, so we need only state the old rules in the new terms.

i. An increase in the demand for commodities in terms of money will raise the price-level of commodities in terms of money. Since securities are substitutes for commodities, their price will rise too; that is to say, the rate of interest will fall.

ii. An increase in the demand for securities in terms of money will raise the price of securities—that is to say, it will lower the rate of interest. Since securities and commodities are substitutes, it will also raise the prices of commodities.

iii. An increase in the demand for securities in terms of commodities will raise the price of securities relatively to the

[1] Cf. Chapter XIII, above.

price-level of commodities; since there is no complementarity present, the value of money must rise in terms of commodities, and fall in terms of securities. In money terms, the price-level of commodities must fall, and the rate of interest fall.

3. These appear to be the formal rules for the working of an economy with inelastic expectations. The second and third of these rules seem quite acceptable at first sight; the first is rather more surprising. Yet it, too, appears to be acceptable when it is worked out in detail, full attention being paid to the precise assumptions under which alone it is claimed to be valid.

Let us say that there is an increase in the demand for some particular commodity; expectations are inelastic, so that the increase in demand must be understood to be temporary, and all consequential changes in prices must be understood to be temporary too. The increase in demand will then be met, so far as is possible, by drawing on stocks or accelerating production; this will damp down the repercussions on other prices, so that it is easily understandable that a large temporary increase in demand may affect the price of the first commodity very little, and may affect other prices to an almost negligible extent. However, all this drawing on the future must have another side to it; sellers selling now rather than in the future must either build up money balances or borrow less (more rapid repayment of loans being reckoned as a form of reduction in borrowing); buyers postponing purchases must either build up money balances or increase their lending. If the reaction is entirely upon the demand for money (as it may be if the times for which purchases are postponed and sales antedated are short), then the rate of interest will be entirely unaffected. But in so far as there is any repercussion upon the rate of interest, it is bound to be in a downward direction.

It must of course be understood that all these repercussions of temporary changes in demand are likely to be small; and repercussions upon the rate of interest are likely to be particularly small, in view of the close substitutability between money and securities. This substitutability is more in evidence if the rate of interest is low than it is if the rate of interest is high (as is made evident by the fact that it is this substitutability which keeps the rate of interest from falling to zero); consequently, if the rate is very low to begin with, no moderate change in data of any kind may be able to shift it; if it is high to begin with, it may be affected much more easily.

4. Let us now proceed to take the elasticity of expectations into account, beginning with the elasticity of price-expectations. In order to allow for this we need to know what the effects of a change in price-expectations are likely to be; that is to say, what sorts of shifts in demand (of the kind we have been discussing) it is likely to produce. It turns out that it can work in two or three different ways. On the one hand, since future goods and present goods are ordinarily substitutes, there is a presumption that a rise in price-expectations will increase the demand for current commodities. If a firm comes to expect higher prices in the future for the goods it produces, it will probably increase its input of factors in the present, and perhaps decrease its output of products. This increase in input (or decrease in output) must be balanced by a corresponding movement in the demand either for securities or for money. The firm may therefore be thought of as shifting its demand from money, or from securities, to commodities; and we know the consequences of such a shift as that. If the increased 'investment' is financed by borrowing, the net change is an increased demand for commodities in terms of securities; this will raise the price-level of commodities, and raise the rate of interest. If it is financed in part by a diminished demand for money, then the rise in the rate of interest will be checked or even abolished; but the rise in commodity prices will be stimulated.

Can anything be said about the relative probability of these two sorts of financing? The most likely reason why 'investment' should be financed by dishoarding is that entrepreneurs have been expecting an opportunity of this sort to come along at some time or another, and have been holding money balances in anticipation of the opportunity. Thus, if it is an entirely new opportunity, it will probably have to be financed by borrowing; if it is not unexpected in itself, but only its date is unexpected, it may be financed by dishoarding. (Something of this sort may well happen on a large scale in the early stages of trade recovery; it is one reason why there may be no particular pressure on interest rates at these early stages.)

On the other hand, if a firm expects higher prices for the factors it plans to employ, it will not necessarily increase its current input

T

of factors; since complementarity over time among factors occurs not infrequently. But if the higher prices are expected to occur in the near future, then its planned rate of expenditure on factors (in money terms) is increased; so that there may be an increase in its demand for money. This would reckon as a shift in demand from securities to money.

There are other reasons, too, why the demand for money may increase. A rise in the expected prices of products implies a rise in the income of the entrepreneur, and this may result in a rise in his expenditure (both his actual expenditure in the present and his planned expenditure in the near future) on consumption goods. This must reckon as a shift in demand to commodities, and probably to money as well, from securities.

The same kind of analysis could be made for the price-expectations of the private individual, though it is hardly worth while to follow it out in detail. There would be some tendency for substitution over time, implying an increased demand for commodities in the present; and, in so far as the rise in price-expectations involves an expectation of increased receipts, there may be an increased demand for money as well.

When we look at all these different tendencies together, it becomes clear that a rise in price-expectations may work itself out in several different ways. The most likely effect is a shift in demand in favour of commodities, mainly at the expense of the demand for securities; this would involve a rise in the price-level of commodities, and a certain tendency for the rate of interest to rise as well. But this is not the only possibility. There are strong reasons making for a shift in demand from securities to money, which would intensify the effect on the rate of interest and put a brake on the rise in prices. Some allowance ought usually to be made for this. And then cases are conceivable in which the shift in favour of demand for commodities would be balanced by a reduction in the demand for money, so that the rate of interest may fail to rise; and it is even possible for a rise in some price-expectations (such as expected prices of factors) to fail to induce a rise in the demand for commodities in general (including the factors in question). However, we should probably be justified if we treat these last cases as exceptional; when we are concerned with a rise in price-expectations which is at all general, they will usually be swamped by forces working in the opposite direction.

5. Somewhat tentatively, then, we may say that the usual effect of a rise in price-expectations is to raise prices and raise the rate of interest; the usual effect of a fall in price-expectations is to lower prices and lower the rate of interest. In a system where price-expectations are elastic, a change in current prices changes price-expectations in the same direction; consequently the rules which we gave previously for the case of inelastic expectations can now be extended to cover the case of elastic price-expectations. The extension is subject to all the qualifications given above; nevertheless, its main lines are fairly clear.

When price-expectations are elastic, all the effects on prices, which we worked out for the case of inelastic expectations, are likely to be intensified; but the rate of interest is always likely to move in the *same* direction as the price-level. Thus, if (i) we start with a shift of demand to commodities from money, the primary effect is to raise prices a little and (if anything) to lower the rate of interest; the secondary effect is to raise prices further, but to *raise* the interest rate. (ii) If we start with a shift in demand to securities from money, the process is similar; the primary effect is to lower the rate of interest, and to raise prices; the secondary effect is to raise prices yet further, and to raise the rate of interest.[1] (But here it must be observed that the secondary effect only occurs if prices are actually raised by the primary effect; if the rate of interest is as low as it will go, or if a fall in interest fails to stimulate the demand for goods, there may be no secondary effect at all.) (iii) If we start with a shift in demand from securities to commodities, the primary effect is to raise prices and raise the interest rate; here the secondary effect only intensifies the primary effect.

It is not at all surprising to find that some of these repercussions in a system with elastic price-expectations look very treacherous; for we know that when the elasticity of price-expectations passes a certain point the system becomes dubiously stable. A world in which an increased demand for securities in terms of money may (even in the end) raise the rate of interest has its instability proclaimed aloud by this condition and this condition alone.

---

[1] Cf. Marshall, *Money, Credit and Commerce*, p. 257: 'The new currency . . . increases the willingness of lenders to lend in the first instance, and lowers the rate of discount. But it afterwards raises prices; and therefore it tends to increase discount.'

As we saw in the last chapter, the instability of the system may be expected to reveal itself only slowly, expectations becoming more elastic as more time is allowed. This is the justification for regarding the primary effects we have just analysed as being impact effects, and the secondary effects as representing further stages in the causal process. However, it must not be supposed that the increasing elasticity of expectations is likely to proceed at all evenly; it is much more probable that the rate at which expectations become more elastic will be very different in different markets. If the first stage of the process is roughly represented by our primary effects, the next stage will be one in which the elasticity of some expectations has increased considerably, while others have not altered much. In this next stage, then, we have to superimpose upon the primary effects the effects of a change in some people's price-expectations for some goods; and that will affect particularly the prices of those goods and of other goods closely allied to them. This is a point of great importance for the detailed working out of a process of price-change. The effects of an initial disturbance upon the general system of prices are not exhausted by the sort of effects upon related goods which we identified in our static analysis. If there is an increase in the demand for commodity X, it is not necessarily those goods which are the closest substitutes for X whose prices will be most affected at a given stage in the causal process; it is quite possible that there may be a greater change in the prices of some goods which are less closely related to X, but which are traded in by persons who have more elastic expectations.[1]

Another consequence of the relative insensitivity of certain price-expectations is the rigidity of wage-rates. Wage-rigidity presumes a certain amount of unemployment; over a certain range, changes in the demand for labour reflect themselves in changes in employment, rather than in changes in wage-rates. So long as the sorts of capacity possessed by the unemployed are fairly well varied, it is reasonable to assume that labour in general is a strong 'substitute' for other goods in general; it follows from this that the employment of labour (and consequently the aggregate volume of production also) will be directly correlated with the price-level we have been discussing, and will obey the same laws. However, as unemployment falls, and as the variety of capacity in the unem-

[1] Is this why it appears to be easier to stimulate a boom by increasing the demand for capital goods than by increasing the demand for consumption goods?

ployed population diminishes, wage-rates must become less rigid; a given rise in prices will then produce a smaller fall in unemployment—or (putting it the other way about) a larger disturbance of prices will be required to produce a given fall in unemployment, unless the increase in demand acts directly upon the particular kinds of labour which are still unemployed.

6. So far we have said nothing about interest-expectations. About the elasticity of interest-expectations there is not much to be said, though that little is of great importance. So long as interest-expectations are inelastic, the long-term rate of interest (which depends mainly upon interest-expectations) must be taken as approximately given; it is largely independent of changes in current demands or supplies. Therefore the rate of interest which we have been discussing must be almost solely a short rate; the long-term rate of interest cannot be much affected by the sort of changes we have been concerned with, unless the change of conditions in the security market is expected to be fairly durable.[1]

Now it is of course reasonable to assume some elasticity of interest-expectations, at least in the secondary stages of any economic process; although (as we saw in the last chapter)[2] highly elastic interest-expectations are less probable than highly elastic price-expectations. Some effect on the long-term rate of interest must therefore be allowed for, in spite of the general tendency of that rate to be rather sticky.

In order to work out this effect, let us begin by examining what would happen if there were to be a general change in interest-expectations which was not induced by any of the changes in demand we have been analysing. Assume, then, for the moment that the short-term rate of interest is given. If interest-expectations rise, without any change in the short rate, it will diminish the discounted values of future sales and purchases (sales and purchases more than a short period ahead); this will ordinarily result

---

[1] There is only one way in which it may be affected. The long rate is an average, not of expected short rates, but of forward short rates, which equal expected rates *plus* a risk-premium. (Cf. p. 147, above.) If a rise in current demand increases this risk-premium, then it may force up the long-term rate, even when interest-expectations are inelastic. Perusal of Mr. Hawtrey's latest work, *A Century of Bank Rate*, makes me feel that I have probably underestimated the importance of this consideration.

[2] P. 262, above.

in a substitution effect reducing the demand for current commodities. This will work out just like the effect of a fall in price-expectations. Various exceptions are possible, but the probable result will be that the money prices of commodities will tend to fall, and the *short* rate of interest tend to fall.

An autonomous change in interest-expectations will therefore lead to a movement of the short rate and the long rate in different directions. People's pessimism about the future course of the rate of interest leads to a fall in securities; this checks the demand for goods, and causes prices to fall; this relaxes the pressure on the short-term market.

If the change in interest-expectations is induced by a change in the current situation in the market for securities (that is to say, if interest-expectations are elastic), the same principles will hold. But now the change in the short rate induces a change in the long rate in the same direction, and that reacts back on the short-term market in such a way as to check the movement of the short rate. If interest-expectations are inelastic, the whole weight of the adjustments in interest we have been discussing is thrown on the short rate; consequently, a large fall in the demand for securities (or increase in the supply) would have a very large effect on the short rate; while on the other hand (since no interest rate can become negative) a large increase in the demand for securities may easily have no repercussions upon (or through) interest rates at all. If interest-expectations are elastic, the pressure is taken off the short-term market and shifted to the long-term market; the danger of short rates rising very high is reduced, and (in view of the additional effect on prices of changes in the long rate) so is the danger of repercussions through interest becoming inoperative because of the minimum below which interest rates cannot fall.

However, as I have said, I do not believe that we can count upon anything more than a small elasticity of interest-expectations. The long rate of interest is much more likely to be governed mainly by fairly long-run prospects; by the danger of credit restriction in the future rather than by current credit policy; by the way in which the banking system is expected to behave in emergencies, and by the extent to which those emergencies are considered likely to arise.

CHAPTER XXIII

THE ACCUMULATION OF CAPITAL

1. ONE more question remains to be considered before we can claim to have completed our task—to have laid down the main lines of a pure theory of economic dynamics. So far, in the terms of our model, we have been concerned only with what happens in a particular 'week'—that is to say, with those repercussions of economic change which might take place immediately, if people were sufficiently alert, and if communications between markets were good enough. Of course, in practice even these repercussions take some time to work themselves out; we have tried to make some allowance for that. But we have still to investigate the working of those repercussions which *must* take time to work themselves out—which are delayed, not by slowness of communication or imperfect knowledge, but by the technical duration of productive processes. In terms of our model, we have to investigate what happens in later 'weeks', as the plans drawn up on the 'first Monday' proceed to unfold themselves. On this matter there is probably a great deal to be said; I think, however, that the important things can be said fairly briefly.

The actual prices established on the second Monday are determined, like those on the first Monday, partly by the desires and expectations of the individuals composing the economy, as they happen to be at that date; to all this everything that has been said in earlier chapters applies, and no new problem is raised. But the prices established at any date are also affected by the capital equipment (in the widest sense) existing at that date; now the capital equipment existing on the second Monday is determined by the activities of preceding weeks, including that which has just elapsed. If, as is theoretically possible but practically almost impossible, the activities of that week have involved the production of goods exactly similar to those which were consumed or used up in the week (no more and no less), then the capital equipment existing on the second Monday may be exactly the same, both in amount and in composition, as that which existed on the first. In such *stationary* conditions there is no new problem to be considered here. But in all other conditions there is a new problem—that of the effect of capital accumulation (or decumulation) on prices.

Suppose that the production plans adopted by some entrepreneurs on the first Monday have involved accumulation of capital during the first week; that is to say, some of the inputs of the first week have been used, not merely to maintain in the future the first week's rates of output and input, but in order to make it possible to produce larger outputs (or employ smaller inputs) in later weeks than in the first week.[1] Suppose that the second week is one in which some of these efforts come to fruition. Then, simply as a result of carrying through the original plans, the equipment existing on the second Monday is such that either the supply of certain goods is greater than in the first week (the 'supply curves' are moved to the right) or the demand for certain goods (or services) is less. Even if tastes and expectations are just the same on the second Monday as on the first, this alteration in equipment has to be allowed for. It would appear (since an increase in supply and a fall in demand act in substantially the same way) that it must lead to a fall in prices, to a tendency for prices in general to be lower (*ceteris paribus*) on the second Monday than on the first.

However, the rule that an increase in supply necessarily leads to a general fall in prices is only bound to hold if the increase in supply is an increase *in terms of money*. It is the supply schedule in terms of money which must be moved to the right. Is that the case here? In order to see whether the second Monday's prices will be higher or lower than the first Monday's, we have to assume the same prices as were established on the first Monday to be established on the second, and then see what excesses of supply over demand (or vice versa) there will be at those prices. The position here is that we have an excess of supply over demand in the markets for those goods for which output has increased (or input diminished) as a result of the carrying through of the plans. But (assuming unchanged tastes and expectations) is that the only change in supplies or demands? Surely not. As a result of the accumulation of capital, the entrepreneurs with the developing production plans will be better off than they were on the first Monday—their prospective net receipts stream will have

---

[1] We do not need a more precise definition of capital accumulation than this for the purposes of this chapter.

risen. This is likely to increase their demands for goods, and therefore does something to offset the fall in prices.

2. The detailed working out of these forces can be best understood if we look at some of the particular cases which can readily be distinguished.

First of all, take the case where the accumulation of capital during the first week has taken the form of constructing some permanent improvement, expected to produce a constant stream of net additions to output, beginning in the second week, and going on into the indefinite future. (This is not in fact a probable case, but it is a simple case with which to start.) Here, even if similar construction goes on during the second week (if there is a cessation of construction it will of course involve a drastic change in conditions), even so the situation in the second week must differ from that in the first in two ways: (1) there is an increased output of certain goods, (2) the entrepreneurs who have made the new construction are better off. Assuming that these entrepreneurs expect unchanged prices and an unchanged rate of interest in the future, then their income has gone up by an amount exactly equal to the value of the additional output.[1] If they spend all this additional income, then there is an increase in the demand for some goods exactly equivalent to the increased supply of others. Thus, as a consequence, some prices will rise and some fall; but there will be some sort of a general price-level which can be said to be unaffected.

However, there is probably a tendency in practice for people to base their expenditure plans on the precept of living within their incomes; this probably (though not necessarily) also involves saving a portion of an increment of income. If they do this, if they spend less than the whole increment of income, then the pressure on prices will be on balance downwards. When accumulation of capital has taken the form assumed, we should thus expect a downward pressure on prices when the capital goods become ready.

This tendency to consume less than the whole of an increment of income is one reason why the accumulation of capital may exert a downward pressure on prices. But it is not the only reason.[2]

---

[1] See above, Chapter XIV.

[2] The peculiar definition of income given by Mr. Keynes (*General Theory*,

For suppose accumulation takes another form from that which we have just been assuming—a more realistic form this time. Suppose that it involves the construction of new capital goods which take a large number of weeks to produce, and only come into action as productive instruments after that period is completed. In this case, if the production of the capital goods were to be started on the first Monday, they would not be ready on the second, so that there would be no increased supply of products on the second Monday. But there would still be a rise in entrepreneurs' incomes in the second week, equal at least to the interest on the value of the construction which has already taken place. The value of their assets is increased by the new construction, and (provided their price-expectations are unchanged) they can expect to be able to consume at least a part of the interest on this increment of value without impoverishing themselves.[1] It is thus not unlikely that their expenditure will rise. There is here no increased output to match the increased expenditure, so that the sole influence on prices tends to raise them.

However, let us go on with the story. Suppose that, instead of the production of the new capital goods being started on the first Monday, it was nearly finished at that date, so that they come into action as productive instruments in the second week. In this case there is a large increase in output in the second week, and there is an increase in entrepreneurs' income; but the rise in income is very small relatively to the increase in output, for the increased receipts of the entrepreneurs have been largely discounted in advance. Even if they spend the whole of the increment of their incomes, the pressure on prices is still downwards; and will still be downwards even if the construction of a new set of capital goods of similar character is begun straight away.

This is, again, only a special case; but it serves to show that increments in output and increments in income need not correspond at all closely. In a process of capital accumulation where

ch. 6) seems to be designed in such a way as to enable him to claim that the tendency to save part of an increment of income is the only way in which capital accumulation depresses prices. I do not see the advantage of this. Surely it is better to use concepts in those senses in which it is natural to use them; and to be prepared to admit that capital accumulation can act upon prices in more than one way.

[1] A simple example, showing in detail the effect on income of a process of capital accumulation, is worked out in the note at the end of this chapter.

the construction period is at all long, where output begins to expand at a much later date than input expanded, income will increase perceptibly before output increases. In what way this reacts upon expenditure will of course depend upon people's habits in drawing up their expenditure plans (and also, in practice, upon the dividend policies of companies). It may be that people are reluctant to expand expenditure before they see the results of their savings materializing in the form of increased output. But while accounting policy may have some tendency to realize this aim in practice (it is certainly most desirable on social grounds that it should), there is no sufficient reason, from the private viewpoint, why it should do so. The natural thing to expect is that a period of active investment will witness an increase in expenditure while the capital goods are being constructed, so that little is left to offset the depressing effect of the increased output when it materializes.

In so far as the proceeds of the increased output are not used to increase expenditure, they must be used either for buying securities (including repayment of loans) or for increasing money balances. There is some reason to suppose that a process of saving (which is what this is) will show itself in part in each of these forms.[1] Whichever form it takes the rules given in the preceding chapter apply. A shift in demand from goods to securities (increased supply of goods works like diminished demand) must lead to a fall in prices and a fall in interest rates; a shift from goods to money must lead to a fall in prices, while it will probably induce (at least in the first place) a rise in the rate of interest.

Of course it must be remembered that this is only one influence at work; it may easily be offset by forces working in the opposite direction. As always, we work under the rule of *ceteris paribus*. In itself, the increased output resulting from the completion of productive processes has a depressing effect on prices; but if any of the forces which ordinarily raise prices are at work simultaneously it may be offset.

On the other hand, it must not be supposed that the fall in prices thus analysed is innocuous; that it is only the price of the product whose output has expanded which will fall, other prices being unaffected. There is a considerable probability that other prices will fall too. In view of the general dominance of substitution relations throughout the whole system (a phenomenon with

[1] See above, p. 242.

which we are by this time well acquainted), a shift in demand from some particular commodity to money will generally reduce other prices; any other particular price taken at random is more likely to fall than to rise. A shift in demand to securities is only likely to reduce other prices relatively to the price of securities; thus, if there is a sufficient fall in the rate of interest, there may be no tendency for other prices to fall. But if the rate of interest does not fall appreciably, or if such fall as occurs is insufficient to stimulate the demand for commodities appreciably, then it is probable that there will still be a fall in the money prices of other commodities, as well as in the price of that commodity whose output has increased. Taking all things together, one would say that this is the most likely eventuality.

If money wages were flexible, they would be particularly likely to fall; but in view of the rigidity of money wages, the first effect on the labour market is likely to be a rise in unemployment.

3. In cases such as we have studied in the last few chapters, where price-expectations are very elastic, the effect of such a fall in prices may be very serious if it is not offset. Even in less extreme cases, where people are slower to adjust their expectations, it may have serious effects on employment, through the rigidity of money wages. Yet all this does not mean that the accumulation of capital is undesirable, awkward though it may be in some of its effects.

For when we look at the changes in the relative prices of goods and services which are brought about by capital accumulation (it is these relative prices which determine real incomes, and it is real incomes which are important from the point of view of economic welfare), they present, in all probability, a decidedly different picture. Let us try to follow through the effect on real wages of a process of accumulation, assuming a sufficient degree of rigidity in expectations to maintain the stability of the system. It will be convenient to start from stationary conditions, and to use these stationary conditions as a standard of comparison. In the first phase of the process of accumulation, when new capital goods are being produced but are not yet completed, there is an increased demand for those resources which are needed to make the capital goods; these resources are likely to consist, in large part, of labour. The demand for labour is thus greater than it would have been if stationary conditions had continued. But the effect of this increased demand on real wages depends to some extent upon the nature of the displaced alternative, at the expense of which the demand for labour has expanded. If the demand is financed by a contraction of expenditure upon consumption goods (saving) then labour is almost certain to be benefited; since the change reduces to an increased demand for labour in terms of consumption goods—and this must raise real wages, the price of labour in terms of consumption goods. However, some attention must be paid to the extent to which the sorts of consumption goods set free by the savers are good substitutes for the sorts of consumption goods desired by the wage-earners.[1] The better substitutes they are, the larger will be the rise in real wages in terms of the wage-earners' own sorts of consumption goods.

If the demand for labour is financed in other ways—if the initial change, for instance, is an increased demand for labour in terms of securities—still the presumption is that the prices of consumption goods will rise less than the price of labour, so that real wages will still rise. (This consequence may be modified if money wages are rigid; in that case real wages must be lowered by a rise in the prices of consumption goods; but labour will still benefit by a rise in employment.)

In the middle phase of the process we have distinguished, when the expenditure of entrepreneurs (and profit-receivers in general) may run ahead of the additional output of commodities, this tendency for an improvement in labour's position may be reversed. For there is now an increased demand for consumption goods in terms of securities, and this is likely to raise the prices of consumption goods relatively to other prices as well. The tendency is still towards rising prices, and thus employment may continue to expand (if money wages are rigid); but, as compared with the first phase, the tendency of real wages is definitely downward.

In the last phase, when the output of consumption goods runs ahead of the expenditure of entrepreneurs (the stage when prices begin to fall and employment may be decreased), the effect on real wages is at first sight necessarily favourable. The change now amounts to an increased supply of consumption goods in

---

[1] Substitution on either the production side or the consumption side will serve.

terms of securities; this will lower the prices of these consumption goods relatively to other prices, therefore relatively to wages. Thus it would appear that real wages will rise, even if money wages are flexible; if money wages are rigid, real wages will rise still more, but of course at the expense of increasing unemployment.

However, this conclusion is subject to an important qualification. We saw in Chapter XVII that when entrepreneurs embark upon a process of accumulation, when they impart a *crescendo* to their production plans, the increase in input at early stages of the plan is likely to be matched, not only by an increase in output at later stages, but also by a fall in input at later stages. This must probably be interpreted to mean, not only that input at later stages is likely to be less than the increased output of the early stages, but also that it is likely to be less than the input which would have been allotted to the later date if conditions had remained stationary. At least, that is the case if ordinary substitution relations hold throughout; if early input and late input are complementary (it is not impossible that they may be) then the new equipment may go on inducing an increased demand for labour to work it, and the demand for labour may go on indefinitely at a higher level than it would have maintained in the original stationary conditions. But in any case it is most improbable that early and late input will be so complementary that they increase in the same proportions; and that is what is needed for there to be no falling off in the demand for labour in the later stages of the plan relatively to the early stages.

Now a rise in output combined with a fall in input (say a fall in the demand for labour) has a very different effect upon real wages from that which would follow from a rise in output taken alone. The depressing effect on prices is of course only intensified (our previous analysis of that is unaffected); but the effect on real wages is much less favourable. The change in prices likely to supervene in the last phase of the process of accumulation is now the same as that which would be generated by a switch from certain kinds of goods and services (among which both labour and the sorts of commodities whose output has been facilitated must be included) into securities. If money wages are flexible, real wages will fall in terms of those things whose output has not been facilitated by the capital accumulation; and will not necessarily rise even in terms of those things whose output has been facilitated. If money wages are rigid, real wages will rise; but there will be a sharp increase in unemployment.

This is the sort of change which must be expected as we pass from the second to the third phase; but we shall see the whole process in better perspective if we compare the last phase of accumulation, not with that which immediately preceded it, but with the stationary conditions from which we started. As compared with that original position, there is not necessarily a fall in the demand for labour at all; there will be if early inputs and late inputs of labour are substitutes, but not if they are complementary. The case where early and late inputs are substitutes may be described as that in which the new equipment, which has been produced, is 'labour-saving';[1] in this case there is a fall in the demand for labour, as a result of the whole process, relatively to the situation which would have arisen if no capital had been accumulated at all. The case in which early and late inputs of labour are complementary is that in which the new equipment requires additional labour to work it, and where this more than counterbalances any displacement of labour by its use.

In this complementary case, the final result of the accumulation process, taken as a whole, is an increased supply of certain commodities, and an increased demand for labour. Assuming the same amount of employment at the end as at the beginning, this will involve a rise in real wages in terms of all goods, but particularly in terms of those goods whose production has been facilitated. In the substitute ('labour-saving') case, the demand for labour is diminished, but the supply of certain goods is still increased. Real wages will fall in terms of other goods, but they may still rise in terms of these goods (unless the new equipment is very labour-saving).

Even in the long run, the accumulation of capital is thus not necessarily favourable to the interests of labour; but there are two reasons why we should expect it to be usually favourable in practice. One is the point which came up in our original discussion of the theory of production—the tendency for complementarity to be the dominant relation among factors employed in the same enterprise;[2] there is no reason why that should not apply here. There is thus no reason to expect new capital to be

---

[1] The unemployment caused is 'Technological Unemployment'.
[2] See above, Chapter VII.

generally labour-saving. But the second point is probably more important. Even if the new capital is labour-saving, it will probably raise real wages in terms of those goods whose production has been facilitated. If accumulation of many sorts of new capital goods proceeds simultaneously, the production of many sorts of consumption goods will be facilitated; so that the goods in terms of which real wages may fall will probably be unimportant relatively to the goods in terms of which real wages are likely to rise. In practice, no doubt, this has been the main reason why accumulation of capital does seem to have been so favourable to the standard of living of labour during the last century; the fact that the things whose production has been facilitated have been particularly articles of mass consumption has worked in the same direction. If there are any goods in terms of which wages have fallen as a result of the accumulation of capital, they are not goods of much importance to the wage-earner.[1]

Note to Chapter XXIII

INCOME DURING A PROCESS OF CAPITAL ACCUMULATION

Suppose that an entrepreneur is in such a position that, if he did not construct any new capital goods, he could look forward to a constant stream of net receipts A, A, A,... going on indefinitely. Then (assuming him to expect constant prices, and constant rate of interest) that amount A would be his income, on any definition. Now suppose him to use an amount B of these receipts for the first r weeks to construct a new capital instrument, which is expected to yield a constant stream of additions to output equal to C from the $(r+1)$th week onwards. His new anticipated stream of net receipts is then

$$A-B,\ A-B,\ ...,\ A-B,\ A-B,\ A+C,\ A+C,\ ....$$

The income derived from this is equivalent to that derived from a constant stream of $(A-B)$'s, together with a constant stream of $(B+C)$'s, beginning only after r weeks. Thus his new income

$$I_0 = (A-B)+(B+C)\frac{1}{(1+i)^r}.$$

[1] Of course, this is not to say that wages may not have fallen in terms of some important goods for other reasons—such, for example, as the increase of population.

His income in the second week will be that derived from a constant stream of $(A-B)$'s, together with a constant stream of $(B+C)$'s, beginning now after $(r-1)$ weeks. Thus

$$I_1 = (A-B)+(B+C)\frac{1}{(1+i)^{r-1}}.$$

Now, it would not have been worth his while to construct the new capital good unless the income secured by constructing it is at least equal to that which would have been secured without. Therefore I_0 cannot be less than A. Suppose, for simplicity (it makes no difference to the argument), that $I_0 = A$.

Then

$$A = A-B+\frac{B+C}{(1+i)^r}. \qquad \therefore\ B+C = B(1+i)^r.$$

$$\therefore I_1 = (A-B)+B(1+i) = A+iB.$$

Similarly,

$$I_2 = (A-B)+B(1+i)^2 = A+2iB \quad \text{(assuming simple interest)}.$$

In the week before the capital good comes into production,

$$I_{r-1} = (A-B)+B(1+i)^{r-1} = A+(r-1)iB \quad \text{(assuming simple interest)}.$$

In the following week,

$$I_r = (A-B)+B(1+i)^r = A+riB \quad \text{(assuming simple interest)}.$$

The increase in income between these last two weeks is thus approximately iB; but the increase in output is C, which equals $B(1+i)^r-B$. Again assuming simple interest, this is approximately riB.

Thus, the longer the period of construction, the more important is the increase in output, relatively to any increase in spending, due to increase in income, which can be expected to offset it at the date when it accrues.

CHAPTER XXIV

CONCLUSION—THE TRADE CYCLE

1. ON coming to the end of such a task as this, one is tempted to turn round and make a lot of general reflections about things in general. There is even one side of one's mind which says one ought to do so; the economic outlook in which we were most of us brought up was based on static theory, so that now, when we have the main outline of a dynamic theory in our hands, and it turns out to be so very different from static theory, we are bound to find it making a difference to our general outlook. Sooner or later, an attempt must be made to assess that difference, and to work out the practical consequences of the new point of view. Some such attempts have been made by Mr. Keynes and by his followers; but it does not seem clear that we need go the whole way with them, for the view of capitalism which is included in their work contains other elements besides those which are necessarily implied in the transition to a dynamic theoretical basis. What is needed is a statement of the minimum change in outlook necessary; but although I have tried to give the materials out of which such a statement could be made up, I do not think I can venture to give it in this place.

For this there are several reasons. One is the mere fact that this book has already run to a considerable length; it has taken a good deal of time to write, and will (I fear) have taken a good deal of time to read—so that I can hardly hope to ask the reader's patience longer. Another is due to the peculiarity of the analytical methods employed, so different from those commonly used by contemporary economists, and particularly different from those commonly used in the town of Cambridge, where this book has been written. This has made it impossible for me to have the advantage of constantly submitting my work in small portions to the judgement of others, in spite of the admirable critical ability which might have seemed to be so near at hand. Criticism will have to come after publication, not before; and I should like to have the advantage of that criticism before expressing my opinions on the widest issues.

Finally, I do not think it is possible to form the needed sort of *Weltanschauung* from theory alone. It is particularly necessary to confront our theory of the dynamic process with our historical knowledge of the development of capitalism before we can reach an economic philosophy with which we can hope to be contented. Obviously, this cannot be done briefly, or without introducing a whole mass of new considerations, which would be out of place in a work of the character I have tried to write.

So I shall content myself with a few tentative reflections.

2. The reader will probably have been impressed (as I have certainly been impressed while writing) with the close concordance between the phenomena of a process of capital accumulation (as we have worked them out in the last chapters) and the phenomena we actually observe during a period of trade boom. It is not necessary, on our theory, that a process of capital accumulation should always pass through exactly the same phases, nor do we observe a trade boom always passing through exactly the same phases. But the general correspondence is so close that we seem to be justified in saying that a trade boom *is* nothing else but a period of intense accumulation.

If anything happens to stimulate the rate of investment by entrepreneurs (what that 'anything' may be, we will leave over for the moment), we have seen just how we should expect things to work out. There will be, first of all, a period of 'preparation', whose only visible effects are (perhaps) a small increase in the demand for factors and (perhaps) a small increase in the demand for money. If (as is usually the case at the beginning of a boom) there already exists a plethora of unemployed labour and a plethora of unemployed money, these increased demands will have practically no effect upon prices in general, and practically no effect on interest rates. The only prices which are likely to be affected are those which are a direct expression of a change in the expectations of the most sensitive persons trading—such as the prices of ordinary shares.

In the second phase, when a start is made with the physical construction of the new capital goods, the increase in the demand for factors becomes much more considerable. This produces a primary fall in unemployment. At the same time, there is a tendency to a general rise in the prices of the more sensitive commodities; and within a little, we may suppose that some industrialists may have had time to develop elastic expectations (at least for that length of time in the future which is mainly relevant for the sorts of production processes in which they are engaged); this would induce a considerable secondary fall in unemployment due to the rise in price-expectations.

Thus the boom proceeds to develop; but from this point onwards there is a parting of the ways. It is possible, first of all, that we may go on to a third phase which is characterized by nothing else but a gradually spreading elasticity of expectations. Optimism diffuses itself throughout the community; as time goes on, more and more price-expectations become elastic; further sets of processes are therefore started and get under way. Unemployment falls yet further; but after a point the expectations of wage-earners (or at least of their Trade Union representatives) become elastic too, and wages start to rise. The boom waxes fast and furious. But there are several ways in which it may get into trouble.

On the one hand, increasing activity of this sort involves an increased demand for money. Up to a point, it will usually be possible to meet this without any strain; but if the boom continues unchecked, that point is bound to be passed sooner or later. The monetary authority will then have to consider whether it is prepared to expand credit indefinitely; if it puts even the slightest check on the expansion of the supply of money, rates of interest will rise. It is even probable that the long rate of interest will rise before there is any action by the monetary authority; since the long rate of interest reflects interest-expectations, the mere apprehension of the possibility of such action by the monetary authority will induce a rise in the long-term rate of interest.[1] However, it does not seem likely that a rise in the long-term rate due to such apprehension would check expansion to an important extent, unless the boom was already flagging from other causes.

Among such other causes we may have to include a mere sense on the part of business men that the boom has gone on about as long as booms do usually go on; so that the mere lapse of time shifts their expectations downwards. Even in a very cycle-conscious world it is hard to attach very much importance to this. More important is the possibility that the expectations of some important sections of the community prove very stubbornly inelastic, so that demand for goods in general fails to expand as rapidly as the more sensitive people had expected it to expand. This may force them, after a time, to revise their expectations downwards: but

---

[1] There may be other reasons for the rise. See above, p. 281, note.

if (as was usually the case with the localized or specialized booms of the eighteenth and nineteenth centuries) the division between sensitive and insensitive people corresponds more or less to a division between people using different banking systems (that is to say, different kinds of money), the check due to this cause may be transmuted into a check through credit restriction, brought about in order to keep the different kinds of money at par.

Most important of all, because of its radical difference from the other braking factors we have listed, is the check which must come from the mere completion of productive processes, from the achievement of the capital accumulation planned in the first stage and now carried out. We saw in the last chapter how this is almost certain to be a depressing influence—though, of course, at any particular stage, it has to struggle against the other influences making for expansion. How powerful it is depends upon the character of the capital accumulation which has taken place; and particularly upon the sensitivity of the markets on which the increased supply (or diminished demand) exerts pressure.

3. There are thus at least two quite different ways in which a general boom can be brought to an end; it may be killed by credit restriction or it may die by working itself out. It ought to be possible to make a rough classification of recorded booms according to their cause of death; but, of course, we should have to be prepared to find that the task of classification was not at all simple —that perhaps in the majority of cases more than one cause was at work to a significant extent. Nevertheless, it makes a great deal of difference what cause is dominant. Not least, it makes a great difference to the course of the ensuing slump.

The leading feature of a slump is not the decumulation of physical capital (though there is usually some decumulation, mainly in the form of working off stocks); it is the mere cessation of accumulation. That is sufficient in itself to produce the typical slump phenomena—downward revision of expectations, leading at once to a fall in ordinary shares; shift of demand from commodities and factors to money and fixed-interest securities, leading to a fall in prices, a rise in unemployment, and (after an initial period of stringency, due to distress borrowing) a fall in interest rates. If all prices were equally flexible, and all price-expectations equally flexible, mere cessation of accumulation would be sufficient to produce a slump without a bottom—the instability of capitalism declaring itself in complete break-down.

That this does not happen is due to price-rigidities, and ultimately, beyond price-rigidities, to people's sense of normal prices. If wage-rates had risen sharply in the last stages of the boom, they may fall again fairly quickly; but this does not necessarily mean that the expectations of wage-earners have become permanently elastic—it may mean no more than a relapse into the old idea of normal prices. Once these norms are re-established, they will impose a limit to the fall in wages, a point at which wages will stick. Similarly, when prices have fallen to a certain extent, there will be some entrepreneurs (those whose expectations are less elastic) who will begin to think that the prices which have now been reached are abnormally low, and who will therefore begin to develop production plans on the basis of a probability of rising prices in the future. It is these things which check the slump, which prevent the depression from developing at once into a break-down.

The importance of this service can hardly be over-estimated; but in spite of that we must be careful not to put too much trust in these factors of stability, not to suppose that they can permanently save the situation. They can do nothing more than provide a breathing-space; if something new supervenes, which converts that breathing-space into recovery, well and good; but if nothing happens to induce a genuine resumption of the process of accumulation, then the stabilizing factors are bound to grow weaker as time goes on. Prolonged experience of low prices will disturb the norms, and induce a further revision of expectations downwards. A secondary slump will set in, far more dangerous than the first, since there is less resistance available to prevent collapse.

This is the reason why the cause of death of the preceding boom is so important. If it was killed by credit restriction, then it is probable that it had not exhausted the investment opportunities on which it was feeding; opportunities were available which would have been exploited if the boom had been allowed to go on, which had to be postponed during the crisis period, but which may be available again in the relatively quiet times of the breathing-space. Their utilization will then convert breathing-space into recovery, and our cycle is complete.

If the preceding boom died a natural death, the situation is much more dangerous. Some entirely new factor is then needed to convert depression into recovery, and therefore to avert the dangers of secondary depression. Now what new factor is likely to be available?

4. It is only possible to make sense of the theory of the trade cycle to which we appear to have been led, to reconcile it, that is, with the most obvious facts of history, if we lay great stress upon the supply of investment opportunities which is provided by invention and innovation. I use these terms in a very broad sense, to include not only the invention of new methods of producing already familiar commodities and the invention of new commodities, but also those changes in tastes, which have to be treated as autonomous changes for our purposes, though it will often be easy enough to trace them to their sources outside the economic field, in politics, or education, or population movements. Any of these causes is capable of providing the sort of stimulus for which we are looking. A shift in demand, for instance, even if it is a mere shift from one consumption good X to another consumption good Y, will suffice to provide a temporary stimulus to the demand for inputs, provided only that it is expected to continue more or less permanently. There is, of course, a fall in the direct demand for labour and raw materials from the X-industry, which may match (or more than match) the increased demand from the Y-industry; there is no stimulus here. But there is also a demand for productive instruments from the Y-industry, and this is not likely to be matched by any appreciable reduction in the demand for productive instruments from the X-industry. The X-industry has its durable equipment already there; assuming that it itself has not been expanding previously, the only demand which can be reduced is a replacement demand, and even if this is reduced to zero, the reduction will not offset the rise in demand from the Y-industry. There is thus a temporary stimulus to the demand for inputs in general, of precisely the kind for which we are looking.

It is perhaps possible to conceive of a capitalistic economy in which innovations came forward at such a regular rate that the whole system was free from recognizable fluctuations. It is perhaps possible, but the freedom from fluctuation would be very precarious. In fact, there is no reason to suppose that the rate of innovation is very regular; and if it is not regular, that in itself is a sufficient reason for a cycle—even a fairly regular cycle—to develop. For, as we have seen, the primary expansion caused by a rate of innovation above the average induces a secondary expansion; and in this condition of boom, the rate of autonomous innovation ceases for a while to be the main determinant of business activity. Or rather, once the boom has taken charge, it becomes difficult to distinguish, even theoretically, between those changes which in other circumstances we should certainly reckon as innovations, and those changes which are induced by the boom. The boom itself may affect the rate of innovation; in the hothouse atmosphere of boom optimism, innovations may be made which would otherwise have never been made at all, and innovations may be introduced at an earlier date than that at which they would otherwise have been tried out. It is particularly for this latter reason that the slump, even when it has reached the stage of breathing-space, may find itself abnormally short of investment opportunities; and we have seen how dangerous a shortage of investment opportunities at that stage may be.

Thus, even if there is no secular trend in the supply of innovations, a moderate degree of irregularity in the supply will be sufficient to generate a cycle. And certainly such irregularity is nothing to be surprised at; it would be much more surprising if it did not occur. Now if such irregularity were the only source of trouble, it would seem to be clear that the objective of a wise economic policy ought to be simply to diminish, in every way possible, the force of the fluctuations so caused. There are two main ways in which this could be done. On the one hand, we have already reached a point in history where the supply of investment opportunities is naturally to some extent under public control (or can easily be brought under such control); this must necessarily be so as the economic functions of the State increase. Fluctuations can then be damped down by adjustment of the timing of public investment.[1] On the other hand, some control can be exercised by monetary policy. This is a much less effective means of controlling the whole cycle, because its efficiency is much greater for purposes of checking the boom than for purposes of checking the slump; it is thus least efficient where it is most wanted. All

---

[1] Cf., for example, U. K. Hicks, *The Finance of British Government*, chs. vii and xiii.

the same, I do not think we ought to favour complete discarding of the weapon of monetary policy. There are two grounds on which it may be desirable to use it for checking a boom; one is to prevent the boom from eating too deeply into the supply of investment opportunities, and the other is to prevent too great a disturbance of price-levels, which may upset people's ideas of normal prices, and thus weaken a stabilizing factor which will have a vital part to play later on.[1]

5. All this assumes, however, that there is no reason to be dissatisfied with the average rate of innovation over a long period; so that the whole problem reduces itself to one of smoothing out fluctuations in the rate of innovation, or rather of smoothing out those larger fluctuations in trade activity which are caused by these primary movements. If that is the whole problem, well and good; but it is not by any means certain that it is the whole problem. We may have to consider the possibility of secular changes in the rate of innovation as well. These may present an even more uncomfortable prospect; but we cannot close our eyes to them altogether.

If the average rate of innovation over a long period took a turn downwards, we should expect, as a first sign, a tendency for booms to die off of their own accord more frequently, and for slumps to spread themselves out more frequently to a dangerous length. We should expect, too, that the booms would be disappointing booms, and the slumps bad slumps, so that the average level of employment over the whole cycle would be low. If it was perfectly clear that the unemployment so caused was secular unemployment, there would be various ways of dealing with it. Hours might be reduced, or the demand for consumption goods expanded by transferring income from those classes less inclined to spend to those classes more inclined to spend, through taxation and public expenditure. But secular unemployment is a difficult thing to recognize; even if the trend of innovation was downwards, it

---

[1] I am well aware that if the monetary authority were to abstain altogether from using interest as a brake, it might, in the end, cause the long-term rate of interest to fall to appreciably lower levels than it would otherwise have done. It is possible that this might assist recovery from future slumps. But I feel myself very doubtful whether, even in the breathing-space, one can count on a degree of confidence sufficient to make the difference between low and very low long-term rates a thing of great importance in promoting recovery. If this is so, the policy of total abstinence in all circumstances would mean risking the sense of normal prices in return for a very distant and very dubious advantage.

would not fall regularly; so that the occurrence of utterly disastrous slumps would, in these circumstances, be rather probable. I do not think one could count upon the long survival of anything like a capitalist system, using that term to mean a system of free enterprise, including free lending and borrowing.[1]

We began our study of dynamic economics by rejecting the concept of a stationary state as an analytical tool. We rejected it then, because it seemed to be no more than a special case, which offered no facility for generalization. We have come in the end to doubt whether it is even conceivable as a special case; to suspect that the system of economic relations we have been studying is nothing else but the form of a progressive economy.

[1] The reasons which have led many people to suppose that this sort of danger is likely to be actual in the twentieth century are, of course, the practical cessation of geographical discovery and the approaching fall in population. These are weighty reasons; yet the trend of innovation in the future is, by its very nature, so difficult to forecast that we cannot deduce imminent peril from these things alone. Nevertheless, one cannot repress the thought that perhaps the whole Industrial Revolution of the last two hundred years has been nothing else but a vast secular boom, largely induced by the unparalleled rise in population. If this is so, it would help to explain why, as the wisest hold, it has been such a disappointing episode in human history.

MATHEMATICAL APPENDIX

1. THE purpose of this Appendix is not merely the transcription of the argument of the text into mathematical symbols; I see little advantage to be got from doing that. When the verbal (or geometrical) argument is conclusive, it gains nothing from being put in another form. What can be gained, however, is the assurance that our argument is completely general; that what has been proved in the text for two, or three, or four, commodities, is true for n commodities. In this Appendix I shall concentrate upon the proof of that generality.

I shall follow the same order of subjects as in the text of the book, and shall mark off the sections of the Appendix according to the chapters of the book to which they refer. I must begin, however, by giving some discussion of a purely mathematical proposition, which is fundamental to what follows. Its relevance will appear almost at once.

2. *A fundamental mathematical proposition.* (1) The general homogeneous function of the second degree in three variables

$$ax^2 + by^2 + cz^2 + 2fyz + 2gzx + 2hxy$$

can also be written in the form

$$a\left(x + \frac{h}{a}y + \frac{g}{a}z\right)^2 + \frac{ab - h^2}{a}\left(y - \frac{gh - af}{ab - h^2}z\right)^2 +$$

$$+ \frac{abc + 2fgh - af^2 - bg^2 - ch^2}{ab - h^2}(z)^2.$$

Since the variables appear only within the brackets, and each bracket is squared, it appears at once that the original expression is positive for all real values of the variables if the coefficients of all brackets are positive, negative if the coefficients are all negative. These coefficients are ratios of the determinants

$$a, \quad \begin{vmatrix} a & h \\ h & b \end{vmatrix}, \quad \begin{vmatrix} a & h & g \\ h & b & f \\ g & f & c \end{vmatrix}.$$

Thus the original expression is definitely positive if all three determinants are positive, definitely negative if the first and third are negative and the second positive.

(2) A similar proposition can be established for any number of variables.[1] The general quadratic form

$$a_{11}x_1^2 + a_{22}x_2^2 + \ldots + a_{nn}x_n^2 + 2a_{12}x_1x_2 + 2a_{13}x_1x_3 + \ldots + 2a_{23}x_2x_3 + \ldots$$

will be positive for all real values of the x's if the determinants

$$a_{11}, \quad \begin{vmatrix} a_{11} & a_{12} \\ a_{12} & a_{22} \end{vmatrix}, \quad \begin{vmatrix} a_{11} & a_{12} & a_{13} \\ a_{12} & a_{22} & a_{23} \\ a_{13} & a_{23} & a_{33} \end{vmatrix}, \ldots, \quad \begin{vmatrix} a_{11} & a_{12} & \cdot & \cdot & a_{1n} \\ a_{12} & a_{22} & \cdot & \cdot & a_{2n} \\ \cdot & \cdot & \cdot & \cdot & \cdot \\ \cdot & \cdot & \cdot & \cdot & \cdot \\ a_{1n} & a_{2n} & \cdot & \cdot & a_{nn} \end{vmatrix}$$

are all positive, negative if they are alternatively negative and positive.

(3) If it is required to find the conditions that the above quadratic form should be definitely positive or negative, not for all values of the variables, but for those values only which satisfy the linear relation

$$b_1x_1 + b_2x_2 + \ldots + b_nx_n = 0,$$

we can proceed by eliminating one of the variables, say x_1. The quadratic form then becomes

$$c_{22}x_2^2 + c_{33}x_3^2 + \ldots + c_{nn}x_n^2 + 2c_{23}x_2x_3 + \ldots;$$

where
$$c_{rs} = a_{rs} - \frac{1}{b_1}(a_{1r}b_s + a_{1s}b_r) + \frac{1}{b_1^2}b_rb_sa_{11}.$$

The required conditions can then be written in the same form as that given in (2) above, with c's in place of the a's; but they can be simplified if we multiply every determinant by the necessarily negative quantity $-b_1^2$. For example,

$$-b_1^2 \begin{vmatrix} c_{22} & c_{23} \\ c_{23} & c_{33} \end{vmatrix} = \begin{vmatrix} 0 & b_1 & 0 & 0 \\ b_1 & a_{11} & 0 & 0 \\ b_2 & a_{12} & c_{22} & c_{23} \\ b_3 & a_{13} & c_{23} & c_{33} \end{vmatrix} = \begin{vmatrix} 0 & b_1 & b_2 & b_3 \\ b_1 & a_{11} & a_{12} & a_{13} \\ b_2 & a_{12} & a_{22} & a_{23} \\ b_3 & a_{13} & a_{23} & a_{33} \end{vmatrix},$$

adding appropriate multiples of the first two columns to each of the remaining columns.

Thus the conditions for the quadratic form being definitely positive

[1] Cf. Burnside and Panton, *Theory of Equations*, vol. ii, pp. 181-2.

subject to a linear condition are that the determinants

$$\begin{vmatrix} 0 & b_1 & b_2 \\ b_1 & a_{11} & a_{12} \\ b_2 & a_{12} & a_{22} \end{vmatrix}, \quad \begin{vmatrix} 0 & b_1 & b_2 & b_3 \\ b_1 & a_{11} & a_{12} & a_{13} \\ b_2 & a_{12} & a_{22} & a_{23} \\ b_3 & a_{13} & a_{23} & a_{33} \end{vmatrix}, ..., \quad \begin{vmatrix} 0 & b_1 & b_2 & . & . & b_n \\ b_1 & a_{11} & a_{12} & . & . & a_{1n} \\ b_2 & a_{12} & a_{22} & . & . & a_{2n} \\ . & . & . & . & . & . \\ . & . & . & . & . & . \\ b_n & a_{1n} & a_{2n} & . & . & a_{nn} \end{vmatrix}$$

should be all *negative* (since the negative factor $-b_1{}^2$ will change all signs); the conditions for its being definitely negative are that the determinants should be alternatively positive and negative.

This is all we need as a purely mathematical foundation; let us now turn to the economics.

Appendix to Chapter I

3. *Equilibrium of the consumer.* We begin by considering an individual, who has a given sum of money M available for expenditure (call it provisionally his 'income') and has opportunities for spending it upon n different commodities. The prices of these n commodities are given to him as determined on the market. Call them $p_1, p_2, p_3, ..., p_n$. Call $x_1, x_2, x_3, ..., x_n$ the amounts of the respective commodities which he buys.

Then, provided he spends all his income, we must have

$$M = \sum_{r=1}^{r=n} p_r x_r. \tag{3.1}$$

Assume for the moment that his wants are expressed by a given utility function $u(x_1, x_2, x_3, ..., x_n)$. The amounts bought will be determined by the condition that u is a maximum, subject to the condition (3.1). They can be worked out by introducing a Lagrange multiplier μ, and maximizing:

$$u + \mu\left(M - \sum_{r=1}^{r=n} p_r x_r\right).$$

The conditions for consumer equilibrium are therefore that

$$u_r = \mu p_r \quad (r = 1, 2, 3, ..., n), \tag{3.2}$$

where u_r is written for $\partial u/\partial x_r$, the *marginal utility* of x_r. The equation thus expresses the equality between the marginal utility of x_r and the price of x_r multiplied by μ (which is accordingly identified as Marshall's *marginal utility of money*).

When μ is eliminated between the equations (3.2), they reduce to

$$\frac{u_1}{p_1} = \frac{u_2}{p_2} = \ldots = \frac{u_{n-1}}{p_{n-1}} = \frac{u_n}{p_n}. \tag{3.3}$$

These $n-1$ equations, together with the equation (3.1), provide n equations to determine the n quantities $x_1, x_2, \ldots, x_n$.

4. Stability conditions. In order that u should be a true maximum it is necessary to have not only $du = 0$ (as above) but also $d^2u < 0$. Expanding these expressions, and writing u_{rs} for the second partial derivative, as u_r for the first, we have

$$du = \sum_{r=1}^{r=n} u_r \, dx_r,$$

$$d^2u = \sum_{r=1}^{r=n} \sum_{s=1}^{s=n} u_{rs} \, dx_r \, dx_s.$$

This latter expression is a quadratic form of the same character as that discussed in § 2 above (since $u_{sr} = u_{rs}$); consequently the conditions for $d^2u < 0$ for all values of $dx_1, dx_2, \ldots, dx_n$, such that $du. = 0$, are that the determinants

$$\begin{vmatrix} 0 & u_1 & u_2 \\ u_1 & u_{11} & u_{12} \\ u_2 & u_{12} & u_{22} \end{vmatrix}, \quad \begin{vmatrix} 0 & u_1 & u_2 & u_3 \\ u_1 & u_{11} & u_{12} & u_{13} \\ u_2 & u_{12} & u_{22} & u_{23} \\ u_3 & u_{13} & u_{23} & u_{33} \end{vmatrix}, \ldots, \quad \begin{vmatrix} 0 & u_1 & u_2 & . & . & u_n \\ u_1 & u_{11} & u_{12} & . & . & u_{1n} \\ u_2 & u_{12} & u_{22} & . & . & u_{2n} \\ . & . & . & . & . & . \\ u_n & u_{1n} & u_{2n} & . & . & u_{nn} \end{vmatrix}$$

$$\tag{4.1}$$

should be alternatively positive and negative.

These determinants will play an exceedingly important part in our subsequent analysis. I shall write the last of them U; and the co-factors of u_r, u_s, u_{rr}, u_{rs}, in U, I shall denote by U_r, U_s, U_{rr}, U_{rs}. Since the n goods can be taken up in any order, it follows directly from (4.1) that U_{rr}/U is necessarily negative.

5. The ordinal character of utility. The equilibrium conditions and the stability conditions for an individual consumer have been written out assuming the existence of a particular utility function u. This is, indeed, the most convenient way of writing them; but it is important to observe that they do not depend upon the existence of any unique utility function. For suppose the utility function u to be replaced by any arbitrary function of itself $\phi(u)$. Then it can be shown that, provided only the function $\phi(u)$ increases when u increases—that is to say, provided $\phi'(u)$ is positive—the equilibrium conditions and the stability conditions will be entirely unaffected by the change in the utility function.

Since $\dfrac{\partial}{\partial x_r}\phi(u) = \phi'(u).x_r$, the equilibrium conditions (3.3) will be unchanged. The equal ratios are simply multiplied by a common factor $\phi'(u)$, which cancels out. (Even if they are written in the form (3.2), they are still unchanged, provided that μ is replaced by $\phi'(u).\mu$. Since μ is arbitrary, it is legitimate to make this alteration.)

Since $\dfrac{\partial^2}{\partial x_r\partial x_s}\phi(u) = \phi'(u).u_{rs}+\phi''(u)u_r u_s$, the stability determinants reduce down similarly. The first determinant becomes

$$
\begin{vmatrix}
0 & \phi'(u)u_1 & \phi'(u)u_2 \\
\phi'(u)u_1 & \phi'(u)u_{11}+\phi''(u)u_1{}^2 & \phi'(u)u_{12}+\phi''(u)u_1 u_2 \\
\phi'(u)u_2 & \phi'(u)u_{12}+\phi''(u)u_1 u_2 & \phi'(u)u_{22}+\phi''(u)u_2{}^2
\end{vmatrix}
$$

$$
= \{\phi'(u)\}^3
\begin{vmatrix}
0 & u_1 & u_2 \\
u_1 & u_{11} & u_{12} \\
u_2 & u_{12} & u_{22}
\end{vmatrix}
$$

and the same reduction can be performed for every determinant in the series. The rth determinant in the series has $(r+2)$ rows and columns; it will therefore have to be multiplied by the factor $\{\phi'(u)\}^{r+2}$. Since $\phi'(u)$ is assumed positive, none of the determinants have their signs changed by the introduction of such a factor; and since it is the signs of the determinants which govern stability, the conditions may be considered to be unaltered by the substitution of $\phi(u)$ for u.

Thus, if we decide (as I think we should) to start, not from a given utility function, but from a given scale of preferences, all we have to do is to confine our attention to those properties of the utility function which are invariant against the substitution of $\phi(u)$ for u. The original equilibrium conditions and the original stability conditions have been shown to be invariant in this way. The remainder of our theory of value will be worked out using invariant properties only, though I shall generally leave it to the reader to check the invariance for himself.

Appendix to Chapters II and III

6. *The effect on demand of an increase in income.* Let us revert to the equilibrium equations (3.1) and (3.2), writing them in the form

$$
\left.\begin{aligned}
p_1 x_1+p_2 x_2+\cdots\ +p_n x_n &= M \\
-\mu p_1+u_1 &= 0 \\
-\mu p_2+u_2 &= 0 \\
\cdots\ \cdots\ \cdots& \\
-\mu p_n+u_n &= 0
\end{aligned}\right\}. \tag{6.1}
$$

Differentiating partially with respect to M,

$$
\left.\begin{array}{l}
p_1\dfrac{\partial x_1}{\partial M} + p_2\dfrac{\partial x_2}{\partial M} + \cdots \quad + p_n\dfrac{\partial x_n}{\partial M} = \mathrm{I} \\[2mm]
-p_1\dfrac{\partial \mu}{\partial M} + u_{11}\dfrac{\partial x_1}{\partial M} + u_{12}\dfrac{\partial x_2}{\partial M} + \cdots \quad + u_{1n}\dfrac{\partial x_n}{\partial M} = 0 \\[2mm]
-p_2\dfrac{\partial \mu}{\partial M} + u_{21}\dfrac{\partial x_1}{\partial M} + u_{22}\dfrac{\partial x_2}{\partial M} + \cdots \quad + u_{2n}\dfrac{\partial x_n}{\partial M} = 0 \\[2mm]
\cdot \quad \cdot \quad \cdot \quad \cdot \quad \cdot \quad \cdot \quad \cdot \quad \cdot \\[2mm]
-p_n\dfrac{\partial \mu}{\partial M} + u_{n1}\dfrac{\partial x_1}{\partial M} + u_{n2}\dfrac{\partial x_2}{\partial M} + \cdots \quad + u_{nn}\dfrac{\partial x_n}{\partial M} = 0
\end{array}\right\}. \quad (6.2)
$$

Solving,

$$
\frac{\partial x_r}{\partial M}
\begin{vmatrix}
0 & p_1 & p_2 & \cdot & \cdot & p_n \\
p_1 & u_{11} & u_{12} & \cdot & \cdot & u_{1n} \\
p_2 & u_{12} & u_{22} & \cdot & \cdot & u_{2n} \\
\cdot & \cdot & \cdot & \cdot & \cdot & \cdot \\
p_n & u_{1n} & u_{2n} & \cdot & \cdot & u_{nn}
\end{vmatrix}
=
\begin{vmatrix}
0 & p_1 & \cdot & \cdot & p_{r-1} & \mathrm{I} & p_{r+1} & \cdot & \cdot & p_n \\
p_1 & u_{11} & \cdot & \cdot & u_{1,r-1} & 0 & u_{1,r+1} & \cdot & \cdot & u_{1n} \\
p_2 & u_{12} & \cdot & \cdot & u_{2,r-1} & 0 & u_{2,r+1} & \cdot & \cdot & u_{2n} \\
\cdot & \cdot & \cdot & \cdot & \cdot & \cdot & \cdot & \cdot & \cdot & \cdot \\
p_n & u_{1n} & \cdot & \cdot & u_{r-1,n} & 0 & u_{r+1,n} & \cdot & \cdot & u_{nn}
\end{vmatrix}.
$$

Since (6.1) $p_s = u_s/\mu$, this can be written

$$
\frac{\partial x_r}{\partial M} = \frac{\mu U_r}{U}. \quad (6.3)
$$

Nothing is known about the sign of U_r; consequently $\partial x_r/\partial M$ may be either positive or negative. (See above, Chapter II, pp. 27–9.)

7. *The effect of a change in price with constant income.* Now suppose p_r to vary, other prices (and M) remaining unchanged. We have from (6.1)

$$
\left.\begin{array}{l}
p_1\dfrac{\partial x_1}{\partial p_r} + p_2\dfrac{\partial x_2}{\partial p_r} + \cdots \quad + p_n\dfrac{\partial x_n}{\partial p_r} = -x_r \\[2mm]
-p_1\dfrac{\partial \mu}{\partial p_r} + u_{11}\dfrac{\partial x_1}{\partial p_r} + u_{12}\dfrac{\partial x_2}{\partial p_r} + \cdots \quad + u_{1n}\dfrac{\partial x_n}{\partial p_r} = 0 \\[2mm]
\cdot \quad \cdot \quad \cdot \quad \cdot \quad \cdot \quad \cdot \quad \cdot \quad \cdot \quad \cdot \\[2mm]
-p_r\dfrac{\partial \mu}{\partial p_r} + u_{1r}\dfrac{\partial x_1}{\partial p_r} + u_{2r}\dfrac{\partial x_2}{\partial p_r} + \cdots \quad + u_{rn}\dfrac{\partial x_n}{\partial p_r} = \mu \\[2mm]
\cdot \quad \cdot \quad \cdot \quad \cdot \quad \cdot \quad \cdot \quad \cdot \quad \cdot \quad \cdot \\[2mm]
-p_n\dfrac{\partial \mu}{\partial p_r} + u_{1n}\dfrac{\partial x_1}{\partial p_r} + u_{2n}\dfrac{\partial x_2}{\partial p_r} + \cdots \quad + u_{nn}\dfrac{\partial x_n}{\partial p_r} = 0
\end{array}\right\}. \quad (7.1)
$$

Solving and simplifying as before,

$$\frac{\partial x_s}{\partial p_r} = \frac{1}{U}(-x_r\mu U_s + \mu U_{rs}) \quad (r \text{ and } s = 1, 2, 3, ..., n).$$

Applying (6.3), this can be written

$$\frac{\partial x_s}{\partial p_r} = -x_r\frac{\partial x_s}{\partial M} + \mu\frac{U_{rs}}{U} \quad (r \text{ and } s = 1, 2, 3, ..., n). \tag{7.2}$$

This equation, originally due to Slutsky, may be regarded as the Fundamental Equation of Value Theory. It gives us the effect of a change in the price of a commodity x_r on the individual's demand for another commodity x_s, split up into two terms, which we have called the Income Effect and the Substitution Effect respectively. Since $x_r = dM/dp_r$, when M is not taken as given, but all x's and all other p's are taken as given, it follows from the equation that the substitution term represents the effect on the demand for x_s of a change in the price of x_r combined with such a change in income as would enable the consumer, if he chose, to buy the same quantities of all goods as before, in spite of the change in p_r. It is obvious that this change in income will be smaller, the less important is x_r in the consumer's budget.

By putting r and s equal (there is no reason why we should not do so), the same equation can be used to split up the effect of a change in the price of x_r on the demand for x_r itself. The equation will then read

$$\frac{\partial x_r}{\partial p_r} = -x_r\frac{\partial x_r}{\partial M} + \frac{\mu U_{rr}}{U}.$$

It follows directly from the stability conditions that the substitution term in this equation must be negative.

8. *Properties of the substitution term.* Most of the rest of the theory of consumer's demand consists in working out the properties of this fundamental equation. First of all, it will be convenient to write it in an alternative form. The substitution term $\mu U_{rs}/U$ is in fact invariant against a substitution of $\phi(u)$ for u as the utility function; consequently it is better to write it in a form which does not make direct reference to a particular utility function. I shall therefore write it in the non-committal form $\mathbf{x}_{rs}$; so that the equations become

$$\left.\begin{aligned}\frac{\partial x_s}{\partial p_r} &= -x_r\frac{\partial x_s}{\partial M} + \mathbf{x}_{rs}, \\ \frac{\partial x_r}{\partial p_r} &= -x_r\frac{\partial x_r}{\partial M} + \mathbf{x}_{rr}.\end{aligned}\right\} \tag{8.1}$$

This is the form in which we shall find it most convenient to use them in our further work.[1]

[1] From some points of view, but not (I think) from all, there is an advantage

Two properties of the substitution term follow at once from what has been said already. I shall first of all write down these properties and then go on to work out some others.

(1) Since the determinants U_{rs} and U are both symmetrical between r and s, $\mathbf{x}_{rs}$ is also symmetrical; that is to say, $\mathbf{x}_{sr} = \mathbf{x}_{rs}$. The substitution terms in $\partial x_s/\partial p_r$ and $\partial x_r/\partial p_s$ are therefore identical; but the income terms are not, in general, equal. Thus, in order for $\partial x_s/\partial p_r$ and $\partial x_r/\partial p_s$ to be equal, it is necessary that $x_r(\partial x_s/\partial M)$ and $x_s(\partial x_r/\partial M)$ should be equal. This implies that $(M/x_r)\partial x_r/\partial M$ and $(M/x_s)\partial x_s/\partial M$ must be equal; i.e. the elasticities of demand for x_r and x_s with respect to income must be the same.

(2) Since U_{rr}/U is negative, and μ is positive, $\mathbf{x}_{rr} < 0$.

(3) The expression

$$0 . U_r + u_1 U_{1r} + u_2 U_{2r} + \dots + u_n U_{nr}$$

forms a determinant in which two rows are identical; therefore it vanishes. But since $u_s U_{rs} = p_s \mu U_{rs} = p_s U\mathbf{x}_{rs}$, we can deduce from this relation a relation between the $\mathbf{x}$'s, viz. $\displaystyle\sum_{s=1}^{s=n} p_s \mathbf{x}_{rs} = 0$.

$\therefore \sum p_s \mathbf{x}_{rs}$ (for all values of s except r) $= -p_r \mathbf{x}_{rr}$ which is necessarily positive.

(4) All our work so far has been based upon two only out of the set of stability conditions (4.1), which two conditions we have reduced to one—that U_{rr}/U is negative. How do the other stability conditions come into the picture? Let us proceed to see.

Let $U_{11.22}$ be the co-factor of u_{22} in U_{11}; $U_{11,22,33}$ be the co-factor of u_{33} in $U_{11,22}$; and so on. Then the stability conditions tell us that

$$\frac{U_{11}}{U}, \quad \frac{U_{11,22}}{U}, \quad \frac{U_{11,22,33}}{U}, \dots$$

are alternatively negative and positive.

It follows (by a well-known property of reciprocal determinants)[1] that

$$\frac{U_{11}}{U}, \quad \frac{1}{U^2}\begin{vmatrix} U_{11} & U_{12} \\ U_{12} & U_{22} \end{vmatrix}, \quad \frac{1}{U^3}\begin{vmatrix} U_{11} & U_{12} & U_{13} \\ U_{12} & U_{22} & U_{23} \\ U_{13} & U_{23} & U_{33} \end{vmatrix}, \dots$$

are alternatively negative and positive.

to be gained if we express the fundamental equation in elasticity form, as can easily be done by multiplying the equation through by p_r/x_s, and grouping the resulting expression into fractions which are independent of units. In my French pamphlet, *La Théorie mathématique de la Valeur* (Hermann, 1937), I have set out a large part of the following argument, using the elasticity method of statement. So the reader can take his choice.

[1] Cf., for example, Burnside and Panton, vol. ii, p. 42.

But these are the conditions that a quadratic form such as

$$\sum_{r=1}^{r=m} \sum_{s=1}^{s=m} z_r \, z_s \frac{U_{rs}}{U}$$

should be necessarily negative, for all values of the z's. (Cf. 2 (2) above.)
Consequently $\sum_1^m \sum_1^m \lambda_r \lambda_s \, \mathrm{x}_{rs} < 0$, for all values of the arbitrary coefficients λ, and for all values of m up to and including n.

We have thus accumulated four rules which must be obeyed by the substitution terms:

(1) $\mathrm{x}_{sr} = \mathrm{x}_{rs}$; \qquad (2) $\mathrm{x}_{rr} < 0$; \qquad (3) $\sum_{s=1}^{s=n} p_s \, \mathrm{x}_{rs} = 0$;

(4) $\sum_1^m \sum_1^m \lambda_r \lambda_s \, \mathrm{x}_{rs} < 0$ for all values of m up to n.

It will be observed that rule (2) is a special case of rule (4). Among other values, the λ's may take values equal to the p's. Thus we have as a special case of rule (4)

$$\sum_1^m \sum_1^m p_r \, p_s \, \mathrm{x}_{rs} < 0 \text{ for all values of } m \text{ less than } n.$$

It follows from this, together with the third rule, that

$$\sum_{r=1}^{r=m} \sum_{s=m+1}^{s=n} p_r \, p_s \, \mathrm{x}_{rs} > 0.$$

This last inequality may be expressed in words in the following way. If we divide the n commodities into two groups in any possible manner and form the expression $p_r \, p_s \, \mathrm{x}_{rs}$ (x_r being taken from one group and x_s from the other), then $\sum \sum p_r \, p_s \, \mathrm{x}_{rs}$ (where r and s vary in every possible way within their respective groups) must be positive.

If we consider a change in prices which is such that the changes in different prices *compensate*, leaving the consumer on the same indifference level after the change as before, the income-term in the fundamental equation vanishes, and we have

$$dx_r = \sum_s \frac{\partial x_r}{\partial p_s} \, dp_s = \sum_s \mathrm{x}_{rs} \, dp_s.$$

Thus $\qquad \sum_r dx_r \, dp_r = \sum_r \sum_s \mathrm{x}_{rs} \, dp_r \, dp_s,$

which by rule (4) is necessarily negative. This is the same proposition as we reached by another route on p. 52 above.

9. *Complementarity*. As in the text of this book, I say that two goods x_r and x_s are substitutes from the point of view of a particular consumer if his $\mathrm{x}_{rs} > 0$; complementary if his $\mathrm{x}_{rs} < 0$. It follows at once from Rule (5) that, while it is possible for all other goods consumed to be substitutes for x_r, it is not possible for them all to be complementary

with it. And it follows from Rule (6) that there is a further limit on the amount of complementarity possible. There are a large number of ways in which the substitution terms between pairs of goods can be taken together in groups, within which the pairs that are substitutes must outweigh the pairs that can be complements. There are $\frac{1}{2}n(n-1)$ different pairs of goods which can be selected out of a group of n goods; these $\frac{1}{2}n(n-1)$ pairs can be taken together in groups of this sort in

$$\frac{1}{2}(C_1^n + C_2^n + \dots + C_{n-2}^n + C_{n-1}^n) = 2^{n-1} - 1$$

different ways. The $\frac{1}{2}n(n-1)$ expressions $p_r p_s \mathbf{x}_{rs}$ $(r \neq s)$ need not all be positive; but there are $2^{n-1} - 1$ different collections of them whose sums must be positive. This is the sense in which substitution is dominant throughout the system as a whole.

10. *The demand for a group of goods.* We have still to consider the most important application of Rule (4). To begin with, it follows from our fundamental equation that the *value* of the increment in the demand for x_s which results from a given *proportionate* change in the price of x_r

$$= p_r p_s \frac{\partial x_s}{\partial p_r} = -p_r x_r \cdot p_s \frac{\partial x_s}{\partial M} + p_r p_s \mathbf{x}_{rs}. \tag{10.1}$$

Here $p_r x_r$ is the amount spent on x_r; $p_s(\partial x_s/\partial M)$ measures the increment in the amount spent on x_s which would result from a rise in income.

Now suppose that the prices of a group of goods $x_1, x_2, \dots, x_m$ $(m < n)$ rise, all in the same proportion. Then the value of the increment in the demand for one of these goods x_s $(s < m)$ is given by summing the above expressions:

$$\sum_{r=1}^{r=m} p_r p_s \frac{\partial x_s}{\partial p_r} = -\left(\sum_1^m p_r x_r\right) p_s \frac{\partial x_s}{\partial M} + \sum_{r=1}^{r=m} p_r p_s \mathbf{x}_{rs}.$$

The value of the increment in demand for the whole group taken together is given by summing again:

$$\sum_{s=1}^{s=m} \sum_{r=1}^{r=m} p_r p_s \frac{\partial x_s}{\partial p_r} = -\left(\sum_1^m p_r x_r\right)\left(\sum_1^m p_s \frac{\partial x_s}{\partial M}\right) + \sum_{r=1}^{r=m} \sum_{s=1}^{s=m} p_r p_s \mathbf{x}_{rs}. \tag{10.2}$$

This has identically the same form as (10.1) and has a corresponding interpretation. Further, since the r's and s's are summed over the same group of goods, it follows from Rule (4) that the substitution term in (10.2) is necessarily negative.

Thus we have demonstrated mathematically the very important

principle, used extensively in the text, that if the prices of a group of goods change in the same proportion, that group of goods behaves just as if it were a single commodity.

11. *The supply side.* Suppose now that an individual, instead of coming to the market with a given quantity of money, which does not vary when prices vary, comes with a certain quantity of goods for sale, so that the amount he has available for expenditure is affected by market prices. To take the general case, suppose that he starts off with quantities $\bar{x}_1, \bar{x}_2, \bar{x}_3, ..., \bar{x}_n$ of the n goods. As a result of trading, he will increase or diminish these quantities, so as to acquire a preferred collection $x_1, x_2, x_3..., x_n$ as before. The first of the equilibrium equations (6.1) must then read

$$p_1 x_1 + p_2 x_2 + ... + p_n x_n = p_1 \bar{x}_1 + p_2 \bar{x}_2 + ... + p_n \bar{x}_n. \qquad (11.1)$$

That is the only alteration which has to be made to the system.

This alteration amounts to replacing M by the quantity $\sum p_r \bar{x}_r$, which is no longer independent of prices. Therefore, when we differentiate the equations, we can no longer put $\partial M / \partial p_r = 0$, but must write $\partial M / \partial p_r = \bar{x}_r$. The first equation of (7.1) then becomes

$$p_1 \frac{\partial x_1}{\partial p_r} + p_2 \frac{\partial x_2}{\partial p_r} + ... + p_n \frac{\partial x_n}{\partial p_r} = \bar{x}_r - x_r.$$

And instead of the equation (8.1) we shall get

$$\frac{\partial x_s}{\partial p_r} = (\bar{x}_r - x_r) \frac{\partial x_s}{\partial M} + \mathrm{x}_{rs}.$$

This only differs from our first fundamental equation in that the income term is now weighted by the *net* amount of x_r acquired.

12. *Market demand.* It is one of the most obvious conveniences of our Fundamental Equation that it can be applied directly to deal with the effect of a change in price on the demand from a group of individuals. If the summations are taken over all members of the group,

$$\frac{\partial}{\partial p_r} \left(\sum x_s \right) = \sum \frac{\partial x_s}{\partial p_r} = \sum \left[(\bar{x}_r - x_r) \frac{\partial x_s}{\partial M} \right] + \sum \mathrm{x}_{rs}. \qquad (12.1)$$

The income term corresponds to the effect on the demand of the group for x_s, when the group's income is increased, but the increment in income is divided among its members in proportion to each individual's previous net demand for x_r. The substitution term is a mere aggregate of individual substitution terms; it must therefore obey the same rules as its components do. If we write the group substitution term $\sum x_{rs}$ in the form X_{rs}, we shall have exactly corresponding rules

$$(1)\ X_{sr} = X_{rs}, \qquad\qquad (2)\ X_{rr} < 0,$$

$$(3)\ \sum_{s=1}^{s=n} p_s\, X_{rs} = 0, \qquad\qquad (4)\ \sum_{1}^{m}\sum^{m} p_r p_s\, X_{rs} < 0,$$

$$(5)\ \sum_{s \neq r} p_s\, X_{rs} > 0, \qquad\qquad (6)\ \sum_{r=1}^{r=m}\ \sum_{s=m+1}^{s=n} p_r p_s\, X_{rs} > 0.$$

Appendix to Chapter IV

13. *Equilibrium of exchange.* Here it is only necessary for us to restate the classical argument of Walras in our own terms.

We have N individuals bringing to the market various quantities of n goods, and exchanging them under conditions of perfect competition. Since we are writing the quantity of the rth good originally at the disposal of a representative individual $\bar{x}_r$, and the amount he ultimately retains x_r ($x_r > \bar{x}_r$ if he is a buyer of that good, $< \bar{x}_r$ if he is a seller), let us write the total quantity originally brought by all individuals together $\bar{X}_r$, the total amount ultimately retained X_r.

The prices of the n goods we shall denote as before by $p_1, p_2, ..., p_n$. But it must be remembered that one good (say x_n) has to be taken as standard of value. Therefore $p_n = 1$. The remaining prices $p_1, p_2, ..., p_{n-1}$ have to be determined.

If the system is to be in equilibrium, the demand for every commodity must equal the supply.

$$\therefore X_r = \bar{X}_r \quad (r = 1, 2, 3, ..., n). \tag{13.1}$$

This gives us n equations corresponding to the n goods; but there are only $n-1$ prices to be determined. However, one equation follows from the rest. Among the equations of equilibrium of a representative individual is the equation

$$\sum_{1}^{n} p_r x_r = \sum_{1}^{n} p_r \bar{x}_r. \tag{11.1}$$

Summing these equations over all individuals, we have

$$\sum_{1}^{n} p_r X_r = \sum_{1}^{n} p_r \bar{X}_r.$$

Since this last equation must necessarily hold, whether the equations (13.1) are satisfied or not, it follows that if $n-1$ of the equations (13.1) are satisfied, the nth equation must be satisfied too. There are therefore only $n-1$ equations to determine the $n-1$ prices.

Appendix to Chapter V

14. *The stability of exchange equilibrium.* Since $\bar{X}_r$ can be taken as constant, the conditions for the stability of exchange can be got by examining the sign of dX_r/dp_r. In order for equilibrium to be perfectly stable, dX_r/dp_r must be negative

(1) when all other prices are unchanged;

(2) when p_s is adjusted so as to maintain equilibrium in the market for x_s, but all other prices are unchanged;

(3) when p_s and p_t are similarly adjusted;

and so on, until we have adjusted all prices, excepting p_r (and of course p_n, which is necessarily 1).

The third of these conditions, for example, implies that dX_r/dp_r is negative, when

$$\left.\begin{aligned}
\frac{dX_r}{dp_r} &= \frac{\partial X_r}{\partial p_r} + \frac{\partial X_r}{\partial p_s}\frac{dp_s}{dp_r} + \frac{\partial X_r}{\partial p_t}\frac{dp_t}{dp_r} \\
0 &= \frac{\partial X_s}{\partial p_r} + \frac{\partial X_s}{\partial p_s}\frac{dp_s}{dp_r} + \frac{\partial X_s}{\partial p_t}\frac{dp_t}{dp_r} \\
0 &= \frac{\partial X_t}{\partial p_r} + \frac{\partial X_t}{\partial p_s}\frac{dp_s}{dp_r} + \frac{\partial X_t}{\partial p_t}\frac{dp_t}{dp_r}
\end{aligned}\right\}. \tag{14.1}$$

Eliminating dp_s/dp_r and dp_t/dp_r

$$\frac{dX_r}{dp_r} = \begin{vmatrix} \dfrac{\partial X_r}{\partial p_r} & \dfrac{\partial X_r}{\partial p_s} & \dfrac{\partial X_r}{\partial p_t} \\[2ex] \dfrac{\partial X_s}{\partial p_r} & \dfrac{\partial X_s}{\partial p_s} & \dfrac{\partial X_s}{\partial p_t} \\[2ex] \dfrac{\partial X_t}{\partial p_r} & \dfrac{\partial X_t}{\partial p_s} & \dfrac{\partial X_t}{\partial p_t} \end{vmatrix} : \begin{vmatrix} \dfrac{\partial X_s}{\partial p_s} & \dfrac{\partial X_s}{\partial p_t} \\[2ex] \dfrac{\partial X_t}{\partial p_s} & \dfrac{\partial X_t}{\partial p_t} \end{vmatrix}.$$

This gives us one of the expressions which must be negative, in order for the system to be stable.

Taking all similar conditions together, and remembering that they must hold for the market in every x_r $(r = 1, 2, 3, ..., n-1)$, the stability conditions emerge in a more convenient form. It is necessary for the Jacobian determinants

$$\frac{\partial X_r}{\partial p_r}, \quad \begin{vmatrix} \dfrac{\partial X_r}{\partial p_r} & \dfrac{\partial X_r}{\partial p_s} \\[2ex] \dfrac{\partial X_s}{\partial p_r} & \dfrac{\partial X_s}{\partial p_s} \end{vmatrix}, \quad \begin{vmatrix} \dfrac{\partial X_r}{\partial p_r} & \dfrac{\partial X_r}{\partial p_s} & \dfrac{\partial X_r}{\partial p_t} \\[2ex] \dfrac{\partial X_s}{\partial p_r} & \dfrac{\partial X_s}{\partial p_s} & \dfrac{\partial X_s}{\partial p_t} \\[2ex] \dfrac{\partial X_t}{\partial p_r} & \dfrac{\partial X_t}{\partial p_s} & \dfrac{\partial X_t}{\partial p_t} \end{vmatrix}, \dots \tag{14.2}$$

(for all values of r, s, t,..., over the range 1, 2, 3,..., $n-1$) to be alternatively negative and positive.

15. Now we know that

$$\frac{\partial X_r}{\partial p_r} = \sum (\bar{x}_r - x_r)\frac{\partial x_r}{\partial M} + X_{rr}. \qquad (12.1)$$

Therefore, since X_{rr} is necessarily negative, the first-order condition of stability can only fail to be satisfied if the income term in the above expression is large and positive. But when the above formula is applied to the group to which we are now applying it (the market as a whole, buyers and sellers together), the income term develops one peculiar property. If $\partial x_r/\partial M$, the increment of x_r which would be bought as a result of a given rise in income, is the same for all persons in the market, the income term will take the form $(\bar{X}_r - X_r)(\partial x_r/\partial M)$; and since, in equilibrium, $X_r = \bar{X}_r$, this means that the income term will vanish. Consequently, if the income term is to be large, it is necessary for buyers and sellers, on the average, to react to changes in income in very different ways. In order for it to be large and positive, the bias must be in such a direction that sellers of x_r are likely to increase their consumption of x_r, when they become richer, much more than buyers of x_r would do in similar circumstances.

Such a strong bias between buyers and sellers is thus one possible cause of instability. In order to investigate whether there can be any other cause, let us assume that there is no such bias in any market, so that all income terms can be neglected.

The stability Jacobians then reduce to the following form

$$X_{rr},$$

$$\begin{vmatrix} X_{rr} & X_{rs} \\ X_{rs} & X_{ss} \end{vmatrix},$$

$$\begin{vmatrix} X_{rr} & X_{rs} & X_{rt} \\ X_{rs} & X_{ss} & X_{st} \\ X_{rt} & X_{st} & X_{tt} \end{vmatrix}, \dots.$$

If the whole system of exchange is to be perfectly stable, these determinants must be alternatively negative and positive.

Now we know from our fourth rule (p. 311) that for every individual in the market, the expression $\sum_{1}^{m}\sum_{1}^{m} \lambda_r \lambda_s x_{rs}$ must be negative, for all values of m up to n, and for all values of the λ's. Summing these expressions over all individuals, we deduce that

$$\sum_1^m \sum_1^m \lambda_r \lambda_s X_{rs}$$

is negative for all values of the λ's, and for all values of m up to n. But this implies that the above determinants are alternatively negative and positive. Consequently the stability conditions must be satisfied, if income effects are neglected.

Asymmetrical income effects are the only possible cause of instability.

16. *Effects of an increase in demand.* Suppose that there is a small increase in the demand for the commodity x_r. This can be dealt with, as in the text (p. 73, above), by inquiring what change of prices would be necessary, under the old conditions, to induce a small excess of supply over demand in the market for x_r, supply remaining equal to demand in the other markets (save that for the standard commodity x_n, at the expense of which the demand for x_r has expanded).

It is directly obvious from the stability conditions that this must imply a rise in the price of x_r.

The effects on other prices can be worked out from the equations (14.1). Suppose first that the effects on all other prices save that of x_s are too small to be considered. Then from the second equation of (14.1) we have

$$0 = \frac{\partial X_s}{\partial p_r} + \frac{\partial X_s}{\partial p_s} \frac{dp_s}{dp_r}.$$

$$\therefore \quad \frac{dp_s}{dp_r} = -\frac{\partial X_s}{\partial p_r} \Big/ \frac{\partial X_s}{\partial p_s} = -\frac{X_{rs}}{X_{ss}} \qquad (16.1)$$

(if income terms are neglected). Since X_{ss} is negative, this means that the price of x_s will rise if x_s and x_r are substitutes, fall if they are complementary.

By writing the formula in the form

$$\frac{p_r}{p_s} \frac{dp_s}{dp_r} = -\frac{p_r X_{rs}}{p_s X_{ss}} = \frac{p_r X_{rs}}{p_r X_{rs} + p_0 X_{s0}}$$

(using the third rule), it follows that p_s will rise less than proportionately to p_r, excepting in the case where there is complementarity between x_s and x_0 (i.e. between x_s and all the other commodities, excepting x_r and x_s, taken together).

Next suppose that the prices of two other commodities, x_s and x_t.

are likely to be affected appreciably. Then from the second and third equations of (14.1) we have

$$\frac{dp_s}{dp_r} = - \begin{vmatrix} \dfrac{\partial X_s}{\partial p_r} & \dfrac{\partial X_s}{\partial p_t} \\[2ex] \dfrac{\partial X_t}{\partial p_r} & \dfrac{\partial X_t}{\partial p_t} \end{vmatrix} \div \begin{vmatrix} \dfrac{\partial X_s}{\partial p_s} & \dfrac{\partial X_s}{\partial p_t} \\[2ex] \dfrac{\partial X_t}{\partial p_s} & \dfrac{\partial X_t}{\partial p_t} \end{vmatrix}$$

$$= \frac{-X_{rs}X_{tt} + X_{rt}X_{st}}{X_{ss}X_{tt} - X_{st}^2} \tag{16.2}$$

(income terms being neglected). In this last expression the denominator is positive, by the stability conditions. The first term of the numerator gives the direct effect on the price of x_s, the second term the effect through the mediation of the price of x_t. If x_t is not closely related to x_r and x_s, this second term will usually be negligible, and the formula reduces to the simpler form (16.1). But if it is closely related, then the indirect effects will work according to the 'substitute of substitutes' rule (cf. p. 74 in the text).

17. Take the last of the whole series of stability Jacobians—which has $n-1$ rows and columns, so that it includes all the commodities excepting the standard commodity and all the variable prices. Call it J. Let J_{rr}, J_{rs} be the co-factors of $\partial X_r/\partial p_r$, $\partial X_r/\partial p_s$ in J. Let $J_{rr,ss}$, $J_{rr,st}$ be the co-factors of $\partial X_s/\partial p_s$, $\partial X_s/\partial p_t$ in J_{rr}.

Then, when indirect effects through *all* other prices are allowed for, we have (cf. the equations 14.1)

$$\frac{dX_r}{dp_r} = \frac{J}{J_{rr}}. \tag{17.1}$$

If we neglect income effects and eliminate the elements X_{rr}, X_{ss}, &c., by means of our third rule, this equation can be regarded as an expansion of dX_r/dp_r in terms of the substitution effects between pairs of commodities (X_{rs}, X_{st}, where $r \neq s \neq t$). What can be said about its dependence upon these elementary substitution effects?

Differentiating (17.1) with respect to X_{st} (where either s or t—but obviously not both—may equal r), we have

$$J_{rr}^2 \frac{\partial}{\partial X_{st}}\left(\frac{J}{J_{rr}}\right) = J_{rr}\frac{\partial J}{\partial X_{st}} - J\frac{\partial J_{rr}}{\partial X_{st}}.$$

It follows from our third rule that $\dfrac{\partial X_{ss}}{\partial X_{st}} = -\dfrac{p_t}{p_s}$, and from a well-known property of reciprocal determinants[1] that

$$J_{rr}J_{ss} - J_{rs}^2 = JJ_{rr,ss};$$

$$J_{rr}J_{st} - J_{rt}J_{rs} = JJ_{rr,st}.$$

Using these propositions, we can carry through the differentiation

$$J_{rr}^2 \frac{\partial}{\partial X_{st}}\left(\frac{J}{J_{rr}}\right) = J_{rr}\left(-\frac{p_t}{p_s}J_{ss} - \frac{p_s}{p_t}J_{tt} + 2J_{st}\right)$$

$$-J\left(-\frac{p_t}{p_s}J_{rr,ss} - \frac{p_s}{p_t}J_{rr,tt} + 2J_{rr,st}\right)$$

$$= -\frac{p_t}{p_s}J_{rs}^2 - \frac{p_s}{p_t}J_{rt}^2 + 2J_{rs}J_{rt}$$

$$= -\frac{1}{p_s p_t}(p_t J_{rs} - p_s J_{rt})^2,$$

which is necessarily negative.

dX_r/dp_r is necessarily negative; consequently we have proved that its absolute size is greater, the greater is the substitution effect between any pair of goods in the system.

Appendix to Chapter VI

18. *Equilibrium of the firm. The conditions of equilibrium.* The firm may be thought of as employing various quantities of factors $y_1, y_2, y_3, ..., y_m$ to produce quantities of products $x_{m+1}, x_{m+2}, ..., x_n$. Its object is to maximize its surplus (or profit)

$$V = -p_1 y_1 - p_2 y_2 - ... - p_m y_m + p_{m+1} x_{m+1} + p_{m+2} x_{m+2} + ... + p_n x_n,$$

subject to a relation (the production function) connecting the x's and the y's. Since, from the firm's point of view, the difference between factor and product is only a difference in sign, it will save trouble if we treat the factors as negative products, writing x_r for $-y_r$ $(r < m)$. We may then say that the firm is seeking to maximize

$$V = \sum_1^n p_r x_r,$$

subject to the condition $f(x_1, x_2, x_3, ..., x_n) = 0$. (It should be observed that the function f is arbitrary, in the same way as the utility function

---

[1] Cf. footnote, p. 310, above.

u was arbitrary. Any function $\phi(f)$, which is 0 when f is 0, would serve.)

Assuming perfect competition, the maximization problem can again be investigated by introducing a Lagrange multiplier, and maximizing $V - \mu f$. Whence

$$d(V - \mu f) = 0,$$

$$d^2(V - \mu f) < 0.$$

From the first of these conditions, we have $p_r = \mu f_r$ $(r = 1, 2, 3, ..., n)$. If μ is eliminated, this gives us $n - 1$ equations, which, together with the production function, determine the n quantities $x_1, x_2, ..., x_n$.

Since V is linear, $d^2V = 0$; the second condition therefore implies that $d^2f > 0$, subject to $df = 0$.

Expanding (as in § 4, but observing the difference in sign), we derive a similar set of stability conditions. The determinants

$$\begin{vmatrix} 0 & f_1 & f_2 \\ f_1 & f_{11} & f_{12} \\ f_2 & f_{12} & f_{22} \end{vmatrix}, \quad \begin{vmatrix} 0 & f_1 & f_2 & f_3 \\ f_1 & f_{11} & f_{12} & f_{13} \\ f_2 & f_{12} & f_{22} & f_{23} \\ f_3 & f_{13} & f_{23} & f_{33} \end{vmatrix}, ..., \quad \begin{vmatrix} 0 & f_1 & f_2 & . & . & f_n \\ f_1 & f_{11} & f_{12} & . & . & f_{1n} \\ f_2 & f_{12} & f_{22} & . & . & f_{2n} \\ . & . & . & . & . & . \\ . & . & . & . & . & . \\ f_n & f_{1n} & f_{2n} & . & . & f_{nn} \end{vmatrix}$$

must *all* be negative. (See 2(3) above.)

We shall find it convenient to employ a notation exactly analogous to that of our utility theory. Thus if F is the last of these determinants, the co-factor of f_{rs} in F will be written F_{rs}. The condition that

$$\frac{F_{rr}}{\mu F}$$

is positive is invariant against a substitution of $\phi(f)$ for f as production function.

Appendix to Chapter VII

19. *Equilibrium of the firm. Effect of a change in price.* Now suppose that p_r varies, other prices remaining unchanged.

The equilibrium equations are

$$\left. \begin{aligned} f(x_1, x_2, ..., x_n) &= 0 \\ \mu f_r &= p_r \quad (r = 1, 2, ..., n). \end{aligned} \right\} \tag{19.1}$$

Differentiating these with respect to p_r,

$$\left.\begin{aligned}
f_1 \frac{\partial x_1}{\partial p_r} + f_2 \frac{\partial x_2}{\partial p_r} + \cdots + f_n \frac{\partial x_n}{\partial p_r} &= 0 \\
f_1 \frac{\partial \mu}{\partial p_r} + \mu f_{11} \frac{\partial x_1}{\partial p_r} + \mu f_{12} \frac{\partial x_2}{\partial p_r} + \cdots + \mu f_{1n} \frac{\partial x_n}{\partial p_r} &= 0 \\
\cdots \cdots \cdots \cdots \cdots \cdots \cdots \cdots \\
f_r \frac{\partial \mu}{\partial p_r} + \mu f_{1r} \frac{\partial x_1}{\partial p_r} + \mu f_{2r} \frac{\partial x_2}{\partial p_r} + \cdots + \mu f_{rn} \frac{\partial x_n}{\partial p_r} &= 1 \\
\cdots \cdots \cdots \cdots \cdots \cdots \cdots \cdots \\
f_n \frac{\partial \mu}{\partial p_r} + \mu f_{1n} \frac{\partial x_1}{\partial p_r} + \mu f_{2n} \frac{\partial x_2}{\partial p_r} + \cdots + \mu f_{nn} \frac{\partial x_n}{\partial p_r} &= 0
\end{aligned}\right\} . \quad (19.2)$$

Solving,

$$\frac{\partial x_s}{\partial p_r} = \frac{F_{rs}}{\mu F}. \qquad (19.3)$$

It is apparent from the form of the stability determinants that the expressions $F_{rs}/\mu F$ will obey very similar laws to those obeyed by the substitution terms in utility theory. By introducing a single change of sign, the rules can be made identical. Let us therefore write

$$\frac{F_{rs}}{\mu F} = -x'_{rs}.$$

Consequently we have as our fundamental equation

$$\frac{\partial x_s}{\partial p_r} = -x'_{rs}, \qquad (19.4)$$

and an exactly similar set of rules:

(1) $x'_{sr} = x'_{rs}$, (2) $x'_{rr} < 0$,

(3) $\sum_{s=1}^{s=n} p_s x'_{rs} = 0$,

(4) $\sum_1^m \sum_1^m \lambda_r \lambda_s x'_{rs} < 0$.

In the form in which the fundamental equation has been written, it gives the effect of a change in price (of either product or factor) on the supply of a product. In order to give the effect on the demand for a factor, it is only necessary to substitute $-y_s$ for x_s. The fundamental equation will then read

$$\frac{\partial y_s}{\partial p_r} = x'_{rs}.$$

The rules are entirely unchanged.

20. *The tendency towards dominance of complementarity among factors.*
The theory of production, worked out in the last two sections, assumes
implicitly that the entrepreneur possesses some fixed productive opportunity, which limits the scale of production, and to which the surplus V
can be imputed as earnings. If no such fixed opportunity exists, then
there is no reason why an equal proportional increase in all factors should
not enable all products to be increased in the same proportion as the
factors have been increased. Mathematically this would mean that if

$$f(x_1, x_2, ..., x_n) = 0,$$

then $$f(\lambda x_1, \lambda x_2, ..., \lambda x_n) = 0$$

for all values of λ. The production function (written, as we have written
it, in its implicit form) would be a homogeneous function of zero degree.

Consequently, by Euler's theorem, $\sum_{1}^{n} x_r f_r = 0$. (Since, by 19.1,
$p_r = \mu f_r$, this implies that $V = 0$.) Differentiating again,

$$f_s + \sum_{r=1}^{r=n} x_r f_{rs} = 0 \quad (s = 1, 2, 3, ..., n).$$

Applying these identities to the stability determinants, it is at once
apparent (by multiplying the 2nd, 3rd,... columns by $x_1, x_2,...$ and
adding to the first) that F (the last of the stability determinants)
vanishes.

Since $x'_{rs} = -\dfrac{F_{rs}}{\mu F}$ this implies that all the x' terms are infinite. It
is not possible for the price of one factor (or product) to change, there
being no change in the prices of all other factors and products, without
upsetting equilibrium altogether. If the price of a product rises, output
will become infinite; if the price of a factor rises, it will become zero.
In the limiting case we are considering, our analysis threatens to break
down altogether.

It is nevertheless instructive to inquire what determines the *direction*
in which the supplies of products or the demands for factors are likely
to be affected, because the rules governing this direction may be expected
to hold even if the limiting case is approached, without being actually
reached. This can be worked out by calculating F_{rs} for the case where
the production function is homogeneous and of zero degree.

We know that F_{rs}

$$= (-1)^{r+s} \begin{vmatrix} 0 & f_1 & \cdot & \cdot & f_{r-1} & f_{r+1} & \cdot & \cdot & f_n \\ f_1 & f_{11} & \cdot & \cdot & f_{1,r-1} & f_{1,r+1} & \cdot & \cdot & f_{1n} \\ & & \cdot & \cdot & \cdot & \cdot & \cdot & & \\ f_{s-1} & f_{1,s-1} & \cdot & \cdot & f_{r-1,s-1} & f_{r+1,s-1} & \cdot & \cdot & f_{s-1,n} \\ f_{s+1} & f_{1,s+1} & \cdot & \cdot & f_{r-1,s+1} & f_{r+1,s+1} & \cdot & \cdot & f_{s+1,n} \\ & & \cdot & \cdot & \cdot & \cdot & \cdot & & \\ f_n & f_{1n} & \cdot & \cdot & f_{r-1,n} & f_{r+1,n} & \cdot & \cdot & f_{nn} \end{vmatrix}.$$

Reducing this down by a double application of the same sort of method as we employed for reducing F above, we find that it becomes equal to $x_r x_s F_0$, where F_0 is the co-factor of 0 in the determinant F, i.e. the principal minor of the determinant. Consequently

$$\mathrm{x}'_{rs} = -x_r x_s \frac{F_0}{\mu F}$$

for all values of r and s.

Since we know that x'_{rr} is negative, it follows that $F_0/\mu F$ must be positive. If x_r and x_s are both products, or both factors, $x_r x_s$ will be positive, and therefore x'_{rs} negative. If one of them is a product and one a factor, $x_r x_s$ is negative, and therefore x'_{rs} positive.

Consequently, as we approach the limiting case under consideration, we must expect to find the factors and products falling apart into two complementary groups; while the 'substitution', which must still be dominant in the system as a whole (factors and products together), will be provided entirely by the factor-product relations.

Appendix to Chapter VIII

21. *The general equilibrium of production.* We must now bring together all the conclusions we have reached up to the present, and use them to give us the working of the static system as a whole. We suppose (as in the text) that the individuals composing the economy provide one (or both) of two kinds of resources: (1) commodities or factors that can be sold on the market directly, (2) 'entrepreneurial' resources which can be employed to produce exchangeable commodities, but which cannot be sold themselves. At any given system of prices, only those entrepreneurial factors will be employed whose employment will yield a positive profit.

Given a system of prices, there will be a certain demand for goods from consumers (the total consumption demand for a good x_r we write

X_r); there will be a supply directly from private individuals ($\bar{X}_r$); and there will be a supply (X'_r) newly produced. The market for x_r is in equilibrium if

$$X_r = \bar{X}_r + X'_r. \tag{21.1}$$

It should be observed that this equation is perfectly general, and can be applied to any commodity, service, product, or factor whatsoever. If x_r is a finished consumption good, whose supply is entirely derived from production, $\bar{X}_r = 0$, and the equation becomes

$$X_r = X'_r.$$

If it is a factor of production, such as labour, X'_r is negative. X_r includes the demand for the direct services of the factor, whether it comes from other people or from the supplier of the factor himself. (This would seem to be the most convenient way of allowing for variations in the supply of a factor.) The equation therefore reads

$$(-X'_r) + X_r = \bar{X}_r.$$

If x_r is a half-finished good, both produced and consumed in the process of production, but sold from one firm to another, both X_r and $\bar{X}_r = 0$ for this reason alone; and the equation becomes

$$X'_r = 0.$$

(The net supply from all firms taken together is zero.)

Thus an equation of the same form will do for all commodities and services. As before, one commodity must serve as standard of value; so that if there are n commodities in all, there are $n-1$ prices to be determined. As before, one equation follows from the rest. Among the equations of equilibrium of a private individual is

$$\sum_{r=1}^{r=n} p_r x_r = \sum_{r=1}^{r=n} p_r \bar{x}_r + V,$$

where V is the profit he draws from the possession of any entrepreneurial resources he may own. Summing these over all persons

$$\sum_1^n p_r X_r = \sum_1^n p_r \bar{X}_r + \sum V,$$

where $\sum V$ is the total of profits throughout the whole economy.

Similarly in any firm $\sum_1^n p_r x_r = V.$ (18.1)

Summing these $\sum_1^n p_r X'_r = \sum V.$

$$\therefore \sum_1^n p_r (X_r - \bar{X}_r - X'_r) = 0.$$

Therefore, if the equilibrium equations (21.1) hold for $n-1$ goods, they must hold for the nth good. There are only $n-1$ independent equations, and the system is determined.

22. *The stability of general equilibrium.* As in the equilibrium of exchange, stability demands that a fall in price in any market should make demand greater than supply. If there is to be perfect stability, this condition must hold (1) if all other prices are constant, (2) if they are adjusted, one by one, so as to maintain equilibrium in the other markets. For imperfect stability, it is only necessary that the condition should hold when all other prices have been adjusted.

The condition can be written $\dfrac{d}{dp_r}(X_r - \bar{X}_r - X'_r) < 0$. But since $\bar{X}_r$ may be regarded as given independently of prices, it can be reduced to

$$\frac{d}{dp_r}(X_r - X'_r) < 0.$$

This can be expanded as in § 14. It appears as the ratio of two determinants, whose representative term is $\dfrac{\partial}{\partial p_r}(X_s - X'_s)$.

We know how to expand this last expression. From (12.1)

$$\frac{\partial X_s}{\partial p_r} = \sum (\bar{x}_r + x'_r - x_r)\frac{\partial x_s}{\partial M} + \mathbf{X}_{rs}$$

(allowing for the change in V when p_r changes).

From (19.4) $\dfrac{\partial x_s}{\partial p_r} = -x'_{rs}$ for every firm in the system; therefore by summation $\dfrac{\partial X'_s}{\partial p_r} = -\mathbf{X}'_{rs}$, where $\mathbf{X}'_{rs}$ must obey the same rules as $\mathbf{X}_{rs}$.

Consequently $\dfrac{\partial}{\partial p_r}(X_s - X'_s) = \sum (\bar{x}_r + x'_r - x_r)\dfrac{\partial x_s}{\partial M} + \mathbf{X}_{rs} + \mathbf{X}'_{rs}$. Since $\mathbf{X}_{rs}$ and $\mathbf{X}'_{rs}$ obey the same rules, $\mathbf{X}_{rs} + \mathbf{X}'_{rs}$ must also obey the same rules.

$\dfrac{\partial}{\partial p_r}(X_s - X'_s)$ therefore obeys the same rules as the $\dfrac{\partial X_s}{\partial p_r}$ we studied in the theory of exchange. Consequently the further analysis of the general equilibrium of production is identical with that of the general equilibrium of exchange; and all the propositions of §§ 15-17 above can be reinterpreted in a wider sense.

Appendix to Chapter XV

23. *The determination of the production plan.* Let us continue to treat factors as negative products, just as we found it convenient to do

Y

in static theory. The problem of the firm, dynamically considered, is to find that stream of outputs, capable of being produced from the initial equipment, which shall have the maximum capital value (cf. pp. 194–6 in the text). If we write

$$x_{r0}, x_{r1}, x_{r2}, ..., x_{r\nu}$$

for the outputs of x_r planned to be sold in successive 'weeks' from the present, then the production function takes the form

$$f(x_{10}, x_{20}, ..., x_{n0}, x_{11}, x_{21}, ..., x_{n1}, x_{12}, x_{22}, ..., x_{n2}, ..., x_{1\nu}, x_{2\nu}, ..., x_n) = 0$$

assuming that the plan extends forward for ν weeks.

The capitalized value of the plan

$$= C = \sum_{r=1}^{r=n} \sum_{t=0}^{t=\nu} (\beta_t^t p_{rt} x_{rt}),$$

where $\beta_t = 1/(1+i_t)$, and i_t is the rate of interest per week for loans of t weeks; p_{r0} is the current price of x_r and p_{rt} is the price the entrepreneur expects to rule in the week beginning t weeks hence. (p_{rt} must be supposed adjusted for risk, in the manner described in the text on pp. 125–6.)

From the point of view of the individual entrepreneur under perfect competition, all β's and all p's are given; consequently, in spite of its seemingly greater complexity, this problem is formally identical with that considered in § 18 above. It is unnecessary to write out the equilibrium equations in full. The laws giving the way in which the production plan will be adjusted to a change in prices or price-expectations will be similar to those given in § 19. But when writing down the six rules which must still be obeyed by the substitution terms, we must remember to replace p_r by $\beta_t^t p_{rt}$; and to sum over all t's as well as over all r's.

Appendix to Chapter XVII

24. *The effect of interest on the production plan.* When we are considering the effects of interest changes on the plan (prices and price-expectations being given), it is convenient to make use of the property that all products whose discounted price-ratios can be taken as given for the problem in hand can be treated as a single product. Consequently we may cease to distinguish between the different sorts of outputs (and inputs) planned for a particular week, and also suppress any explicit reference to prices in our formulae. From now on x_t will represent the expected money value of the outputs and inputs, planned for the week starting after t weeks, taken all together—that is to say, the surplus planned for the week in question.

Adopting this simplification, we may say that the entrepreneur is endeavouring to maximize

$$C = \sum_{t=0}^{t=\nu} (\beta_t^t x_t)$$

subject to the condition $f(x_0, x_1, ..., x_\nu) = 0$.

The effect of a change in the rate of interest for loans of t' weeks on the surplus x_t will be given by

$$\frac{\partial x_t}{\partial(\beta_{t'}^{t'})} = -\mathbf{x}'_{tt'},$$

while among the six rules which the $\mathbf{x}$''s must observe is the rule (3),

$$\sum_{t'=0}^{t'=\nu} (\beta_{t'}^{t'} \mathbf{x}'_{tt'}) = 0. \tag{24.1}$$

In order to get the effect on the surplus x_t of a general change in rates of interest, observe first that

$$\frac{d(\beta_{t'}^{t'})}{d\beta_{t'}} = t'\beta_{t'}^{t'-1}$$

and therefore

$$\frac{\partial x_t}{\partial \beta_{t'}} = -t'\beta_{t'}^{t'-1}\mathbf{x}'_{tt'}.$$

Consequently, if the discount ratios (β) for loans of all periods change in the same proportion, the effect on x_t is given by

$$\frac{dx_t}{d\beta} = -\sum_{t'=0}^{t'=\nu} t'\beta_{t'}^{t'-1}\mathbf{x}'_{tt'} = -\sum_{t'=0}^{t'=\nu} t'\beta^{t'-1}\mathbf{x}'_{tt'} \tag{24.2}$$

if the rates of interest per week for loans of all periods are equal, and the discount ratios therefore equal.

Using (24.1) this can be written

$$\beta\frac{dx_t}{d\beta} = \sum_{t'=0}^{t'=\nu} (t-t')\beta^{t'}\mathbf{x}'_{tt'}.$$

When this latter expression is written out in full, it becomes apparent that the term in $\mathbf{x}'_{tt}$ will vanish. But it is $\mathbf{x}'_{tt}$ which—by Rule 2—is necessarily negative; if no complementarity is present, all the remaining $\mathbf{x}'_{tt'}$ will be positive. This means that if the rate of interest falls (β rises), there will be a substitution in favour of x_t at the expense of all surpluses earlier in date than x_t, and against x_t in favour of all surpluses later in date. This is the normal rule, but it may be complicated by complementarity.

25. *The average period of the plan.* As in Chapter XVII, we define the average period

$$P = \frac{\sum\limits_{0}^{v} t\beta^t x_t}{\sum\limits_{0}^{v} \beta^t x_t}.$$

$$\therefore \sum_{0}^{v} (P-t)\beta^t x_t = 0.$$

Differentiating with respect to β, but holding β^t constant, in accordance with the rule on p. 220 above, we get

$$\sum_{0}^{v} \left[\frac{dP}{d\beta} \beta^t x_t + (P-t)\beta^t \frac{dx_t}{d\beta} \right] = 0.$$

$$\therefore \beta C \frac{dP}{d\beta} = - \sum_{0}^{v} \left[(P-t)\beta^{t+1} \frac{dx_t}{d\beta} \right] \quad \text{(since } \sum \beta^t x_t = C\text{)}$$

$$= \sum_{0}^{v} \sum_{0}^{v} [(P-t)t'\beta^{t+t'} x'_{tt'}] \quad \text{(from 24.2)}.$$

Now from (24.1) $\sum\limits_{t=0}^{t=v} \beta^t x'_{tt'} = 0$. $\therefore \sum\limits_{t=0}^{t=v} (t'P\beta^{t+t'} x'_{tt'}) = 0$ for all values of t'.

$$\therefore \beta C \frac{dP}{d\beta} = - \sum_{0}^{v} \sum_{0}^{v} tt'\beta^{t+t'} x'_{tt'}. \tag{25.1}$$

If we write $t\beta^t = \lambda_t$, the double sum on the right of this last equation becomes

$$\sum \sum \lambda_t \lambda_{t'} x'_{tt'}$$

which we know, from rule (4) in section (19) above, to be necessarily negative for all values of the λ's. The right-hand side of the equation (25.1) is therefore necessarily positive; consequently $dP/d\beta$ is necessarily positive. A rise in β means a fall in the rate of interest; consequently a fall in the rate of interest must lengthen the average period of the plan.

ADDITIONAL NOTE A
The Generalized Law of Demand

1. It was shown on p. 52 above that for any change in prices which leaves the consumer on the same indifference level, the value of the collection of goods purchased after the change in price, assessed at the prices ruling before the change, must be greater than the value of goods previously purchased, assessed at the same prices. For the second collection of goods lies on the same indifference surface, but the first collection was the only point on that surface which was attainable with the previous total expenditure. Thus if p_r $(r = 1, 2,..., n)$ be the prices ruling before the change, $p_r + dp_r$ be the prices ruling afterwards; if x_r be the quantities purchased before, $x_r + dx_r$ be the quantities purchased afterwards; it follows from this principle that, along a given indifference surface

$$\sum p_r x_r < \sum p_r (x_r + dx_r). \qquad \therefore \sum p_r \, dx_r > 0.$$

(For an infinitesimal movement, it follows from our rule 3, on p. 311 above, that $\sum p_r \, dx_r = 0$, as it should do, because of the contact between the 'indifference curve' and the 'price-line'. The new rule holds for more than infinitesimal displacements.)

If we begin with the second position, and go back to the first, we have for the same reasons

$$\sum (p_r + dp_r)(x_r + dx_r) < \sum (p_r + dp_r) x_r. \qquad \therefore \sum (p_r + dp_r) dx_r < 0.$$

It follows from these two inequalities that $\sum dp_r \, dx_r < 0$, as has been shown for infinitesimal displacements in section 8 of the mathematical appendix.

2. Two applications of the above propositions are worth mentioning. One relates to the theory of index-numbers. We have, from the second of the above inequalities, that

$$\frac{\sum (p_r + dp_r)(x_r + dx_r)}{\sum p_r (x_r + dx_r)} < \frac{\sum (p_r + dp_r) x_r}{\sum p_r (x_r + dx_r)},$$

and from the first

$$\frac{\sum (p_r + dp_r) x_r}{\sum p_r (x_r + dx_r)} < \frac{\sum (p_r + dp_r) x_r}{\sum p_r x_r}.$$

Consequently

$$\frac{\sum (p_r + dp_r)(x_r + dx_r)}{\sum p_r (x_r + dx_r)} < \frac{\sum (p_r + dp_r) x_r}{\sum p_r x_r}.$$

The first of these is the Paasche index-number of prices (weighted by the quantities consumed in the second of the two situations); the second is the Laspeyre index-number (weighted by the quantities consumed in the first). Thus it follows from our propositions that, under the conditions assumed, Paasche's index-number must be less than Laspeyre's.

This result has, however, only been proved to hold when the consumer remains on the same indifference level—that is, although there has been a change in relative prices, there has been no change in real income. If there is a change in real income, then there will be an income effect, which may possibly distort the orthodox relation between the index-numbers, which may thus be looked upon as a relation in the world of substitution effects. *A fortiori* when the argument is applied to a group of consumers, instead of a single consumer, there may be disturbances due to redistribution of real income, resulting from the change in prices. (Some of these qualifications are discussed in Bowley, 'Earnings and Prices', *Review of Economic Studies*, June 1941.)

Finally, it should be emphasized that the argument is concerned with the effect of changing prices on the behaviour of a consumer, or consumers, with given wants. If the change which has taken place is a change in wants, with given productive capacity, rather than a change in productive capacity with given wants, then it may be that we should expect the relation between the index-numbers to be reversed.

3. The other application is concerned with the generalization of the fundamental proposition about consumer's surplus, given on p. 41 above. It was there proved that if the price of a particular commodity falls, the compensating variation in income must be greater than the difference between the cost of purchasing the quantity previously purchased, at the old and at the new prices. The same argument can evidently be used in the case of a more complex price-change, say a fall in two or three prices simultaneously. When one price is reduced from p to $p+dp$ (dp being taken as negative), the compensating variation is greater than $-x\,dp$; when several prices are reduced, the compensating variation is greater than $-\sum x\,dp$. For it is still true that if the prices were reduced, and at the same time income was reduced by $-\sum x\,dp$, the same quantities of goods as before could be purchased, so that the consumer could not be worse off; but new opportunities of substitution would be open, which were not open in the old situation, so that he will ordinarily be able to make himself better off. If he is to be no better off, he must lose more than $-\sum x\,dp$.

Consider the mathematical expression of this theorem. We know that in a position of equilibrium

$$u = u(x_1, x_2, ..., x_n), \qquad M = \sum p_r x_r, \qquad u_r = \mu p_r \quad (r = 1, 2, ..., n).$$

From these $n+2$ equations, it is in principle possible to eliminate the $n+1$ variables $x_1, x_2, ..., x_n, \mu$; we are left with a single equation between $M_1 p_1, p_2, ..., p_n, u$. Consider this as an expression of M in terms of the remainder. The partial derivations of M with respect to the prices (u being treated as constant) give us the compensating variations in M (income) which offset particular changes in prices and leave the utility level u unaffected. (Since we are only concerned with cases in which u is treated as constant, the indeterminateness in the utility function is immaterial to the argument.)

The compensating variation corresponding to a general change in prices will thus be given by

$$dM = \sum_r \frac{\partial M}{\partial p_r} dp_r + \tfrac{1}{2} \sum_r \sum_s \frac{\partial^2 M}{\partial p_r \partial p_s} dp_r\, dp_s,$$

proceeding to the quadratic approximation, as is always necessary in consumer's surplus problems.

Now $\dfrac{\partial M}{\partial p_r} = x_r + \sum p_s \dfrac{\partial x_s}{\partial p_r}$ (from the second of the equilibrium equa-

tions), while with u constant $0 = \dfrac{\partial u}{\partial p_r} = \sum_s u_s \dfrac{\partial x_s}{\partial p_r} = \mu \sum_s p_s \dfrac{\partial x_s}{\partial p_r}$ (from

the third equilibrium equation); thus with u constant, $\sum_s p_s \dfrac{\partial x_s}{\partial p_r} = 0$

and therefore $\dfrac{\partial M}{\partial p_r} = x_r$.

Consequently it also follows that $\dfrac{\partial^2 M}{\partial p_r \partial p_s} = \dfrac{\partial x_r}{\partial p_s}$, taken along the same indifference surface; and this $= \mathbf{x}_{rs}$. The quadratic term thus reduces to $\tfrac{1}{2} \sum \sum \mathbf{x}_{rs} dp_r\, dp_s$ (or $\tfrac{1}{2} \sum dx_r dp_r$ taken along the indifference surface); and this, as we have seen, is negative definite.

Thus $dM = \sum_r x_r dp_r + \tfrac{1}{2} \sum_r \sum_s \mathbf{x}_{rs} dp_r\, dp_s$. For a fall in prices, all these terms are negative, and the compensating variation is therefore numerically greater than $-\sum x dp$. For a rise in prices, the first two terms will be positive, and the compensating variation is therefore less than $\sum x\, dp$.

Further discussions on the theory of consumer's surplus, which have taken place since this book was first published, have shown that it is necessary to distinguish between the compensating variation, which measures the change in income which offsets a given change in prices, and the equivalent variation, which is the change in income, taking place in the initial price-situation, which induces the same change in utility as is induced by the price-change. Since the change in utility, resulting from a given change in prices, is equal and opposite to the change in utility which results from an opposite change in prices, the equivalent variation, for a change from price-system A to price-system B, is the same as the compensating variation for a change from price-system B to price-system A. We can thus calculate the equivalent variation for a change of prices from p_r to $p_r + dp_r$ ($r = 1, 2,..., n$) by considering the compensating variation for a change from $p_r + dp_r$ to p_r. Substituting in our formula (and remembering that the relevant quantities must now be adjusted for a change in prices *without* offsetting change in income, so that we must expand by the use of our fundamental equation (p. 309), *not* by proceeding along the indifference surface) we have for the equivalent variation, proceeding as before to the quadratic approximation,

$$-d'M = \sum_r (x_r + dx_r)(-dp_r) + \tfrac{1}{2} \sum_r \sum_s \mathbf{x}_{rs}(-dp_r)(-dp_s)$$

$$= -\sum_r (x_r + dx_r)dp_r + \tfrac{1}{2} \sum_r \sum_s \mathbf{x}_{rs}\, dp_r\, dp_s$$

$$= -\sum_r x_r\, dp_r - \sum_{rs} \frac{\partial x_r}{\partial p_s} dp_r\, dp_s + \tfrac{1}{2} \sum_r \sum_s \mathbf{x}_{rs}\, dp_r\, dp_s$$

$$= -\sum_r x_r\, dp_r + \sum_s x_s\, dp_s \sum \frac{\partial x_r}{\partial M} dp_r - \tfrac{1}{2} \sum_r \sum_s \mathbf{x}_{rs}\, dp_r\, dp_s.$$

Thus

$$d'M = \sum_r x_r\, dp_r - \sum_s x_s\, dp_s \sum \frac{\partial x_r}{\partial M} dp_r + \tfrac{1}{2} \sum_{rs} \mathbf{x}_{rs}\, dp_r\, dp_s.$$

This is the same as the formula for the compensating variation, except for the inclusion of an income term, which corresponds to the difference in the marginal utility of money on the two indifference surfaces on which we are respectively proceeding.

It will be noticed that there is a symmetrical relation between the two variations and their bounds, $\sum x\, dp$ and $\sum (x + dx)dp$, which correspond to the inner and outer rectangles $kpzk'$, $kz'p'k'$ on Fig. 10 (p. 38 above). For Equivalent variation

$$= \sum (x + dx)dp - \tfrac{1}{2} \sum \sum \mathbf{x}_{rs}\, dp_r\, dp_s$$

$$= \sum x\, dp - \sum x\, dp \sum \frac{\partial x}{\partial M} dp + \tfrac{1}{2} \sum \sum \mathbf{x}_{rs}\, dp_r\, dp_s;$$

Compensating variation

$$= \sum x\, dp + \tfrac{1}{2} \sum \sum \mathbf{x}_{rs}\, dp_r\, dp_s$$

$$= \sum (x + dx)dp + \sum x\, dp \sum \frac{\partial x}{\partial M} dp - \tfrac{1}{2} \sum \sum \mathbf{x}_{rs}\, dp_r\, dp_s.$$

The increment in the triangle under the demand curve $(kpp'k')$, measured by taking pp' to be approximately a straight line, is $(x+\frac{1}{2}dx)dp$, and this is exactly half-way between the equivalent and compensating variations.

The above is a simplified and improved version of an argument which first appeared in my paper 'Consumers' Surplus and Index Numbers', *Review of Economic Studies*, 1942. It relates only to what I have subsequently called 'price-variations' as distinguished from 'quantity-variations' ('The Four Consumer's Surpluses', *Review of Economic Studies*, 1944). A more comprehensive study of the theory of consumer's surplus would extend beyond the scope of this book.

ADDITIONAL NOTE B

The Imperfect Stability of the Temporary Equilibrium System

As a result of the work of Professor Lange[1] and of Dr. Mosak,[2] I now feel that the argument of Chapters XX and XXI requires a little qualification. The modifications I should now introduce do not destroy the main lines of the argument, and I have therefore thought it best to leave the text unaltered. What follows is really an extended footnote. Most of it is an extract from a review of Lange's and Mosak's books which I published in 1945 in *Economica*.

The crucial questions (on which the argument of these chapters turns) are those of the effect of a rise (or fall) in the prices of all goods (including factors) in the same proportion: (a) rates of interest remaining unchanged; (b) consequential changes in rates of interest being allowed for. Since the prices of all goods change in the same proportion, we need not distinguish, for the purposes of this problem, between one good and another; we can lump them all together, and talk about changes in the 'price-level' of current goods. Similarly, in problem (a) the constancy of rates of interest enables us to treat money and bonds[3] as a single 'commodity', so that we have only two 'commodities' in our system, and all the technical difficulties are reduced to a minimum. There remain some rather formidable difficulties about the assumptions on which we are proceeding, and here it is evident that in the text I was not sufficiently careful.

[1] Lange, *Price Flexibility and Employment*, Cowles Commission, 1944.
[2] Mosak, *General Equilibrium Theory in International Trade*, Cowles Commission, 1944.
[3] Correctly substituted by Lange (p. 15) for my 'securities'. The prices of ordinary shares will of course adjust themselves to the price-level of commodities.

If there is a rise in the price-level, and the rate of interest is constant, it is only possible for there to be a positive substitution effect in favour of future goods, if price-expectations have a less than unity elasticity. If price-expectations have a unity elasticity, there can be no substitution effect. This is what I maintained, and this I think is agreed. Further, the demand and supply for 'money plus bonds' simply reflects the demand and supply for future goods; thus there can be no substitution effect in favour of 'money plus bonds'.

What, however, of the income effect? In principle, there will be an income effect, because the initial holdings of 'money plus bonds' by different people will differ; in fact, it may be that some people will begin the week with positive holdings of 'money plus bonds', other people with negative holdings. A rise in the price-level means a fall in the real value of these holdings, and this will affect the distribution of purchasing power within the community. Where my analysis seems to have been defective is that it did not take sufficient trouble with this income effect. (I was too much in love with the simplification which comes from assuming that income effects cancel out when they appear on both sides of the market.)

Two cases need to be distinguished. In the one case the only money in our economy is a pure credit money. It is money, not a bond, in the sense that it bears no interest; nevertheless it merely registers a debt from one of the 'individuals' (who may be a bank) in the economy to another. In this case the positive and negative holdings of money must have been initially equal, just as the positive and negative holdings of bonds must certainly have been equal. A rise in the price-level must consequently make some 'individuals' better off to exactly the same extent as it makes others worse off. If the income effects set up by these two movements are symmetric, the net income effect will be zero. The system is in neutral equilibrium. This is Wicksell's case, and here the income effect is sufficiently allowed for in our discussion of past contracts, p. 264 above.

We shall return to this case in a moment. For the present let us contrast it with the other. If credit money is not the only sort of money, but there is also some 'hard' money of whatever kind (it may be metallic money, or it may be a governmental note issue, fixed on principles which are assumed to lie outside our system)—then the positive holdings of money must more than balance the negative; so that even if income effects are symmetrical, a fall in the real value of money will diminish real purchasing power, and the stability of the system will be maintained by the income effect. Of course, even in this case, the system is not necessarily stable. Its stability may be upset by asymmetric income effects; and it may be that that would be quite likely to happen, once the usual stabilizing effect of the substitution effect is removed. Instability through asymmetric income effects is, however, a perfectly general possibility, which runs through static, as well as dynamic, analysis.

So much for the first problem, that of the stability of a system with constant interest rates. It is not surprising to find that when we allow for repercussions on interest rates, we have to maintain the same distinction. We have seen that a pure credit economy, with symmetric income effects, is in neutral equilibrium when rates of interest are held constant. *In such a case it is not very evident why the rate of interest should move, when it is free to move.* For the creation of money, in such an economy, will depend upon willingnesses to lend and borrow, just like the creation of bonds. The maintenance of the same *real* system, at a higher price-level, should give an inducement to a creation of money, sufficient to support the higher price-level. The system is not merely imperfectly stable; it is in neutral equilibrium even when all repercussions are allowed for.

On the other hand, the economy with some 'hard' money is not merely likely to be kept stable by the income effect here discussed; it is also likely to find that at the higher price-level there is insufficient hard money to support this price-level, so that there is a stabilizing effect through the rate of interest as well as the stabilizing income effect. This is the case with which, in the text, we were mainly concerned; our analysis therefore seems to hold, except that the income effect should have been allowed for, and it was (I regret to say) overlooked.

This income effect in the 'hard' money case seems to be the same point as that which has lately been made by Professor Pigou in his criticism of the Keynesian theory.[1] I cannot myself attach much practical importance to it, but I have no doubt that it is valid theoretically, and in principle it ought to be allowed for.

ADDITIONAL NOTE C

Professor Samuelson's Dynamic Theory

Perhaps the most important development which has occurred between 1938 and 1946 in the general field of analysis covered by this book has been the appearance of the theory of 'dynamic stability' due to Professor Samuelson.[2] Professor Samuelson's theory is much too complex to be

---

[1] Pigou, 'The Classical Stationary State', *Economical Journal*, 1943; *Lapses from Full Employment*, 1945, ch. 5.

[2] P. A. Samuelson, 'The Stability of Equilibrium: Comparative Statics and Dynamics', *Econometrica*, 1941; 'The Stability of Equilibrium: Linear and Non-Linear Systems,' *Econometrica*, 1942; 'The Relation between Hicksian Stability and True Dynamic Stability', *Econometrica*, 1944. See also O. Lange, *Price Flexibility and Employment*, Appendix; and Lloyd A. Metzler, 'Stability of Multiple Markets: The Hicks Conditions', *Econometrica*, 1945.

discussed at all adequately in the space now at my disposal; besides, I cannot pretend that I am yet sufficiently at home with it to have made up my mind about it. But it is much too important to be left without any reference.

My discussion of static equilibrium in this book was intended as no more than a preliminary to what I called economic dynamics; thus the discussion of static stability was deliberately and explicitly timeless. And when I passed on to my dynamics, the discussion of *stability* remained timeless, at least in this sense: that I assumed the process of adjustment to temporary equilibrium to be completed within a short period (a 'week'), while I neglected the movement of prices within the week, so that my economic system could be thought of as taking up a series of temporary equilibria. In adopting this device, I was following in the tradition of Marshall, though I was of course aware that the assumption of an 'easy passage to temporary equilibrium' required more justification when it was applied to my problem of many markets than it did when applied to Marshall's case of the single market. I endeavoured, in the note on pp. 127-9 to provide that justification, but I did not pretend to be very satisfied with the results. However this was all I could do with the technique which was at my disposal.

Professor Samuelson has turned some much heavier mathematical artillery than mine on to this precise issue, and has undoubtedly made important progress with it. He drops the assumption of a quick and easy passage to temporary equilibrium, assuming instead that rates of price-change are functions of differences between demands and supplies. His whole theory thus becomes dynamic—in a different sense from mine, but one which is perhaps more acceptable to mathematicians. The argument runs in terms of differential and difference equations, instead of my ordinary equations; it thus develops interesting possibilities of oscillation and periodicity.

In terms of this new technique, my static theory can be 'dynamized'; it is possible to inquire into the stability of the static system in the sense of investigating whether the movements set up when a system is initially out of equilibrium will converge upon an equilibrium position. Since Professor Samuelson's system has a new degree of freedom, it is not surprising that his stability conditions are different from mine and more elaborate than mine; his system may fail of stability, not only for my reasons, but because of a lack of adjustment between rates of adaptation in different markets, or rates of response by persons trading. All this opens a most promising line of investigation, which is clearly by no means exhausted by the work hitherto done on it.

Professor Samuelson's work thus represents an important advance in our knowledge of the mechanics of related markets; his 'dynamizing' of static theory is a notable achievement. But I still feel that something is wanted which is parallel to *my* dynamic theory, and I miss this in Professor Samuelson's work. By my hypothesis of essentially instantaneous adjustment, I reduced the purely mechanical part of my dynamic theory to the simplest terms—it is now quite evident that I over-simplified it. But in so doing I did leave myself free to make some progress with the less mechanical parts—expectations and so on. I still feel that this procedure has its uses, and I should be sorry to abandon it altogether in favour of a pure concentration on mechanism. It may well be that for econometric work a theory of Professor Samuelson's type is all we need; it gives a superb model for statistical fitting. But for the understanding of the economic system we need something more, something which does refer back, in the last resort, to the behaviour of people and the motives of their conduct. It may well be that ways will be found by which we can retain these advantages as well as the advantages of a mechanical theory; but I do not think that they have been found just yet.

There is a striking parallelism between the work which has been done by Professor Samuelson in general equilibrium economics and that which has been done on the theory of the trade cycle by Mr. Kalecki and other econometrists. One of the greatest economic questions which remains to be settled is whether the trade cycle is more easily to be explained in terms of mechanical periodicities which can be expressed by difference equations, or whether a temporary equilibrium theory of the Keynesian type is ultimately the more potent. The answer to that question will no doubt incidentally settle the question—of approach and method, rather than of detail—which remains at issue between Professor Samuelson and myself.

INDEX

Acceptability, general acceptability of money, 165–6.

Acceptances, 143.

Agriculture, Ministry of, 110.

Allen, R. G. D., 19, 28 n., 96 n.

Average costs, 82.

Average period, general definition, 186; average period of a plan necessarily positive, 201; average period of production and rate of interest, 218–22; average periods of expenditure and receipts, 234.

Backwardation, 138.

Balancing the budget, 270 n.

Bank charges, 167 n.; bank deposits and notes as money, 163; bank reserves, 241; banks and the control of interest rates, 170 n.

Bankruptcy, 264.

Barter, Marshall's Appendix on, 127; barter of present commodities against future commodities, 141.

Bills, reasons for the payment of interest on, 164; very close substitutes for money, 168.

Böhm-Bawerk, 117, 153, 192, 213, 218; the fundamental error in his theory, 222.

Bowley, A. L., 28 n., 330.

Capitalism, methods of avoiding disequilibrium under, 135–9.

Cassel, G., 116 n.

Catastrophes and wars causing windfall losses, 180 n.

Clark, J. B., 116 n.

Commodity, extension of the concept, 33–4.

Compensating variation, 40, 330–2.

Complementarity, definition of, 43; its reversibility, 44; extreme complementarity, 77 n., 130 n., 222 n.; technical complementarity, 92; dominance of complementarity among factors as a group and among products as a group, 95–8. *See also* Substitution.

Consumer's surplus, 38–41, 330–2; and taxation, 41.

Cost of investment, as an influence on the short rate of interest, 164–5.

Cournot on perfect competition, 85 n.

Crescendo, 187, 223; measure of, 188 n.

Debt deflation, 265.

Depreciation, 171, 187, 196.

Determinateness of exchange equilibrium, 59; of equilibrium of production, 101; of temporary equilibrium, 155–8, 333–5.

Dichotomy between 'real' and 'monetary' economics, 159–60.

Discount ratio defined, 185.

Discrimination on capital market, 144.

Disequilibrium, defined, 132; causes of, 133; and risk, 134.

Distribution, effects of the accumulation of capital on, 288–92.

Dupuit, 38.

Dynamics, definition of economic, 115.

Edgeworth, 13, 42, 128.

Elasticity of expectations defined, 205; working of a system with inelastic expectations, 250, 275–6; with elastic expectations, 254–5; elasticity of interest-expectations, 260, 281–2.

Elasticity of substitution, 96 n.

Elimination of the odd equation, *see* determinateness.

Equilibrium, meaning of, in statics, 58; in dynamics, 131.

Equilibrium over time defined, 132.

Equivalent variation, 333–5.

Ex ante and *ex post* definitions of Income, 178; Income *ex post* irrelevant to conduct, 179; definitions of saving and investment, 181–3.

Excess demand, 63; income effect on, 64.

Expectations, their place in dynamic theory, 117; the assumption of definite expectations, 124–5; expectations and monopoly, 125; and risk, 125; influence of actual prices on price-expectations, 204.

False prices, 128–9.

Foreign exchanges, as a case of multiple exchange, 75 n.

Foresight, perfect, 140.

Forward exchanges, 138 n., 142 n.

Forward trading, 135; its cost, 139; long lending as forward trading, 144.

Fundamental equation of value theory, 309.

Generalized law of demand, 52, 311, 329.

Georgescu-Roegen, N., 19 n.

Giffen, 35.

Gold mining, 210.